SEEING OURSELVES
MEDIA POWER AND POLICY
IN CANADA

SEEING OURSELVES
MEDIA POWER AND POLICY
IN CANADA

Edited by

HELEN HOLMES AND DAVID TARAS

University of Calgary

Harcourt Brace Jovanovich Canada Inc.

Toronto Montreal Orlando Fort Worth San Diego Philadelphia
London Sydney Tokyo

Canadian Cataloguing in Publication Data

Main entry under title:

Seeing ourselves: media power and policy in Canada

Includes bibliographical references.
ISBN 0–03–922755–3

1. Mass Media – Canada.   I. Holmes, Helen, 1944–
II. Taras, David, 1950–

P.92.C254 1992   302.23'0971   C91–094885–2

Editorial Director: *Heather McWhinney*
Developmental Editor: *Lorraine Doherty*
Editorial Assistant: *Charlene Sue Low Chee*
Director of Publishing Services: *Steve Lau*
Editorial Manager: *Liz Radojkovic*
Editorial Co-ordinator: *Carol Tong*
Production Manager: *Sue-Ann Becker*
Production Assistant: *Denise Wake*
Copy Editor: *Wendy Thomas*
Cover and Interior Design: *Dave Peters*
Typesetting: *Bianca Imagesetting Inc.*
Assembly: *Louisa Schulz*
Printing and Binding: *Webcom Limited*

∞   This book was printed in Canada on acid-free paper.
1 2 3 4 5   96 95 94 93 92

*We would like to thank our families for their wonderful support
and dedicate the book to
Lindsey and Paula Holmes and Daphne, Joel, and Matthew Taras.*

ACKNOWLEDGEMENTS

Our thanks go to the Faculty of General Studies at the University of Calgary for offering us the tangible, intellectual, and moral support that make such a volume possible. We appreciate, too, the financial support of the Secretary of State, Canadian Studies Directorate. Lorraine Doherty of Harcourt Brace Jovanovich Canada gave us her help and enthusiasm. Copy Editor Wendy Thomas did a masterful job improving and sharpening the manuscript and Editorial Co-ordinator Carol Tong did a fine job shepherding the book through to publication. We owe a debt to Margaret Coté for her willingness to type and retype a number of the articles and for her patience and calm in dealing with us. We also want to thank Janet Harkness, who assembled Appendix A. External reviewers David Spencer, Stanley Cunningham, and Walter Nagel, assigned by Harcourt Brace Jovanovich, had insightful criticisms and thoughtful comments. The contributors to this volume brought a wealth of ideas and an enthusiasm for the project that made our work much more pleasurable than it might have been. Our students, through their interest in Canadian media and their many questions, provided the motivation to undertake this project in the first place.

We wish to acknowledge those who gave us permission to use previously published material in this text:

William Boot. Campaign '88: TV Overdoses on the Inside Dope. Reprinted from the *Columbia Journalism Review*, January/February, © 1989, by permission of the author and the publisher.

Communications Canada. *The Broadcasting Act of 1991*. Reprinted with permission of the Minister of Supply and Services Canada, 1991.

Communications Canada. The Development of Canadian Broadcasting. From *Report of the Task Force on Broadcasting Policy*, copyright 1986. Reproduced with the permission of the Minister of Supply and Services Canada, 1991.

Richard Ericson, Patricia Baranek, Janet Chan. Representing Order. From *Representing Order: Crime, Law and Justice in the News Media*. Reprinted by permission of the University of Toronto Press.

Robert Hackett, Richard Pinet, Myles Ruggles. From Audience Commodity to Audience Community. From *After Bennett*. Eds., Warren Magnusson, Charles Doyle, R.B.J. Walker, and John DeMarco. Copyright 1986 by New Star Books. Reprinted with the permission of the publisher.

Joshua Meyrowitz. Television: The Shared Arena. This article originally appeared in *The World & I* in July 1990. Copyright 1990 by Joshua Meyrowitz. Reproduced by permission of the author.

PUBLISHER'S NOTE TO STUDENTS AND INSTRUCTORS

This textbook is a key component of your course. If you are the instructor of this course, you undoubtedly considered a number of texts carefully before choosing this one as the one that would work best for your students and you. The authors and publishers spent considerable time and money to ensure its high quality, and we appreciate your recognition of this effort and accomplishment. Please note the copyright statement.

If you are a student, we are confident that this text will help you to meet the objectives of your course. It will also become a valuable addition to your personal library.

Since we want to hear what you think about this book, please be sure to send us the stamped reply card at the end of the text. Your input will help us to continue to publish high-quality books for your courses.

CONTRIBUTORS

Helen Allison	University of Calgary
Patricia Baranek	Ontario Ministry of Health
William Boot	Seattle Post-Intelligencer
Janet Chan	University of New South Wales
Jeffrey Derevensky	McGill University
Peter Desbarats	University of Western Ontario
Nancy Duxbury	Simon Fraser University
Ross A. Eaman	Carleton University
Richard Ericson	University of Toronto
Seth Feldman	York University
Robert Hackett	Simon Fraser University
Helen Holmes	University of Calgary
Tom Kent	Royal Commission on Newspapers
Carolyn Klein	McGill University
Stephen Kline	Simon Fraser University
Martin Laba	Simon Fraser University
William Leiss	Simon Fraser University
Rowland Lorimer	Simon Fraser University
Janice Dickin McGinnis	University of Calgary
Joshua Meyrowitz	University of New Hampshire
Richard Pinet	Simon Fraser University
Marc Raboy	Université Laval
Gertrude J. Robinson	McGill University
Myles Ruggles	Simon Fraser University
Robert A. Stebbins	University of Calgary
David Taras	University of Calgary
John Herd Thompson	Duke University
Linda Trimble	University of Alberta
Gail Guthrie Valaskakis	Concordia University

CONTENTS

PART III: MEDIA POWER AND SOCIAL CHANGE

INTRODUCTION

As *Seeing Ourselves* goes to press, Canada is in the midst of a profound constitutional crisis that threatens to destroy the political order that has prevailed for over 125 years. The 1990s are certain to be a time of dramatic change as global forces are leading to greater economic and political integration on one hand and to disintegration on the other. While countries in Europe, North America, and East Asia have established powerful trading blocs based on freer trade and harmonized policies and regulations, in Canada, what was formerly the Soviet Union, and Yugoslavia, dissolution and threats of dissolution have brought profound uncertainty. In these instances, questions are being raised about how citizens can exercise their rights and express their choices in the face of large impersonal forces.

Although there has been a great deal of debate in Canada about how to reform the institutions of government—such as proposals for an elected Senate, a new division of powers between Ottawa and the provinces, distinct powers for Quebec, consulting citizens through referendums—little has been said about the role of the mass media. Yet the mass media are among the most powerful determinants of societal values, and they have strongly shaped the ways in which Canadians see themselves. Few scholars would dispute the fact that the mass media have the capacity to create common cultural boundaries, a common cultural space. These boundaries and spaces encompass much of the globe and are threatening national cultures almost everywhere. At the very least, the media have a role in setting the agenda; they often tell us which issues, events, people, and experiences are important and which are not. Todd Gitlin has described the impact of the mass media: "They name the world's parts, they certify reality as reality."

Seeing Ourselves explores whether the public's real needs and desires are being served and reflected by the owners, advertisers, and regulators who control the messages that have become so much a part of our lives. The interests of governments, corporations, and citizens often clash. Each has its own interests to protect. Through institutions such as the CBC, Radio-Canada, and the National Film Board, the government is a major stakeholder in the mass media, and it is also a protector and broker among powerful interests in society. The interests of corporations are more clear cut; corporations want to glean as much in profits as they can. In some instances, this means insisting that the government take a hands-off approach; in other instances, it means turning to the government for subsidies and tax breaks. Citizens, as readers, listeners, audiences, and consumers, also have levers of influence that they can control, although their voices are often muted, inarticulate, and disorganized. Our intention is not to trumpet a particular theory or explanation but to introduce students to issues that we believe are central to democracy. The book will describe Canada's main media institutions and the struggles for power and control that are never far below the surface.

There are at least three great democratic challenges that confront the Canadian mass media system as we approach the twenty-first century. The first is the degree to which citizens will be able to see their own reflections in, and to exercise control over the media. In examining the problem of the mass media and citizens' rights, one is struck by a fundamental irony. To some degree readers, viewers, and listeners have more choices at their disposal than ever before. New technologies such as VCRs, cable, satellite, direct broadcasting services, and personal computers have reduced costs and given people a dazzling array of choices: dozens of TV channels, hundreds of magazines, an endless stream of books and videos, and countless data bases. VCRs have liberated viewers from the tyranny of network schedules and have given them a measure of autonomy; advances in interactive television allow viewers to choose camera angles and call up facts and information at their own discretion; pay-per-view TV and the new electronic journalism available through personal computers will expand choices to an even greater degree by the late 1990s.

Yet even as Canadians enjoy this great new harvest of media options, there are indications that the messages they are exposed to contain more uniformity and less variety than ever before. Media ownership has fallen into the hands of mega corporations that, in their drive to maximize efficiency and profits, often produce homogenized products. One can argue that the choices available to the public are actually quite limited; they are restricted to what can be done for the most profit and what reinforces the status quo. Essays in this volume by Robert Hackett and his associates, Tom Kent, Rowland Lorimer and Nancy Duxbury, Seth Feldman, Linda Trimble, and Stephen Kline and William Leiss deal in varying ways with how control is exercised by or regulated with the agreement of powerful corporations.

A second great challenge is whether the mass media in Canada can promote national cohesion and identity. A distinct Canadian media system survives against enormous odds: the country is spread over vast distances; not only are there sharp linguistic and regional divisions, there is enormous competition from the American media. Indeed, Canada has developed two very different but thriving media systems, one in English Canada and the other in Quebec. The two systems have become separate universes with little contact, sharing, or exchange. Marc Raboy's article explains how the CBC and Radio-Canada long ago parted ways, developing different priorities and sensibilities, reflecting different realities.

It is difficult to conceive of political integration without some level of cultural integration and without some attempt to bridge the psychological divide that separates the two linguistic communities. Some understanding, some sympathy, some connectedness has to exist for the country to be able to survive. Creating pathways that would allow French- and English-speaking Canadians to share common cultural experiences, whether through television co-productions, seeing each other on the news, or translating books and songs, requires a commitment of money and imagination. Failure to do so may severely damage Canada's long-term prospects for survival.

A less grave but in many ways similar situation exists within English-speaking Canada. Regions are separated by enormous physical and psychological distance. English-speaking Canadians need to have unifying experiences that will allow them to see and talk to each other more fluently and more often.

A third challenge is whether Canada's media system can continue to withstand the pressure of increased American cultural influence. Economies of scale, the power of new technologies, and a retreat by the federal government from supporting the CBC and other cultural institutions has meant that American television, films, videos, books, and magazines dominate Canada's cultural landscape. John Thompson's article in this volume cites statistics compiled by Rick Salutin on the extent to which Canadian culture has been overrun:

> Only 3 to 5 per cent of all theatrical screen time in Canada goes to Canadian films; 97 per cent of profits from films shown in Canada go out of the country, 95 per cent to the U.S.; 95 per cent of English-language TV drama is non-Canadian; Canadian-owned publishers have only 20 per cent of the book titles; 77 per cent of the magazines sold here are foreign; 85 per cent of record and tape sales are non-Canadian; . . . Canadian plays are the alternative theatre here (Salutin, 1987, pp. 205–6).

The fear is that, as time goes on, Canadians are becoming more like Americans simply because Canadians and Americans are breathing the same cultural air. American standards, some argue, have become the measure by which Canadians judge whether Canadian culture is worthwhile. For instance, some complain that Canadian television drama is too similar to American television drama because Hollywood has set the standard for what Canadian television drama should look like.

Whether Canada can reclaim its culture has enormous consequences for the country's future. To some extent it's the ultimate public interest. Northrop Frye has described the notable achievements that took place in the 1960s and 1970s:

> It is of immense importance to the United States itself that there should be other views of the human occupation of this continent, rooted in different ideologies and different historical traditions. And it is of immense importance to the world that a country which used to be at the edge of the earth and is now a global Switzerland, surrounded by all the world's great powers, should have achieved the repatriating of its culture. For it is essentially what has happened in the last twenty years, in all parts of Canada; and what was an inarticulate space on a map is now responding to the world with the tongues and eyes of a matured and disciplined imagination (Frye, 1982, p. 70).

Whether the Canadian imagination can respond again in the 1990s to the challenges that it faces is addressed in several of the articles in this volume.

The book focuses in the first section on the role that governments, corporations, and interest groups have played in shaping the mass media. The lead article, by Robert Hackett and his colleagues at Simon Fraser University, describes the impact that corporate ownership of the media has had in British Columbia. Corporate concentration of media ownership exists to approximately the same or to an even greater extent elsewhere in the country. In their view, the concentration of ownership has distorted the news process. The media reflect the interests and ideology of their owners rather than the needs of the communities they serve. The audience is little more than a commodity that is sold to advertisers. The authors propose a different vision: that the media system should include vibrant alternative media that would be owned and run democratically and would reflect community interests. Tom Kent, a former journalist and public servant, headed the Royal Commission on Newspapers, which was struck by the Trudeau government in 1980 to determine whether corporate concentration was strangling competition and stifling free expression. In the article written for this volume, Kent describes how the Commission operated, the pressures it was under, and its recommendations for change. The government's failure to act on the Kent Commission's recommendations raises some disturbing questions about the extent to which power remains concentrated in very few hands. Without the discipline of competition and with the absence of government regulation, many newspapers will continue to place profits ahead of journalistic responsibility or the public interest.

"The Development of Canadian Broadcasting Policy," the first chapter in the 1986 Caplan-Sauvageau Report of the Task Force on Broadcasting Policy, describes the evolution of public broadcasting in Canada. The federal government, through the publicly owned and financed CBC and through various regulatory regimes, dominated broadcasting at the national level for almost 30 years before private television emerged to challenge that predominance. The need to foster a Canadian identity in the face of American penetration and to serve a diverse population thinly spread out over a vast territory was the impetus for a public rather than a private broadcasting system. Broadcasting was seen as a basic building block of national development. In the article that follows the chapter from the Caplan-Sauvageau Task Force Report, Ross Eaman of Carleton University analyzes the problem of how the public interest is to be determined and how the CBC has attempted to measure and reflect what is at best an amorphous concept, easy to acknowledge in the abstract but difficult to grasp in the day-to-day reality of running a constellation of networks and services. Eaman suggests that the CBC has had to strike a balance between public demands and the financial and organizational needs of a large corporation.

Peter Desbarats, Dean of the Graduate School of Journalism at the University of Western Ontario and a former television journalist, argues that private networks may be just as effective as the CBC in carrying the flag of Canadian identity. Traditionally painted as "the villains of the piece" because their hunger for profits has been made at the expense of producing quality Canadian programs, the private networks now have, according to Desbarats, an "inner-directed drive toward more and better quality Canadian content." Whether Canadians are better served by a system that is anchored by a strong public broadcaster or whether broadcasting should be further tilted to allow private networks to dominate to an even greater degree continues to be the subject of intense debate.

The Broadcasting Act is the legal foundation and "social contract" for those who have been given the right to use the airwaves. Bill C-40, the Broadcasting Act of 1991, which is the first new legislation on broadcasting enacted since 1968, appears in Appendix B. It enshrines new power relationships, new definitions of purpose, and a new code of responsibility. But as Marc Raboy points out in his contribution, which appears in the second section of the book, the decision not to have the Act require that the CBC promote national unity reflects a deep rift in Canadian society. As he indicates, the debate over this provision of the Act produced a great deal of soul-searching.

The trials and tribulations of the Canadian film industry are described by Seth Feldman, an associate dean of Fine Arts at York University. The article chronicles the difficult struggle to maintain a Canadian presence in an industry that is dominated by Hollywood films and a Hollywood-controlled distribution and publicity system. Governments in Canada have intervened from time to time in attempts to stem the gravitational pull of talent and investment to the United States. Although many of the films made in Canada are simply thoughtless imitations of American films because financial success can be ensured only by appealing to American audiences, a number of brave and talented filmmakers, Denys Arcand and Anne Wheeler among them, have succeeded by telling a Canadian story.

A similar tale of woe can be told about Canadian publishing. While the federal government subsidizes and protects Canadian publishers, Rowland Lorimer and Nancy Duxbury of Simon Fraser University's Canadian Centre for Studies in Publishing argue that Canadian publishing is almost a "lost" industry. Canadian publishers share a small and linguistically divided market with giant media companies that operate internationally and enjoy economies of scale. The battle of the Canadian Davids and global Goliaths is such that, as the authors put it, "Without government support cultural publishing in Canada is finished. . . ."

Advertising is often a battleground between corporate interests and the rights of citizens. Stephen Kline and William Leiss, both of Simon Fraser University, examine how the ruthless pursuit of corporate gain led to ads that glamorized alcohol and cigarettes and exploited children. Over the years, the medical community and organized interest groups have pressured governments to regulate the advertising of products that might endanger or misinform the public. Although its legality has been questioned in the courts, a complete ban has been placed on cigarette advertising. Yet regulators are handicapped in at least two ways; the messages that do get through are tremendously powerful and sophisticated, and advertising in the American media that is received in Canada cannot be controlled. The authors also question whether the advocacy advertising indulged in by governments and corporations distorts the public's ability to learn the truth about issues such as the environment. The capacity for an informed debate is seriously jeopardized.

The last article in this first section is by Linda Trimble, a political scientist at the University of Alberta. Trimble describes the intense struggle waged between women's groups and broadcasters over the making of the Canadian Radio-television and Telecommunication Commission's (CRTC) guidelines on sex-role stereotyping. The end result was a policy of half measures that didn't fully satisfy any of the parties involved. This look at the regulatory process reveals how organizational strength and sheer persistence are necessary in order to bring meaningful change.

The book's second section deals with the media's impact on nation building. Marc Raboy of Laval University argues that Canadian broadcasting policy suffers from deep schizophrenia. The English- and French-language broadcasting systems developed separately, have distinct traditions, and reflect different needs and aspirations. Whether the two systems, the two solitudes of Canadian broadcasting, reflect a division within society that is ultimately irreparable and whether a different, more unified system might have helped to heal these gaping social and political wounds are questions that remain unanswered. On another front, David Taras argues that Canada's airwaves are inundated not only by American television programs but by Canadian programs that have been made to look like American programs. In addition, the explosion of channels and services brought by satellite and cable, along with other developments, has created information "overload" or "clutter." Messages about Canadian issues and events are no longer reaching large numbers of Canadians. The informational spinal cord that sustains Canadian identity may now be severed.

John Thompson, a Canadian historian who teaches at Duke University in North Carolina, describes the struggles waged between successive Canadian and American governments over Canada's desire to protect its cultural industries. The Free Trade Agreement has raised the stakes considerably. Canadian cultural protectionism so disturbs the Americans that it has the potential to become a "political time bomb with an uncertain fuse" threatening to blow the agreement apart. As Canada enters into a wider North American free trade agreement with the United States and Mexico, Canada will find it difficult to keep cultural industries off the bargaining table.

Ironically, the dilemmas faced by Canada as a nation are faced within Canada by its aboriginal peoples. They have maintained their cultural heritage in the face of overwhelming forces. Among other threats, the new cultural space created by television has challenged traditional Native values and undermined the social order. Gail Valaskakis of Concordia University describes how Native peoples in the North were able to establish, with the help of the federal government, their own broadcasting service. This service may be as critical to their cultural survival as the old traplines were to their physical survival.

The last section of the book examines the role played by the media in producing social change. "Television: The Shared Arena" by Joshua Meyrowitz is one of only two articles in the volume (the other is by William Boot) that have been written by Americans about the American experience. These articles were chosen because they give us important insights about the impact that mass media has had in Canada. Meyrowitz's description of television's powerful effects pertains as much to Canada as it does to the United States. His argument is that television has transformed almost all basic human relationships. It has blurred childhood and adulthood, broken down social and economic barriers for women, and reduced the power and prestige of political leaders by levelling their authority. Television has destabilized traditional values; the old social moorings are no longer in place. Society is only beginning to come to terms with the far-reaching changes of the television age.

Richard Ericson and his colleagues take the opposite position. In their classic description of the functions played by news, they contend that news represents and supports the social order. By focusing on what is out of place—crime, deviance, the alluring, the shocking, and the sensational—news helps to maintain and reinforce societal values. In their view, "law and news are both fundamentally concerned with policing." News, inasmuch as it gives people a way of ordering their world, upholds the status quo.

The second American piece chosen for this collection is William Boot's scathing critique of the media's role in U.S. presidential elections. Although it can be argued that policies and substance have not been totally evaporated by image politics in Canadian elections, Boot's article allows us to ask whether this is the direction that Canadian elections are taking. If elections can be decided by "demon visuals" and the ability to "sound-bite" (used as a verb in Boot's article), then fundamental reforms have to be considered. The Mulroney government established a Royal Commission on Electoral Reform and Party Financing, which when it reported in 1992 called for significant changes in the electoral system. It remains to be seen whether Canadian politicians will have the courage to change a system of which they have been the chief beneficiaries.

While Meyrowitz claims that dramatic changes have taken place in the roles that women play in society, Gertrude Robinson of McGill University offers a more sobering assessment. Her analysis of the experiences of women who have attempted to forge careers in the mass media reminds us that old stereotypes and barriers remain. On one issue, however, women's rights groups and ultraconservatives seem to be fighting for similar goals. The law on obscenity has become a lightning rod provoking strong reactions from many different groups in society. Obscenity is particularly contentious because some view the issue as primarily a battle over freedom of expression, while others see it as a struggle against those who would degrade and demean the human spirit. Moreover, the right to private fantasies often clashes with the need for public virtue. Janice Dickin McGinnis, a lawyer and historian at the University of Calgary, guides us through the legal tangles in the current law and the confusion and controversy that have been generated by proposed changes.

A great concern for many is the impact that the media can have on children. Networks, advertisers, and companies that make cereals, toys, and junk food know that children can be easily influenced. Children's TV is the Wild West of television—corporate gunslingers use a great deal of ammunition and there is almost no law to protect the innocent. Educational psychologists Jeffrey Derevensky and Carolyn Klein review the scholarly literature about the effects that television watching can have on children. Although TV can be an effective tool for learning and development, overexposure to certain kinds of programming can cause problems. Television is not just a vehicle for entertainment and escape; it can condition and mould behaviour.

Helen Holmes and Helen Allison explore the claim made by some scholars that the CBC has never attempted to create Canadian heroes. They look at two characters in "Street Legal," CBC's long-running series, as potential if not genuine heroes who reflect and embody the ideals and concerns of the country. The characters show a greater caring for the collective good, a greater respect for order, and a more genuine concern for societal problems than can be detected in comparable American shows. The question, of course, is whether Canadian heroes and values will continue to thrive on Canadian television or whether Canadian producers will sacrifice the Canadian characteristics of their programs in order to sell them in the lucrative American market. Perhaps we have seen the last of the Canadian "hunks"?

The last two articles are on football and hockey in Canada. Sports play a critical role in fashioning and reflecting societal values and occupy a large portion of media time and space. The two authors, Robert Stebbins and Martin Laba, respectively a distinguished sociologist and a leading authority on popular culture, see football and hockey as integral to national development. Whether we see these sports as elaborate spectacles or rituals, corporate showpieces or a last vestige of lost innocence, the CFL and the NHL are highly respected symbols of Canadian identity. Corporate ruthlessness, the fans' growing taste for brutality and violence, and rapid Americanization and internationalization bring to the fore the issue of whether the right values are being fostered in Canadian sports.

Appendix A is a collection of statistical tables and charts on the state of the media in Canada, compiled by Janet Harkness. Readers may find these contain useful background information for many of the articles in this book.

Whether the public interest is well served by the mass media is a question that is of immense importance to the future of Canadian democracy. *Seeing Ourselves* does not arrive at any definitive answer. Our goal is to explore the shape and texture of the Canadian media system with the students who will read this book. Public broadcasting, newspaper barons, private radio and television, corporate advertisers, community-owned radio, the CRTC, a myriad of laws and regulations as well as the wishes of ordinary citizens are part of a patchwork quilt of often competing interests and visions. The media system is not an empty vessel without values, interests, or a point of view. It is a contested battleground. The brutal reality with regard to the Canadian mass media is that, as Thucydides wrote many centuries ago about a long-forgotten war, "The strong do what they can, the weak suffer what they must."

REFERENCES

Frye, N. (1982). *Divisions on a ground*. Toronto: Anansi.

Salutin, R. (1987). Keep Canadian culture off the table—Who's kidding who. In *If You Love this Country* (Ed., LaPierre, L.). Toronto: McClelland and Stewart.

PART I

REGULATING MEDIA POWER

FROM AUDIENCE-COMMODITY TO AUDIENCE-COMMUNITY: MASS MEDIA IN B.C.

Robert Hackett, Richard Pinet,
and Myles Ruggles

Canadians live in a world of second-hand experience. Our understanding of social reality derives not just from personal involvement or from speaking to other people, but from images and reports transmitted by the mass communications media. Canadians spend about seven hours a day with the media—more than at any other activity except work and sleep. The mass media form a key institution through which our understandings and judgements of the social world are reinforced and challenged. They help produce and reproduce the dominant values and meanings that most people learn to accept as "common sense," to the exclusion of possible alternatives.

At the start, then, we must emphasize a paradox. The mainstream media inhibit popular democracy in British Columbia not by those shortcomings and blunders that critics usually identify, but by their very successes and routines. The problem is not that the media are "biased," but that their very standards of "objectivity" reinforce dominant definitions of social reality; not that the media impose an alien ideology or manipulate audiences, but that they are able to win the consent and participation of audiences. By examining some structural characteristics of the mass media in British Columbia, as well as some of the implications of these structures, we can begin to understand how the mainstream media both create and reinforce dominant values and meanings.

MAINSTREAM MEDIA IN BRITISH COLUMBIA

Media critics, including blue-ribbon bodies such as the Kent Commission, have repeatedly expressed concern about the way the media are owned and organized in British Columbia.[1] Perhaps the most obvious point is that the dominant media (except for the CBC) are privately owned, profit-oriented corporations. This means that the editorial content provided by these media is regarded by their management not as a public service, but as a business cost to be met as inexpensively as possible.

For example, it is cheaper to purchase syndicated columns that recover their costs over a national or continental market than it is to pay local writers. This is why so much coverage of international events in Canadian media is supplied by large American news agencies: it is cheaper to print or modify their copy than it is to send Canadian reporters overseas. Similarly, it is relatively cheap for a broadcaster to buy the exhibition rights to expensively made U.S. programs, which can recover their costs in the huge American market and which have sophisticated production values and audience appeal. The average Canadian TV show costs much less to *produce* than its American counterpart, but it is more expensive for the broadcaster to *purchase*, since it is often difficult to market beyond Canada. Moreover, its necessarily lower budget gives the program less appeal to audiences and advertisers than similar American programs. It is therefore little wonder that as presently organized, television does very little to enable British Columbians to express their own cultural values or to engage in communication with each other.

Corporate ownership also implies a hierarchy of decision making within the organization, with ownership ultimately determining the key hiring and resource allocation decisions, and with management accountable primarily to the dominant shareholders rather than to the audience or to those who work in cultural activities. It also suggests that the media owners are likely to be tied to the business community through shared social interest, background, and interaction, as well as through interlocking directorships. Indeed, sociologist Wallace Clement has found that the "media elite"—the directors and senior managers of Canada's largest media companies—are really part of a broader "corporate elite" (Clement, 1975). It is not surprising that most mainstream media have a "basic commitment to the business community's views on public issues rather than to a wider range of interests" (Audley, 1983, p. 27).

Ownership is not only private. It is also highly concentrated. For example, Western Broadcasting indirectly controls 63.2 percent of BCTV, whose 6 p.m. "Newshour" is B.C.'s most watched TV news show; it indirectly controls CKNW and CFMI, respectively Vancouver's most popular AM and FM radio stations; it owns Victoria's CTV affiliate CHEK-TV; and it has a 50 percent interest in Okanagan Valley Television Company, which owns CHBC, the Penticton-Kelowna-Vernon TV station. All of British Columbia's seventeen daily newspapers (down from nineteen in 1981) are now published by three "chains"—companies that own two or more newspapers.

Chain ownership carries the danger of homogenized content. Newspapers rely increasingly on group or chain news services rather than their own writers to cover federal and provincial legislatures. The chain tends to impose a common stylistic mode on its various "links," and there is always the threat of centralized control of editorial policy. Chain ownership is especially worrisome when it results in regional monopolies. None of B.C.'s seventeen dailies face local competition from a paper published by a different company. Southam, which accounts for two-thirds of British Columbia's daily newspaper circulation, owns both Vancouver dailies through Pacific Press. Thomson, with a reputation for "cheapskate journalism," owns all three papers in the Okanagan. And in southeastern British Columbia, Sterling, in which Toronto financier Conrad Black has a major stake, controls all four dailies.

British Columbians were made starkly aware of the trend toward newspaper monopoly by the corporate manoeuvres of August 1980. Thomson, which earlier in the year had swallowed up F.P. Publications, sold its share in Pacific Press to Southam, leaving the latter with a Vancouver monopoly. Meanwhile, Thomson merged the two Victoria papers it had acquired from FP into the *Times-Colonist*. In the view of municipal politicians and Kent Commission researchers alike, the merger has resulted in a marked decline in the quality, diversity, and geographical range of the newspaper's municipal affairs coverage.

It is true that newspapers compete for audience attention and advertising revenues with the electronic media, but the latter generally do not attempt to compete with newspapers as alternative sources of in-depth information. When newspaper competition gives way to monopoly, diversity of public expression may be threatened. Moreover, monopoly media are particularly given to trimming editorial spending, not because they lack resources, but because there is little incentive to do otherwise. If you already reach the whole market, there may not be much point in spending money on more reporters or better-researched stories. One-newspaper towns are dependent on the extent to which the local newspaper's owners take their journalistic responsibilities seriously. The problem is that owners who spend more than the necessary minimum are vulnerable to takeover bids by less generous and more profit-oriented corporations.

These tendencies are made even more problematic by the trend toward ownership of the media by conglomerates with extensive non-media holdings. The archetype is the Thomson family's corporate empire, which includes interests in wholesaling, retailing (Hudson's Bay, Zellers), real estate, oil and gas, insurance, and financial and management services. This increases the risk of the abuse of power in that the media outlet may be used to support, or at least to avoid embarrassing, other parts of the corporate empire.

The hazards inherent in corporate ownership of the media are not the result of malevolence or conspiracy. They are the consequences of commercialism. The market actually puts a limit on what elites can do with the media, for the media can only make a profit by appealing to a saleable audience. The era of the swashbuckling press baron using his newspaper as a vehicle for his own views is largely over. The mass media are there to make money, rather than to promote particular ideas.

ADVERTISING AND AUDIENCES

In 1980, Canada's newspaper industry earned about $1.16 billion. About 78 percent of that revenue derived from advertising—national, local, classified, and inserts. Advertising also accounted for over half of the 1982 revenues for the broadcasting industry, notwithstanding the importance of cable TV subscription fees and government funding for the CBC (Kent Report, 1981, p. 110). Even the CBC, with a mandate to provide a "public service" alternative to commercial broadcasting, depends on advertising for about one-fifth of its operating revenue and relies in part on private/commercial affiliates to broadcast its programming across the country. In addition, CBC TV feels compelled to compete for audiences with private/commercial stations that fill the airwaves with popular U.S. entertainment shows.

The standard argument in defence of market relations, advertising, and the commercial media is that all firms simply respond to the demands of consumers. But if this is so, why are such vast sums spent on advertising? It is clear that advertising is effective and that it is intended to manage consumer (and political) demand.[2]

The main product of the commercial mass media—what they sell in the market-place in order to make money—is not the programming or editorial content. After all, when we buy a copy of a newspaper, we are paying only a fraction of its total production costs. And the programming on commercial TV appears to be free of charge. Yet we know that media outlets are not charitable institutions. The main product of the media is the audience, whose willingness to pay attention is sold to advertisers, who pay on the basis of audience size and demographics.

Those who defend advertising as the basis of the media argue that commercialism ensures responsiveness to audience tastes, because advertising rates are related to the size of the audience. They also claim that it ensures financial independence from the government and hence makes possible the "freedom of the press." But market relations can inhibit popular democratic communication just as easily as the state.

In fact, the systematic pressure to produce profitable audiences has acted historically as a powerful form of political censorship. As the market for mass-produced consumer goods emerged, the financial basis of the press shifted from readership sales and political subsidies to advertising by the producers of brand-name products. Advertisers were interested in two kinds of audiences: the affluent, who had sufficient disposable income to purchase luxury products; and the mass audience, whose lack of purchasing power as individuals was offset by its huge size. Because advertisers were prepared to pay more for each affluent reader than for each mass reader, the former had a disproportionate say in determining which media survived. As the media and advertisers sought a wealthier audience, content changed to reflect the interests and concerns of the affluent. As the Kent Commission admitted, "It was left-wing viewpoints that tended to be under-represented as commercialism increased its hold" (Kent Report, 1981, p. 15). Such market-imposed censorship is consistent with, but not dependent upon, the intentions and manipulations of owners.

Similar problems are introduced by the way information and entertainment programming—which we are accustomed to regard as media content—works as a "free lunch" to entice an audience for the most important content—the commercials. The match between program and ad content can be so close that the line blurs between the two. Both reflect the lifestyle of the desired audience and promote the forms of consumption appropriate to it. The commercials are often more interesting than the programs—which is not surprising, since they are so much more expensively produced.

In short, commercial media do not simply "give people what they want." They give some of the people part of what they want. The media satisfy precisely those needs that are compatible with the marketing of commodities. Needs that no one can make money from or that threaten our consumer culture are left unattended. These include the need for democratic communication.

THE LIGHT OF THE SUN

The way commercialism affects the media becomes clearer if we take a brief look through a copy—any copy—of the province's most read newspaper, the Vancouver *Sun* (average weekly circulation, about 230 000). The patterns do not differ substantially from day to day. Several features are apparent.[3]

First, in what is still described as a *news*paper, at least half is devoted to advertising. In the You, Home, Travel, Sports, and Leisure sections of the *Sun*, everything—both news and advertising—is targeted at the consumer of airline, cruise ship, and hotel services, of spectator team sports, suburban homes, and gardens, furniture, films, and fitness. The ads corroborate, fill in the picture, urge the reader to fulfil the curiosity whetted by the surrounding articles.

What about the *real* news in the *Sun*'s bastion of integrity, Section A? News editors pride themselves on their autonomy from the marketing and advertising departments. In the sense that advertisers do not directly influence editorial copy at a large metropolitan daily, this autonomy is real. But there are more subtle constraints. Consider the narrative form of the typical "hard news" story. It is an "inverted pyramid," with the "facts" of the story presented in descending order of (perceived) importance. The story has no particular conclusion; should more advertising space be required, the article can be reduced by deleting as many sentences as necessary from the bottom up. The news and commentary also are shaped by a consumerist orientation. Oil price increases are interpreted in terms of what they will cost the driver "at the pump." Labour/management conflict is interpreted in terms of the disruption of services to the consumer. We, as readers, are asked to take the standpoint of the abstract "average" consumer.[4]

Although consumerism may have progressive aspects (for example, it may promote consumer protection legislation), it is also a barrier to change. For one thing, it neglects the sphere of production and our varying relations with it. It overrides the identity of the huge majority (about 77 percent) of Canadian income earners as employees. The interests that employees or workers have in common—improved wages, safer working conditions, more control over the workplace—are fragmented and disguised in media accounts of the industrial world. Particular groups of workers struggling for better conditions are pitted against "the public" or "consumers" in these accounts. The more militant the workers are, the more they are cast as deviants: witness the media barrage directed against striking postal workers. Consumerism also encourages an acceptance of meaningless, routinized, or unsatisfying work in exchange for the pleasures of commodity consumption. To the extent that we accept our positioning as consumers and opt into privatized lifestyles, the sphere of public discourse is diminished. Our collective ability to take charge of the conditions of our lives is reduced (Keane, 1984).

The targeting of news narrative toward consumer audiences also serves to obscure inequalities of income. These inequalities involve contrasts of lifestyle, expectation, and consumption patterns so great that those at the upper and lower ends of the income scale can hardly be termed consumers in the same sense. To address the various users of mass media as "consumers" both mystifies social relations and obstructs the emergence of the social consciousness needed to change those relations. Yet such a form of address is imperative for commercial media, which must attract both advertisers and audiences—audiences prepared to purchase advertisers' commodities.

A number of other ways in which the *Sun* addresses its readers have profound political implications. A definition of politics is suggested by the very layout of the paper. Politics is confined to the public world reported in Section A and is thus separated from the personal and private world of home, lifestyles, and travel, as well as from the bottom-line world of business. That all forms of social and economic power, including corporate control of economic resources, are political, and that personal life and extra-parliamentary movements are important sites of political activity, are denied by the very way in which the paper is organized.

The Business section is useful mainly for the small minority of Canadians who own stock or who regularly employ (and lay off) workers. It is not helpful for those who would subject business to more effective social control. We do not even expect to find a Worker section in a Canadian daily. The comics and light features amuse the young and work-weary. The amusements go with the styles and forms of consumption the advertisements encourage.

The political news is aimed at those who enjoy or feel obliged to watch the spectacle without becoming politically active. The columns of political commentary on pages A4, A5, and A6 give outsiders an "inside" look into the rituals, strategies, and personalities of the powerful—but very little information that would help citizens themselves intervene in the political process. Politics is covered as a spectator sport in which we can cheer or jeer the active participants and every few years help decide the winners and losers. Much political coverage focuses not on the players, their interests, the issues, or what is at stake, but on the "horse race." This is exemplified by the media obsession with polls on voting preferences. The exercise of power outside the electoral and parliamentary area (in corporate boardrooms or bureaucrats' offices, for example) largely escapes the media spotlight. For different reasons, extraparliamentary organizing of grass-roots movements for social change is also ignored—unless the organizations stage photogenic or disruptive protests. And although it sells papers (and advertising), protest that goes beyond what the media present as responsible, serious, and legitimate politics is almost automatically discredited.

The news in general is presented as a mixture of the conflictual, the whimsical, the curious, and the inspiring. It is about the actions and statements of the powerful, and about threats to, or disruptions of, "normal" daily life, dominant social values, and established institutions. The *Sun* does *not* scan the world in terms of how established institutions and their ruling elites may systematically jeopardize the well-being of the less powerful. On the contrary, one of the key principles of news selection and construction is the assumption that society is characterized by a basic harmony of interests and consensus of values (allowing us to get on with the really important business of consumption). The *Sun* presents conflict in ways that take for granted the permanence and legitimacy of existing institutions, power structures, and official information sources.

The paper depends for information on the elites who benefit most from the appearance of consensus: leaders of the major electoral political parties (especially Cabinet ministers), and the official spokespersons of established institutions—the police, business, organized interest groups, government departments. The journalistic reliance on official and bureaucratic sources extends beyond quoting their opinions and statements. It can extend to the incorporation into news reports, sometimes without attribution, of official definitions of reality. A good example is the unemployment rate calculated by Statistics Canada, which, some observers charge, excludes many people who would like full-time work. Similarly, crime reporting is based on how the "phases" of each case are structured by the police and judicial bureaucracies: arrest, arraignment, preliminary hearing, trial, sentencing, and so on. These institutionally structured events also structure the media's reporting. Possible alternative perspectives, such as treatment of the prisoner or the patterns of social violence associated with crime, are generally hidden from public view.

The problem of access is particularly important in the coverage of overseas stories. Coverage of non-Western societies is sparse and dominated by accounts of disasters, coups, atrocities with political implications, and the misfortunes that befall whites. If the press simplifies the richness and complexity of economic and political life in the West, it virtually ignores the Third World. The problem arises partly from the domination of the flow of news by several Western-based international news agencies. For the most part, by presenting the outside world as a place of danger and disruption, these agencies help to reinforce our attachment to the system in which we live.

It would be unfair to suggest that the patterns of news coverage we have noted here are unique to the *Sun*. On the contrary, they are typical of the commercial mass media. What we have said here would apply, with little alteration, to BCTV or the commercial radio stations. This is the reason for our concern: we are dealing not with the failings of a particular paper, but with the *successes* of the commercial media in shaping our understandings of the world.

MASS MEDIA AND DEMOCRATIC POLITICS

The mainstream media are not monolithic. Debate and dissent, controversy and criticism do not appear, even in the pages of the *Sun*. Charges of biased coverage are frequently headlined in letters to the editor. Columnists such as Vaughn Palmer and the late Marjorie Nichols have offered somewhat different views of provincial politics. (Indeed, they have reflected the whole range of opinion to the right of the NDP.) Opposition as well as government statements are reported, and sometimes even demonstration organizers are quoted. The commercial media could hardly do otherwise if they wish to retain their credibility and mass audience appeal.

Nevertheless, these media do subtly position their audiences as mere consumers, provide a general conception of politics that downplays dissent and discourages participation, interpret social conflict in terms of a presumed consensus, and allow greater access to official and Western perspectives. Moreover, the film, print, and broadcasting media have been highly susceptible to monopolization because efficiencies of scale, in the form of extended distribution systems, easily overwhelm the market power of more localized, culture-specific production. These are the consequences of the structural imperatives of generating advertising revenue, minimizing editorial expenses, and enticing audiences with content that both attracts their attention and encourages the purchases of advertisers' commodities. The kinds of communication equipment produced; the financing, production techniques, editorial and journalistic routines that make up the institutional structures of the mass media; the media's sources, agenda, intended audience, and the propositions made to those audiences—the very shape of public language itself—are all moulded by the requirements of market relations.

It is important to understand that these effects can occur without appearing to violate the journalistic norms of balance and objectivity. We are not alleging conspiracy or even "bias." A conspiratorial view sees the media's reinforcing of "establishment" viewpoints as a result of the power and deliberate intentions of owners and advertisers. The reality is more complex. The common-sense notions of "bias" and "objectivity" are inadequate for understanding the ideological role of media, or for organizing to change it, for the following reasons. First, "objectivity" implies the possibility of value neutrality in reports of social reality. Not only is this possibility philosophically dubious, but we have already seen that the values of consumerism—free choice in the marketplace, etc.—are firmly embedded in the routines of "objective" news production. Second, "bias" implies that the main problem with news is that it is deliberately manipulated. Our discussion of the structure of B.C. media suggests that they are shaped by impersonal market forces, particularly the imperative of selling audiences to advertisers, more than by the partisan prejudices of some elite of media owners or news managers. Therefore, adherence to the norms of objectivity is precisely the means by which the media retain the consent of audiences. Indeed, charges of bias against particular media reports are given a hearing, and even encouraged, through such manageable avenues as letters to the editor and complaints to the Press Council. This is because the example of the media's own occasional departures from the norms of objectivity highlights and legitimizes the "objectivity" of the majority of their reports.

Thus the hegemonic function of the media is achieved through the active participation of the audience. Readers and viewers may challenge particular media accounts. But such challenges underline audiences' acceptance of both the routines of conventional journalism, and the media's right to monopolize the representation of public life—so long as the media do so "objectively." It is less a matter of an elite telling us what to think than a set of structures that establishes the conditions under which dissent can be voiced.

The attempt to develop more popular, democratic media must involve more than a struggle to change the explicit political content of the media or to put popular representatives on media boards of directors. We have to change the way we experience mass communications, create a new relationship to the media, become *speakers* as well as listeners and readers. Mass communication must express the popular initiatives that transform our roles as citizens.

The fate of the CBC indicates what happens when the state creates institutions that leave intact our way of relating to institutional authority. The CBC is the closest approximation of a non-commercial mass medium in British Columbia and in Canada at large. It is publicly owned. Its radio services and part of its television service are non-commercial. Unfortunately, the CBC has to fit into a pattern of mass communications and audience relations established by the commercial media. The government expects it to operate a commercial television service to offset the costs of public service broadcasting. If it fails to attract large audiences, the CBC is vigorously criticized in the commercial media and in Parliament. Adherents of the commercial media resent paying for a service they do not use. As a result, the CBC tries to make itself more popular, and this means imitating the commercial media. The gap between commercial and public broadcasting is narrowed, and the alternative offered by the CBC becomes more apparent than real.

Obviously, public ownership is not the whole solution to the problem of the commercialized media, valuable as the CBC and its provincial counterparts may be. In a sense, we get the media we deserve. The commercialism of our society—the dominance of the market and the big corporations, the emphasis on getting and spending, the neglect of public life—is reflected in the nature of the media, both private and public. The government-owned media reproduce the conventional relationship between the state and its citizens: the CBC speaks from on high to a passive audience. The ethos of journalism, the understanding of politics as a spectator sport, the perspective of the consumer carry over from the private to the public media. Breaking through this web of relationships means establishing ourselves as the agents of democratic communication and refusing to be sold as a passive audience to private corporations or government leaders. The question is how.

New Media Relations

Things can be done to maximize the democratic potential of the existing media. Movements for social change should continue to use the opportunities presented by the contradictions and "leaks" within the media in order to influence its content. Journalists, technicians, and printers can attempt reform from within. Critics can continue to expose the more blatant biases, reveal the limitations of journalistic norms of objectivity and balance, and increase popular receptivity to alternative journalism. It might be possible to institutionalize a pressure group to sponsor public debates on questions of media structure and orientation, conduct studies, undertake public education, and lobby for progressive legislation on the media industry. Ordinary readers, listeners, and viewers can become involved in criticizing the media and enforcing their demands by boycotts or other forms of protest.

All this involves a politics of audience resistance and transformation. The danger is that such a politics may be simply negative. People need positive outlets for their energy. This means creating new, authentically democratic media. Without such media, it is impossible to establish new relations within the audience or to develop the popular capacity for collective action.

These media should be alternative in a number of senses. Their internal operations should be co-operative and democratic rather than organized into a rigid and hierarchical division of labour. The political news they report should not be confined to elections and governments' actions. The statements of official spokespersons and leaders of the dominant electoral parties should be treated with less prominence and greater scepticism. Conversely, more attention should be given to the response of the ordinary people affected by governmental and corporate policies. Readers, listeners, or viewers should be regarded as participants in a community rather than as commodities whose attention can be bought and sold. The information supplied to (and by) audiences should help them build an alternative political culture and take collective control of their lives, rather than encourage consumption. While the conventional media focus on events that threaten or disrupt established institutions and values, the alternative media should reveal how these institutions and values themselves affect the well-being and rights of ordinary people. Alternative media should be willing to report on ongoing social and political *processes* without being restricted by a dependence on "hard news" *events.*

An instructive example of an alternative medium in British Columbia is Vancouver Co-operative Radio (CFRO, 102.7; 104.9 on most cable systems). Like all Canadian radio stations, Co-op Radio must be 75 percent owned by Canadian citizens. But any member of the audience may, subject to this rule, buy shares and annual memberships, which are the core of the station's financing. Members in good standing have one vote each, regardless of the size of their shareholding, in the annual General Meeting that elects directors. Co-op Radio is thus controlled through an open and democratic process that vests ultimate power in the public as subscriber-members of the audience.

All programming is produced by shareholder-volunteers. Program applications are considered by a programming committee and by the Board. Volunteers organize themselves into program collectives, dividing up the roles of studio operator, producer, host, reporter, and so on. The material they produce ranges from local music, drama, and poetry to coverage of city hall, labour issues, provincial, national, and international news and analysis, and programs of interest to a wide range of minority groups. All of this material is originated and produced by the audience itself to meet its own cultural and political needs. Listeners become speakers.

Co-op Radio is by no means perfect, but it is an example of an authentically democratic medium of communications. It is not dependent on advertisers (like the commercial media), or on the state (like the CBC), or even on the unions (like the now-defunct *Solidarity Times*). It is an organization of its own listeners. Only as such can a medium of communications be empowering, enabling people to change the commercial society they confront. As CFRO demonstrates, democratic change in the media of communications need not wait on the election of a progressive government. On the contrary, establishment of alternative media is essential to building popular democratic movements, without which the hope of progressive social transformation is in vain.

NOTES

1. See especially Canada, Royal Commission on Newspapers (Kent Commision), *Report,* (1981) Ottawa; Leonard Kubas and the Communications Research Centre, *Newspapers and their readers*, Research Study for the Royal Commission on Newspapers, Vol. 1, (1981), Ottawa; Eugene Malleman, et al., *The newspaper as a business,* Research Study for the Royal Commission on Newspapers, Vol. 4. (1981) Ottawa; Special Senate (Davey) Committee on Mass Media, *Report* (1970) Ottawa; and Peter S. Anderson and Warren Brownridge (1983), *Canadian communications intercorporate ownership*, 2nd ed. Vancouver: Peter Anderson.

2. See, for example, Stuart Ewen (1976), *Captains of consciousness: Advertising and the social roots of the consumer culture,* New York: McGraw-Hill; Dallas W. Smythe (1981), *Dependency road: Communications, capitalism and consciousness in Canada*, Norwood, NJ: Ablex.

3. Since this paper was completed, the *Sun* has acquired a new format and a new name (the *Vancouver Sun*), has moved the editorial pages to Section B, pages 4 and 5, and has added more American wire-service copy. Our general argument is unaffected by these changes, which are largely cosmetic.

4. Graham Knight, (1982), Strike talk: A case study of news. *Canadian Journal of Communications, 8* (3), 61–79; Robert A. Hackett (1983), The depiction of labour and business on national television news. *Canadian Journal of Communication 10* (1), 23–29; Todd Gitlin, *The whole world is watching* Berkeley: University of California Press, p. 282.

REFERENCES

Audley, P. (1983). *Canada's cultural industries*. Toronto: James Lorimer/CIEP.

Canada. Royal Commission on Newspapers (Kent Commission). (1981). *Report*. Ottawa.

Clement, W. (1975). *The Canadian corporate elite*. Toronto: McClelland and Stewart.

Keane, J. (1984). *Public life in late capitalism: Towards a socialist theory of democracy*. Cambridge: Cambridge University Press.

Kent Commision. See Canada. Royal Commision on Newspapers. (1981).

THE TIMES AND SIGNIFICANCE
OF THE KENT COMMISSION

Tom Kent

At this distance, the most significant question about the 1980–81 Royal Commission on Newspapers is why its work came to nothing except the production of useful material for journalism students.

Was anything more intended? Some people think not. Governments sometimes appoint commissions or other inquiries in order to appear to be concerned about a politically difficult problem that in truth they prefer to evade. The inquiry is then a tactic of defusion. While it pursues its normally slow course, circumstances will change, or at least time will wear the sharp edges off the problem. Inconvenient recommendations can be ignored; government action, if any, can be limited to what has by then become hardly controversial.

In the case of the newspaper Commission, however, evasion was not the original intent. I shall first describe the beginnings of the Commission, in enough detail to demonstrate that the government was motivated, initially, by a genuine desire to do something to improve the condition of the Canadian newspaper industry. Its trouble was that it did not know how that objective could be achieved.

Was it that the Commission failed the government? Naturally, I do not think so. In the main part of this article, I shall describe how we came to our conclusions and, I hope, demonstrate again that they were—and are—the practicable way to induce the newspaper industry to serve, more comprehensively, accurately, and fairly, the information needs of Canadian society.

Although I think, with the wisdom of hindsight, that some of the detail should be different, essentially our recommendations were and are the reforms that the public interest requires. The furious criticism was entirely negative. And the experience of the past decade has fully confirmed the Commission's view that, if nothing was done, ownership of the newspaper industry would continue to become more and more concentrated and the public service provided by most newspapers would deteriorate rather than improve.

Was nothing done because the government was frightened by the newspaper owners who so hated the Commission's recommendations? Certainly it was frightened, but the question is why. There was no doubt at any time that any significant action affecting newspapers would be vehemently opposed by their owners. The government knew that when it appointed the Commission; if it had therefore wanted a do-nothing report, it would not have chosen the commissioners it did.

I was a declared critic of the press and had been involved in many government interventions in the economy; Borden Spears had had a large part in the critical study of the media by the Senate committee chaired by Keith Davey; and Laurent Picard's previous media role had been in its public sector, as president of the CBC.

In the event, the criticism of the Commission's report was so violent precisely because it was so entirely lacking in substance. There was only an empty claim to be defending not the profits but the freedom of the press. In fact, the Commission's proposals gave the government no control whatever over what was printed. The only pressure that would have been created was pressure on newspaper owners to be content with less vast profits in order to spend more money on the content of their papers. What the content was, what news was reported, and what opinions were expressed remained entirely at the free discretion of the press. All that was under attack was monopoly profit, and a determined government would have had no difficulty in demonstrating the self-interest of the objectors.

There was precedent for this. Most newspapers had denounced the government with similar vehemence in 1965, claiming that freedom of the press was under attack from a measure whose effect, in truth, was that it might reduce the sales value of some of their properties. This was the legislation providing that advertising directed to Canadians not be admitted as a business expense and deductible from taxable income if it is placed in publications not Canadian-owned. One effect was to prevent newspaper owners selling out to foreigners. The government of 1965 was far more politically vulnerable than the 1980 Trudeau government, but it faced the publishers down. It implemented the legislation, and a campaign that was so evidently self-interested could not be sustained even by the press. The legislation has remained untouched for 26 years.

The question, therefore, is why the government's will to take on the newspaper owners faded between the autumns of 1980 and 1981. In the concluding part of this article, I shall point to political factors unrelated to the newspaper problem. The lesson to be learned is more general. Powerful vested interests can be overcome, when the public interest is asserted against them because there are moments when circumstances temporarily weaken them. That was true of the newspaper industry in the shock of the transactions of 1980. Within a year, however, the balance of power had shifted.

The conclusion for public policy is that those who want to assert the public interest, whether political parties or other organizations, are likely to succeed only if they are ready in advance with practical ideas to press as soon as circumstances create the opportunity for reform. The time is often brief. To start only then to devise specific policy is to let the opportunity pass. If proposals of the nature of the Commission's had been in someone's pocket in September 1980, they would probably have been implemented. The fundamental failure was that the policy was not ready then. In its absence, a relatively speedy inquiry was the best that could be done, but it was a poor substitute. Much as I hoped otherwise, in retrospect the reality is that the opportunity had been lost before the Commission's work was done.

This is not to say, however, that the Commission's work is wasted for all time. It will not be if, but only if, the lesson is learned and if the Commission report provides a base for practical, up-dated measures ready when the next opportunity comes.

THE START

The Royal Commission was established in response to public shock. On August 27, 1980, the two big English-language chains shared out most of the Canadian daily newspaper business. Together they had almost 60 percent of the circulation of English-language dailies. In order to end direct competition between them, they immediately and simultaneously closed two long-established papers. In Ottawa, the Thomson company abandoned its *Journal,* leaving the market to Southam's *Citizen.* In Winnipeg, Southam abandoned the *Tribune,* leaving that city to the Thomson *Free Press.* In Vancouver, Thomson sold its afternoon *Sun* to Southam, which already owned the city's other daily, the morning *Province.* To tidy things up, Thomson also transferred to Southam its minority interest in the *Gazette,* which had already become the only English-language paper in Montreal because of the recent demise of the *Star.*

This arrant exercise of corporate power, in a business of so much public concern, was deeply shocking to many people. It was obvious, however, that little, if anything, could be done through existing law on the restriction of competition. There was nothing to forbid two companies choosing separate cities in which to publish newspapers. If any offence at all had been committed, it was at a technical level and no possible penalty could alter the situation. The law could not compel competition among companies that chose to abandon their activities in some locations.

The federal Cabinet was therefore in the position of feeling that action was required but not knowing what it could be. The shock nevertheless produced a prompt response. The next day, August 28, I was asked to be a one-man Royal Commission, charged to report quickly on the effects of the concentration of newspaper ownership and suggest what, if anything, could be done about it.

There were two reasons for saying no. One was personal: I had recently joined Dalhousie University as Dean of Administrative Studies and it would not be fair to walk away from the job at the beginning of the academic year, which a one-person commission would require. If that was the form of the inquiry, someone else must be found for it. Secondly, I doubted the wisdom of the form. Any proposals of real effect would be violently opposed by the newspaper proprietors, with all their power. A very hasty, one-person commission would be too vulnerable to criticism. On the other hand, I had seen enough of Royal Commissions to know that if they have many members they almost certainly drag on too long; the inquiry would probably become an evasion of effective action, despite the government's good intentions.

After overnight reflection, therefore, I suggested a compromise. The Commission should have three members, one of whom should be able to give virtually full time to it. Unlike most Royal Commissions, it should operate under the sense of urgency of a firm date to report, but with enough time for the investigation not to be vulnerable to a charge of superficiality. I suggested ten months, with an end date of July 1, 1981.

Within that framework, I could reconcile chairmanship of the Commission with other responsibilities.

The Order-in-Council establishing the Commission was passed on September 3. It gave broad powers to inquire into the newspaper industry and report on "such measures as might be warranted to remedy any matter that the Commission considers should be remedied as a result of the concentration of the ownership and control of the industry and the recent closing of newspapers." The same Order named me as chairman. The other two commissioners—Laurent Picard and Borden Spears—were appointed on September 15. The late Borden Spears was effectively a full-time commissioner; he made, with wisdom and dedication, the most important contribution to the Commission. Holding our first meeting on September 17, we at least started smartly.

It was not easy to get all our investigations underway as promptly as our deadline required. The bureaucratic machine could not be moved to produce financial authorizations with much less than its usual slowness. Anyone who organizes a quick inquiry for government should be warned that success depends on some people being willing to start work on trust, waiting perhaps several months to receive their fees or even reimbursement of expenses.

The Decline and Fall of Competition

Nevertheless, the work was pushed quickly enough to yield, by the turn of the year, some preliminary, if negative, views.

The first was a conclusion to sadden many journalists. The traditional kind of newspaper competition, in Canada, was dead and gone forever. This was the competition that used to quicken pulses, the head-to-head contest between two similar newspapers both aiming for a broad community coverage, usually reflected in their emphasis on home delivery of an afternoon paper. Such competition probably continued as long as it did in Ottawa and Winnipeg because the two newspapers had, until early 1980, been the properties of chains—Southam and F.P. Publications—that maintained strong newspaper traditions and were reluctant to kill the *Tribune* and the *Journal* though their return on capital was small or even negative.

The decline of competition has been dictated by the economics of the media business. Daily newspapers draw only about 20 percent of their revenues directly from their readers, 80 percent from advertising. In other words, we pay for most of the cost of newspapers not when we buy them but when we buy the goods and services whose prices include the charge for advertising in the newspapers. When newspapers were the only mass media, their advertising volumes could support two or more dailies in many communities. The electronic media have narrowed the range of products for which newspapers are the efficient medium: real estate, used automobiles, jobs, groceries, and so on. Such advertisers want a broad community reach. They can get it most economically if the community has only one newspaper to read. If there are two, the one that gets ahead is increasingly favoured by advertisers. It can then afford to spend more on the circulation war with its competitor. The advantage widens. The second paper becomes unprofitable.

In such a situation, the lure of success is strong. Competition is killing, but once a paper is alone in a community, it can earn rates of profit beyond the dreams of most industries.

In large communities, the monopoly does not have to be complete. The growing volume and sophistication of advertising are reflected in market segmentation. In wealthy Toronto, there is scope for a paper directed to business and affluent people, and contemporary technology allows simultaneous printing at several locations, enhancing the paper's effectiveness for some types of advertising. So we have the "national" *Globe and Mail*. In big cities, there is also room beside the newspaper of general appeal for a morning tabloid, designed primarily for a quick read when commuting or taking a break at work; it again provides a particularly effective medium for some advertisers.

Obviously there is, in Toronto especially, some competition between the *Globe and Mail, Star,* and *Sun.* It is, however, competition at the margins of largely segmented markets. It is very different from the head-to-head competition that disappeared in most Canadian cities long before the 1980 shock in Winnipeg and Ottawa.

Nevertheless, the Commission had to consider whether competition could be restored. In more densely populated countries, particularly in western Europe, it continued, with evident benefits for the free, democratic discussion of public policies. Even there the trend to fewer newspapers was evident, but in many countries— Sweden, Norway, Denmark, the Netherlands, Belgium, West Germany, France—it had been kept partially at bay by various kinds of government subsidy or tax concession. There were adequate safeguards against political manipulation of the assistance, and the effect had been to sustain a broad expression of differing opinion in lively debate.

It seemed possible that Canadian politics would have been healthier if similar measures had been taken when there were still numerous communities with second newspapers. But now subsidizing would be directed not to preserving existing newspapers but to creating new ones. We could not entertain faith that partisanship and favouritism of one kind or another would be avoided. Such use of tax money was not acceptable.

A better alternative, urged on us by a number of thoughtful journalists, was labelled "print CBC." That is, the government should establish and finance a public corporation, with the same independence as the CBC, to publish a national newspaper with regional variations. Certainly CBC news and public affairs, particularly on radio, provided more information and wider, more thorough discussion than would otherwise be available to most Canadians.

It was reluctantly, therefore, that we thought a parallel in print not feasible. The CBC was created when radio was young. It participated with private stations in an expanding industry. In the case of television, it was in on the ground floor. Private stations came after, and their profitability lay in buying U.S. programs rather than making their own. The CBC therefore, has a special role as an instrument of nationwide communication and national identity that would be little served without the use of public money.

Newspapers are different in many ways. Most have a history of partisan association, and although this has generally weakened, because in most cities the surviving newspaper seeks to be acceptable to all conventional opinions, it is still true that people expect newspapers to be politically identified, whereas radio and TV, appearing more recently, do not have, overtly at least, such associations. A publicly financed newspaper would therefore be more readily suspected of pro-government bias than is the CBC.

In this, history would be reinforced by technology. The electronic media are the means by which politicians reach directly to people in their homes. However much some may feel that television and radio coverage is unfair to them, that the CBC's commentary is biased or subversive or whatever, they have a countervail; much of the time, the medium brings them directly to the public, speaking their own words. That does not make the CBC's independence of the government that finances it altogether easy, but it helps.

In print, however, the reporting is all. The politicians' personalities are conveyed only indirectly, through the medium. The temptation for the government to interfere, to press for reports as it liked them, would therefore be stronger than is feasible in dealing with television. It would be heightened by there being, in almost all communities, less competition in print than there is for the CBC on the air. Even if politicians in fact kept their hands off newspapers for which they voted the funds, there would be constant suspicion and complaint. The journalists operating the papers would have a hard time establishing their reputation for objectivity so firmly that criticism could be contained to a manageable volume. To succeed, they would have to be extremely careful, at the expense of both depth and liveliness in their reporting.

We therefore saw for "print CBC" a miserable choice: either it would yield to political pressures to some degree and be manipulative; or it would establish and retain its independence only by being bland and very dull, an expensive nullity. In neither case would the use of taxpayers' money be justified.

CHAINS

At this point we concluded we could not realistically recommend public policies that would increase the number of newspapers and restore competition. This was not to say that new, privately owned papers were impossible. The technological revolution of computerized photocomposition, which swept through the industry during the seventies, had already greatly strengthened weekly newspapers. Combined with satellite communication, it was enabling the *Globe and Mail* to become a nation-wide paper. Conceivably there were more large cities where the new production technology would make another daily economic. But it could be so only within the confines of market segmentation imposed by advertising considerations. Any new dailies would almost certainly follow the trend toward morning tabloids, creating only marginal competition. Moreover, the capital investment involved made it unlikely that they would diminish concentration and conglomeration.

The decline in the number of newspapers had overlapped with the growth of chain ownership. Many journalists were understandably inclined to see a causal connection and to blame the chains for closing newspapers. Our analysis did not support this. There was, however, a sense in which chains lessened competition, because newspapers are significant in the public affairs not only of their local communities but also regionally and nationally. Any democrat will think first of the New Brunswick situation. It can be accepted as an economic necessity that the English-language daily press is limited to one newspaper business in each of the province's three major cities: Saint John, Moncton, and Fredericton. But that still gives three sources of information and opinion on the affairs of the province and of the nation. There could be marginal competition for circulation areas and substantial competition in reporting and commenting that would be influential in forming provincial opinion. There is no economic reason why that benefit of separate ownership should be denied to the people of New Brunswick. In fact, of course, the papers in all three cities are owned by the Irving family—which also owns television and radio stations, as well as much of the province's industry.

This was and is an extreme case, but nationally the extent of concentration that the Commission had to examine was horrifying to a believer in the virtues of political and economic freedom. In 1980, the two big chains—Southam and Thomson—together had close to 60 percent of the circulation of English-language dailies. Other chains (i.e., companies owning dailies in two or more communities) enjoyed about another 15 percent of circulation. Independent ownership was limited to barely more than a quarter.

That was the result of rapid change. Only ten years earlier, the share of independent papers in English-language circulation had been almost 40 percent, more than half as big again as it had become by 1980. In 1970, there were three big chains. Southam and F.P. Publications each had about 22 percent of total circulation; Thomson owned numerous papers but they were in smaller cities, so that its share of circulation was only a little over 10 percent.

The FP chain, put together at great speed in the 1960s, was a troubled organization, soon ripe for dissolution. In 1980, Thomson purchased it all and then sold some to Southam. This not only accentuated concentration but also changed its character; whereas FP had been simply a newspaper company, Thomson was a conglomerate for which newspapers were one among diverse business interests.

The transformation of the French-language daily press had been no less dramatic. In 1970, independently owned papers had accounted for just over half of the circulation. By 1980, one chain alone had expanded to 46.5 percent, there were two other chains with 43.5 percent between them, and the circulation of independent papers was a mere 10 percent of the total.

Was this massive concentration of ownership driven by compelling business considerations comparable to those that had eliminated head-to-head competition? The answer was no. By its nature, a daily newspaper must be managed on the spot. A head office for the geographically dispersed units might provide some benefits in specialized services and some economies in purchasing and administrative organization. Such factors were, however, of minor significance. The chains themselves did not seriously claim otherwise. They could not, since their primary defence of chain ownership was to assert that their papers were virtually independent, operating with almost no interference from head office.

One argument that had been made in the past was that a chain could afford to maintain an unprofitable newspaper that would have to close if it were independent. That argument had disappeared in August 1980 with the closures in Ottawa and Winnipeg.

The substantial benefit to the public from chain ownership could be that the pooled resources of a number of newspapers enable them to provide better coverage of news outside their own localities—of national and international affairs—than is possible for one paper alone. Southam can claim this virtue. In 1980, its news service had six bureaus in Canada and five abroad. The quality of its staff—who were paid superior salaries and allowances—made it a bright light in Canadian journalism. But of the print media, it was alone. FP had, shortly before its demise, put a similar service into place; when Thomson took over, it was promptly killed. The Southam service, standing alone, was hardly in itself a justification for the massive concentration of newspaper ownership.

THE PURPOSE OF THE PRESS

To determine what could reasonably be done about that concentration, it was necessary to define the role of newspapers in Canadian society and examine, in the language of the Commission's terms of reference, "the consequences of the present situation in the newspaper industry for the political, economic, social and intellectual vitality and cohesion of the nation as a whole."

Freedom of the press is sometimes championed by the press as if it were a property right: to own the means of publication creates a special right to self-expression. In truth, of course, the press has distinctive power, but in a democracy its *rights* are those that belong to every person. Freedom of opinion and expression is, in our society, universal. It is meaningful, however, only if people also have freedom of access to the information required to form opinion. That is not only factual information; it is also awareness of varied interpretations of events and the range of views about what might or should be done to influence future events.

The importance of the media is that they are the most general source of such information. To provide it is their responsibility to society. The function is both increasingly important and increasingly difficult as communication quickens, as we are all drawn into greater interdependence, as the complexity of scientific advance requires increasing specialization and makes general understanding harder to secure.

Newspapers have had to cede immediacy to the electronic media. Newscasts, however, can hold attention only if each item is short enough for people who are not interested in it to wait for the next item rather than turn off or tune out. The newspaper reader, in contrast, easily skims or skips what is of little or no interest and welcomes detail about what is of interest. Therefore, the newspaper's coverage is, compared particularly with TV, more comprehensive and more detailed. Most of us may use the electronic media for our quick fix on the news, but it is still to print that we must turn for anything near the information that the effective citizen of a democracy requires in order to form his or her opinions. And it is in newspaper files that the record of much of our public affairs is stored.

Journalists are the gatekeepers of most of our information. They select what will reach us and present it to us as they see it. Their first duty is to get their facts right, but facts alone rarely tell a story. To make sense, they must be put in context. There can be no pretence to a cold objectivity in journalism. The truth about public affairs is always the truth as someone sees it. Journalism is of good quality if that someone has the breadth of view that comes from knowledge and experience, the fairness of mind that comes with awareness of the range of opinions and interpretations besides those dominant at the particular time and place. Moreover, such individual qualities of the journalist can be effectively exercised only if the staff of the newspaper is large enough to permit a considerable degree of specialization and to provide an interplay of opinions within the paper.

It is snobbery to pretend, as is often done by defenders of the press as it is, that these standards are relevant only to newspapers aimed at the sophisticated minority of readers. A fair and accurate report has limited value if it is also dull. To make a significant report interesting to the general reader requires at least as much knowledge, understanding, and time, and more writing ability, than to do it for people who already have much of the background information.

A similar defence of the status quo is that people get the newspapers they want or deserve. The truth is that few have any choice. They might like to read more national and international news, but in order to get the local news as well, they have to buy, say, the Cape Breton *Post*. What they get is what can be produced by the staff Thomson considers to be the minimum necessary expense of the paper.

The skills, knowledge, and experience required for good journalism are fully comparable to those required in most professional work. The glamour of journalism may make it relatively easy to obtain recruits, but newspapers will hold enough people of the required ability only if the salaries and conditions of work for experienced journalists are comparable to those of other professional workers. The newspaper industry will better fulfil its responsibility to Canadian society only if it employs more journalists, pays them better, plans their career development to give broader experience, than is now the practice of most newspapers.

The managing editor of the Toronto *Mail* made the central point very simply more than a hundred years before the Royal Commission: "A daily newspaper is good or bad according to the money expended on the preparation of its news." But there is no business incentive for newspapers to spend more than they do. This is the central point underlying the concentration of newspaper ownership.

CONGLOMERATION

Newspapers compete with other media for some kinds of advertising, their principal source of revenue. The distinctive product of the newspaper—the day's news in print—goes into the space between the ads, the "news hole" as it is known to the people who put the paper together after the space required by the day's advertising has been allocated. The special case of the national *Globe and Mail* apart, what is put into most of the news hole has little bearing on the paper's revenues. People who want a general-appeal newspaper published in the locality have no choice; they take the one that is available or they do without. Some potential readers are driven away by very poor content. Above a low minimum level, however, most newspapers have little circulation and revenue to gain by improving the quality of their news coverage.

What is visibly related to newspaper's content is its costs. The news hole can be filled quite cheaply with wire-service copy, syndicated material (mostly American), and handouts from interested parties. The paper can then manage with a small reporting staff. It does not require of its editorial staff the background, ability, and time to assess and select material so that the reader has an intelligible account of significant news, national, international, or even local.

To produce better newspapers is more costly. It is not done for profit. It is done at a reduction of profit, because there is some continuing sense that newspapers are more than a business. In theory, that is recognized by all Canadian publishers. The statement of principles adopted by their association in 1977 declared:

> The operation of a newspaper is in effect a public trust, no less binding because it is not formally conferred, and its overriding responsibility is to the society which protects and provides its freedom. The newspaper keeps faith with its readers by presenting the news comprehensively, accurately and fairly . . .

and so on. But keeping faith costs money, and newspaper publishers vary greatly in their willingness to incur the cost.

The Royal Commission was able to calculate, for 82 newspapers over three financial years ending in 1980, their editorial expense (i.e., total expenditure on content) as a proportion of total revenue from advertising and circulation. The proportions varied from over 20 to under 10 percent.

It was notable that Quebec newspapers tended to spend relatively more than those of English Canada, perhaps because the Quebec market was more competitive. Elsewhere, some of the more extreme ratios could be explained by financial troubles. But those, in an industry that was as a whole highly profitable, were very few. The variations in the expenditure ratio had no relation to circulation, or, within English Canada, to location. They could be explained only by the policies of their owners, by the balance struck between the rate of profit—generally high, or very high—and the quality of the newspaper's service to the public.

The newspapers that spent more than the industry average, in ratio to their revenues, included eleven of the Southam papers, plus its Vancouver *Sun*, which until 1980 had been in the FP chain; three other former FP papers; a number of independents, notably *Le Devoir*, the London *Free Press*, Kingston *Whig Standard*, and Toronto *Star*; and—it must be noted in fairness—the Irving papers in two of their three cities.

The newspapers spending less than the industry average included three Southam papers; the two Armadale (i.e., Sifton) papers in Saskatchewan; the former FP paper in Winnipeg; the Toronto *Sun*; and independents in a number of cities, of which the largest was Halifax. The list was dominated, however, by Thomson. Of the 38 papers with the lowest spending relative to revenues, 28 were, and had been before 1980, Thomson-owned.

The dynamics of newspaper concentration were all too plain. A newspaper is worth more as a business the less its proprietor is concerned with serving the public interest by comprehensive, accurate, fair reporting of the news. Profit can be maximized by cutting editorial costs to a minimal level. Newspapers can then be milked for most attractive cash flows with which to build expanding business empires. That is how the Thomson fortune was developed to embrace oil in the North Sea, media in other countries, and much of the department store business in Canada. Thomson's purchase of the FP papers meant the absorption, in one gulp, of a large part of the press into a corporate structure within which newspapers are run not by newspaper people but by accountants who are indeed remarkably successful in cutting costs, extracting in profits the resources that would be needed to produce good newspapers, and channelling them into other ventures.

Southam read the signs. That was the reason for the drama of August 27, 1980, the reason why Southam made the arrangements with Thomson that freed it from the losing Winnipeg *Tribune* and consolidated its position in Ottawa, Vancouver, and Montreal. While growing to a chain, Southam had remained essentially a newspaper company, caring enough about the quality of journalism to spend appreciably more than a simple dedication to maximizing profit would have required. Precisely for that reason, Southam was vulnerable to takeover by a conglomerate with exclusively financial motives. Its management has in fact been largely occupied, throughout the 1980s, in fending off the danger. To that end it has cut some costs and made an alliance with the Toronto *Star*. These actions are unlikely to do more than put off the evil day. Within our present legal and financial structure, it is inevitable that a separate newspaper industry, distinct from other business, will disappear. The remaining independents and Southam will be progressively absorbed into conglomerate corporations; they will all be run by people whose interest is not in the newspapers' role of maximizing public information but in their contribution to the profits and growth of business empires.

This will be justified as market economics, but it is not. The point of conglomerates is to distort markets by cross-subsidization; enterprises that yield large cash flows in relation to the capital employed, such as newspapers, are used to support or promote weaker ventures, saving those from full exposure to the tests of the market. The consequence in the case of newspapers is that public information is impoverished. Its quality is vital to a democratic society, but the effect of our financial structure is to undervalue the importance of providing information. Revenues generated by the media, which could be used within them, are siphoned off as monopoly profits to be invested in other activities.

There is a second major consequence. The structure of media ownership concentrates political influence. This is not to suggest that the owners dictate what appears from day to day in each of a chain of newspapers. Some may occasionally interfere directly, from a whim or for the sake of a sacred cow or in pursuit of a particular vendetta. Generally, however, the captains of finance are too busy for such indulgences. They put the media into the charge of people who are, from their point of view, safe: people whose careers then depend on their accurate sense of the kind of paper the corporation wants. The corporation does not sit in the newsroom but its interests are a strongly felt presence shaping the kind of paper emerging from the presses.

RESTRAINT

The Commission's investigations showed clearly the strength of the business forces leading to further conglomerate control. Unless countervailing measures were taken, the press's responsibility for informing democracy would be further devalued.

What countervail was possible, however, when the trend had already gone as far as it had in 1980? In the Commission's view, it was too late for the simplistic solution of breaking up the chains. Such concentration of ownership ought never to have been allowed. But it had. It had proceeded entirely naturally under our business system; the law had not said of newspapers, as it had of banks, that they were different from other businesses.

However strong the case for a law that changes the future, a responsible government must be careful about its retroactive effects. A wholesale break-up of chains would be a major disruption of organizations that had evolved legitimately under the law as it had been. True, the resulting concentration of newspaper ownership had become so monstrous that the disruption could be justified, but only if two conditions were met. We had to be confident both that large improvements in the press would follow and that there was no less disruptive way of securing the public interest. We could not have that confidence.

There was no possibility that small investors, co-operatives, journalists, etc., would produce enough equity capital to be the successful bidders for many of the scores of newspapers that would be put on the market. Most would pass to groups with other substantial business interests. There could be no guarantee that their journalistic conscience would put the quality of information service to the public ahead of a high rate of return on investment. True, it was unlikely that new ownership would make any of the Thomson papers worse; but it was probable that some of the Southam papers would deteriorate. And, intent apart, there was the risk that inexperienced management would reduce the resources available for reporters and editors.

Chain ownership had, in short, gone too far to be now destroyed. The Commission proposed prohibitions on its further growth, and on future purchases of newspapers by other business interests. We could not, however, regard this standstill as sufficient unless there was also correction of the worst cases in which concentration of ownership had also lessened competition.

In some communities, there was common ownership of the daily paper and television or radio stations, or even both television and radio, covering the same area. Such concentration of power was prevented even in a country as business oriented as the United States. To end it in Canada required no drastic action, since radio and television licences are given for limited periods. They could simply not be renewed when next under review, unless of course the company chose to sell its newspaper instead. (This was the one commission recommendation on which the Trudeau government acted, only to have the policy reversed by the Mulroney government.)

The unnecessary restriction of competition that had the most serious consequences had come about only recently. Thomson's nationally printed *Globe and Mail* was to some degree an alternative to local papers—papers owned, in so many communities, by Thomson. There was obvious danger that Thomson would use the excuse to bother even less than it would otherwise have done about national and international news in the local papers; people who wanted that service could buy the Thomson *Globe and Mail* instead or, even better, as well. To stop this unnecessary lessening of competition, the Commission recommended that Thomson should be required to choose, to divest itself either of all its other papers or (the practical choice) of the *Globe and Mail*.

The other worst cases were those of the provinces—Saskatchewan and New Brunswick—that had two or three principal cities with newspapers, but only one proprietor. The Commission proposed that Sifton and Irving should each be required to sell one of their papers.

COUNTERVAIL

These were, in our view, minimal proposals for lessening the concentration of ownership. They dealt with the worst cases in which competitive diversity within the media was unnecessarily constrained. They did not touch the general problem: the impoverishment of the information available to Canadians because the resources generated within the newspaper industry are so heavily drained into monopoly profits. For that, we turned to other policies.

Apart from public ownership, which we had rejected as a prescription for newspapers, government has two methods of intervention when "free" enterprise serves the public poorly, usually because of some degree of monopolization. One method is regulation in its many forms. The other, often more appropriate and certainly more so for the media, is to alter the impact of the incentives under which business operates. Markets are deficient when the "invisible hand," in Adam Smith's phrase, does *not* induce people following their own interests to act in ways that in fact serve the public interest. The time-honoured methods by which government may strengthen the inducement include tax advantages, tariffs for infant industries, services free or below cost, and cheap capital, as well as outright grants.

The Commission identified a tax measure that would bear directly on the choice between public service and profit. This choice was reflected, as noted above, in the wide variation in the proportion of their revenues that newspapers spent on their content. The Commission proposed to make preference for profit over content more expensive. A company publishing a newspaper that spent less than the industry average for the previous year in proportion to revenue would have to pay a surtax equal to 25 percent of the deficiency; if the newspaper spent more than the industry average, 25 percent of the extra would become a tax credit. There would thus be a large reduction in the net profit after tax obtainable by spending less rather than more on a newspaper's content.

This would be achieved without significant cost to the Treasury in any one year, since the credits would be approximately equalled by the surtaxes. There might, of course, be some cost in the long run, if the policy achieved its purpose, if the total profits of newspapers were reduced in favour of, say, reporters' salaries taxed at lower rates than the companies were. But any such net loss to the Treasury would be trifling beside the public benefit of improvement in the newspapers.

We could not be greatly confident, however, about the extent of the improvement that would come from this one measure. Some more money would be spent, but how well? It might be a long time before the weaker papers had either the will or the capacity to make their news coverage more comprehensive, accurate, and fair. There was need for a supplementary measure, and an instrument for it was obvious.

In the days when they were almost entirely independent of each other, Canadian newspapers had organized the co-operative news agency, Canadian Press. CP had provided, particularly in the 1940s, a distinguished service. But in the postwar period it had not kept pace with the revolutionary changes that brought the nation and the world so much closer to us all. Instead, CP's international coverage had been all but eliminated; news from one part of the nation to another depended on heroic work by insufficient staff; most damagingly for national unity, twenty years after the Quiet Revolution CP's coverage of Quebec for English Canadians, and of the rest of Canada for readers of French, remained pathetically inadequate.

The main reason for the inadequacies was clear. The assessments that are the core of its financing must be agreed on by most of the member newspapers. Thomson, with its multitude of papers, does not need the support of many others, almost as parsimonious, in order to control the scale of the CP service.

It seemed to the Commission that improvement was essential to the newspaper industry's contribution to, in the words of our terms of reference, the "vitality and cohesion of the nation." We could see no method except a financial incentive. It should be available not only to CP but to any competitor that serviced a significant number of papers in varied ownership. We proposed that a news service that spent more (after allowance for inflation) than it had done in a base year on Canadian news and on international news from Canadian sources should receive—after the event—a grant equal to half of the increased expenditure.

The details of both these financial proposals—the tax credit/surtax for individual newspapers, and the grant incentive to news services—were carefully structured so that a government could not use either the threat or the promise of changes as an incentive to influence the opinions of the press. Their aim was purely to increase the resources that newspapers put into their service of information to the public. The two measures together, we thought, would in time induce greater willingness to forgo some newspaper profit for the sake of the public interest in more information and so facilitate fuller discussion of public affairs.

ACCOUNTABILITY

We were concerned, however, that the attitudes of newspaper managements might make many of them slow to respond even to strong incentives to shift their preferences between profit and expense. We therefore decided, after some hesitation, that the incentives should be reinforced by measures to strengthen the influence of journalists and of the local community of the conduct of a chain newspaper.

It is a paradox of the press that, while professionally dedicated to exposing other organizations and persons to public view, it is extremely secretive about its own affairs. Not only does it resist any kind of external accountability; internally its management styles are among the least participative now to be found in major businesses.

There are exceptions. Some of the world's greatest newspapers operate under trust deeds that limit the returns to shareholders, retain other earnings for the development of the papers, and ensure editorial independence. Other distinguished publications achieve the same character less formally, but by firm tradition. None, however, is an English-Canadian newspaper. While all the publishers professed, through their association, to recognize that the operation of a newspaper is a public trust, we saw no possibility of legislation to enforce that status. Since they compete with other media for their main revenue—from advertising—newspapers could not be held to be monopolies in the sense that would justify a legal limit on their rate of profit.

The Commission therefore proposed a lesser change that would somewhat enhance the sense of public accountability in the operation of chain-owned newspapers. In essence, it was that each paper should be conducted in some respects under conditions similar to those imposed by companies legislation on a business corporation.

A corporation must have, in its registered articles of association, a statement of its purpose. We proposed that a chain-owned newspaper would be required to publish a definition of its objectives as a medium of information. Second, that its owner be required to identify the person with contractual responsibility for fulfilling these objectives. At present in chain newspapers, the actual division of responsibility between head office, the publisher appointed for each paper, and its editor is, to say the least, obscure. Furthermore, though the larger chains are public companies and therefore required to publish annual reports, these say little or nothing about individual newspapers. To cure this, we proposed that each paper should be required to produce and print an annual report of the paper's performance in relation to its declared objectives.

A company report is open to question and criticism at the annual meeting of shareholders. Some equivalent was needed if the newspaper's report was not to be mere puffery. The Commission therefore proposed that each chain newspaper should have a small advisory committee. Appointees of the company, journalists elected by the staff, and independent members from the community would sit in equal numbers, under a chair chosen by the independents. The committee would review the paper's annual report, and the paper would be required to publish the comments. This would make it difficult for the report to be entirely remote from reality.

The Commission was under no illusion that this process would in itself work any sudden transformation in all chain newspapers. It would, however, somewhat enhance the status of journalists relative to newspaper managements, and it would be likely, in conjunction with our tax proposals, at least gradually to induce a stronger consciousness of public responsibility in the operation of chain papers.

The Commission proposed that its various recommendations be consolidated in a Newspaper Act, somewhat analogous to the Bank Act. Such administration as it required would not, however, be entrusted to a minister and a government department. It would be the responsibility of a Press Rights Panel of the Canadian Human Rights Commission. It would thus be independent of the Cabinet. With the wisdom of hindsight, one of the minor changes that I would make in the Commission's recommendations would be to make that independence so explicit, through the method of appointment of the panel, that even the most prejudiced of newspaper proprietors could not seriously contest it.

DEFEAT

There was, of course, no doubt that the proprietors of newspapers would vehemently object to the Commission's proposals. Their large profits were at stake. Since they could not make that an effective public argument, their recourse was to wrap themselves in the flag of freedom of the press. They could adduce no argument for that. The proposals were directed entirely to restraining the business interests of newspaper owners, to changing the environment of their operations so that they would put more resources into service of the public's right to information. The Commission made no recommendations that would give government any control of the information that the newspapers chose to provide or that would limit in any way the newspapers' freedom to report what and as they wished and to express whatever opinions they liked. On the contrary, the effect of more resources going into the content of newspapers, of larger staffs and the rest, would be that newspapers could be more effective in their role as critics of government.

The public interest was not, however, the newspapers' concern. It was profit. Their unstated but plain domination by business self-interest combined with the poverty of the arguments they deployed to provide the clearest possible demonstration of the accuracy of the Commission's analysis and the need for the reforms it proposed. The campaign against the Commission implicitly recognized this. It was fury and bombast without substance, vehemence and invective and misrepresentation to cover the lack of an arguable case.

In fairness to the journalists who complied with their owners' attitudes, it should be remembered that for much of history everywhere, and still today in many countries, it is government that suppresses or limits the freedom of the press. Journalists inherit a long-bred suspicion of government action that affects the press in any way. A considerable recasting of traditional thinking is required in order to recognize that now the enemy is within, that the main barrier to accurate, comprehensive, fair reporting is created by the dominance of business interests in the concentrated ownership of newspapers.

To understand the force of habit is not, however, to justify the mindless ferocity of the campaign against the Commission. Previous experience had partly prepared me for the onslaught.

In 1965, the Pearson government introduced a measure to prevent further foreign ownership of Canadian newspapers and magazines. There was at the time danger that other American publications would follow the example of the Canadian edition of *Time* and that some principal newspapers—notably the *Globe and Mail* and *La Presse*—might be sold to foreign owners. The simple but effective defence was to provide that the cost of advertising directed primarily to the Canadian market would not be allowed as a deduction from taxable income if it was placed in a publication that was not Canadian-owned.

The opposition to this was not quite as widespread as to the Commission's proposals. The Toronto *Star*, with its nationalist sentiments, supported it, and St. Clair Balfour, the broad-minded head of the Southam organization at that time, was personally sympathetic. The advertising tax was a purely preventive measure. It did not affect the profits of existing newspapers. Its adverse business effect was to reduce the potential capital worth of a newspaper; if it was up for sale, the bidders would be restricted to Canadians. This mattered not only to proprietors who might want sooner or later to sell, but also to companies that, in the way of conglomerates, use the worth of their existing assets as security for loans to finance further acquisitions.

Most newspapers therefore attacked the proposal. Their cry that they were defending the freedom of the press was too patently baseless for editorials to carry much weight, but the lobbying of politicians, both by proprietors individually and by their association, was intense. It was also vituperative in its attacks on Walter Gordon and me, who were presumed (correctly) to be the principal authors of the government measure. The Winnipeg *Free Press* even went so far as to depict Walter Gordon in the category of enemies of freedom, along with Hitler and Stalin in an editorial cartoon.

Although the experience prepared me for the nature of the attack, it also lulled me into overoptimism. In 1965, we had a minority government, exposed to the possibility of an election at any time. For such a government to incur the self-interested enmity of most newspaper owners was a serious undertaking. Nevertheless, the Pearson government stood firm against the storm. It implemented the publications measure as proposed.

The Trudeau government of 1980 was in a much happier situation. It had just won a remarkable election victory and, with a secure majority, had four years to justify itself. As I showed at the beginning of this chapter, its concern about the condition of the press was initially serious. It wanted a prompt report, and the composition of the Commission showed that it did not want a do-nothing report. I did not expect that every one of our extensive recommendations would be accepted as proposed. Political wisdom would call for some concessions to criticism, some compromises that would not mollify the owners but would take the edge off any sympathy they might enlist. At first, however, I thought that the main substance of our reforms was achievable.

I was wrong, for four reasons.

The Commission was appointed in 1980 by a fresh, buoyant, take-on-the-world government. It reported in 1981 to a government already in deep decline, mired in economic problems that it did not know how to deal with, beset by so many critics on so many fronts that, despite its majority, its enthusiasm for controversial action was greatly depleted.

Second, the Trudeau Cabinet lacked the unifying sense of direction of successful administrations. The Prime Minister had his pet purposes, notably the patriation of the Constitution and the entrenchment of a Charter of Rights and Freedoms, which he pursued with determined willingness to fight. His interest in most other issues, however, was sporadic, academically abstract rather than purposeful. And where he did not give strong leadership, his Cabinet was generally confused and indecisive.

Third, it was particularly unfortunate for the Commission that it was early constitutional change that preoccupied Mr. Trudeau. The newspaper owners would undoubtedly put up constitutional arguments to delay, if not frustrate, some of our proposals. Their lawyers would claim that in the Newspaper Act the federal authority was usurping powers that properly belonged to the provinces. Their case might be as thin as we thought, but even so, the raising of the issue would not help the Prime Minister at a time when he was trying to negotiate the provinces into acceptance of a restraint on all legislative power, provincial as well as federal, through the Charter. In retrospect, we might have done more to avoid this difficulty by making our own suggestions for the form of federal-provincial co-operation that would most smoothly implement our proposals.

The fourth factor was an unforeseeable misfortune. Publication of our report was soon followed by the MacEachen Budget of the fall of 1981. It proposed important changes in the tax system. As always, a storm of protest came from many special interests; and as usual, the protest was strengthened by the weaknesses in detail that, for many years now, have characterized much of the work of the Department of Finance. The government made a humiliating retreat from most of its proposals. Consequently the last thing it wanted to undertake, after having been so lately so badly burned, was another tax measure.

This was fatal to our central proposal, the tax credit/surtax, which would have been the easiest to implement, the quickest to take effect, and would have exercised, in combination with the news service subsidy, the most direct influence to improvement in the newspapers' fullfilment of their responsibility to a democratic society.

It was not to be. The legislation that the government did prepare was only a small step toward the implementation of our ideas, and even that was never proceeded with. The government's will had failed. The victory of the newspaper owners was complete. The Commission had failed.

Yet this did not have to be, and it need not be the end of the affair. My experience and observation of politics have convinced me that reforms are not frustrated because vested interests are strong. They are strong, much of the time, but there are also occasions when they become paper tigers, easily swept aside. They go unswept because few people recognize the importance of timing. They are not ready with practical measures to undertake when the time is ripe.

The newspaper crisis of 1980 is a clear case. If there had been practical proposals on the table, no Royal Commission would have been needed. The government would have made decisions while the shock of August 27 was vivid. It would not have lost its nerve.

Proposals could have been ready. The crisis had been long in the making. The Davey Committee of the Senate had diagnosed much of the problem a decade earlier. The crucial event, the purchase of FP by Thomson, had taken place at the beginning of 1980. The transactions of August 27, which caused so much horror, were merely the visible working out of the implications of the Thomson takeover. It was that, seven months earlier, which should have rung the alarm bells for alert reformers.

The Liberal party was then in opposition. It is sad to reflect how different the outcome would have been if the party had seen that the state of the newspaper industry created an issue for which policy should be prepared. Alternatively, suppose that an independent body, such as the Institute for Research on Public Policy, had recognized that the newspaper situation called for prompt study. (This does not imply criticism of anybody else; I was at the time a member of the Institute board and did not offer the suggestion.) Most appropriately of all, suppose that a school of journalism had become constructively concerned about the effects that heightened concentration in the industry would have on the future employment of its graduates.

Under any such auspices, it would not have been difficult to set up a volunteer task force to recommend what might be done by public policy. Elaborate investigation by a Royal Commission was not essential. It only made precise what many journalists and observers of the media knew already in general. If the task force had employed the talents of, say, a professor of journalism, a working journalist, an economist, a lawyer with business experience, a political scientist, a retired public servant, then some months of spare-time work could have been sufficient to arrive at conclusions of much the same nature as those to which a commission was required to proceed judiciously. I am not suggesting that the proposals would have been identical, but it is likely that they would have been to similar effect. And if they had been available in September, when the shock of the Thomson-Southam manoeuvres was vivid, their implementation would have been practicable.

The newspaper industry will not be static. Its profits responded buoyantly to the economic expansion of the later 1980s. The investment community, rarely conspicuous for either the breadth or the length of its sight, seems to have needed the Commission to make it fully aware of the financial attractiveness of newspapers. Consequently our report, when not acted upon, was perversely beneficial for the prices of newspaper shares. The aftermath of the recession of 1990–91 could be different. Newspapers have been losing readership, as is hardly surprising when there has been so little adjustment of their content to the new information age. In consequence, their profit rates may not rebound to the former heights. Nevertheless, it is unlikely that the financial system's impulse to takeovers will be subdued for long. There will be new dramas in the newspaper industry, and the financial operators will again arouse public concern.

For sanity, we have to presume that our federal politics will not be in permanent malaise. The time will probably come when policy to revitalize newspapers is again a feasible item of the government agenda. To take the Royal Commission report off the shelf will not be sufficient. Probably its proposals could be improved; certainly they will require some adaptation to changed circumstances. It will not do to start the thinking then.

That is the most important working conclusion from our experience. The necessary motto for reformers, in this as in other matters, is similar to that of the Boy Scouts: be prepared—for the day when some conjunction of circumstances creates a will for change; that day belongs to those who have practical ideas ready. If this is understood by some of the people who recognize our democracy's need for a better information service from the press, then in the end the work of the Commission may not have been wasted.

THE DEVELOPMENT OF
CANADIAN BROADCASTING POLICY

Report of the Task Force on Broadcasting Policy

The search for public policy for the Canadian broadcasting system has now gone on for almost six decades. A small but honourable cottage industry, it has been the subject of some dozen reports by commissions, royal or otherwise, committees, and task forces. As well, there have been several studies by parliamentary committees and CRTC committees, along with a half-dozen major government statements and the *Broadcasting Acts* of 1958 and 1968. We tread a well-worn path indeed.

At this point some may say enough is enough. Robert Fowler, our distinguished predecessor who chaired both a royal commission and a committee, remarked that he thought it doubtful whether broadcasting could survive many more investigations.

With the utmost respect, we demur. Certainly we sympathize with Mr. Fowler's weariness after two reports in seven years. What he could not know, however, was that those two reports, in 1957 and 1965, would be the only major studies ever undertaken dealing in detail with the entire Canadian broadcasting system until our own. The Massey Commission and the Applebaum-Hébert Committee looked at broadcasting in the larger context of Canadian culture, and various studies have reported on specific aspects of the broadcasting system. But there has never been a comprehensive study of the efficacy of the 1968 *Broadcasting Act*, notwithstanding the enormous changes that have affected Canadian broadcasting over the past eighteen years.

In short, the widely expressed view that the archives of Ottawa are filled with a succession of largely neglected studies and committee reports is something of a caricature, a symbol, perhaps, of the substantial mythology that envelopes Canadian broadcasting.

If anything, therefore, a study such as ours is long overdue. Existing policy and the legislative framework for the broadcasting system is based in some respects on a rapidly vanishing reality, and in certain inevitable ways is both inappropriate to and inadequate for the emerging era. Our mandate reflects this situation.

The Canadian broadcasting system is one of the great achievements of our nation. In the face of formidable geographical, technical, political, financial, and linguistic obstacles; in the face of unparalleled problems inherent in our contiguity with the United States, the greatest purveyor of entertainment (or "culture," as Canadians think of it) in human history; Canada has evolved a radio and television system that, like the country itself, mostly works. There have, of course, always been flaws and imperfections, some of them significant, reflecting both the difficulties that had to be met and surmounted and the way the nation has developed.

The Canadian broadcasting system has many strengths and virtues. Our task, however, is not to dwell on these. Formulating public policy is a matter of trying to make what already may be working well work better. That is why our mandate is to investigate the system, to understand its development, dilemmas, and failures, in order to recommend ways and means for its improvement.

A PERSPECTIVE

When this Task Force was created in 1985 it was appropriate for the Minister of Communications to quote the stirring words of Prime Minister R.B. Bennett who introduced public broadcasting to Canada in 1932.

> . . . this country must be assured of complete Canadian control of broadcasting from Canadian sources. Without such control, broadcasting can never be the agency by which national consciousness may be fostered and sustained and national unity still further strengthened . . . (House of Commons, 1932, pp. 3035–36).

The Minister's citation was appropriate not because of the continuity of party—on the contrary, political partisanship has been the least divisive of the factors affecting broadcasting policy—but rather because of the remarkable continuity of generations. Over and over again we were impressed by the durability of the issues and dilemmas of the broadcasting system. Not even the physical presence of satellites above could constrain us from wondering if there were ever anything new under the broadcasting sun. At the very least, we can say with confidence that the nature of public policy in Canadian broadcasting reflects the constancy of the problems it is designed to solve.

Indeed, our very first predecessor, the Aird Royal Commission on Broadcasting, was appointed in circumstances strikingly like those in which we find ourselves.

The Age of Radio

During the 1920s, radio in Canada represented still another manifestation of the waning of British influence and the waxing of American. But there was also a growing sentiment that recognized Canadian culture as being distinct from both British and American. There was already a movement underway to protect Canadian magazines by allowing them tax and postal concessions and by imposing tariffs on American imports. There was also fitful interest in encouraging a Canadian film industry. The Canadian Press news agency was made viable through government subsidy. As the twenties wore on, however, and virtually every city and town established a radio station or two, it was through broadcasting that more and more Canadians felt the constant barrage of American influence—both from stations across the border and from Canadian stations acting largely as relays.

The originator of public broadcasting in Canada was Sir Henry Thornton, president of the Canadian National Railways, who opened a radio broadcasting service for train travellers, hotel guests, and employees in 1923. While nearly all the radio stations were privately owned and were broadcasting mostly American material, the CNR service used Canadian performers for concerts, talks, and other programming.

Aird

It was in this atmosphere of perceived crisis that Prime Minister Mackenzie King created the first inquiry into broadcasting in Canada. The 1928 Royal Commission on Radio Broadcasting was chaired by Sir John Aird, president of the Canadian Bank of Commerce. Its three members established the pattern for later enquiries—meetings across the country, consultations with key parties, the receipt of written submissions, careful consideration of alternative broadcasting models—and submitted its singularly brief report, a scant nine pages of text, in 1929. The Commission had received, the report noted, a considerable diversity of opinion. "There has, however, been unanimity on one fundamental question—Canadian radio listeners want Canadian broadcasting." Yet, it said, "the majority of programmes heard are from sources outside of Canada" (Aird Commission, 1929, p. 6).

The Aird Commission recommended the adoption of a British or European model of public broadcasting rather than the commercial American one. The commissioners believed only a national publicly owned system could achieve a genuinely Canadian broadcasting system. Private broadcasters, they concluded, could not raise sufficient revenues from advertising to satisfy the need for Canadian programming.

The Commission set a coverage goal of "good reception over the entire settled region of the country," an expensive enterprise in a country with the geography of Canada. And it dealt with quality of transmission rather than with quality of content, recommending tougher legislation to deal with sources of interference to broadcast signals.

It was the physical plant and organization of broadcasting that Aird and his colleagues saw as a federal responsibility. Content was to be a provincial responsibility. "It is desirable . . . that provincial authorities should be in a position to exercise full control over the programs of the station or stations in their respective areas," the Commission said. But it added, "As to what extent the provinces should participate in effecting this control, of course, is a matter which could be decided between themselves and the Dominion Government authorities" (Aird Commission, 1929, p. 7).

At the time of the Aird Commission, owners of radio receiving sets were required to pay an annual licence fee of two dollars. Aird and his colleagues suggested increasing fees to cover part of the cost of the proposed broadcasting service, which was the practice followed in Britain and other European countries. They further recommended that sponsorship of programs, but not commercials for particular products, should form another source of financing. Finally, they proposed an annual government subsidy to broadcasting, to be reviewed every five years.

The debate surrounding the Aird report also set the pattern of a remarkably consistent series of recurring issues that have been as much of a challenge to our generation as they were to Aird's. Canadian programming versus American, public ownership versus private, the responsibilities of the public broadcaster versus those of the private sector, the subsidizing of culture versus the protection of commercial interests (often called "cultural industries"), the commercial needs of the private stations versus their national obligations, regulation of content versus freedom of expression, federal authority versus provincial, annual financing of the national broadcaster versus long-term financing, technology versus programming as the driving force of the system. The long search for sensible public policies for a nation that in some ways defied common sense was well underway by 1929.

Bennett, Spry, and Massey

One could scarcely question the devotion to private enterprise of either Sir John Aird or Prime Minister R.B. Bennett, who actually introduced public broadcasting to Canada. Yet both found overwhelming the argument that state control was needed to avoid being swamped by American broadcasting, supported by its mighty domestic market. Public control would also serve the aims of coverage and fair allocation of a scarce natural resource. Bennett laid before Parliament in 1932 three memorable principles:

> First of all, this country must be assured of complete control of broadcasting from Canadian sources, free from foreign interference or influence. Without such control radio broadcasting can never become a great agency for communication of matters of national concern and for the diffusion of national thought and ideals, and without such control it can never be the agency by which national consciousness may be fostered and sustained and national unity still further strengthened . . .

> Secondly, no other scheme than that of public ownership can ensure to the people of this country, without regard to class or place, equal enjoyment of the benefits and pleasures of radio broadcasting . . .

> [Thirdly] The use of the air . . . that lies over the soil or land of Canada is a natural resource over which we have complete jurisdiction under the recent decision of the Privy Council (and) I cannot think that any government would be warranted in leaving the air to private exploitation and not reserving it for development for the use of the people (House of Commons, 1932).

The Aird Commission had recommended provincial control of programming, in consultation with Ottawa. By the time of Bennett's speech, broadcasting had been placed firmly in federal jurisdiction. Quebec, supported by New Brunswick, Manitoba, and Saskatchewan, had challenged federal jurisdiction, but the Courts ruled in favour of the Dominion.[1]

With jurisdiction over broadcasting now settled, the creation of a centralized public broadcasting organization proceeded in two stages. The Canadian Radio Broadcasting Commission, established by the Bennett Conservative government in 1932, was remodelled into the Canadian Broadcasting Corporation by the King Liberal government in 1936; because it was public, not a state, broadcaster, the crucial arm's-length principle was enshrined as a key characteristic. By providing for the inclusion of both publicly owned and privately owned stations, however, the new system institutionalized the CBC's reliance on private stations for distribution, even though Aird clearly hoped such stations would be eliminated as quickly as possible.

By 1936 a number of fundamental assumptions and principles had become the accepted guidelines for Canadian broadcasting. These were:

1. Canada's airwaves are owned by the public, and should be administered by the national government in trust. Transmission frequencies, therefore, may not be owned, but users may be extended the privilege of using one in the public interest.

2. The broadcasting system should be Canadian in ownership.

3. Service should be extended to all Canadians.

4. Payment for the system should come from a blend of public and private sources.

5. Programs should be of high standard and primarily Canadian, but high standard programs should also be obtained from other sources.

The system as it emerged in 1936 followed almost exactly the model devised by the main lobbying organization for public broadcasting, the Canadian Radio League, headed by Alan Plaunt and Graham Spry. "The State or the United States," Spry had proclaimed in one of the great slogans of Canadian history, and indeed the power given the broadcasting arm of the state was mighty. The CBC was called upon not only to provide a national radio service, but also to license and regulate such parts of the national broadcasting system it did not directly own and operate, namely, the private stations.

Predictably this development had been strenuously opposed by the association of the private stations, the Canadian Association of Broadcasters, formed in 1926, and such powerful commercial interests as the Canadian Pacific Railways, which had always objected to CNR radio. The CAB, tending to reflect its larger members, objected to the regulation of private stations by the public broadcaster, which they viewed as a competitor. This attitude was not always shared by the smaller CBC-affiliated stations, which generally had good relations with the Corporation.

Despite the political battles that often swirled around it, the CBC proved the accuracy of the Aird Commission's assertion that Canadians wanted Canadian programming. The Corporation provided it, helped rally the country during the war, and steadily built a constituency that would come to its defence in future challenges. Then, as now, however, the situation was complicated by Canadians' undeniable appetite for American as well as Canadian programming, and providing this service was also a major task for both an under-funded public broadcaster and a commercially driven private sector.

The Massey Royal Commission, appointed in 1949 under the chairmanship of Vincent Massey, later Governor General, to look into national development in the arts, letters, and sciences, represented a major step forward from the cultural beachhead established by Ottawa after the broadcasting ruling in 1932. It was the first time the federal government had asserted so capacious a responsibility in culture; broadcasting was but a part of the Massey Commission's terms of reference. In brief, the Commission rejected the position of the Canadian Association of Broadcasters and strongly endorsed the existing system.

Essentially, the CBC emerged from the Massey examination smelling like roses. The Commission's report reaffirmed that the broadcasting legislation called for "one national system." The private stations were licensed only because they could play a useful part in that single broadcasting system, and the CBC properly exercised control over "all radio broadcasting policies and programs in Canada." The report continued:

> The principal grievance of the private broadcasters is based, it seems to us, on a false assumption that broadcasting in Canada is an industry. Broadcasting in Canada, in our view, is a public service directed and controlled in the public interest by a body responsible to Parliament (Massey Commission, 1951, p. 283).

The Massey report noted that radio coverage had expanded from 50 percent of the population in 1936 to 90 percent in 1950, a considerable achievement in view of the special Canadian coverage problems: two languages, five time zones, and sparse settlement. While Aird had been chiefly concerned with the physical plant and organization for a national system, Massey stressed that "the quality of the programs which the Canadian listener receives must . . . be the test for the justification of a national system of radio" (Massey Commission, 1951, p. 25).

The theme of cultural sovereignty found strong expression in the Massey report. "Many Canadians in the 1920s . . . began to fear that cultural annexation would follow our absorption into the American radio system just as surely as economic and even political annexation would have followed absorption into the American railway system 50 years earlier" (Massey Commission, 1951, p. 24). Massey opposed networks of private radio stations because they "would inevitably become small parts of the American systems" (Massey Commission, 1951, p. 287).

By 1951, the year of the Massey report, the age of radio was giving way to the era of television, and the Commission warned presciently about the implications of the imminent ascendance of the magical new medium, pointing out that "the pressure on uncontrolled private television operators to become mere channels for American commercial material will be almost irresistible" (Massey Commission, 1951, p. 301). What Canada would need in television, it decreed, was a regime similar to the one governing radio.

In its sensible way, the Massey report highlighted both the accomplishments and the inadequacies of the radio broadcasting system and insightfully drew attention to the dilemmas that would plague the television age to an even greater extent.

Fear for cultural sovereignty in the face of American broadcasting penetration has remained a perpetual theme for some six decades, but by Massey's time a certain consensus had emerged that the state had an obligation to support Canadian "culture," however the term had been defined and however Canadians disagreed on the magnitude of that obligation.

THE AGE OF TELEVISION

During the period of the Massey Commission, from 1949 to 1951, television was just beginning to build in the United States and its prewar existence in the United Kingdom was largely unknown in Canada. But its entry into Canada—initially by spilling over the border—altered the Canadian broadcasting scene forever. Just three years after the introduction of television into Canada, a royal commission on broadcasting was created, as Massey had recommended.

The first reality to be faced reflected the historic dilemma of broadcasting in Canada. From the beginning, 60 percent of Canadians had over-the-air access to the television programming of the American networks. Throughout the 1950s, a distinctive physical characteristic of those Canadian cities within 50 miles of the international border was the proliferation of roof-top television aerials for receiving stations from Plattsburg, Buffalo, and Bellingham. It was a veritable peaceful American invasion of the living rooms of Canada—and Canadians welcomed the invaders with open arms.

For the representatives of both the state and the private sector the central issue, as always, was cost. Television posed a far greater challenge than radio to Canadian resources. Television production is vastly more expensive than radio production. Television programs produced in the United States could recover their costs in that market and therefore be available to Canadian broadcasters at very low rates. Private broadcasters had always tried to minimize costs but they now realized that while the capital costs of moving into television were very high, they could draw upon the product of the American networks as well as Hollywood movies at rates much lower than the cost of producing comparable programs in Canada. To do this it was more urgent than ever to shake off the regulatory yoke of the CBC.

The government chose not to provide the CBC with the additional capital investment to build a complete national television network on its own. In the years after the CBC's owned and operated stations in Montreal and Toronto commenced service in 1952, private stations were licensed as affiliates. Thus, the historic pattern was repeated and the national broadcasting system became dependent upon a combination of public and private stations.

At the same time, some perceived that the new medium threatened national cultural sovereignty to an unprecedented extent. Whatever its own preferences, the CBC was obliged because of both cost and demand to procure some programs abroad, especially for the English-language service. The American networks, in a fierce competition for audience, promoted their programs aggressively and this marketing inevitably spilled over into Canada. As a result, American programs were being marketed in Canada far more effectively than Canadian programs, allowing the private broadcasters to assert that Canadians preferred American programs. But the Canadian desire for Canadian programs, noted by Sir John Aird and every review since, persisted. The Fowler Commission was now formed against a background of considerable dissatisfaction with the existing broadcasting system and a feeling that things had to be sorted out before television developed too far.

The Fowler Commission and the Fowler Committee

Robert Fowler, a lawyer and president of the Canadian Pulp and Paper Association, was appointed to head the Royal Commission on Broadcasting in 1955. In its report issued two years later, the Commission carried over into the age of television the main features of radio broadcasting. It gave the Graham Spry battle cry more formal expression:

> We cannot choose between a Canadian broadcasting system controlled by the state and a Canadian competitive system in private hands. The choice is between a Canadian state-controlled system with some flow of programmes east and west across Canada, with some Canadian content and the development of a Canadian sense of identity, at a substantial public cost, and a privately owned system which the forces of economics will necessarily make predominantly dependent on imported American radio and television programmes (Fowler Commission, 1957, p. 10).

The commissioners went right to the heart of the matter:

> . . . if the less costly method is always chosen, is it possible to have a Canadian nation at all? The Canadian answer, irrespective of party or race, has been uniformly the same for nearly a century. We are prepared, by measures of assistance, financial aid and a conscious stimulation, to compensate for our disabilities of geography, sparse populations and vast distances, and we have accepted this as a legitimate role of the government in Canada (Fowler Commission, 1957, p. 9).

The Fowler report said there was not enough advertising revenue in Canada for a private system that could both cover the country and provide Canadian programming. In the spirit of Aird and Massey, the report concluded that stations on such a system would "necessarily become outlets for American networks and programs."

> This would result not because the private broadcasters are unpatriotic citizens or because they lack a sense of Canadian consciousness or responsibility; it would result from economic pressures on the private operator which make it easy and inexpensive to import American programs and difficult and costly to produce any substantial volume of Canadian programs (Fowler Commission, 1957, p. 11).

Fowler and his colleagues held that for the foreseeable future, Canadian radio and television broadcasting would be a single mixed system of private and public ownership regulated and controlled by an agency representing the public interest and responsible to Parliament. The Commission also went to some length to justify regulation of broadcasting content on several grounds: scarcity of frequencies, the absence of a tradition of self-regulation that would create "recognized standards of performance," the influence on programming of commercial sponsors, and the pressure of American economic forces.

> It is not the freedom of the private operator or the commercial spon-
> sors that is important; it is the freedom of the public to enjoy a
> broadcasting system which provides the largest possible outlet for
> the widest possible range of information, entertainment and ideas
> (Fowler Commission, 1957, p. 86).

The private broadcasters won partial success in their battle for separate status in Fowler's recommendation that a Board of Broadcast Governors be created that would regulate both the CBC and the private stations. Full recognition of their position came in 1958 from the Progressive Conservative government in legislation providing for regulation of the private sector by the BBG and a continuing CBC board responsible to Parliament. It was the BBG that began the practice of imposing Canadian content requirements on private broadcasters, although it had great difficulty in making them meaningful.

What followed the Fowler report was reminiscent of the beginnings of public radio broadcasting, when the recommendations of a royal commission appointed by the King government were dealt with by the Bennett government and then the Liberals returned to office with amendments. Now, the Diefenbaker Conservatives, after deal-ing with the recommendations of a royal commission appointed by the St. Laurent Liberals, were succeeded by the Pearson Liberals who, in the nature of things, felt some amendments were needed. In 1964, Robert Fowler was called back into service to act as chairman of an advisory committee on broadcasting, which reported the fol-lowing year.

The heart of the Fowler Committee recommendations lay in its proposal to create a Canadian Broadcasting Authority, to replace both the BBG and the CBC's Board of Directors, with "full powers and authority to regulate, supervise, control and develop the Canadian broadcasting system." Its basic task should be

> ... to develop a coordinated policy for the provision of broadcasting
> services to the Canadian people—to all the people, by all the broad-
> casting stations publicly and privately owned (Fowler Committee,
> 1965, p. 98).

Between Fowler's two reports, the BBG had taken the momentous step of licensing CTV, a private English television network, and TéléMétropole, a private French-language television station in the large Montreal market. In one stroke, the balance between the public and private sectors had been fundamentally altered.

The gamble initially seemed shrewd. The new licensees, proud and determined, believed they had major contributions to make to Canadian culture in return for winning their cherished prize and did not hesitate to make grand commitments to fulfil those obligations. Alas, the practical realities foreseen by Massey and Fowler soon exerted their force. The private networks were licensed in 1961; four years later the Fowler Committee was scathing in its comments about the record of private broad-casters.

> ... the program performance of the private stations ... bears very
> little relationship to the promises made to the BBG ... Undertakings
> given to obtain the grant of a public asset have largely been ignored,

and the program performance has generally fallen far short of the promises made. The BBG has been powerless to deal with this . . . A promise made by a broadcaster to obtain a license . . . should be an enforceable undertaking, and not a theoretical exercise in imagination or a competitive bid in an auction of unrealistic enthusiasm (Fowler Committee, 1965, p. 107).

THE BROADCASTING ACT AND AFTER

It was against this background that the Minister of Communications, Judy La Marsh, drafted the government's 1966 White Paper On Broadcasting, which duly led to the Broadcasting Act of 1968 (although a key provision of the White Paper, to finance the CBC through five-year statutory grants, was excluded from the final legislation). The Act, with certain amendments, still governs the Canadian broadcasting system today. [Editor's note: The 1968 Broadcasting Act that was in place when this article was first published has been replaced by the 1991 Broadcasting Act.]

The intent and implications of the Act were perfectly clear: to institutionalize the major principles of and objectives for the broadcasting system as they had been overwhelmingly re-affirmed ever since the Aird report four decades earlier, and as they were supported by all political parties.

We will refer only to the highlights of the 1968 Act. It created a new overall regulatory body, the Canadian Radio-Television Commission (today's Canadian Radio-television and Telecommunications Commission), with broad powers including licensing, detailed regulation, and the imposition of conditions of licence. The CBC, though it kept its own board, was put under the jurisdiction of the CRTC. The whole was affirmed as "a single system . . . comprising public and private elements," to be "owned and controlled by Canadians so as to safeguard, enrich and strengthen the cultural, political, social and economic fabric of Canada" (House of Commons, 1970, s.3[a], 3[b]). But the mandate of the CBC was spelled out with considerable precision while that of the private sector was left quite vague. "The national broadcasting service," as the CBC was described, was to be a "balanced service of information, enlightenment and entertainment for people of different ages, interests and tastes covering the whole range of programming in fair proportion." And it was to be "in English and French, serving the special needs of geographic regions and actively contributing to the flow and exchange of cultural and regional information and entertainment" (House of Commons, 1970, s.3[g]).

No comparable obligations were placed upon the private sector, and it was logical to infer that private broadcasters did not carry quite the same burden of state policy as did the CBC. Indeed, the new Act relieved them of the burden established in the 1958 Act to provide programming that was predominantly Canadian in content and character, although they must use "predominantly Canadian creative and other resources." Also, the 1968 Act explicitly stated that where a conflict arose between the public and the private broadcasting sectors, the public element should predominate.

The 1968 Act created the framework within which the broadcasting system has operated for the past eighteen years. Invariably, the operations of all the players have been made to seem to be in harmony with the wording of the Act. Over the years, the

CRTC has significantly diluted the notion of a "predominantly Canadian" broadcasting system, always in the name of the Broadcasting Act. While the private sector acknowledges its responsibility to the national obligations implied in the Act, realistic commercial goals dictate maximum allowable American programming in prime time. The CBC attempts to be all things to all people, with resources sufficient only to be some things to some people. The Department of Communications and the CRTC have tried to determine how technological change could be accommodated within the confines of an Act passed before some of the new technology had ever been conceived. The cable industry has sought justification for its own massive expansion in an Act in which it was a mere afterthought.

In fact, the realities of today's broadcasting system would have astonished the framers of the 1968 Act. That is why it is time for a new Canadian Broadcasting Act.

Broadcasting's Changing Environment

The 1968 Act came toward the end of the postwar generation, a period of an expanding world of broadcasting for an expanding country. The large postwar influx of people into the cities from the country, together with the baby boom and heavy immigration, was transforming urban Canada, creating an environment in which mass media flourished. The period was one of rapid growth in real income—more money to buy the goods and services whose advertising supported broadcasting, more money to pay the taxes that supported broadcasting, more money to buy equipment. Television spread to full coverage of the population in Canada faster than in any other country.

In Quebec, CBC's French television service had been moulded into an instrument of social transformation, revealing a people's identity to itself and unleashing a sense of national awareness that would sweep into public life and dominate Canada's domestic politics for a generation—the "Quiet Revolution." In the rest of Canada, television spurred nationalism in a reactive way, by serving as the conduit for an increased flood of American pop culture into the Canadian market. But the pressure of inexpensive American programming noted in the first Fowler report drastically curbed the efforts of even the CBC to give English Canada the kind of self-expression that Quebec was enjoying.

The unhappy irony was that Canadian television was booming in a way that reflected less and less the goals set out in the 1968 Act. The Fowler Committee recommended that broadcasting goals be enshrined in legislation to underline the deal between the state and those who had won the privilege from the state of holding a broadcast licence. "All broadcasting agencies," it declared, "both public and private, are recipients of public support in the right to use scarce public assets. They must pay for these valuable rights by giving a responsible performance, and the state is fully entitled to ensure that the trust is honored" (Fowler Committee, 1965, p. 98).

On the other hand, there was the implicit demand upon the state to protect Canadian broadcasters in order that they could provide sometimes uneconomic cultural services. In dealing with expanding cable operations, for example, Fowler had warned that cable systems could pose a threat to broadcasters. While cable operations had been brought under the 1968 Act as "broadcasting receiving undertakings" and were therefore an element of the broadcasting system, subject to CRTC regulation, there existed no clear legislative guidance as to the basis on which cable should be regulated. In the years that followed, the CRTC declared that it was obligated to treat the cable industry in such a way as to protect local broadcasting industries and their sources of revenue.

Yet while the Commission would not allow Canadian radio and television stations to affiliate to American networks, it then agreed that cable systems could provide local carriage of the full program schedules of all the American television networks. Thus was born a tension between Canadian broadcasters and cable systems that persists to this day.

Clearly, cable television mattered. The Fowler Commission report demonstrated an appreciation of the new delivery system, assessing correctly the effect cable would have both in bringing yet more American programming into Canada and in segmenting audiences. Technology such as cable, communication satellites, and computer control were gradually changing the nature of broadcasting.

Under the arm's-length tradition of keeping control of broadcasting independent from political interference, the CBC and later the BBG and CRTC were formally free of governmental direction. From the start, governments followed instead a policy that might be called direction by inquiry: a parliamentary committee or outside inquiry of some kind made an investigation and submitted recommendations upon which the government acted. Certainly, our own Task Force fits neatly into this pattern.

We will examine many of these policy questions in detail as a basis for our own recommendations for change, and give a brief summary of important policy developments since the passage of the 1968 Broadcasting Act.

The importance of the new communications was given institutional form within the newly created Department of Communications in 1969, when it took over responsibility for spectrum management and the technical side of broadcasting policy. Two years later the Telecommission, a group appointed by the new Minister to guide policy formation in the early days of the Department, observed in its report, *Instant World*, that:

> . . . the means to implement broadcasting policy are part of the technology of telecommunications and may be improved by new systems and devices. Cable systems, for example, may one day become the predominant broadcasting channels in urban communities, but satellite transmission and new terrestrial modes will also contribute to the effectiveness of national broadcasting policy, and thus to the health of the body politic (Department of Communications, 1971, p. 5).

In a 1973 green paper on communications policy commissioned by the DOC, the Liberal government laid the groundwork for combining telecommunications with broadcasting under the mandate of the CRTC. The green paper had offered a sweeping view of communication policy "counter-balancing the strong north/south pull of continentalism" and "fostering national unity and identity in a Canada of admittedly diverse cultural and regional components." More than ever before, it said, "it is clear that the technologies and economic aspects of communications are intimately related with their social and cultural implications" (Department of Communications, 1973, p. 4).

The 1973 green paper had seen the need for broad policy direction from government to the proposed combined agency for broadcasting and telecommunication policy. This integrated approach was needed because of "the evident and growing tendency for many formerly distinct systems of electronic communications to become interconnected, more integrated, and more powerful." In the atmosphere of the strained federal-provincial relations of the 1970s, this sounded to many provinces, particularly Quebec, like a massive federal bid to move into telecommunication and cultural jurisdiction claimed by the provinces. Ottawa's offers to share control were turned down. The federal government then proceeded to implement its views to the extent possible within federal jurisdiction.

In 1976, the CRTC was expanded to include telecommunications, its initials remaining the same but its name changing from Canadian Radio-Television Commission to Canadian Radio-television and Telecommunications Commission. In 1978, a new telecommunications act covering both broadcasting and telecommunications was introduced in the Commons by the Minister of Communications but came to nothing. The bill—Bill C-16—was notable for taking a broadcast concept and applying it to the whole of telecommunications in its section 3 (a):

> Efficient telecommunications systems are essential to the sovereignty and integrity of Canada, and telecommunications services and production resources should be developed and administered so as to safeguard, enrich and strengthen the cultural, political, social and economic fabric of Canada (House of Commons, 1978).

A Decade of Studies

Reverting to the strategy of leadership by inquiry, the government appointed the Clyne Committee in 1978 to look into the challenges to Canadian sovereignty posed by the new communications. The chairman, J.V. Clyne, was a former justice of the British Columbia Supreme Court. Noting that Canadians were "already being swamped with foreign broadcast programming," Clyne and his colleagues urged an inquiry into making the CBC more effective since its broadcasting services were "the main national instruments for the preservation of Canadian social and cultural sovereignty."

The Committee made 26 recommendations, many of them extremely detailed, but the overall tone of their report may be judged by its final words:

> We conclude our work . . . with an exhortation: with all the force at our command, we urge the Government of Canada to take immediate action to alert the people of Canada to the perilous position of their collective sovereignty that has resulted from the new technologies of telecommunications and informatics; and we urge the Government of Canada and the governments of the provinces to take immediate

action to establish a rational structure for telecommunications in
Canada as a defence against the further loss of sovereignty in all its
economic, social, cultural and political aspects (Clyne Committee,
1979, p. 76).

While the Clyne Committee took its starting point in integrated communications technology, the Federal Cultural Policy Review Committee, co-chaired by Louis
Applebaum and Jacques Hébert, started with the whole spectrum of cultural services
and policies as its purview. As an update of the Massey inquiry, Applebaum-Hébert too
had broadcasting included in its terms of reference. Indeed, their 1982 report concluded
that the CBC was the very heart of Canadian culture, and that private broadcasters must
be called upon to make a larger contribution to new Canadian programming on
English television. This has been a finding of our own Task Force as well.

In fact, there has hardly been an inquiry that has not agreed on the overriding
dilemma of the Canadian broadcasting system: how can Canadians be offered a
serious choice of Canadian programming in a system in which (a) American
influences are inescapable, (b) market forces dictate American programming, through
both production costs and advertising benefits, and (c) Canadians themselves want
access to Canadian as well as American programming.

On the other hand, the Task Force finds itself in substantial disagreement with
many of the recommendations made by the Applebaum-Hébert Committee to resolve
this central dilemma. Some of their proposals, notably calling on the CBC to end in-
house production of performance programming, would have seriously undermined the
very principles they affirmed.

It is the CRTC, under the profound powers granted it by the 1968 Act, that has day-
to-day responsibility for regulating Canadian broadcasting. While the federal
government has pursued a succession of projects to obtain power of direction over the
CRTC, the Commission has continued, as it is entitled, to operate independently, holding hearings on issues, deciding on policy, making regulations, and putting these
decisions into effect, with varying degrees of informal consultation with the government and the Department of Communications.

After years of debate, provincial educational television services were licensed in
the early seventies and were later given wide latitude as to the programming and policies they could pursue. The beginnings of community broadcasting were approved.
Through the late seventies, however, notwithstanding substantial pressure from the
DOC to introduce pay-TV, the CRTC kept the door closed against pay on the grounds that
it could not operate in a manner consistent with the 1968 Act and that it would be "disruptive" to the existing broadcast industry.

Eventually the CRTC itself adopted the practice of appointing task forces on major
issues, beginning with a committee under CRTC vice-chairman Réal Thérrien on service to Native peoples and remote areas—an increasingly vexing issue—and on the
introduction of pay television. As pressure grew, the Committee felt it had little choice
but to recommend pay-TV when it reported in 1980. But it optimistically persuaded
itself that the chief justification for introducing pay-TV was the stimulus it would give
to the Canadian program production industry and the provision of new Canadian ser-

vices. The Committee paved the way for both the licensing of the Canadian Satellite Communications (CANCOM) service to remote and underserved areas and the licensing of satellite-to-cable specialty and pay-TV services.

In the meantime, the Trudeau government, after its return to office in 1980, had been pursuing the aim of bringing together policy making on the means of communication and the cultural content of communication, including broadcasting. Soon the federal cultural agencies and programs of aid to cultural industries were transferred from the Secretary of State's department to the Department of Communications. Cultural policy in this new setting took on a more commercial and industrial coloration, with what some considered an undue emphasis on the economic impact of cultural activities and the desirability of designing Canadian cultural products and services to maximize their export potential rather than recognizing their social and cultural function as a means of Canadian expression. The DOC was particularly anxious to link culture, which it sometimes described as a form of software, to the potential of new communications technologies.

The Department of Communications' 1983 broadcasting strategy for Canada—its very first—consisted of four initiatives. The first suggested a reversal of the CRTC's long-standing emphasis on the role of private broadcasters and the related need to set reasonable limits to cable's impact on fragmenting their market. Cable was to become the state's "chosen instrument," with all programming to be available on cable, described as the "most cost-effective means of significantly expanding the viewing choices of most Canadians." The second was to create a Canadian Broadcast Program Development Fund starting at $35 million and reaching $60 million in its fifth year. The third was to give the government the long-sought power of direction over the CRTC on general policy matters, through Bill C-20. The fourth, reflecting a newly emerging controversy, was to abolish licence requirements for individual satellite reception dishes. Actually, a fifth initiative was an integral part of the strategy but came later in the budget: a new excise tax on cable subscriptions to offset the cost of the program development fund.

Because technological change was multiplying channel capacity, the government concluded that the only way for Canada to compete was to increase its own programming capacity, especially in areas where foreign programming dominated Canadians' viewing time. "As a general principle," the government's 1983 policy statement said, "the Canadian broadcasting system must make available a significant amount of Canadian programming in each program category—for example, the drama, children's and variety categories (Department of Communications, 1983a, p. 9).

As the first major comprehensive broadcasting initiative since the 1968 Act, this strategy left something to be desired. It overestimated the immediate effects of technological change in expanding channel availability and the related ability to finance attractive programming. It miscalculated in its expectations that DBS—direct-to-home broadcasting satellites—would soon be a reality.

In institutionalizing the status of cable, the Department's strategy was legitimizing cable's overriding function of bringing more American programs to more Canadians. It effectively accepted a class system for broadcast recipients, since some Canadians, for economic or geographical reasons, were in no position to receive cable. (We have had to accept the same reality, but as a challenge to the policy maker.) In *Building for the Future*, a follow-up document on the CBC (Department of Communications, 1983b) the government imposed greater national obligations on the Corporation without providing commensurately greater funds to do the job. Indeed, in the eight years prior to the release of *Towards a New National Broadcasting Policy*, the government had systematically whittled away the resources of the Corporation. Now it had its mandate expanded on the basis of already diminished funding.

On the other hand, the creation of the Broadcast Fund as part of the Canadian Film Development Corporation, which became Telefilm Canada, was a move adopted from the Clyne and Applebaum-Hébert reports. The purpose of the Broadcast Fund was to meet the programming goals of the broadcasting strategy and to strengthen the Canadian program production industry. The abolition of licences for individual dishes was a welcome acknowledgement of a situation that could not be addressed effectively by prohibition in any event. And the new tax on cable users would offset the cost of producing Canadian programs. Unfortunately, the cable industry has been able to convey the notion that it is the cable operators, rather than the individual subscribers, who are carrying that burden.

The new strategy also reflected the fifteen-year tug-of-war between the CRTC and the federal government, represented by the Department of Communications, over the formation of broadcasting policy. While the DOC pressed for development of new technology in such applications as communications satellites and the Telidon electronic print services, the CRTC, by its very mandate, naturally gave priority to Canadian broadcasters and programming. To some, it seemed that the CRTC was encroaching on the prerogative of government and Parliament to make national policy, hence the pressure for a power of direction over the regulatory agency. On the other hand, some feared such direction, reluctant to see government interfering in the operations of an autonomous agency dealing in the realm of ideas and freedom of expression.

Within government there was also tension. Those connected with arts and culture felt that the technological side of the DOC, which constituted the whole of the Department before arts and culture was added in 1980, was controlling broadcasting policy, which should be essentially cultural in nature. It was only in 1985 that broadcasting policy was made a responsibility of the cultural affairs sector of the Department, with consequences yet to be determined.

The Age of Integrated Communication

Over the next few years, Canada must overhaul many aspects of broadcasting and telecommunication policies to accommodate a new age of broadcasting. After a first age dominated by over-the-air radio, and a second dominated by over-the-air television, we are already well into a third age characterized by integrated communications. New systems for the delivery, production, and reception of programming are greatly expanding the capacity for selectivity, the technical quality, and the scope of service.

Today, improvement in selectivity means for many Canadians a plenitude of channels by satellite and cable; in future it could mean almost unlimited capacity for selection of content, at a price. Today, improvement in technical quality means the arrival of stereophonic, "smart" television sets—smart because of digital microprocessing capacity that restores the picture to the quality on a studio monitor; in future it could mean high-definition, wide-screen TV comparable to 35-mm film, displayed on a flat panel. Today, increased scope of services means new video and specialty services, and the experimental beginning of text, graphics, commercial exchange, and monitoring services; in future, as screen definition and portability improve, it may mean a whole range of electronic publishing in the home. When we explore the technology of the new era in greater detail, we shall see the problem of determining public policy for such an undetermined future.

But whatever kind of Buck Rogers future is in store for us, surely the Canadian tradition demands that we must continue to entrench the Canadian presence in our broadcasting system, and we must adopt policies to do so in a new world in which substantially greater choice may be available to Canadian viewers. More than ever, broadcasting must be seen as a fundamental part of cultural policy. It must be program-driven, not hardware-driven as in its first decades.

While our terms of reference called upon us to look ahead to the year 2000, and while there are major changes on the horizon, we see them coming in stages rather than overnight. The third age of broadcasting, radically different from its predecessor though it may be, is an evolution not a revolution. The ages of broadcasting overlap. Rather than disappearing, old services tend to find new niches. The new age of broadcasting, already partly upon us, brings extraordinary possibilities of conservation as well as innovation. In Canada, we have the skills and talent to be in the forefront of this new age, to make the new technologies work for us.

The members of this Task Force agree with Aird and his colleagues that broadcasting services in Canada, today as a half-century ago, should "continue equal to that in any other country"—and that they should offer, so far as possible, a truly Canadian service for those millions of Canadians who have demonstrated their belief in one.

NOTES

1. In *Re Regulation and Control of Radio Communication in Canada*, [1932] A.C. 304.

REFERENCES

Aird Commission. See Canada. Royal Commission on Radio Broadcasting. (1929).

Canada. Committee on Broadcasting (Fowler Committee). (1965). *Report*. Ottawa.

Canada. Consultative Committee on the Implications of Telecommunications for Canadian Sovereignty, Telecommunications and Canada (Clyne Committee). (1979). *Report*. Ottawa.

Canada. Department of Communications. (1973). *Proposals for a communication policy for Canada: A position paper of the government of Canada*. Ottawa.

Canada. Department of Communications. (1983a). *Building for the future: Towards a distinct CBC*. Ottawa.

Canada. Department of Communications. (1983b). *Towards a new national broadcasting policy*. Ottawa.

Canada. Department of Communications, Telecommission. (1971). *Instant world*. Ottawa.

Canada. Parliament. House of Commons. Bill C-16. November 9, 1978.

Canada. Parliament. House of Commons. c. B-11. Broadcasting Act, R.S.C. 1970.

Canada. Parliament. House of Commons. *Debates*. May 18, 1932.

Canada. Royal Commission on Broadcasting (Fowler Commission). (1957). *Report*. Ottawa.

Canada. Royal Commission on National Development in the Arts, Letters and Sciences (Massey Commission). (1951). *Report*. Ottawa.

Canada. Royal Commission on Radio Broadcasting (Aird Commission). (1929). *Report*. Ottawa.

Fowler Commission. See Canada. Royal Commission on Broadcasting. (1957).

Fowler Committee. See Canada. Committee on Broadcasting. (1965).

Massey Commission. See Canada. Royal Commission on National Development in the Arts, Letters and Sciences. (1951).

PUTTING THE "PUBLIC"
INTO PUBLIC BROADCASTING

Ross A. Eaman

The CBC should be in a position to regularly feel the entertainment pulse of its sponsors, or customers, the Canadian Radio Audience, and should be quick to detect, and act upon, those signals which indicate pleasure, displeasure, or perhaps actual antagonism.
                                        E.C. Stewart, February 23, 1948

Taking a poll of the passengers on a ship would be a risky way to navigate.
                              Letter to CBC Board of Directors, August 25, 1959

In 1972 the Canadian Broadcasting Corporation conducted a national survey to find out what Canadians thought about its television services. This was not the first or last survey of this scope or kind carried out by the CBC. A decade earlier, the CBC had surveyed Canadians on their views about its overall performance; it completed another survey of this type in the mid-1980s; and it made plans for a similar study in 1991. But there was one line of questioning on the 1972 survey that has not, to my knowledge, been included on any other major CBC-sponsored surveys. This was the question of whether Canadians feel they have an adequate say in the kind of programming provided to them; or, more specifically, whether television "provokes feelings of frustration in viewers because of their lack of personal control over, or interaction with, the television available to them."

In asking this question, the 1972 survey made no distinction between CBC TV and other television networks. Nor did it give any explanation of what was meant by "control" or "interaction." But the results suggested that many Canadians might like to be more involved in the determination of program services. Among anglophones, 53 percent said they "often" found their lack of control over television to be frustrating, 40 percent "occasionally" had such feelings, and only 7 percent were "rarely" or "never" troubled in this manner. For francophones, the percentages were 33, 46, and 20 respectively (CBC Research Department, 1974, p. 33). Although it would be unwarranted to draw any general conclusions from the results for a single question on one survey, the 1972 survey does, at least, point to the possibility that Canadians would like more input into what they watch on television (or listen to on the radio).

This raises the question, however, of whether it would actually be in the best interests of Canadians to allow them a greater voice in shaping broadcasting services. In particular, what would happen if the CBC decided to design its radio and television programming to serve the needs and desires of Canadians *as expressed by Canadians themselves*? Would the CBC be rapidly transformed into a preponderantly mass entertainment medium with little or no room for arts, culture, and information? Would levels of Canadian content plummet, especially on television, through massive imports of American programming? Would services that exist largely for the benefit of minorities have to be abandoned or at least be reconstituted in the interests of the majority? Or might it be that Canadians as a whole would favour essentially the same kind of programming mix and balance that now exists? Might it even be that Canadians overall would prefer greater amounts of Canadian, cultural, and minority-interest programming?

The larger problem addressed by these questions concerns the kind of relationship that should exist between the CBC and the Canadian public. Before considering the possible results of greater public input, therefore, we need to examine the nature of the CBC as a public broadcasting organization, the various mechanisms that might enable the public to be heard and their relative effectiveness, the potential role of audience research in this regard, and the kind of audience research that must be conducted if it is to serve as a meaningful conduit between the public and the CBC. In general, it will be argued that the results of CBC audience research provide no basis for fearing public opinion as a guide to programming policy. But before audience research can fulfil its potential, it needs to be treated less as the scientific measurement of audiences and more as a divining rod for discovering the underlying wisdom within the Canadian public.

THE NATURE OF PUBLIC BROADCASTING

The CBC is a publicly owned broadcasting organization. But what does this really mean? Clearly, it does not mean, as some critics still allege, that the CBC is government controlled. Although the CBC, as a Crown corporation, is ultimately accountable to Parliament for its general policy, it has, with very few exceptions over the past 55 years, maintained its independence from the government of the day in its actual operations. It does, of course, receive close to four-fifths of its funding from the federal government. Does this mean, in the case of the CBC at least, that publicly owned broadcasting is simply publicly *funded* broadcasting?

The national broadcasting services of the publicly funded CBC fulfil many particular needs. But the underlying purpose of channelling public funds into broadcasting is to provide the public with an agency that is primarily responsive to its needs rather than those of the marketplace or the state. The question is: who is to decide what these needs are and which ones should be given priority? It could be argued that if broadcasting is to be truly public, then a public broadcasting agency should enable the citizens of a country or region to decide for themselves the kind of service they want. In other words, the purpose of public ownership should not simply be to ensure that broadcasting serves the public interest; it should be to allow the public, rather than the market or the state, to determine wherein its interest lies.

Public broadcasting has seldom been defended on this basis in Canada. Instead, it has been justified on the grounds of the threat of American cultural imperialism, the dangers of rampant commercialism, or the economic incapacity of the private sector to produce an adequate amount of high-quality Canadian programming. These may well be valid reasons for state support of broadcasting in Canada. But they are not necessarily permanent problems nor the only ones that can be dealt with best through publicly owned facilities. Moreover, insofar as it embraces the democratic value of public participation, public ownership would be justifiable even if none of these factors was operative. It is a worthy ideal in and of itself, not just a means to other desirable ends.

Democracy exists to the extent that institutions and processes are characterized by accountability, equality of treatment, and participation. A political system, for example, is democratic to the degree that the government is accountable to the public, treats all members of the public equally, and provides opportunities for public participation in the decision-making process. Other institutions, including broadcasting organizations, can also be assessed in terms of these attributes. The CBC, for example, is at least partly democratic insofar as it is accountable to Parliament, which is ultimately accountable to the electorate. It is even more democratic if it seeks to provide service for all Canadians more or less equally. But to be fully democratic, it must also provide for meaningful public input into the determination of its basic practices and priorities.

Public participation in the shaping of CBC services is, however, an extremely problematic ideal. In the first place, it must be pursued within the context of the CBC's mandate as legislated by Parliament through the Broadcasting Act. If the public disagrees with this mandate, then it must seek to influence Parliament, not the CBC, to effect its change. Yet at the same time, as Lord Bryce once suggested in *Modern Democracies*, public opinion can deal only with broad principles; it cannot address matters that are highly specific or technical. This means that public input into CBC decision making can occur only in areas that are sufficiently general as to give rise to public opinion, but not so fundamental as to have been decided by the terms of the Broadcasting Act.

Although aspects of programming such as the amount of Canadian content and the balance of local, regional, and national programming would probably meet this criterion for public participation, it is by no means obvious how Canadians could be enabled to express their views about these things in a coherent and useful way. Indeed, there are many who would argue that the average Canadian does not have sufficient knowledge or understanding to hold considered views about such matters. According to this argument, it would be better for Canadians to have those with special knowledge of broadcasting make such decisions for them. Against this, it could be countered that with regard to programming, at least, Canadians are certainly qualified to speak about their needs and desires. After all, in an average week, English-speaking Canadians watch about 21 hours a week of "conventional television" (that is, excluding watching movies and so forth on their VCRs) (CBCRD, 1988, p. 7).

THE PLATONIC OR REITHIAN APPROACH

The question of whether Canadians as a whole should have a say in the programming practices and priorities of the CBC runs parallel in many respects to the larger issue of political knowledge and participation. From Plato and Aristotle to the present day, philosophers have debated whether the average citizen possesses sufficient knowledge to make a positive contribution to the political decision-making process. Plato argued that only the elite has the requisite knowledge to make policy in the interests of the community. He allowed that all citizens have the right to partake of the benefits of a well-run state, but he wanted power to reside in the hands of philosopher-kings on the grounds that they alone are capable of perceiving absolute and eternal truth.

The Platonic tradition in political philosophy has had its counterpart in broadcasting theory and practice. One of its most forthright and articulate defenders was J.C.W. Reith, the first Director-General of the British Broadcasting Corporation. Reith was one of the few prominent broadcasting executives to reflect at length upon the nature of public broadcasting, and he strongly influenced early CBC managers such as Gladstone Murray. It is, therefore, worth considering, at least briefly, his views about the relationship between broadcasters and the public.

Like many advocates of public broadcasting between the First and Second World Wars, Reith believed that it held the potential to link the theory of democracy to "real life." He thought that it might be "the tempering factor that would give democracy for the first time under modern conditions a real chance of operating as a living force throughout the extended community as long ago it operated in the city-state." The press had failed in this regard because "the freedom it had always claimed was not necessarily accompanied by an obligation to give unconditional elucidation or points of view opposed to those of its owners. Moreover, no particular press organ reached the whole community." Reith felt that broadcasting might become "the integrator for democracy," but to do so it would have to occupy a neutral position, free from both government interference and the pressures of the commercial sector. In his view, a public corporation with wide autonomy and a monopoly over broadcasting was the only way to fulfil this requirement (Reith, 1949, pp. 135–36).

Reith never had any doubt that it was the BBC's duty to determine for itself what was in the public interest. As a result, he was hostile not only to government interference in the management of the BBC but also to the idea of basing its programming on what the public wanted. Reith's emphasis on the public-service aspect of BBC programming was combined with a strong belief in the necessity of preserving a "high moral tone." To criticism that listeners did not like BBC programs, his characteristic reply was: "It is occasionally indicated to us that we are apparently setting out to give the public what we think they need—and not what they want, but few know what they want and very few what they need" (Altman, 1962, p. 13).

"I am certain of this," Reith said in about 1930, "that to set out to give the public what it wants—as the saying is—is a dangerous and fallacious policy, involving almost always an underestimate of public intelligence and a continual lowering of standards." In his view, "it is not insistent autocracy but wisdom that suggests a policy of broadcasting carefully and persistently on the basis of giving people what one believes they should like *and will come to like*, granting, of course, discretion, understanding and resolution on the part of those who carry it out. The supply of good things will create the demand for more" (Reith, 1949, p. 133).

Reith's approach to programming has been endorsed by many Canadian supporters of public broadcasting. For example, the members of the Royal Commission on National Development in the Arts, Letters and Sciences, which was chaired by Vincent Massey in 1949–51, were concerned not only about the "general ignorance of the Canadian public" about the CBC, but also about the quality of the CBC's talks programming. In particular, they thought it "important to express" their "dissent" from the policy whereby "speakers with no special knowledge or reputation in their fields may be engaged because they have a natural facility for broadcasting and also, apparently, because the popular approach of the amateur is thought to have a special appeal to the average listener." They favoured "the principle of the BBC that the popular talk should be in quality and authority comparable to the scholarly" (Massey Commission, 1951, p. 296).

Parliament, Formal Enquiries, and Advisory Councils

Like the BBC, the CBC is indirectly accountable to the public through Parliament. As their elected representatives, members of Parliament speak to a degree for all Canadians. But this constitutes a very limited and imperfect relationship between the CBC and the public. In the first place, Parliament is expected to maintain an arm's-length relationship with cultural agencies such as the CBC and not exert any influence over specific content. Otherwise, agencies such as the CBC could become tools of government influence and propaganda. Secondly, Parliament is not well designed to represent the public *as a broadcasting audience*. Individual members of Parliament are seldom chosen on the basis of their views on broadcasting. They rarely consult their constituents about broadcasting matters. And they do not constitute a representative cross section of Canadian audiences.

A better way for the public to make its views known to those in charge of broadcasting is through formal enquiries such as royal commissions and task forces. These have generally consulted widely before drawing up their recommendations. However, presentations to such enquiries tend to come from formally organized groups, many of them representing vested interests such as station owners, radio and television dealers, advertisers, and educators. As the Massey Commission admitted, "Most of the briefs and most of the interviews came to us from organized societies. We heard little from the citizen who represented no one but himself" (Massey Commission, 1951, p. 268). The Fowler Commission believed that it had "heard the voice of Canada," but of the 276 briefs that it received, only 30 were from private citizens (Peers, 1979, p. 67). By their very nature, moreover, formal enquiries are not continuous. They do not provide the basis for regular public input into broadcasting policy or programming. Because of this, there have been periodic calls for the creation of permanent advisory councils on broadcasting.

The idea of advisory councils first arose during discussions of the Aird Commission report. When the CBC's predecessor, the Canadian Radio Broadcasting Commission, was created in 1932, there was a provision for provincial advisory councils, though none were actually formed during its short life span (Weir, 1965, p. 152). The new Canadian Broadcasting Act of 1936 allowed the CBC to "provide for the appointment of advisory councils to advise it as to programmes." During Gladstone Murray's tenure as the CBC's first general manager, councils were set up across the country, but they did not last for very long. And although the Massey Commission recommended that they be re-established, the Royal Commission on Broadcasting, chaired by Robert Fowler in the mid-1950s, more or less put an end to the idea. "It would," it said, "be not only impractical but wrong in principle to set up a whole series of advisory groups." The problem, in its mind, was not that a few persons from each province or community would not comprise a representative cross section of the population. It was rather that they would "to a large extent . . . usurp one of the important functions which the board of governors has been established to discharge, and that is to represent the people of Canada" (Fowler Commission, 1957, p. 43).

KATE AITKEN'S PANEL

As specified by the 1936 Broadcasting Act, the CBC Board of Governors consisted of nine members "appointed by the Governor in Council and chosen to give representation to the principal geographical divisions of Canada." Clearly, it was more representative than the three commissioners who had headed the CRBC. But it still could not presume, by virtue of its own composition, to represent the diverse views of Canadians about CBC programming. It was for this reason that Kate Aitken offered in 1959 to organize a voluntary panel of listeners and viewers for the purpose of learning what Canadians thought about CBC radio and television programming. A popular lecturer and radio broadcaster for over three decades, "Mrs. A." had recently been appointed to the CBC Board (which had been reconstituted as the Board of Directors by the 1958 Broadcasting Act). She thought that the CBC should try to be more responsive to the public in the formulation of programming policy and secured the unanimous approval of her colleagues for her panel project.

Aitken proposed that some five hundred politicians, religious leaders, and heads of service clubs each nominate 15 "responsible and responsive" citizens for membership on the panel. She anticipated that of the seven thousand nominees, between two and three thousand would agree to serve as members. Moreover, her original idea seems to have been that the panel members would simply watch and listen to CBC programs at will and, over the course of a year, write letters to CBC headquarters with their comments and suggestions. She would then prepare a synopsis of the responses for the Board's consideration. In return for their help, the participants would receive one-year subscriptions to *CBC Times*, a weekly publication that included program schedules.

The Toronto *Daily Star* got wind of Aitken's project and published a critical story that, in Aitken's opinion, was "inaccurate, untrue and malicious" (Aitken, 1960, p. 3). Other newspapers quickly picked up the story and generally echoed its negative sentiments. "The really disturbing thing," *Maclean's* editorialized on September 26, "is that such a featherhead project was actually approved, without audible protest, by the CBC board of directors and the CBC management." Both the *Star* and *Maclean's* rejected the idea that CBC programming should be guided by the views of a panel of listeners and viewers. "If Mrs. Aitken's idea is that the CBC should be directed by the prejudices and inexpert opinions of 2,500 people," the *Star* asked on October 24, "why did she accept a directorship on the new CBC board at all? Why not let them direct, and throw the CBC to the winds." While reassuring its readers that Aitken's "well-meant folly" would probably be "quietly dropped" after a couple of months (which it more or less was), *Maclean's* took pains to point out that her scheme "repudiate[d] the whole philosophy and purpose of the CBC." In its view, "the CBC was created to give Canadians something different," whereas the views expressed by a panel would either cancel each other out or else reduce CBC programming to "the lowest common denominator of unanimous acquiescence."

FROM PUBLIC TO AUDIENCE

Aitken was not alone in thinking that more needed to be done to develop a closer relationship between broadcasters and the public. In an address to the Vancouver Institute on November 21, 1959, Alan Thomas, a professor in the College of Education at the University of British Columbia, lamented that the means available for the public to communicate to broadcasters were "crude and grossly ineffective. The Audience generally has had only one weapon, that of refusing to give its attention to the emission." Thomas made this assessment in the course of outlining a novel framework for interpreting the history of Canadian broadcasting. This consisted of examining the development of broadcasting in terms of the influence and interaction of three forces: the Market, the Public, and the Audience. In Thomas's view, "The most important unifying force in the country today is the Audience, created and secured by repetitive mass programming." But he thought that the failure to understand and explore this mysterious new phenomenon had "prevented broadcasting from playing its full role, and thus hampered the free and democratic development of the country" (Thomas, 1960, pp. 3, 23).

To understand how Thomas reached this conclusion, we need to begin by clarifying what he meant by "the Public." In the most general sense of the term, the public refers to the people or inhabitants of a community, state, or nation. However, a number of social scientists have used the term in a more limited and specialized sense. For example, Herbert Blumer used it to refer to "a group of people (a) who are confronted by an issue, (b) who are divided in their ideas as to how to meet the issue, and (c) who engage in discussion over an issue" (Blumer, 1946, p. 188). For Thomas, the public comprises those citizens who keep themselves informed about a country's affairs through the vehicle of print. "The Public as we know it and as we commonly use the word has basically been given its character by the influence of book and newspaper" (Thomas, 1960, p. 4).

Thomas thought that because of the local and regional character of the print media in Canada, the emergence of a Canadian public has been highly problematic. "Canada's major problem has been the difficulty of . . . creating a genuine public out of a set of separate and geographically determined communities." From the outset, therefore, broadcasting has been seen as a vital means of creating a Canadian public. But what has not been fully realized is that broadcasting contributes its own characteristics to the society it mobilizes. It has not merely created what used to be called the "listening public." Rather it has brought into existence the puzzling phenomenon of "the Audience," which, Thomas insisted, "is an entity in its own right and must be understood as such" (Thomas, 1960, pp. 5, 9).

During the early years of mass communication research, audiences were viewed as essentially passive. The Massey Commission reflected this conventional approach when it criticized "the indifference of the listeners [to the CBC] who enjoy or resent their fare in silence. The reticence of the CBC matches the passivity of its audience" (Massey Commission, 1951, p. 41). By then, however, researchers were beginning to realize not only that audiences play an active role in deciding what they will pay attention to, but also that different segments of the audience react to the same message in different ways (Bauer, 1964, pp. 319–28; 1973, pp. 141–52). In this vein, Thomas pointed out that the *Oxford Dictionary* includes among its definitions of the word "audience," "the action of hearing, attention to what is spoken, to give audience, to give ear, to listen," adding that "at least the dictionary is assistance in restoring a meaning nearly lost, that is that the Audience is essentially active" (Thomas, 1960, p. 6).

Thomas thus thought that it was a mistake to regard the Audience "merely as the Public, prostrate, isolated, and defenceless." He acknowledged that the audience is fundamentally conservative in the sense that it has little tolerance for broadcasts that attempt to change what it thinks, as opposed to what it thinks about. But he also argued that the audience has the potential to play a greater role than the traditional consumers of print media. "Having created an audience out of our population, we must now find a way to make this audience responsible and articulate" (Thomas, 1960, pp. 9, 8, 23).

THE ORIGINS OF NORTH AMERICAN AUDIENCE RESEARCH

A copy of Thomas's paper eventually made its way to the CBC's research library. At some point, someone scrawled on the last page (where Thomas called for steps to make the audience "responsible and articulate") the comment: "Hasn't this man ever heard of a thing called audience research!" The author of this remark was, in all probability, a member of the CBC's Bureau of Audience Research (now called simply the Research Department), which had been set up in 1954. And the implication was that audience research enables listeners and viewers to exert an influence over what is broadcast. As Neil Morrison, the first director of the Bureau, put it in his progress report to the Board of Governors in 1957, "essentially, audience research provides a channel of communication from Canadian audiences back to their national broadcasting system. The findings constitute an evaluation and criticism of the CBC's program service" (Morrison, 1957, p. iv).

This conception of audience research was a natural extension of Morrison's underlying faith in democratic principles. As national supervisor of talks and public affairs, he had worked to make CBC public-affairs programming a vehicle by which Canadians could communicate their views to the governing powers. It followed that he should see audience research as a way of enabling the CBC to be more responsive to the needs of the Canadian public. At the same time, however, Thomas could be forgiven for failing to recognize this point. Although Morrison envisaged audience research as a form of audience relations, it was by no means obvious in the late 1950s whether the management of the CBC perceived the role of audience research in the same manner.

The main impetus behind audience research in North America was not to facilitate public input into program planning, but rather to provide advertisers and their agencies with the data necessary for making efficient and effective use of radio and television. Systematic audience research began in North America around 1930, a full decade after the introduction of radio. It was not until advertisers became seriously interested in radio that any effort was made to study audiences scientifically.

Before advertisers could make extensive use of radio, however, a method had to be developed for measuring the size of audiences. The general solution to this problem lay in sampling. This is now a highly developed and widely used statistical technique for rapidly and at low cost obtaining reliable data about a population. It is based on the scientific principle that a small number of items selected at random will reflect with a known degree of precision the characteristics of a large group of items. The first attempt to measure radio audiences through sampling was undertaken by Archibald M. Crossley, the head of a small American market research company. In 1930, the Association of National Advertisers (ANA) agreed to endorse the formation of a radio audit bureau—to be called the Cooperative Analysis of Broadcasting—if Crossley would assume responsibility for its costs. In return for its endorsement, the ANA required Crossley to work under the direction of a governing committee and consult with an advertising agency advisory committee. It also specifically excluded the networks from its ranks (Beville, 1988, pp. 4–11).

Crossley conducted the first continuing survey of American network radio audiences and produced what came to be known as the "Crossley ratings." These consisted of estimated percentages of *listening* households tuned to particular network programs. Since Crossley's day, usage of the term "rating" has changed. In the strict sense, it now refers to the estimated percentage of *all* radio (or television) households in a given area tuned to a particular program. At the same time, it is also used in a more general sense to refer to all quantitative measurements of audience size, including audience shares and cumulative audience figures.

Crossley hoped to provide his clients not only with ratings but with demographics; that is, with breakdowns of the audience composition for various programs. As *Printer's Ink* reported optimistically on March 20, 1930, "The listening habits of the different sexes, the different age groups and the different financial classes will be compared. Fluctuations in public preference for programs will be studied closely in the hope that answers to questions will indicate what are the factors that make programs popular" (Vol. 150, no. 12, p. 36). The reports issued by Crossley failed to live up to this advance hoopla. But since Crossley's day, audience measurement services have placed increasing emphasis on supplying advertisers with this kind of data to enable them to target specific groups with their messages.

Crossley developed what came to be known as the telephone recall method to obtain data on network radio listening. This consisted of selecting numbers from telephone directories and asking respondents to recall what they had listened to the previous day. This had two major benefits for the advertisers who made up Crossley's clientele. First, because telephone ownership was still largely restricted to the upper and middle classes, Crossley's sample was biased in favour of those radio listeners who were most likely to purchase the advertisers' products; that is, to the "commodity audience." Second, because it required respondents to perform an incredible feat of memory, it deflated audience estimates and thereby reduced advertising costs. (Meehan, 1990, pp. 122–23).

The exclusion of broadcasters from the Cooperative Analysis of Broadcasting together with the underestimation of audiences stemming from the recall method left the door open for a second ratings service in the United States. In 1934, Montgomery Clark and C.E. Hooper set up a competing radio audience measurement service using what was called the coincidental telephone method and gave the American networks the opportunity to subscribe. Invented by George Gallup at Drake University, this new method simply asked people what they were listening to at the time of the telephone interview. The Hooperratings, as they came to be known after Clark left the company in 1938, measured the percentage of radio households (whether listening or not) tuned to network broadcasts. With the support of the major American networks, Hooper not only began to rival but to overtake Crossley in the radio ratings field. Despite providing higher audience estimates than Crossley, Hooper was able to attract advertisers by targeting potential consumers more accurately and providing his service at a reduced cost (Beville, 1988, pp. 11–13; Meehan, 1990, pp. 123–25).

By then a new competitor with yet another method for measuring radio audiences had joined the fray. In the mid-1930s, Robert Elder and Louis F. Woodruff of MIT had built and tested an electronic meter for recording listening, but lacked the financial resources to develop it commercially. As a result, they sold their audimeter to Arthur C. Nielsen, the head of a successful market research business. By the late 1940s, the meter-based Nielsen Radio Index (NRI) had achieved 97 percent coverage of U.S. households, and plans were laid for expanding into television. In 1950, after CBS decided to cancel the Hooperratings service and rely on Nielsen, Hooper sold his national ratings service to his arch rival and withdrew to the local radio and television ratings scene (Beville, 1988, pp. 17–21).

Neither Crossley nor Hooper made any effort to expand their services into Canada. But in 1940, Walter Elliott, who had set up a small market research company in Montreal, travelled to New York to learn about the coincidental telephone method first-hand from Hooper. Together with his partner, Paul Haynes, he established the first continuous radio audience measurement service in Canada. Beginning with monthly radio reports for Montreal (English and French), Toronto, Vancouver, and Winnipeg, the Elliott-Haynes service encompassed 36 cities by the end of the 1940s (though only the original four were surveyed monthly) and added another ten radio markets during the 1950s. In 1952, after two years of experimental research, the company also began issuing monthly reports on television audiences in Canada, including 42 markets by 1960 (Elliott-Haynes, n.d.).

Although the coincidental telephone method was generally regarded as a more accurate and valid measurement tool than the recall method, it still suffered from serious weaknesses when applied to Canadian broadcasting in the 1940s. Because it was easier and more economical to conduct telephone surveys in large urban centres, there was a tendency to ignore rural areas. At the time, however, nearly 50 percent of Canadian households were located on farms and in small towns with populations of less than 10 000, and the CBC attracted a substantial proportion of its audience in such areas through its regional transmitters and numerous affiliates. As a result, the Elliott-Haynes surveys underestimated the overall audience for CBC radio. As an independent study of radio audiences in Saskatchewan concluded, it is "easy to see . . . how woefully inadequate coincidental telephone surveys in a few urban centres can be in such an area as Saskatchewan, or for that matter in many other parts of Canada" (CBC, 1949). Despite this, the private stations and their lobbying agency, the Canadian Association of Broadcasters, pointed to the Elliott-Haynes ratings as supposed proof that Canadians overwhelmingly preferred their programs to those of the CBC.

Given these circumstances, the CBC welcomed the development of an alternative method of audience measurement in which representative panels of Canadians kept diaries of their listening (and viewing) during a stated period of time. Developed by International Surveys Limited (ISL), which Paul Haynes set up in 1946 after parting company with Elliott, the panel-diary technique did not have to restrict sampling to urban areas served by toll-free telephone coverage, but could include all types of homes. ISL claimed that this enabled it to produce ratings that could be projected; that is, they could be applied not only to Canada as a whole but to different regions and city sizes. Moreover, by operating its radio panel in conjunction with its consumer panel, ISL was able not only to produce ratings quite economically but also to relate listening and viewing habits with purchasing behaviour.

The panel-diary technique also had its shortcomings, however. Participants tended not only to under-report programs in off-peak periods but also to write in what they thought they should be listening to or watching. There was a higher co-operation rate among households whose members had more education and higher socio-economic status. And keeping diaries became progressively more bothersome as the number of program choices increased and new technologies made it easier to switch from one program to another. As a result, the CBC tried to interest the A.C. Nielsen Company in extending its meter-based television ratings system into Canada. Nielsen had entered Canada in 1944 after pressure from American branch plants to provide market research services. But Nielsen considered it too expensive and difficult to set up a meter operation in Canada. In 1959, it began providing the Nielsen Broadcast Index for Canadian advertisers and broadcasters, but it did so by means of the panel-diary technique rather than by meters.

By the early 1960s, Nielsen was the dominant television ratings service in the United States, and it gradually strengthened its position in Canada as competitors such as Penn-McLeod, ISL, and McDonald Research fell by the wayside. In both countries, however, it left the task of radio audience measurement to other companies. In Canada, this facilitated the growth of a co-operative audience measurement service called the Bureau of Broadcast Measurement (BBM). The BBM had been created by the Canadian radio industry in 1944 to provide stations with information about their "circulation" (defined as the area in which a station has a significant share of regular listeners) to facilitate local advertising. A similar non-profit organization called the Broadcast Measurement Bureau (BMB) had been set up in the United States a few years earlier to conduct station coverage surveys. For a time, the Canadian organization (later renamed the BBM Bureau of Measurement) worked in collaboration with its American counterpart, using the same mail ballot technique and conducting its surveys simultaneously. But whereas the BMB was soon forced out of existence by private companies, the BBM steadily expanded its audience-measurement operations.

Although Nielsen gradually eliminated technical flaws in its meters, the criticism remained that meters record only that television sets are turned on, not that anyone is watching. It was not until 1987 that Nielsen overcame this objection by introducing "people meters." These are small computerized devices wired into television sets and connected to a central computer. Each time a set is turned on, flashing red lights appear on the screen until the computer is told which members of the household are present. The meter automatically records the age and sex of each person watching, the program being watched, and the length of time it is watched. This information is stored digitally and collected silently in the middle of the night through a telephone call from the central computer.

Nielsen and the BBM reached a tentative agreement whereby the former would extend its people-meter service into Canada under the auspices of the latter. However, the BBM failed to secure the approval of its members for this co-operative arrangement. On September 18, 1989, therefore, Nielsen proceeded to introduce people meters to Canada on its own. In the meantime, the BBM decided to develop its own electronic ratings service. In February 1990, it began tests in Montreal and Toronto using a meter built by the Montreal firm, Les Entreprises Videoway. As a result of this initiative, negotiations between the BBM and Nielsen were resumed and there were signs of a new agreement early in 1991. These signs proved to be premature, however, and it remains unlikely that the BBM and Nielsen will agree to co-operate in the use of people-meter technology.

Whereas previous methods of measurement balanced the requirements of broadcasters and advertisers, people meters seem biased in favour of advertisers. In the first place, because viewers have to press a button every so often to record their presence (as well as to indicate channel changes), people meters still tend to underestimate audiences. Second, by restricting its sample to cable households, Nielsen has once again found an extremely effective method of targeting the commodity audience, especially in the United States where cable is not as widespread as in Canada. It is not surprising that the American networks discontinued their subscriptions to the Nielsen people-meter service.

The Limitations of Ratings

Measurements of audience size are essential if broadcasting is to be financed through advertising. But those who have conducted such measurements have not been content to rest their case here. Instead, they have advanced the additional argument that ratings are the basis of cultural democracy in broadcasting. Through radio audience measurement, C.E. Hooper declared, "the radio industry seeks to furnish people with the programs they prefer, and not with programs which some advertiser or company executive *believes* they prefer, nor yet with those which some reformer asserts they *ought* to prefer. The determination of the public's radio program preferences and desires is the basic function served by radio audience measurement" (Chappell and Hooper, 1944, pp. 1–2). "Nothing in American life," Martin Mayer wrote in 1979, ". . . is so democratic, so permeated with egalitarianism, as the use of television ratings to influence program decisions. Whatever the failings of Nielsen ratings, they do assert the equality of souls" (Mayer, 1979, p. 12).

This argument overlooks three points. First of all, as already noted, virtually all the measurement methods that have been developed over the years have a bias toward the commodity audience (those members of the middle class between 18 and 49 years of age). As Meehan points out, this serves to disenfranchise not only minority groups, such as intellectuals and the elderly, but also the public as a whole. Second, ratings measure only the relative popularity of programs shown at the same time. Since the nature of these programs will often vary considerably, this is not a true measure of how much these programs are liked or wanted. It is like placing candidates for different political offices on the same ballot. And third, the idea of broadcasting as a cultural democracy in which programs succeed or fail through a public vote ignores the fact that some people have, in effect, more votes than others. That is, the ratings system necessarily gives the greatest impact over programming to those persons who spend the greatest amount of time listening or watching. Since heavy listeners and viewers also tend to be less discriminating than lighter listeners or viewers, ratings do, in fact, have a negative effect on program quality.

This is not to say that cultural democracy is not a laudable objective, but only that ratings do not actually facilitate its achievement. Ratings do not provide a direct indication of the extent to which a program was enjoyed or appreciated; they only indicate that it was preferred on that occasion to others broadcast at the same time. Nor do they enable the public to indicate programming that it would like to receive. They merely create the illusion that broadcasters give the public what it says it wants.

QUALITATIVE CBC AUDIENCE RESEARCH

If audience research is to facilitate public participation, it must involve qualitative as well as quantitative analysis. In the context of audience studies, quantitative research consists of measurements of the *size* of audiences. These measurements may pertain to programs, stations, or networks in cities, regions, countries, or even larger geographic units. They may be expressed as ratings, share of audience figures, or cumulative audience totals. They may also be broken down by age, gender, socio-economic status, and so forth. In the final analysis, however, all these measurements relate to audience size.

Qualitative research, in contrast, seeks to evaluate audience *reactions* to radio and television programming (as expressed in any form other than audience size). It may pertain to particular programs, program segments, program series, types of programming, and general programming objectives. It may relate to content, form, and even such things as program scheduling. In some cases, moreover, it may express audience reactions in quantitative form, such as a numerical enjoyment index. Within the social sciences, this would qualify it as quantitative research. In the field of audience research, however, the term "qualitative" is used to designate studies of audience reactions, regardless of how the results are expressed.

The most obvious form of audience reaction to programming consists of unsolicited audience mail and spontaneous telephone calls. Val Gielgud of the BBC no doubt overstated the case when he complained in 1930 that letters from listeners were written for the most part by "ego-maniacs, cranks, axe-grinders or the incorrigibly idle who can find nothing better to do" (Briggs, 1965, p. 263). But the fact is that audience mail and telephone calls make up a self-selected sample and cannot, therefore, be regarded as representative of the audience as a whole. Among the CBC's own studies that lent confirmation to this point was one conducted in 1960 in connection with the Corporation's decision to carry American election-night coverage of the presidential contest between Nixon and Kennedy. Although most callers were critical of the decision, a scientific survey revealed that 85 percent of viewers were glad to have had the opportunity to see the broadcast and that most viewers were favourable in their appraisal of the coverage (CBCRD, 1961).

While the CBC research unit continued to make periodic analyses of audience mail, it turned its attention to other methods of assessing audience reactions, including several developed by the BBC. Reith had remained unconvinced of the need for audience research, commenting in 1936 that if anything was to be done in this area, "I do not think that it need be very much, and certainly nothing formal" (Briggs, 1965, pp. 267–68). But within a couple of years, a Listener Research unit was organized within the BBC. In addition to quantitative audience measurement (its "listening barometer") through daily personal interviews with a scientifically selected sample of 2500 to 3000 listeners (and later viewers), the unit undertook qualitative research using fixed regional panels. The volunteers for the panels, each of whom served for several months, recorded their "likes" and "dislikes" on cards and the results were presented in the form of an "appreciation index."

In the early 1950s, the CBC considered establishing similar panels of its own, but was deterred initially both by the costs involved and the fact that the focus of the BBC panels was extremely broad, covering only programs as a whole and one or two of their features. Moreover, more promising approaches in both respects seemed to be offered by two American initiatives in program evaluation. The first of these had been developed in the 1930s by Frank Stanton, head of CBS's research department, and Paul Lazarsfeld, a professor at Columbia University. The Stanton-Lazarsfeld program analyzer, affectionately known as "Little Annie" in CBS circles, involved having a small group of people listen to a pilot program in specially designed seats. The seats were equipped with buttons that enabled their occupants to record their reactions to the program (green for like, red for dislike) as it progressed. A follow-up discussion period was used to probe for reasons that particular programs or program segments were liked or disliked.

The CBS program analyzer could be used to pre-test or post-test programs and involved a minimum of staff and space. It also produced a large amount of qualitative data. But it did so by virtue of the small number of people in its test groups, which meant that its results could not be said to be truly representative. It was for this reason among others that the CBC decided to experiment initially with an alternative system developed by the Horace Schwerin Research Corporation in New York. This involved recording minute-by-minute reactions to test programs by having several hundred people (listener or viewer "juries") mark questionnaires at specified intervals. The Schwerin system also used follow-up sessions, although the large number of people involved reduced their effectiveness. In 1952, Schwerin entered into a partnership with Canadian Facts Limited to offer the service in Canada, and three years later the CBC began testing programs in Toronto using the Schwerin technique.

Despite its use of a larger sample, the Schwerin system also failed to produce data that could be directly projected to a larger population. As a result, the CBC conducted numerous surveys to ascertain audience reactions to various aspects of CBC programming. By the early 1960s, however, it had become clear that this approach was too time consuming and labour intensive. Arthur Laird, the new director of research, decided, therefore, to establish two national audience panels (one anglophone, one francophone).

The national audience panels, which still operate today, were originally designed to gather both quantitative and qualitative information. In addition to recording their program selections, panel members were asked to indicate their level of enjoyment for specified programs. These reactions were then tabulated in the form of an "Enjoyment Index" (EI). This practice has been expanded to include individual characters and specific program elements such as story line, dialogue, acting, pace, settings, photography, and even humour. But it is questionable whether this really adds more depth, or merely extends the oppressive ratings mentality. For example, a report for the "Complex Offer" episode of "Street Legal," which was broadcast on November 17, 1989, summarizes the results for characters as follows:

> EIS . . . are between 3 and 6 points higher than the season-to-date averages. Leon's EI of 84 is his highest ever, and Chuck's EI of 77 moves him into the upper 70s range for the first time. While Carrie's EI of 84 is generally consistent with her high average of 81, Olivia's EI of 80 shows a marked increase from her average EI of 75 this season. Dillon's EI of 76 and the 75 by Nick are higher than their single previous ratings, and Alana's EI of 71 and Gloria's 72 are quite respectable first-time figures (CBCRD, 1990b, p. 1).

Even individual subplots are rated according to enjoyment ("the drunk driving case was given the highest score of 81"). It is difficult to see how this kind of "qualitative" feedback is consistent with the needs and integrity of those producing the program. Should they try to make certain characters more "enjoyable"? Should they write in a few more drunk-driving segments?

The problem with panel operations is that they do not enable participants to provide active as well as passive feedback; that is, they do not indicate what they would like the CBC to do differently, but merely what they think about what the CBC is already doing. It is for this reason in part that use is made of small group techniques. In November of 1989, for example, concern over apparent fluctuations in the size of the audience for "The National" (as indicated by the new people meters) led to the decision to examine the newscast through focus-group testing. This involved holding in-depth discussions with small groups of regular news viewers at the InFocus research facility in Toronto. The two-hour sessions were recorded on audio tape and observed through one-way mirrors with the knowledge of the participants. Because the total sample was restricted to 60 persons, the findings cannot be taken as representing all viewers' opinions. Nonetheless, the sessions shed considerable light on certain attitudes toward "The National" (CBCRD, 1990a).

What the Public Thinks of the CBC

The CBC has periodically arranged for large-scale surveys to find out what the Canadian public thinks about its operations (Opinion Surveys Limited, 1941; Gruneau Research, 1952; CBCRD, 1963, 1974, 1986). Although none of these surveys has been designed specifically from the standpoint of finding out what kind of CBC Canadians would really like to have, many of the questions that have been asked do enable us to ascertain whether the CBC would be radically altered—and if so, in what direction—if it acted upon the expressed desires of the public.

By the 1970s, if not earlier, television had become the most prevalent in-home leisure activity. As the CBC Research Department observed in connection with its 1972 survey, "When viewers are asked to explain what it is about any particular television program that makes it preferable to others, one of the most common responses is in terms of relaxation, time-killing, escape, and passivity. To watch television is, for many people, to relax" (CBCRD, 1974, p. 12). It might be thought, therefore, that were the public allowed to determine programming policy, it would fill the television schedule with pure entertainment. But the matter is more complex than this.

Apart from the fact that many people relax and escape by watching news, public affairs, and other non-entertainment programming, a minority of the adult population considers relaxation to be the only or even the main appeal of television. Most people consider that television fulfils other functions as well, such as serving as a watchdog on government or as an ombudsman (CBCRD, 1974, pp. 21–22). In addition, the tendency to perceive (or not perceive) television as being largely for relaxation and escape does not seem to be confined to any particular demographic group (CBCRD, 1974, p. 15). There are no grounds, therefore, for thinking that an elite would necessarily view it differently.

Although CBC TV's viewers are not very different from those who view other television services, it is possible that Canadians would prefer that CBC play a markedly different role than the commercial networks. Over the years, Canadians have consistently supported the idea of using the CBC to foster an indigenous culture, pursue educational goals, and promote understanding between different cultural groups. In its first national survey of public opinion about the CBC, for example, the CBC Research Department found that 94 percent of Canadians agreed that it is important the the CBC "help Canadians in all parts of Canada to understand and learn about each other," while 89 percent felt that it was important for the CBC to "help French Canadians and English Canadians to understand and learn about each other" (CBCRD, 1963).

When offered a choice between more entertainment programming and more cultural and information programming, slightly more than two-fifths of the participants in the 1984 national survey chose to leave things as they were, and one-fifth said they would prefer more culture and information and slightly less than one-third favoured more entertainment. Even without allowing for the fact that the distinction between these two categories is by no means clear cut and participants were not given any indication of current levels of each kind of programming, this indicates that public opinion would not justify a substantial increase in entertainment programming (CBCRD, 1986, p. 33).

The same is also true for foreign programming. Only about one-quarter of those surveyed indicated that they would like more American and/or European programming, while a slightly larger number preferred more Canadian programming. About two-fifths said they would prefer to leave things as they are. One area in which English-speaking Canadians indicated they would like to see a change was in the relative balance of network and regional programming.

The main point that needs to be kept in mind, however, is that audience research must proceed on the basis of three types of principles. The first category consists of principles set forth in the Broadcasting Act and other government regulations. The second category comprises principles generated within audience research itself as a scientific as well as a democratic activity. An example would be the principle that one must evaluate the quality of programs from the standpoint of the audience for which they are intended. The third category is made up of principles established on the basis of the expressed needs and desires of the Canadian public. An example *might* be the principle that the CBC should give priority to those types of programs that are not available either in sufficient quantity or with the desired degree of quality on other broadcast media outlets. (A corollary of this is the principle that the emphasis of CBC programming might vary from one region or locality to another.) Only when an overall programming philosophy has been developed on the basis of these three categories should audience research proceed to more specific programming matters.

There must, of course, be a balancing act between the value of public input and the practical requirements of running a large broadcasting organization. Nonetheless, it is particularly important that the CBC, as a public broadcasting agency, use its audience research facility so as to be as responsive as possible to the expressed needs of Canadians. This is the surest guarantee that it will continue to serve the public interest and thereby retain the public support on which its survival depends.

REFERENCES

Aitken, K. (1960). *Report on national radio-television study.* CBC Central Registry, AR3-1-20.

Altman, W. (1962). The rise and fall of the BBC monopoly. In *TV: From Monopoly to Competition* (Eds., Altman, W. et al.). London: Institute of Economic Affairs.

Bauer, R.A. (1964, May). The obstinate audience. *American Psychologist, 19.*

Bauer, R.A. (1973). The audience. In *Handbook of Communication* (Eds., Schramm, W., et al.). Chicago: Rand McNally.

Beville, H.M., Jr. (1988). *Audience ratings: Radio, television, and cable*. Rev. ed. Hillsdale, NJ: Lawrence Erlbaum Associates.

Blumer, H. (1946). The mass, the public, and public opinion. In *New Outline of the Principles of Sociology* (Ed., Lee, A.M.). New York: Barnes and Noble.

Briggs, A. (1965). *The golden age of wireless*. Volume II of *The History of Broadcasting in the United Kingdom*. London: Oxford University Press.

Canada. Royal Commission on Broadcasting (Fowler Commission). (1957). *Report*. Ottawa.

Canada. Royal Commission on National Development in the Arts, Letters and Sciences (Massey Commission). (1951). *Report*. Ottawa.

Canadian Broadcasting Corporation. (1949). *Saskatchewan survey*. As prepared from a report by Canadian Facts, Limited.

Canadian Broadcasting Corporation Research Department. (1961, January). *Canadian audiences to the 1960 U.S. election-night telecast: A study of the reactions of Canadian TV viewers to the showing of the U.S. telecast on Canadian television*. Unpublished report.

Canadian Broadcasting Corporation Research Department. (1963, June). *What the Canadian public thinks of the CBC*. Unpublished report.

Canadian Broadcasting Corporation Research Department. (1974, February). *What the Canadian public thinks of television and of the TV services provided by the CBC*. Unpublished report.

Canadian Broadcasting Corporation Research Department. (1986, January). *How Canadians feel about the CBC*. Unpublished report.

Canadian Broadcasting Corporation Research Department. (1988, March). *CBC television in the 1990s: The audience's perspective*. Unpublished report.

Canadian Broadcasting Corporation Research Department. (1990a, February). *The National: Findings from focus group tests on the use and viewing of national television newscasts*. Unpublished report.

Canadian Broadcasting Corporation Research Department. (1990b). *Street Legal: CBC English network panel results—"Complex offer."*

Chappell, M.N., & Hooper, C.E. (1944). *Radio audience measurement*. New York: Stephen Daye.

Elliott-Haynes Limited. (n.d.). Pamphlet entitled *From little acorns grow...*

Fowler Commission. See Canada. Royal Commission on Broadcasting. (1957).

Gruneau Research. (1952, March). *Canadian public opinion toward radio and the Canadian Broadcasting Corporation*.

Massey Commission. See Canada. Royal Commission on National Development in the Arts, Letters and Sciences. (1951).

Mayer, M. (1979, March). The Nielsens versus quality. *American Film.*

Meehan, E.R. (1990). Why we don't count. In *Logics of Television: Essays in Cultural Criticism* (Ed., Mellencamp, P.). Bloomington and Indianapolis: Indiana University Press.

Morrison, N.M. (1957). *Audience research progress report for [CBC] board of governors.* Unpublished report.

Opinions Surveys Limited. (1941, February). *A study of radio listening habits made for the Canadian Broadcasting Corporation.*

Peers, F. (1979). *The public eye: Television and the politics of Canadian broadcasting, 1952–1968.* Toronto: University of Toronto Press.

Printer's Ink. (1930, March 20). p. 36

Reith, J.C.W. (1949). *Into the wind.* London: Hodder & Stoughton.

Stewart, E.C. (1948, February). *A report on a study of Elliott-Haynes survey data and its usefulness to the Canadian Broadcasting Corporation.*

Thomas, A. (1960, April). Audience, market, and public: An evaluation of Canadian broadcasting. *Occasional Papers on Adult Education, 7.* University of British Columbia: Department of University Extension.

Weir, A.E. (1965). *The struggle for national broadcasting in Canada.* Toronto: McClelland and Stewart.

PRIVATE TELEVISION: THE VILLAIN OF THE PIECE SEEN IN A NEW LIGHT

Peter Desbarats

Since the beginning of Canadian television in the 1950s, competition between public and private television[1] systems has been portrayed as a medieval morality play with private television cast as the villain. In recent years, however, the history of private broadcasting in Canada has been revised to provide a more complex picture of the relationship between the two systems. At the same time, after years of awkward and disappointing attempts to "Canadianize" the industry by regulation, technological and market developments are forcing private television to play a larger role as a producer and distributor of Canadian programs. This seems destined to continue, supported by public subsidies for independent television production.

Coincidentally, an international trend to increase the role of private broadcasters in countries previously dominated by public radio and television systems, reflected in Canada by reductions in funding and activities of the Canadian Broadcasting Corporation, has further blurred old black-and-white distinctions between public and private television systems.

THE TRADITIONAL VILLAIN OF THE PIECE

Private television in Canada was less than a decade old when the Special Senate Committee on Mass Media began its inquiry and set the tone for public discussion of the industry's shortcomings. The Committee decided that private television broadcasters collectively had achieved a level of performance "perhaps best described as neanderthal" (Special Senate Committee, 1970, p. 240).

Formulating a critique that would be repeated over and over again in the decades ahead, the Committee stated in its report that "the vast majority of private broadcasters have done the minimum required of them by law, and no more. . . . They have been content to let the networks fill the prime-time hours with imported programmes; they have been happy to take whatever the networks would supply free; they have filled the rest of their hours with as much syndicated material as possible, producing themselves as little as possible." This lacklustre performance had been exhibited even by "immensely profitable" private television stations. In sum, the Committee confessed that it could not find "any reason at all why some of the healthy profits of private broadcasting might not be turned into something more than the legal minimum of Canadian programmes" (Special Senate Committee 1970, p. 206).

This critique, with minor variations, has remained the orthodox view of private television among most academics, journalists, and other critics of popular Canadian culture for the past twenty years. Robert Fulford, for example, showed how potently vitriolic criticism of private television still was in 1987 when he thundered from the editor's chair at *Saturday Night* that "private TV simply doesn't do what TV is supposed to do. It never has, and long experience suggests that it never will" (Fulford, 1987, p. 6). Targeting the dominant group of Bassett-owned stations within the CTV network, Fulford claimed that they had never made "more than the most meagre and pitiful contribution to the entertainment business of which they are ostensibly a part. . . . Their record, over a whole generation, amounts to the most appalling regulatory failure in modern Canadian history," he continued, "and calls into question not only the role of the federal regulators in broadcasting but the very idea of private television in Canada" (Fulford, 1987, p. 5).

But Fulford's tirade, while illustrating the undimmed fury and frustration of private television's critics almost twenty years after the Special Senate Committee's report, also indicated an important shift of focus from broadcaster to regulator. By the end of the 1980s, the critics hardly seemed to know where to place primary responsibility for what they regarded as an unmitigated fiasco—whether to blame the private broadcasters for ignoring regulations enacted to improve their performance, or the federal regulatory authority, the Canadian Radio-television and Telecommunications Commission, for failing to enforce its own regulations.

One of the most detailed criticisms of private television published in the past decade, Herschel Hardin's *Closed Circuits—The Sellout of Canadian Television*, was essentially an attack on the record of the CRTC. Hardin said that the federal regulators, "by handing out licences on the basis of certain promises and then backing off denying renewal when the promises were not fulfilled . . . created an Americanized broadcasting structure that was never intended and never envisaged in the legislation that the agencies were created to implement" (Hardin, 1985, p.167).

Criticizing the regulatory agency, however, proved to be a more complex task than launching diatribes against the allegedly greedy capitalists who owned private television stations. Anyone could understand the proposition that profit had replaced public service as a corporate objective in the boardrooms of the private stations. Quoting the famous dictum of the 1965 Fowler report that "the only thing that really matters in broadcasting is program content; all the rest is housekeeping," one analyst in 1987 insisted that "actually, the only thing that *really* matters in *private* broadcasting is the bottom line; all the rest is window dressing" (Mill, 1987, p. 2). It didn't require a Ph.D. to grasp this message, particularly if the criticism was accompanied by statistics, as it was in this case, showing that CTV's profit as a percentage of revenue in 1986 was 22.9 percent compared to a general industrial average of less than 6 percent (Mill, 1987, p. 3).

Focusing on the regulator required more complex analysis and tended to produce a lower degree of invective. Compare the tone of the Special Senate Committee's report, for instance, with the assessment 16 years later by the Federal Task Force on Broadcasting Policy. While the Committee suggested that Canadian broadcasters should develop a "concept of broadcasting as something other than a form of strip-mining" (Special Senate Committee, 1970, p. 204), the Task Force in 1986 found "encouraging signs" in the industry's performance. "We believe it is fair to ask them to do more," it gently suggested, "and to do more in a continuing and systematic way" (Caplan-Sauvageau Task Force, 1986, p. 418). The change of tone was the result of a realization that remedying the shortcomings of private television would require more than Dickensian repentance by the Scrooges of the industry.

In the 1980s, critics of private television had to face the fact that several decades of regulatory pressure designed to increase private stations' Canadian programming had produced disappointingly little in the way of results. Why was this? The simplest and commonest reason given was that private broadcasters, possessing a great deal of economic and political clout, had simply thumbed their collective nose at the CRTC and had been able to get away with it. While this was true to some extent, groups such as the Task Force, with the resources to do research in depth, discovered other and more substantial reasons for the apparent timidity of the CRTC. They had to do with such concrete factors as the size of the Canadian population, the lack of television production experience and resources in the Canadian private sector, and above all, the availability of relatively cheap American productions. Attempting to overcome these barriers to the creation of a truly Canadian private television production industry, or even trying to imagine how to do it, was a far tougher task than fulminating against the owners of television stations.

The traditional criticism of private television had been based on the assumption that a few million dollars, taken from the pockets of the owners and given to Canadian television producers, would solve the problem. No one ever demonstrated that this was true. On the contrary, the experience of the late Al Bruner, who drove Ontario's Global TV into bankruptcy in its first season in 1973–74 on a rich diet of new and imaginative Canadian programming, seemed to indicate that many complex factors were involved in the "failure" of private television.[2]

There was no doubt that profits at some private stations were grotesquely out of proportion when compared with the economy-model local television shows produced by these same stations. But there was also no guarantee that simply throwing the owners' money at the problem would resolve it.

Coercion to spend more on Canadian production was the principle behind content regulations enacted and re-enacted over the years by the CRTC. No matter how the formulas were juggled to force private broadcasters to air more Canadian productions, particularly during prime evening time, the results were always disappointing.

Licensing new stations to provide more competition and more outlets for Canadian programming proved to be even more unproductive. Experience showed that the new Canadian-owned stations became additional conduits for U.S. programming; as the number of Canadian stations in a community increased, viewing levels of American programming went higher and higher (Starowicz, 1989). The new private stations were described by one observer on the public broadcasting side, Mark Starowicz, executive producer of CBC's "The Journal," as "pocket video slums, unable to climb out of an economic niche equivalent to a small U.S. station surviving on syndicated re-runs." Their biggest problem, as Starowicz defined it, was not a lack of entrepreneurial leadership or excessive greed but the fact that they "did not generate enough critical mass to allow investment in quality drama" and other types of Canadian production (Starowicz, 1989). Their inability to act as channels of Canadian culture was related to the size of the market and the structure of the industry, complicated by the proximity, across the Canadian border, of the world's most productive television entertainment industry.

The experience of the owners of Quebec's francophone private television stations provided additional evidence that their counterparts in English-speaking Canada might have behaved differently under other conditions. In the 1984–85 season, for instance, English-language broadcasters, both public and private, spent 21 percent of their programming budgets on foreign programs, while French-language broadcasters spent only 6 percent (Caplan-Sauvageau Task Force, 1986, p. 429). Francophone broadcasters, located in a strong market for domestic product and deprived of ready access to suitable foreign programming, traditionally have spent relatively heavily on Canadian production. Although their motive was primarily commercial, it contributed to the cultural development of their own community. The same commercial motive produced different results in English-speaking Canada, where private broadcasters in 1984–85 paid $133 million for imported television shows that cost up to $5 billion to produce in the United States and that were eagerly watched by Canadian viewers.

"It is not surprising that private broadcasters find this an attractive proposition," noted the 1986 Task Force, "particularly when these shows come with the backing of extensive publicity and advertising that spills into the Canadian market" (Caplan-Sauvageau Task Force, 1986, p. 433).

HISTORY REVISITED AND REVISED

Other factors in the 1980s contributed to a blurring of the distinctions between private and public television broadcasters that had given such zest to the old morality play. As state ownership of various types of enterprises fell into disfavour, first in the United States and western Europe and then with a cataclysmic rush in the Soviet bloc, public broadcasters found themselves working against the current of public opinion and political fashion. In western Europe, one country after another "Canadianized" its broadcasting system by eliminating state monopolies and permitting competition by commercial broadcasters; this orderly process became, in the Soviet bloc, a confused dismantling of previously dominant and protected state publishing and broadcasting enterprises and their replacement by almost unregulated private sector activity, at least in the short term.

In Canada, public broadcasting had to contend not only with this hostile international tendency but with the beginnings of a revisionist school of broadcasting history that threatened its philosophical underpinnings.

Until very recently, histories of Canadian broadcasting have usually been produced by authors closely connected to and in sympathy with the Canadian Broadcasting Corporation. These histories tended to downplay the importance of private broadcasting, particularly in the critical early years of radio; they typically portrayed the beginnings of public broadcasting in Canada as a kind of virgin birth inspired by the purest national and cultural motives. In the 1980s, more extensive research by historians with different backgrounds and approaches to the subject began to produce a more complicated version of the nativity of the CBC.

At the University of Western Ontario, Dr. Michael Nolan, an historian with experience as a journalist in private broadcasting, produced in 1986 a biography of Alan Plaunt, a major figure in the development of Canadian radio, that contained the outline of a revisionist history of Canadian broadcasting. It called for "a clearer understanding . . . of the cultural myth surrounding the broadcasting industry and a fuller grasp of the commendable role played by the private sector, especially in the early days." [3]

In this and other writings, Professor Nolan began the task of rescuing from official neglect the accomplishments of private radio broadcasters in Canada during the industry's initial years. He demonstrated, for instance, that the support by many Canadian newspapers of a highly effective lobby in the 1920s to promote public broadcasting was based in large part on the newspapers' fear that commercial radio would develop into a significant competitor for advertising. For the newspapers, arguments in favour of cultural nationalism were convenient instruments of commercial advantage.

"That private broadcasters operated stations with a crude radio technology . . . during this pioneer period to provide programs that had sizable Canadian audiences is an historical development that officialdom today sometimes seems reluctant to acknowledge," wrote Professor Nolan in 1984. "These stations were in existence a full fourteen years before the formulation of a comprehensive federal policy which had, at its core, the notion that radio should serve as an electronic instrument for cultural uplift" (Nolan, 1984, p. 34).

Revisionist history was reinforced by more careful study of the cultural effects of television on Canadians' sense of national identity, particularly in English-speaking Canada. (In Quebec, of course, television has long been credited as being instrumental in promoting the social, religious, and political changes that contributed to the "Quiet Revolution" of the 1960s.) Private television traditionally had been criticized for carrying imported programs that would "Americanize" Canada; one of the main arguments for public television was that it would prevent this cultural subversion. But by the end of the 1980s, after three decades of private television, cultural activity in English-speaking Canada showed no sign of withering away. On the contrary, according to Canada's foremost media historian, the Canadian experience showed that fear of television as "the instrument of assault on particular cultures . . . can easily be exaggerated by anxious nationalists" (Rutherford, 1990, p. 491).

In his 1990 history of the first fifteen years of Canadian television, Paul Rutherford concluded that "the fears of . . . the highbrows back in the early 1950s, that the Americanization of the airwaves would somehow undo Canada, weren't realized.

"True enough, the accessibility plus the popularity of Hollywood entertainment made virtually impossible the survival of an indigenous and vigorous PopCult in

English Canada," he stated. "But this so-called colonization of the imagination didn't prevent the flowering of the arts and letters that has been so notable a feature on the cultural landscape of English Canada over the past three decades" (Rutherford, 1990, p. 50).

THE ROCKY ROAD TO DAMASCUS FOR PRIVATE TELEVISION

One can argue that the morality-play approach to private television served Canada reasonably well in the first few decades of the industry. It provided a philosophical basis for maintaining a strong public television system and for closely regulating its private competitors, even if rules setting quotas for Canadian content didn't always achieve the desired results. During the 1980s, however, as the historical and nationalist themes of the morality play came into question, technological and commercial developments forced private television into new patterns of behaviour.

In the early decades of Canadian television, public and private broadcasters operated in markets with limited numbers of competitors. Most communities were served by only two Canadian stations, the CBC and a private broadcaster, with the CBC providing only restricted competition for advertisers. In many markets, the demand for television advertising surpassed the available supply. Under these conditions, the temptation to "strip mine" the territory was overwhelming.

Even competition from U.S. stations, unregulated in the days when Canadian viewers near the border used antennas to pick up American channels, came under CRTC control as cable systems brought both Canadian and U.S. channels to more and more homes. Legislation introduced in the mid-1970s required cable systems to replace a foreign signal with a local one if the same program was being shown simultaneously, thus protecting the audience and the advertising revenue of local broadcasters. At the same time, Bill C-58 used tax regulations to discourage Canadian companies from advertising on U.S. stations close to the border. This comfortable market provided Canadian stations with little incentive to invest in Canadian programming apart from news, current affairs, and sports, which had always attracted large Canadian audiences. In those areas, there was vigorous competition between public and private Canadian stations, and standards of production were high. In the entertainment programming that makes up most of the television schedule, American programs continued to dominate the Canadian market. Even the publicly owned Canadian Broadcasting Corporation competed with private stations for the rights to popular U.S. shows.

In the past decade, Canadian broadcasters have felt the cold winds of competition blowing through this cosy world. The licensing of new private Canadian stations and specialty channels has fragmented a television audience already diminishing because of growing numbers of VCRs in homes and changing lifestyles.

These developments have not been exclusive to Canada. In the 1980s, network audiences in the United States started to shrink for the first time in the history of the industry. "The really serious thing is the loss of one or two percent of the audience every year," according to Bill Munro, editor of the *Washington Journalism Review* and a former producer for NBC News. "And there is no horizon for that stopping" (TV network, 1988)."

The fragmentation of the television audience and its movement away from conventional television programming toward other types of on-screen entertainment—or, in some cases, abandoning the couch-potato lifestyle entirely for more active pursuits—has forced all broadcasters to review and revise programming.

On the public side, CBC television was influenced by the success that CBC radio had achieved in meeting competition from television in the 1960s and 1970s. Faced with the loss of its mass audience for sports, drama, and other types of entertainment programming, CBC radio had discovered a new sense of national mission by focusing on news and information programming. In the 1980s, CBC television followed this example by concentrating much of its dwindling resources on news and current affairs (Desbarats, 1990, pp. 40–49).

Private broadcasters and the Canadian Radio-television and Telecommunications Commission, locked in a cozy embrace that threatened to turn into a dance of death under the new market conditions, were slower to respond. The CRTC continued to tinker with Canadian content rules by tying them to station profitability and more specific content requirements. This enabled the industry to focus on fewer productions of higher quality rather than trying to spread low-cost Canadian productions across the schedule. Starting in 1983, higher subsidies were provided to independent producers through the Broadcast Program Development Fund of Telefilm Canada, although about half of these private-sector productions ended up on the CBC rather than on private stations (Vipond, 1989, pp. 156–57). After a private broadcaster, André Bureau, began a five-year appointment as chairman of the CRTC in 1983, the regulatory agency relaxed restrictions on cross-ownership (simultaneous ownership of properties in various media, both print and electronic) and on concentration of ownership in radio and television. "The nub of Mr. Bureau's big-is-dutiful approach," according to a 1989 report of the Consumers' Association of Canada, "was to encourage the development of enterprises financially strong enough to tackle the Canadianization of peak-hour drama and entertainment programming, then to impose more demanding Canadian programming requirements in their conditions of licence" (Creery, 1989). None of these changes, at the time, seemed to represent the breakthrough needed to reform private television, but collectively they now can be seen as the beginning of an important new phase.

THE LIGHT AT THE END OF THE TUNNEL

It was significant that, by 1989, even organizations such as the Consumers' Association, long critical of concentrated media ownership, had come to the conclusion that regulation of private television had failed to produce the desired results and now threatened to become even less productive in a competitive world of proliferating video technologies.

"The licensing of supervised concentration in the electronic media is one of many ways in which Canada's paternalistic broadcasting regime is limiting freedom of expression and enterprise to the detriment of the public," the Association stated in the 1989 report cited above. "Consumers would benefit from a new policy to dismantle program control, leave competition and content questions to general laws, and retain only those controls needed to regulate technical matters and assure non-discriminatory service at reasonable rates from common carriers and monopolies."

Other students of the broadcasting system have tended to agree that the old structure of content restrictions is now often counter-productive and should continue to be replaced by incentives. A 1986 survey of research literature on the economics of Canadian broadcasting showed an apparent trend among experts toward the opinion that "attempts to force private broadcasters to act against their own self-interest can never be made effective" (Hoskins & McFayden, 1986, p. 36). On the other hand, "there is no evidence, even where protective measures are successful in boosting broadcasters' profits, that these additional profits lead to additional expenditures on Canadian programming." Larger subsidies for Canadian productions would appear to be a more effective method, particularly if the subsidies can be justified on cultural and economic grounds (Hoskins & McFayden, 1986, p. 37). In her 1989 study of the mass media in Canada, Mary Vipond concluded that "better ways must be found to ensure that Canadian alternatives to the products of U.S. media also exist. The banning of imported products is unacceptable, but stimulation of the creation of local works, by quotas or other devices, is quite legitimate" (Vipond, 1989, p. 183).

Worried by continuing declines in audience numbers and the prospect of reduced levels of profit in the decade that opened with the recession of 1990, private broadcasters also have been re-examining old assumptions. If North American television viewers are switching off because they find much of the American entertainment on the small screen boringly predictable and cluttered with commercials, that is particularly grim news for the private Canadian stations that have prospered for decades on imported U.S. programs. Once this programming base starts to erode, and if the CBC continues to dominate network television news and to compete strongly in local news markets, private Canadian television will experience decreases in profitability, ratings, and political clout. The only apparent alternative to this dismal prospect is more and better Canadian programming on private stations to provide viewers with a reason for watching Canadian rather than American television, or not watching television at all.[4]

This option is now more appealing than it was in the past because of the rising cost of imported American programming in a world of increasing competition for programming of any kind, in Canada and internationally, and because of higher prices paid overseas for quality Canadian television programs.

Private television already has started to move in this direction. By 1987, more than two-thirds of the programming budgets of private broadcasters was spent on Canadian programming (Canadian Association of Broadcasters, 1989, p. 2). In 1990, one of the first major decisions by CTV's new president, John Cassaday, was to upgrade the network's news and current affairs programming. In its strategic plan for the 1990s, the Canadian Association of Broadcasters recognized that "government policy, the need to be both distinctive in the marketplace and locally relevant, and the rising cost of foreign programming, combine to exert increased pressure for high quality Canadian programming" (Canadian Association of Broadcasters, 1989, p. 7). The first two points of the CAB's seven-point strategy for the new decade were:

1. "Strengthen the Canadian character of the broadcasting system and strengthen the capacity of private broadcasting to play its foundation role in the system.

2. "Develop an all-industry strategy to produce and exhibit Canadian programming that Canadians want to watch."

"Stations' programming to please governments and regulators, rather than their audiences, will be tuned out," predicted CAB President Michael McCabe. "In today's expanding 100-channel universe if we're not good, we're gone. . . . In the 1990s more hours of Canadian content just won't mean that much" (McCabe, 1989, p. 19).

Apart from the usual rhetoric, the CAB's plan for the 1990's contained the seeds of a strong inner-directed drive toward more and better quality Canadian content on private stations, not for national or cultural reasons but as a strategy for survival in a decade when conventional and fibre-optical cable systems, direct-broadcast-to-home satellites, improved VCR and videodisc systems, and the introduction of high-definition television will increase the already stiff competition for the television audience.

This development reveals a growing rapprochement between the objectives of private broadcasters and those who in the past would have been their sternest critics. The morality play has become a piece of existentialist theatre and the villainous private broadcaster a complex modern hero.

NOTES

1. There were 93 private television stations in Canada in 1989, according to the Canadian Association of Broadcasters' strategic plan of July 1989, *Taking the lead—Private broadcasting strategies for the 90s.* According to the same document, the industry employs more than 8000 people, attracts more than $1 billion annually in advertising, and pays more than $300 million a year in salaries.

2. The author was anchor and Ottawa Bureau Chief for Global TV from 1973 to 1980.

3. Professor Nolan's book *Foundation: Alan Plaunt and the early days of CBC Radio* was published in 1986 by CBC Enterprises.

4. Even as this paper was being prepared, the CRTC was considering yet another proposal designed to lure more viewers from the programming of private television: a service called "Viewer's Choice," which would permit cable subscribers to phone in orders to view films that they have selected from a menu provided by the new service.

REFERENCES

Canada. Task Force on Broadcasting Policy (Caplan-Sauvageau Task Force). (1986). *Report.* Ottawa.

Canada. Special Senate Committee on Mass Media. (1970). *Report.* Vol. 1. Ottawa.

Canadian Association of Broadcasters. (1989, July). Taking the lead—television strategic plan and analysis. Internal report.

Caplan-Sauvageau Task Force. See Canada. Task Force on Broadcast Policy. (1986).

Creery, T. (1989, May). *Supervised concentration—big-is-dutiful in Canadian broadcasting regulations.* A report to the Council of Regulated Industries by the Consumers' Association of Canada.

Desbarats, P. (1990). *Guide to Canadian news media*. Toronto: Harcourt Brace Jovanovich, Canada.

Fulford, R. (1987, July). Promises, promises. *Saturday Night*.

Hardin, H. (1985). *Closed circuits—The sellout of Canadian television*. Vancouver: Douglas & McIntyre.

Hoskins, C., & McFayden, S. (1986). The economic factors relating to Canadian television broadcasting policy: A non-technical synthesis of the research literature. *Canadian Journal of Communication, 12* (1).

McCabe, M. (1989, December 15). Challenges and priorites. *Cable Communications*.

Mill, M. (1987, May/June). CTV's troubles set—If profitability is the accepted god, are viewers not the ultimate losers as TV economics get most of the attention? *Content*.

Nolan, M. (1984, January). Canadian broadcasting history: A time for revision. *Broadcaster*.

Rutherford, P. (1990). *When television was young: Primetime Canada 1950–1967*. Toronto: University of Toronto Press.

Starowicz, M. (1989). *Citizens of video-America—What happened to Canadian television in the satellite age?* Speech delivered to a symposium on "Television, Entertainment and National Culture" sponsored by Duke University and Laval University in Quebec City.

TV network news in U.S. losing audience, discovering budgets. (1988, March 2). *Globe and Mail*, pp. B1–B4.

Vipond, M. (1989). *The mass media in Canada*. Toronto: James Lorimer.

THE CANADIAN FILM INDUSTRY

Seth Feldman

"Brazil," according to its weary cynics, "is the country of the future and always will be." To the equally weary cynic, the same might be said of Canadian cinema. For Canadians, the promise of a viable film industry is usually met with a well-weathered incredulity. Both the private and public sectors have promised us Hollywood North. And they have done so far too often. But have we really gained nothing at all? The question we will be asking here is not: has Canada succeeded or can Canada succeed in creating a Hollywood North? Rather, the question is, is that criterion relevant as a measure of what has been accomplished? Similarly, the reality of Canadian cinema today must be measured against what it—or indeed any national cinema—can be. There is also a second question: have we built a cinema culture in which Canadian audiences are used to taking Canadian cinema seriously?

PARALLEL HISTORIES

The answers to both questions are best searched for in a historical context. Because cinema itself is part industry, part public policy, and perennially the product of changing social and artistic norms, the standards for judging Canadian cinema have evolved over time. During the medium's first decade, the potential for an indigenous Canadian film industry was taken for granted. There was no question of having to establish a Hollywood North because there was very little in the way of a Hollywood South. As the American industry developed, it became the model against which other national cinemas were measured. Yet that model has always been changing, subject to internal and external demands.

The several stages of cinema's invention came to fruition in the 1890s, the Lumière brothers' public screening of December 28, 1895, being the convenient if somewhat apocryphal date usually cited. In reality, work on the new medium had taken place simultaneously in a number of industrialized nations. The earliest stages of film dissemination mirrored its global origins. Typically, a French, American, or British crew arrived both to shoot and screen filmstrips lasting barely a minute. The event would catch the attention of a local photographer, showman, or other entrepreneur. In some nations—most notably Japan—the new medium was venerated as a technological wonder. In most places, it was soon submerged into the general run of novelties and entertainments. Either way, one of the selling points of the earliest cinema was its ability to present moving pictures from all over the world. Films from the original producing nations and the local offshoots circulated globally, their intertitles (when they had intertitles) easily replaced with local translations.

In Canada, the emergence of cinema fits well within this paradigm. The first screenings took place on June 27, 1896, in Montreal and on July 21 in Ottawa. Before the turn of the century, foreign and Canadian cameramen had shot footage throughout the country. By 1914, American companies alone had shot more than 100 films here. The consolidation of that footage into longer productions also kept pace with world trends. In 1903, Joe Rosenthal of Desbarats, Ontario, made *Hiawatha, The Messiah of the Ojibway Indians*, one of a number of works that make up a body of early Canadian narrative films. In 1908, Ernest Leo Ouimet produced the first of a long series of newsreels and documentaries in Montreal. Other independent producers followed.

If anything distinguished Canadian cinema during this period, it was the relative sophistication with which the medium was being used as an informational tool. In 1903–04, the Canadian Pacific Railroad hired the Edison Company to produce 35 short travelogues and thirteen short dramas to lure immigrants and tourists to the Canadian West. These were deemed a highly successful addition to the CPR's long-established photo and poster advertising campaigns. The public sector was also aware of the effectiveness of informational filmmaking. Beginning in 1915, the federal government, as well as the governments of Ontario, Quebec, Saskatchewan, and British Columbia sponsored documentaries with increasing frequency.

The end of this first period of cinema history came with the emergence of the feature film as the medium's prevailing format. By 1905, the development of acting, filming, and editing techniques allowed filmmakers to sustain audience interest in a single film for ten to fifteen minutes (one full projector reel). This norm for a cinematic narrative steadily increased to half an hour, an hour, and finally the now-conventional hour-and-a-half to two hours of a feature film.

Canada was part of the worldwide experimentation in increasingly longer films. The Canadian Bioscope Company of Halifax made the first Canadian feature, *Evangeline,* in 1913. But the breakthrough film was D.W. Griffith's 1915 American epic, *Birth of a Nation*. The unprecedented success of that work upped the ante of filmmaking as a whole. Films would now require substantial capital, teams of specialists working in elaborate production facilities, and a far-flung distribution system to theatres large enough to earn back costs. Southern California, with its good weather, varied topography, and distance from the supervision of New York investors, seemed like the ideal location for the newly centralized industry. Hollywood also grew at the expense of the European industries, most of which were shut down for the duration of the First World War.

By the 1920s, Hollywood was attracting the best film talent in the world, a process that drained the pool of human resources available to national cinemas. Mary Pickford and Mack Sennett were among the first Canadian contributions. Hollywood was also a blender of international styles, successfully domesticating German Expressionism, Soviet Constructivism, and French Surrealism. Canada's contribution was less a style than subject matter: the Mounties, bush pilots, and indeed the entire array of what

Pierre Berton calls "Hollywood's Canada" (Berton, 1975). During the inter-war period, Canada was in the avant-garde of cultures that came to know themselves through their Hollywood (mis)representations. Lewis Selznick, one of the founding geniuses of Hollywood, stated the situation quite plainly in 1922: "If Canadian stories are worthwhile making into films, companies will be sent into Canada to make them" (Morris, 1978).

Canada's first response to the primacy of Hollywood was the concept of Hollywood North. Speaking in 1925, D.W. Griffith himself offered the assurance that the industrial structure he had helped create could be recreated north of the border: "You in Canada should not be dependent on either the United States or Great Britain. You should have your own films and exchange them with those of other countries. You can make them just as well in Toronto as in New York" (Morris, 1978).

Even before Griffith's pronouncement, the notion of a Canadian film production centre had no lack of supporters. In 1919, Adanac Films of Toronto built a permanent studio in Trenton, Ontario. That same year, "Ten Percent Ernie" Shipman, an Ottawa-born entrepreneur with some experience in the American entertainment industry, sold Calgary investors on the idea of establishing a filmmaking centre. In the next four years, Shipman also brought the concept to Winnipeg, Ottawa, Sault Ste. Marie, and Saint John. These various Hollywood Norths financed seven films, some taken from the works of Canadian authors. The first of these, *Back to God's Country*, was an unqualified success. Subsequent titles fared less well. In the end, Shipman got in the habit of leaving town with his films undistributed and books unaudited. He left Canada altogether in 1923. The following year, Adanac's Trenton studio was sold to the Ontario Government Motion Picture Bureau.

Shipman and Adanac served to prove the limitations of the Hollywood North strategy. What success they had was more the product of an alternative production system, a model of regional, locally financed production that, flawed as it was, led to the production of feature films. This alternative cinema was the second Canadian response to Hollywood. It would be invoked in 1927–28 with the production of *Carry On, Sergeant!* Financed entirely by private investors, that First World War epic was the most ambitious Canadian undertaking prior to the creation of the Canadian Film Development Corporation in 1967. However, the regional model's greatest success (as measured by numbers of films produced) came in Quebec between 1944 and 1953. Two companies, Renaissance Films and Quebec Productions, made some nineteen feature films.

The production of locally made feature films was, at best, sporadic. The filmmakers worked in isolation. The few people who wrote about the films seldom saw them as Canadian cinema or indeed anything more than the curiosities they were. Most Canadians never had a chance to see the films at all. Movie theatre chains were either owned or dominated by the increasingly aggressive American studios. By 1930, Famous Players alone owned nearly a third of the nation's screens. The Hollywood studios insisted on block booking—forcing theatre owners to show nothing but a given studio's work if they wanted to show any of it at all. At the same time, Hollywood's publicity machine insured that even the few independent theatres showed little interest in relatively obscure non-Hollywood productions.

Governments did little to improve the situation. While the Radio League won its battles for the Canadianization of its medium, the federal government backed down on the issue of foreign control of the film industry. In 1930, Famous Players was cited under the Combines Investigation Act. The following year, the studio was found to have contravened the Act, and yet nothing was done. Nor did the federal government show any interest in subsidizing feature film production. By the end of the 1920s, the Weimar Republic had underwritten the mammoth UFA studio, and the golden age of Soviet cinema had been sponsored by the new Communist government. But beyond the creation of the Canadian Government Motion Picture Bureau in 1923, there was no desire to use federal funds to make movies.

The federal government's apathy toward the industry went so far as to subvert the one piece of legislation during the inter-war period that did encourage Canadian feature production. In 1928, the British Parliament established a quota on the screening of foreign films. Thanks to Westminster's inclusion of Commonwealth films under the scheme, 21 "quota quickies" were produced in Hollywood branch plants in Western Canada. Made for the least possible money by skeleton crews and third-rate actors, most of the quota quickies were ultimately screened during the morning hours in empty British cinemas. The Canadian government did nothing to discourage these abuses. In 1938, the British, disgusted by Canadian quota quickies, specifically excluded Commonwealth productions from the theatre quotas. The branch plants instantly disappeared.

PURPOSE AND STYLE

At the end of the inter-war period, Canada had only one successful cinema strategy. Building on the early documentaries and the publicly financed informational films, the tiny Canadian industry began to attract some notice for its non-fiction films. The Canadian Government Motion Picture Bureau had a growing catalogue of practical if not terribly glamorous information films. By the end of the period, the Bureau had also produced two widely screened feature-length documentaries: Frank Badgley's *Lest We Forget* (1935) and his film, *The Royal Visit* (1939). Private-sector filmmakers also produced notable work. Beginning in 1925, Albert Tessier shot 70 ethnographic films of life in rural Quebec. In 1932, Gordon Sparling made the first of his 85 newsreels under the title, *Canadian Cameos*. And throughout the 1930s, Bill Oliver earned an international reputation for his wildlife films.

On the eve of the Second World War, Canada was ripe for John Grierson. Grierson had coined the term "documentary" in 1926 and had gone on to produce and influence hundreds of British films. In the late 1930s, he had also pioneered what would later be called "the non-theatrical circuit," a means of distributing documentaries and special-interest films outside movie houses. Grierson was invited in 1938 to review the state of Canadian government filmmaking. The result of his investigation was the National Film Act establishing the National Film Board as a co-ordinating agency for all public involvement with the medium. In October 1939, Grierson became the first Film Commissioner. The wartime need for propaganda and Grierson's own skill as a bureaucrat transformed the new agency into a documentary studio employing nearly

800 people, including a stellar collection of American, British, and refugee European filmmakers. During the Second World War, the Film Board produced more than 500 films and distributed them throughout Canada, the United States, and Britain. In 1942, it won an Oscar for its newsreel, *Churchill's Island*.

Grierson contributed not only quantity but also purpose and an aesthetic to Canadian filmmaking. The generation of young Canadians employed by the wartime Film Board learned to think of the medium as a pulpit to be used in the service of precisely defined social objectives. Whether they focused on global or domestic issues, Grierson's bombastic documentaries were made to transform reality into salable ideas. Ernst Borneman, one of the editors at the wartime Board, provided one of the better descriptions of the Grierson aesthetic:

> Since visual, music and effects tracks were running side by side in a highly complex three-part counterpoint, and since the visual by itself constantly skipped from place to place all over the globe, it became doubly important for the commentary to draw the other two tracks and the visual together into a single continuity and this had to be done in such a manner as to make its points through the spectator's subconscious as well as through his conscious. Aside from active verbs and pseudo-quotations ("The experts say that . . .") the most important innovation here was the use of metaphors and similes created by a juxtaposition of an incidental aspect of the visual and an incidental aspect of the commentary in such a way that they became meaningfully, though to the spectator imperceptibly, welded together . . . (Borneman, 1977, pp. 48–58).

Borneman goes on to provide examples in which, generally, the object photographed loses its literal identity in favour of a metaphorical meaning conducive to the message of the film (e.g., the shot of a city skyline is shown under commentary describing "the new horizons of adventure").

The Griersonian aesthetic coupled with the new importance of film per se gave Canadians their first hint of continuity in the development of a national cinema. After the Second World War, Parliament would question the need for a film board. The Board would become a prime target in the Canadian Red Scare. But the quantity and sense of purpose of the Board's productions as well as masterful lobbying by Grierson and his successors kept it intact.

In the late 1940s, with the coming to power of the first generation of Canadians at the Board, the authoritarian voice-over documentary began to give way to experiments with less assertive, more contemplative work. The best films of the Board into the early 1960s represented a calculated dismembering of the authoritative voice in favour of a self-generated and necessarily ambiguous definition of the image. These included *Paul Tomkowicz: Street Railway Switchman* (Roman Kroitor, 1954), *City of Gold* (Wolf Koenig and Colin Low, 1957), *The Days Before Christmas* (Terrence Macartney-Filgate and Wolf Koenig, 1958), *Back Breaking Leaf* (Terrence Macartney-Filgate, 1959), *Universe* (Roman Kroitor and Colin Low, 1960), and *Lonely Boy* (Roman Kroitor and Wolf Koenig, 1962). All these works insisted upon the vulnerability of cinematic perception and, cumulatively, drew a portrait of the world as open text, free of any geo-political preconception. Peter Harcourt's description of them is the antithesis of Ernst Borneman's description of the previous generation's documentaries:

> There is something very Canadian in all this, something which my own Canadianness prompts me to attempt to define. There is in all these films a quality of suspended judgement, of something left open at the end, of something undecided. . . . There is something rather detached from the immediate pressures of existence, something rather apart (Harcourt, 1977, pp. 67–77).

At the same time that the Film Board was developing its documentary aesthetic, it was pursuing other avenues in Canada's strategy of alternative filmmaking. The animation unit achieved a growing recognition as Norman McLaren's *Neighbours* won the NFB's second Academy Award in 1952. Non-theatrical distribution expanded and came to include television. The Film Board's in-house laboratory was in the forefront of developing lightweight portable filmmaking equipment. By the early 1960s, this would make possible not only cinéma vérité documentaries, but community-based filmmaking and low-budget feature films.

All of these developments took place during a hiatus in Canadian feature film production. At the end of the war, with the Hollywood studio system at its zenith, the idea of a Canadian feature film industry seemed all but absurd. In 1948, the federal government would acknowledge as much in secretly agreeing to what the Motion Picture Association of America called "The Canadian Cooperation Project." In exchange for some location shooting, mention of Canada in Hollywood scripts, and American distribution of NFB shorts, Canada agreed to do nothing that would interfere with the distribution of American features. The government also agreed to provide no federal support or encouragement for a feature film industry.

The Canadian Cooperation Project was not a bad idea given the priorities of the postwar period. The federal government was trading something it didn't have (i.e., a feature film industry) for the good will of a very influential sector within the economy of Canada's major trading partner. The deal would last until 1958. But no one could have predicted the change in the structure of Hollywood that would take place during those ten years. No sooner was the Canadian Cooperation Project enacted than the American studios lost an antitrust suit that forced them to divest themselves of their theatre chains. The industry's prestige suffered as Hollywood personalities were dragged before the House Un-American Activities Committee. Most importantly, the advent of television cut deeply into Hollywood's well-established distribution and marketing system. By the late 1950s, weekly movie attendance in the United States was less than half what it had been before the beginning of network television broadcasting.

At the same time, the very idea of Hollywood's hegemony was beginning to slip. The postwar generation of filmgoers and film critics became increasingly interested in the work of non-Hollywood directors such as Ingmar Bergman, Federico Fellini, and Akira Kurosawa. When the French studio system faced near collapse in the late 1950s, more than 60 new directors (including Jean-Luc Godard, Francois Truffaut, and Claude Chabrol) proved they could make highly successful, individualistic low-budget features. In the 1960s, this New Wave model was repeated throughout Europe.

Canada returned to feature filmmaking with its own New Wave. The most important manifestations were in post-Quiet Revolution Quebec, where a number of young filmmakers had completed their apprenticeships with the National Film Board's French Unit. The unit had already made six features when Claude Jutra made his feature film debut with *À tout prendre* in 1963. The next year, Gilles Groulx directed a minor masterpiece of Separatist angst, *Le chat dans le sac*. Also in 1964, Gilles Carle was asked by the Film Board to produce a documentary on snow removal in Montreal. He turned the project into his first feature, *La vie heureuse de Léopold Z*. Jean Pierre Lefebvre launched his career with *L'homoman*. In 1965, Michel Brault, the cinematographer for much of the Quebec New Wave, produced his own first feature, *Entre la mer et l'eau douce*.

Compared to the charged political atmosphere in which Quebec viewed its New Wave features, the English-Canadian films of the period caused only the smallest stir. The first feature was Don Haldane's *The Drylanders*, made at the Film Board in 1963. But the best-known work of the period was a film that, like *La vie heureuse de Léopold Z*, was made out of an NFB documentary assignment. Don Owen's *Nobody Waved Goodbye* (1964) was an improvisational drama of teenage alienation in suburban Toronto. Even that film had to prove itself in a New York "art house" theatre before the NFB distributed it in Canada (one Canadian theatre owner continued to describe it as "amateur night in Hicksville"). Still less exposure was given to the micro-budgeted first films of directors who would go on to better things: Larry Kent (*The Bitter Ash*, 1963, and *High*, 1967); David Cronenberg (*Stereo*, 1969); Ivan Reitman (*Cannibal Girls*, 1970); Jack Darcus (*The Great Coups of History*, 1969); and Peter Rowe (*Buffalo Airport Visions*, 1967). Other promising English-Canadian directors had their careers stalled or stymied altogether by the raging public disinterest. These included John Hofsess (*The Palace of Pleasure*, 1966, and *The Columbus of Sex*, 1967); Robert Fothergill (*Countdown Canada*, 1970); David Secter (*Winter Kept Us Warm*, 1965); and Clarke Mackey (*The Only Thing You Know*, 1971).

English-Canadian features were hampered by the perennial problems of American competition in general and continued disinterest of film theatres in particular. In Quebec, films could recoup their investments in a small number of urban theatres. Theatre owners and their audiences recognized the work as part of an important—and marketable—cultural dialogue. Outside Quebec, neither the dialogue nor the recognition existed. Sympathetic theatre owners were few and widely scattered. And Hollywood was quick to respond to any proposal that would limit access to the Canadian theatres that *Variety* counted in its totals of the American domestic market. At the same time, the NFB was wary of feature film production and amateurish in its efforts at distribution. The CBC had problems with the production values, language, and sexual content of the English-Canadian New Wave.

For English Canada, the great loss of the New Wave period was more than the enforced obscurity of its own films. There was also a tragic lack of resources and foresight that left much of the Quebec New Wave untranslated. As the nation moved toward the October Crisis, there was little access in English Canada to cinema's meticulously drawn picture of the mood and aspirations of a restless Quebec. Unfortunately, it was a mistake that continues to be repeated.

THE FIRST AGE OF SUBSIDY

Despite the difficulties inherent in feature film production, there was, by the mid-1960s, a growing consensus that Canada was ready for a feature film industry. The federal government's reponse was the creation of the Canadian Film Development Corporation in 1967. In theory, the CFDC was a bank whose job it was to loan seed money to projects whose profits would then replenish the fund to provide seed money for yet more films. In practice, the agency often found itself investing far more than seed money and seldom receiving any return on its investment. Potential filmmakers complained of arbitrary or politically motivated funding decisions and endless red tape. Policy analysts wondered whether the CFDC's first priority was to fund commercially or artistically viable proposals. Quebec producers complained of a bias toward anglophone filmmaking. And the CFDC did little to address the ongoing problem of distribution.

Augmenting the CFDC initiative was the establishment of the 100 percent Capital Cost Allowance in 1974. This generous tax shelter was meant to attract private capital that would match the government's seed money. The CCA generated the mythical figure of the upscale citizen eager to exchange his or her savings for the opportunity to appear under the klieg lights on opening night. The reality was that most investors found themselves lured into projects that had little chance of succeeding—or even of being completed. The glamour of Canadian cinema was soon replaced by embarrassment at the resulting product and no small degree of anger at producers, lawyers, and accountants who grew quite wealthy manipulating the system. There was also a good deal of discussion as to how Canadian these films really were. Despite an elaborate point system used to "certify" Canadian content, it was often hard to see how the resulting product advanced the national ethos.

But if the goals of the CFDC and the CCA were to convert a small but promising New Wave into a permanent institution, they did stumble onto some degree of success. In Quebec, the emerging directors matured. Gilles Carle made a dozen feature films during the 1970s while Jean Pierre Lefebvre made eight. Michel Brault, who continued as cinematographer on (seemingly) everyone else's films, directed the definitive drama about the October Crisis, *Les Ordres* (1974). Denys Arcand grew tired of censorship battles over his Film Board documentaries and turned to feature filmmaking. His *Réjeanne Padovani* (1973)—in which actors bearing a striking resemblance to the provincial premier and mayor of Montreal end a shady construction deal with a murder—furthered his bad-boy image. A very short list of other important Quebec feature filmmakers to emerge in the 1970s would have to include Mireille Dansereau (*La vie rêvée*, 1972), Francis Mankiewicz (*Le temps d'une chasse*, 1972), André Forcier (*Bar salon*, 1973), and Micheline Lanctôt (*L'homme à tout faire*, 1979). The overall highlight of the decade, though, was the result of one of the Film Board's periodic efforts to join the feature film boom. Claude Jutra made his (and perhaps the nation's) greatest film, *Mon Oncle Antoine* in 1971.

As it was from the beginning, the work of the Quebec *auteurs* was characterized by an ethos of *entre nous*. The films were thoughtful, wry, political, full of references to the events and personalities of Quebec culture. Even soft-core pornography, such as Claude Fournier's enormously popular *Deux femmes en or* (1970) played upon common perceptions of a well-formed culture. In Quebec, the screen reflected the sizable and thoughtful audience participating in the cinematic dialogue. Films caused scandals, sparked public debate, and served, on the whole, as proof of the reborn society's continuing cultural development.

Quebec films attracted little attention in English Canada. This is one of the few things they had in common with anglophone Canadian features of the 1970s—English product continued to enjoy very little public attention. Perhaps as a result of being made and screened in a vacuum, the films themselves tended to be self-pitying, immature, culturally vacuous, and often bereft of any reason for existence other than as an exercise in feature film production. Robert Fothergill, who as a CFDC script reader and film critic in the 1970s, saw an inordinate amount of this work, wrote: "It is very rare indeed to find an English-Canadian film in which a male character of some worth and substance is depicted as growing towards self-realization, achieving or even working towards a worthwhile goal, playing a significant part in any kind of community, or establishing a mature loving relationship with a woman" (Fothergill, 1977). It almost goes without saying that female characters were marginal at best, the losers' victims.

Despite this low-grade existential crisis (on and off screen), genuine talent did emerge and develop in English-Canadian feature films during the 1970s. The breakthrough film of the period was Don Shebib's *Goin' Down the Road* (1970), whose naïve maritimers seem in retrospect to have been prototypes for SCTV's the Great White North and fodder for Margaret Atwood's *Survival*. Peter Pearson made his fine realist drama, *The Best Damned Fiddler from Calaboogie to Kaladar* (1968), at the Film Board. He went on to the private sector to direct *Paperback Hero* (1973) and to CBC for the twin political dramas, *The Insurance Man From Ingersoll* (1975) and *The Tar Sands* (1976). In the latter work, the likable loser is Peter Lougheed (who responded with the very un-Canadian gestures of suing and winning his case).

The most popular anglophone feature of the period and most likable (albeit moral) failure were Ted Kotcheff's *The Apprenticeship of Duddy Kravitz* (1974) and the very young Richard Dreyfuss as Duddy. Craig Russell in Richard Benner's *Outrageous* (1977) ends the film by dancing to the observation that he is "alive and sick in New York." Other work in this vein is Don Owen's *The Ernie Game* (1967), William Fruet's *Wedding in White* (1972), Zale Dalen's *Skip Tracer* (1977), and Clay Borris's *Alligator Shoes* (1980).

Of those who tried to break away from the loser film, the most notable was Paul Almond, a long-time CBC director, who attempted a self-consciously artistic triology: *Isabel* (1968), *The Act of the Heart* (1970), and *Journey* (1972). Joyce Wieland almost succeeded in merging the experimental and feature traditions in her work, *The Far Shore* (1975). Jack Darcus continued to exorcise his personal demons in seldom-seen films, most notably *Proxyhawks* (1971) and *The Wolfpen Principle* (1974). Two of the most commercially successful filmmakers of the 1970s were David Cronenberg and Ivan Reitman. Cronenberg's horror films (*Crimes of the Future, The Parasite Murders, Scanners*) and Reitman's *Meatballs* (1979) provided work for the infrastructure of the fledgling industry while having very little to do with anything Canadian. But the financial champion of the first age of subsidy was Bob Clark, whose 1981 film *Porky's* (in which American lads come of age in a Southern brothel) holds the record for most profitable Canadian feature.

THE SECOND AGE OF SUBSIDY

The mixed results of the 1970s brought about a re-examination of federal film policy. Unhappiness with the abuses of the Capital Cost Allowance led to a series of amendments to the tax legislation enacted in 1976, 1978, 1982, 1983, and 1987. The objective of each of these reforms was either to increase Canadian content or tighten the means by which the tax credit could be claimed. Each initiative brought a jolt to the industry by both threatening its sources of capital and by disturbing the legal continuity necessary to attract investors. After 1987, the CCA became an insignificant incentive.

A similar unhappiness with the track record of the CFDC resulted in that agency's 1983 metamorphosis into Telefilm Canada. The change was aimed directly at the stalemate in film distribution. Most of Telefilm's budget went to a Broadcast Program Development Fund of $254 million over five years. The money was to provide one-third of the budgets of Canadian programs (not necessarily films) with guaranteed prime-time "windows." This move coincided with the licensing of pay-TV services which, it was hoped, would be primary users of the new funding.

As the CCA regulations tightened, and as Telefilm turned more toward mini-series and other television formats, provincial governments attempted to take up the slack in feature film production incentives. The first provincial agency was Quebec's La Société générale des indépendant culturelles, created in 1977. It was followed by the Alberta Motion Picture Development Corporation (1981), Manitoba Film (1984), the Ontario Film Development Corporation (1986), and Saskfilm (1989). Including grants by the government of Nova Scotia, these agencies in 1988–89 accounted for 27 percent of the $138.5 million in public funding expended on feature filmmaking (OFDC, 1990). During the 1980s, Quebec also experimented with its own 150 percent and 166 percent tax write-offs.

Because of provincial activity, total public support for feature filmmaking was, by the end of the 1980s, higher than it had ever been. But this was only a small part of the incentive for the development of the industry. Federal and provincial arts councils provided support for small-budget narrative films, experimental films, and documentaries. Provincial and municipal film offices donated free services to film crews. Public funding also increased for ancillary activities and institutions: film festivals, cinémathèques, film publications, and film studies programs in secondary and post-secondary schools. What Canada bought for all its film incentives was a ticket to the worldwide infrastructure that "Hollywood" had become. The lines between film and television production (not to mention cable, video, and merchandising) were blurred. Both capital and markets had become—as they were in the beginning of cinema—international. Japanese corporations were less interested in the Japanese film industry than they were in acquiring Hollywood studios. These studios, in turn, paid less attention to their own back lots than they did to the product (films, television series, made-for-television films) they commissioned from independent companies—of any size or in any nation. Large and small producers shot films anywhere that provided a financial advantage, including the cost efficiencies of a local service industry.

In English Canada, one of the most frequently cited icons of 1980s filmmaking was the imported garbage used to disguise Canadian cities as New York or Los Angeles. American-style television series such as *Night Heat* or the very American escapades of Reitman's *Police Academy* films were the most visible manifestations of a growing number of cross-border deals. Supporters argued that the people spreading garbage on the streets of Toronto and Vancouver were surrounded by ever larger numbers of Canadians in increasingly responsible positions. Canadian cameramen, editors, and sound technicians won the respect of their Hollywood counterparts. The American projects in Canada also sustained a full range of specialty services—from entertainment industry lawyers and financial services to laboratories, caterers, and equipment rental agencies.

In the spirit of 1980s' entrepreneurship, the discussion of Canadian cinema centred less on the films themselves than it did on the economics of the industry. The Toronto Festival of Festivals' Trade Forum and the Banff International Television Festival were among the most successful events to advertise themselves as the places where skills were acquired and deals hatched. Experts provided tips on the packaging of financial backing from the increasingly complex array of public and private sources. There were regular panels on the mysteries of international co-production, the selling of television rights, and the open-ended possibilities of home video.

Among the speakers at the decade's trade forums were the young owners of small film companies whose output of innovative work mushroomed during the 1980s. Atlantis Films spent the first half of the decade making its reputation with documentaries such as John Walker's *Chambers: Tracks and Gestures* (1982) and with adaptations of short stories. By the end of the decade, its multi-faceted operations included the production of a variety of film and television formats in Canada and Europe. At the same time, Rhombus Media won international recognition for its extraordinary films on the performing arts. Nelvana Films specialized in television series and animation. Playing With Time sold its *Degrassi* television series throughout the English-speaking world; *Degrassi*'s dubbed version is one of the rare cases of an anglophone production succeeding in Quebec.

The small companies were not alone in taking advantage of the internationalization of the film industry. The 1989 Canadian feature film output included eleven international co-productions (Thompson, 1990). Television movies such as Kevin Sullivan's *Anne of Green Gables*, Francis Mankiewicz's *Love and Hate*, and Eric Till's *Glory Enough for All* cracked international markets—an achievement made all the more satisfying by their Canadian subject matter. Canadian features—most notably Denys Arcand's *Decline of the American Empire* and *Jesus of Montreal* and Patricia Rozema's *I've Heard the Mermaids Singing*—have enjoyed substantial theatrical runs outside (and even inside) Canada.

From the perspective of film culture, the most significant beneficiaries of the over-all boom in the 1980s were a new generation of feature filmmakers who succeeded in making low-budget personal features. Phillip Borsos's *The Grey Fox* (1982) was the first such work of the decade. It earned him a ticket to Hollywood—and a ticket back to make the most costly Canadian film to date, *Bethune* (1990). Atom Egoyan stayed in the greater Toronto area to direct three seminal post-modern dramas: *Next of Kin* (1986), *Family Viewing* (1987), and *Speaking Parts* (1989). Sandy Wilson released her autobiographical *My American Cousin* in 1985, a film that did well enough to per-mit a sequel, *American Boyfriends* (1989).

Wilson's very British Columbian tales were emblematic of the rise of regional film-making during the decade. Alberta-based Anne Wheeler directed two important works, *Loyalties* (1985) and *Bye Bye Blues* (1989). In Nova Scotia, Bill MacGillivray made the features *Aerial View* (1979), *Stations* (1984), and *Life Classes* (1988). Winnipeg pro-duced a neo-surrealist school of animation highlighted by films such as Richard Conde's *The Big Snit* (1985) and Cordell Barker's *The Cat Came Back* (1988). A simi-lar sensibility produced startling short films by John Paizs and Arthur Kroeker as well as Guy Maddin's midnight cult film, *Tales from the Gimli Hospital* (1988).

In the 1980s, Quebec's cinema was characterized by the continued development of its *auteurs*. Arcand's work received the most recognition. But other *auteurs* also con-tinued to produce notable work, as exemplified by Francis Mankiewicz's *Les bons débarras* (1980), André Forcier's *Au clair de la lune* (1982), and Gilles Carle's *Maria Chapdelaine* (1983). The decade's new talents included Léa Pool, best known for *La femme de l'hotel* (1984) and Yves Simoneau, who turned from the psychological thriller *Pouvoir intime* (1983) to the poetic *Les fous de Bassan* (1986). Perhaps the most striking new talent of the decade was Jean-Claude Lauzon, whose *Un zoo, la nuit* (1987) added a new depth to the traditional *policier*. At the other end of the spectrum, producer Rock Demers released a series of extraordinary children's films.

If Canadian filmmaking in the 1980s owed its prosperity to the decade's cult of free enterprise, it is not surprising that Canada's two largest public filmmaking agencies, the CBC and the National Film Board, found themselves under attack. Even before the Conservative government introduced its own version of Reaganism/Thatcherism, both institutions were encouraged to farm out more of their work to private-sector film-makers. After the Conservative victory, the CBC was forced to do so amid continuing budget cuts. The Corporation's large overhead (to be increased in 1992 with the open-ing of the Toronto Broadcast Centre) left less and less room to manoeuvre. The situation came to a head in December 1990, when the Corporation was forced to choose between its ambitious drama program and its presence in local television mar-kets. By deciding to cut local television, it at least partially reaffirmed the 1980s' redefinition of itself as a "window" for the nationwide distribution of moving imagery.

The National Film Board faced a far more serious challenge. Private-sector film-makers had always seen the Board as unfair competition. With the rise of a large and diverse independent film industry, they argued that the civil service filmmakers were an inefficient anachronism. In 1982, the Federal Cultural Policy Review Committee (Applebaum-Hébert) bought the argument. For the first time, a federal task force pub-licly recommended that the NFB be divested of all production. The Committee suggested that a much-reduced Board remain only as a research and training centre. Predictably, the Board responded with considerable indignation. However, in 1984, it underwent a massive restructuring that cut a number of peripheral activities and aimed to reallocate resources in order to provide greater support for private-sector filmmakers. This did not protect it from cutbacks that further constrained its own production. As a result of the cutbacks, the Board's in-house filmmakers found themselves making fewer films. Some of the best left the Board entirely. In 1988, even the film commissioner, François Macerola, quit in mid-term to pursue more lucrative prospects in the private sector.

The filmmakers who remained at the National Film Board found themselves increasingly discouraged. In the early part of the decade, the women of Studio D made the Board's most popular film to date, Bonnie Sherr Klein's *Not a Love Story* (1981) as well as another Oscar winner, Terri Nash's *If You Love This Planet* (1982). Under the new policy, Studio D's directors were reassigned while the Studio itself became a conduit for funding to independent women filmmakers. In the same way, the Board chose to invest heavily in independent feature films. Its $5-million drama fund went only to outside producers. Far less support was forthcoming for the in-house Alternative Drama Programme that nevertheless released three popular theatrical features: Giles Walker's *90 Days* (1985), John Smith's *Sitting in Limbo* (1986), and Cynthia Scott's *Company of Strangers* (1990).

By the time it celebrated its fiftieth anniversary in 1989, the National Film Board appeared to have adapted all too well to the spirit of free enterprise. The best work it did was in its regional centres aiding independent filmmakers—a seemingly redundant function given the number of other granting agencies. At the same time, alternative *raisons d'être* proved elusive. Community activism had peaked with Challenge for Change, a program that ended in 1980. The tradition of Quebec nationalist documentary that began with the work of Pierre Perrault in the early 1960s came to a head with Denys Arcand's *Le confort et l'indifférence* in 1981. Environmental concerns, feminist issues, and animation were increasingly left to the independents. Even the Board's historical underpinnings were being questioned. In 1988, Joyce Nelson's book, *The Colonized Eye*, second guessed Grierson's entire agenda for Canadian filmmaking and Canadian culture.

There was an aesthetic crisis as well. The contemplative documentary as pioneered by the Board in the 1950s seemed to have run its course. The style's ultimate practitioner was Michael Rubbo, whose films from *Sad Song of Yellow Skin* (1970) to *Margaret Atwood: Once in August* (1985) were about whether the film itself could come to terms with its subject. Rubbo quit the Board in 1985.

The transformation of the National Film Board from the centre of Canadian documentary to a support mechanism for the genre did little to interfere with the high quality of Canadian documentary as a whole. Donald Brittain, the most urbane and literate of Canadian filmmakers, had, from the mid-1960s, used the Board as a resource. Packaging deals between the NFB and the CBC, he made superb films such as *Fields of Sacrifice* (1963), *Memorandum* (1966), *Dreamland* (1974), *Volcano* (1976), *The Champions* (1978), and *Canada's Sweetheart* (1988). By the time of his death in 1989, Brittain was the closest English Canada had come to producing a cinematic sage.

During the 1980s, other documentarians expanded on Brittain's model. They used all the resources of the polyglot funding system to produce a rich crop of work. One of the two best depictions of the early 1980s recession, Mary Jane Gomes and Emil Kolompar's *Downside Adjustments* (1983), was made by independent filmmakers working with arts council grants. The other, Allan King's *Who's in Charge?* (1983), was a commission from CBC. Working at the Film Board, Paul Cowan upset a good many people with his debunking of Billy Bishop in *The Kid Who Couldn't Miss* (1982). Working with the Board and the CBC, Sturla Gunnarsson and Robert Collison produced *Final Offer* (1986), a film that won a number of international awards for its depiction of labour relations. The full variety of public and private resources was used to produce Holly Dale and Janis Cole's *Hookers on Davie* (1984), Brigitte Berman's Oscar-winning *Artie Shaw: Time Is All You've Got* (1984), and Ron Mann's *Comic Book Confidential* (1989).

INTO THE NINETIES

The 1980s were to have ended with a grand celebration of Canadian cinema. Coinciding with the fiftieth anniversary of the National Film Board, the Academy of Canadian Cinema (best known for its glitzy Oscar clone, the Genie Awards) was to have staged a year-long tribute. In 1988, the entire event was cancelled. Its organizers cited cutbacks not only in their budget but in support for the industry as a whole. Tax incentives were gone. Telefilm had overextended itself and, shades of the old CFDC, had sunk its money into a number of questionable projects. The 85-cent dollar that followed free trade frightened off American producers. Their fear—abetted by predictions of an approaching recession—was rapidly transmitted throughout the new cinema infrastructure. No one felt like celebrating.

Perhaps the gloom was shortsighted. At the dawn of the 1990s, the production of feature films in both Canada and the increasingly independent Quebec has achieved a degree of stability that will survive upheavals in both public policy and the marketplace. One conservative estimate suggests that there are more than 40 000 Canadians involved in some aspect of film production (Toronto Women in Film, 1990). In 1989, they had worked on 93 feature films, nearly double the number produced a decade before (Thompson, 1990). The amount spent on certified Canadian productions topped $275 million in 1988, down from a peak of $370 million the year before but still substantially above the $100-million range in which the industry sat throughout the mid-1980s (OFDC, 1990).

More important than these figures is the fact that feature films have become only a part of total film production. Diversification—into television, co-production, specialty films, and film services—has guaranteed a continuity of Canadian cinema. The more that diversification is recognized, the more impressive the total figures become. Revenue earned by all filmmakers in 1988 was $622 million, more than four times what it had been a decade before. In Ontario alone, the direct economic output of the entire industry (including production, distribution, and exhibition of all film and video) in 1988–89 was estimated at more than $2.7 billion. The indirect economic output nearly doubled that figure (OFDC, 1990).

Looking beyond the current economic downturn, the prospects for the Canadian film industry will be most strongly affected by factors prevailing in the economy as a whole. Free trade may be expected to discourage public subsidy and regulation, put competitive pressure on wages, and integrate the Canadian industry more fully into the North American sphere. The opening of Eastern Europe, with its long-established national film industries, may well draw off co-production funding that would otherwise have gone to the Canadian industry. In the longer term, cultural protectionism in the post-1992 European Economic Community may inhibit Canadian distribution (however, at present, Canada has been specifically excluded from legislation limiting co-productions with non-EEC members).

Against these dismal prospects must be weighed the continued public-sector commitment to the industry. In 1988, Telefilm, despite its difficulties, was given a new Broadcast Fund, some $250 million over the next four years. Its Feature Film Fund was provided with $200 million to take the industry into the early 1990s. Also in 1988, Telefilm announced a Feature Film Distribution Fund and a Non-Theatrical Production Fund. Other agencies and levels of government seem equally committed to investments that have paid off in generating jobs and secondary economic spinoffs. Ontario, for example, created its own $15-million production fund in 1989. Quebec's Société generale des industries culturelles (SOGIC) provided $11 million for feature film production in 1990.

Changing technology may also play a significant role in the continued viability of the Canadian film industry. Digital techniques will continue to reduce the costs of professional standard production values. In the long term, digital technologies coupled with high-definition television will introduce theatrical quality into broadcasting. This will, in turn, lead to new alliances between the performing arts and the Canadian film and television industries—a marriage that may serve to sustain both. The National Arts Centre's "electronic touring" is a pioneering effort in this regard.

The groundwork for electronic distribution has already been laid with the rise of home video during the 1980s. In 1982, home video accounted for only 2 percent of film distribution income. By the end of the decade, more than a third of an average film's expected revenues came from video sales and rentals—a figure expected to rise to nearly one-half by the mid-1990s (OFDC, 1990). The majority of titles in video stores and on pay-per-view cable outlets will continue to be big-budget, largely American productions. But just as small publishers can survive with specialty audiences, independent filmmakers will find new outlets for their work. Consumers are already buying videotapes in art galleries, bookstores, and directly from the non-film institutions that commissioned them. With these and other new outlets come increased possibilities for capitalizing small- and medium-budget productions.

But what will be produced? If there was a reason not to celebrate Canadian Film Year, it had less to do with the ultimate health of the industry than with its sense of purpose. What, exactly, was this cultural industry supposed to do for the society that funded it? What proportion of its products would continue to be indistinguishable from the "international style" of their American counterparts? And, moreover, by what standards should we judge the Canadian product?

In 1988, Bruce Elder, the most prolific and outspoken experimental filmmaker in Canada, published a manifesto entitled "The Cinema We Need." In it, he condemns narrative film per se (and, to a lesser extent, documentary) as the manifestations of a broader acceptance of technological causality. For Elder, the structure of narrative cinema—from its corporate producers to the design of each film's shooting and editing—mirrors the values of a culture that habitually narrows its options to meet the dictates of predetermined ends. Certainty becomes the essential value.

Elder's way out is a recognition that Canada need not accept the teleological bias of Hollywood's use of technology. Citing Canadians such as Innis, McLuhan, and Grant as humanist alternatives to technological determinism, he argues that we deserve better:

> The makers of the cinema we need will be those who have the strength to abide with doubt and uncertainty and still open themselves up to unfolding situations, allow themselves even to be remade by experiences the destiny of which they cannot foresee. It is only through this process that truth will arrive . . . (Elder, 1988, pp. 260–71).

Elder writes from within the third tradition in Canadian cinema: experimental filmmaking. That practice can be traced back to John Grierson's grudging admission that the NFB could afford one animator. In 1941, Norman McLaren (and his much under-rated assistant, Evelyn Lambart), began the Film Board's production of unconventional animation and experiments with cinematic formats. Filmmakers such as Arthur Lipsett and Derek May enhanced the NFB's efforts. Some technologically based experiments continue in projects such as the Board's work with IMAX large-screen formats. But for the most part, the importance of experimental film at the NFB peaked with the Expo 67 films, of which Colin Low and Roman Kroitor's *Labyrinth* is the best remembered.

Centennial year also saw the return of Michael Snow and Joyce Wieland to Toronto from New York. Their work—most notably Snow's *Wavelength* (1967) and Wieland's *Reason over Passion* (1969)—announced the arrival of a new artistic sensibility in Canadian experimental film. Jack Chambers's *Circle* (1968-69) and his (and perhaps the genre's) masterpiece, *Hart of London* (1970), cemented the recognition Canada was beginning to obtain. Other artists such as Greg Curnoe and David Rimmer became part of an experimental movement that expanded in the 1970s to include Elder, Al Razutis, Kirk Tougas, Rich Hancox, Vincent Grenier, and Andrew Lugg. In the 1980s, a network of independent production and distribution co-operatives encouraged the participation of yet more new talent: Chris Gallagher, Phillip Hoffman, Patricia Gruben, Brenda Longfellow, Midi Ondera, Barbara Sternberg, and Blaine Allen (to mention a very few).

Canada's experimental filmmakers have won a degree of public funding which, while minuscule by industry standards, is generally superior to that enjoyed by their counterparts in other nations. In art museums, festivals, and cinémathèques around the world, their work has repaid that support several times over. Hence, from a strictly aesthetic perspective, Elder's "The Cinema We Need" and his 1989 book, *Image and Identity*, are not entirely fanciful in positing experimental filmmaking as a model for the industry as a whole. Not surprisingly, the call for a reallocation of resources away from narrative filmmaking was forcefully rebutted in a collection of articles appearing in *Cinema Canada* (the entire exchange has since been reproduced in *Documents in Canadian Film*—see references). Nor was it a particularly realistic proposal given the economic interests at stake. But what remains important in Elder's manifesto is its public declaration that Canadian cinema be planned as a proactive assertion of a national ethos rather than a reaction to the prevailing trends in industrial development.

English-Canadian cinema has not yet emerged as a forum or indeed an indicator of popular sentiment. For all its advances, the Canadian feature film industry as a whole continues to fill less than 3 percent of screen time at the nation's movie theatres (OFDC, 1990). Worse still, the discussion generated by these films is far down the list of factors determining the national agenda. One indication of this was the failure in 1990 of *Cinema Canada*, the most important English-language journal concerning itself with the nation's films. No one has come forward to replace it.

For most citizens of this country, there is still no Canadian *Gone With the Wind* or, more realistically, no cinematic equivalent of *The Stone Angel*, Glenn Gould, or the Group of Seven. And there may never be. With the current internationalization and fragmentation of the medium—not to mention the fragmentation of the country itself—it may be more difficult than ever for a single classic film to strike a chord in the entire nation's imagination. Nor will it be easy for our best filmmakers to avoid the temptations of the international style. Documentaries come and go, and experimental cinema continues to be marginalized. The best that can be said is that, as we approach the centenary of film in Canada, Canadian cinema has taken on all the attributes of a continuing presence. Canadians are used to its potential as well as its disappointments. If the unabashed classic or classics do emerge—or if the achievements of documentary and experimental filmmaking are recognized as part of a pantheon—fewer people will be surprised.

REFERENCES

Berton, P. (1975). *Hollywood's Canada: The Americanization of our national image*. Toronto: McClelland and Stewart.

Borneman, E. (1977). Documentary films: World War II. In *Canadian Film Reader* (Eds., Feldman, S,. & Nelson, J.). Toronto: Peter Martin Associates.

Elder, B. (1988). The cinema we need. In *Documents in Canadian Film* (Ed., Fetherling, D.) Peterborough, ON: Broadview Press..

Elder, B. (1989). *Image and identity: Reflections on Canadian film and culture*. Waterloo, ON: Wilfrid Laurier Press.

Fothergill, R. (1977). Coward, bully or clown: The dream-life of a younger brother. In *Canadian Film Reader* (Eds., Feldman, S., & Nelson, J.). Toronto: Peter Martin Associates.

Harcourt, P. (1977). The innocent eye: An aspect of the National Film Board of Canada. In *Canadian Film Reader* (Eds., Feldman, S., & Nelson, J.). Toronto: Peter Martin Associates.

Morris, P. (1978). *Embattled shadows: A history of Canadian cinema, 1895–1939*. Montreal: McGill-Queen's University Press.

Ontario Film Development Corporation. (1990, June 29). *Socio-economic impact assessment of the Ontario film and video industry, Phase I.*

Thompson, P. (Ed.). (1990). *Film Canada yearbook,1990.* Toronto: Cine-Communications.

Toronto Women in Film and Video. (1990, January 10). *A statistical profile of women in the Canadian film and television industry.*

BOOK PUBLISHING IN CANADA: THE FIGHT FOR SURVIVAL

Rowland Lorimer and Nancy Duxbury

Those great American publishing houses control the book trade of the continent—they are gradually rooting out the last remnant of bookmaking and book-publishing in Canada. . . . Canadian book publishing has become almost a lost industry among us, and with it Canadian authorship fails likewise, for authorship without publishers is like the voice of one crying in the wilderness.

William Kirby, 1884[1]

A contrast often drawn between Canada and the United States is that Canada evolved gradually through negotiations with Great Britain while the United States was born of revolution. This contrast is frequently used to obscure the reasons for a vast difference in style between the two countries, especially in the area of entrepreneurship. But this tired contrast takes on new life in the case of book publishing.

EMPIRE EXPANSION AND INFORMATION FLOWS

In the traditional view, the European discovery of the Americas occurred accidentally as Columbus attempted to reach the Orient by travelling west. In fact, we know that inhabitants of Northern Europe had ventured along the North American coast long before Columbus and, no doubt, these travellers had traded with the indigenous peoples.

Columbus's trip was different in that it fed into aggressive empire building made possible by improved transportation technology (sailing ships and navigation). Not only Spain, but also Spain's rivals, were not long in learning the results of Columbus's voyages. The exploitation of such natural riches as gold, fish, fur, and timber was just the beginning. The European empires also began an investment of human and financial resources to create the new-found lands' hinterlands to feed their metropoli. Missionaries worked with commercial traders from the beginning, believing that the spread of Christianity and European culture was both good and necessary. However, with the coming of settlers to organize colonial resource extraction and production for European markets, a much-expanded effort at creating a hinterland economy was begun.

The flow of ideas that resulted from this expansion of empire was consistent with overall centre-hinterland dynamics. At the beginning, the missionaries and settlers unpacked the few volumes of ideological baggage they could afford to bring with them. Later, other individuals and institutions brought books to the colonies and lent or sold them to those who had the desire and ability to read. Whether they were for children or adults, these books played the very important role of keeping the ideals and imaginations of the colonists rooted to empire central. As Parker (1985) puts it:

> From the outset the book trade was organized to import books and periodicals, just as other mercantile activities brought in manufactured goods: this was a corollary of being a colony, which existed to absorb excess populations and to serve as a market for home products, as well as to ship out raw materials (p. 13).

Flows of information in the opposite direction, from colony to empire, were of a particular type. They began with the journals of the explorers, many of which were published and helped define for Europeans the nature of these unknown lands and the riches they offered. These works were followed by other non-fiction and then by works of fiction by members of the European elite who had passed some time in the colonies. The leading theme, stated in myriad forms, was the contribution these outposts of empire offered to the organizing centres in Europe.

How Britain regarded the place, the rights, the people, the ideas generated, and business development in the colonies was reflected in a series of restrictive licensing laws and paper taxes that eventually were superseded by the Imperial Copyright Act of 1842. This act "gave protection throughout the Empire to works first published in London or Edinburgh, and made provision for prohibiting [importation of] unauthorized foreign reprints of British copyright works in British territory" (Parker, p. 106). A book produced in the colonies had no copyright protection in the Empire and none in the United States but only "the protection of location." This failure to extend to her colonies rights enjoyed by citizens of England and Scotland had played a large part in encouraging the thirteen British colonies south of the forty-ninth parallel to band together and declare themselves a separate nation.

Both before and after U.S. independence had been achieved, British copyright was a contentious issue. As far back as 1790, and continuing through to the 1800s, American printers acquired new popular British writing and printed cheap editions in the United States. Unencumbered by the need to pay royalties to authors, they then distributed such works as widely as possible at great profit. The piracy of British writing was essential to the founding of the American book publishing industry. The handsome profits made by these printers allowed them to evolve into publishers and begin to consider publishing American authors.

Beyond the political tensions between nations that this international piracy produced, such policies had their drawbacks, particularly for American writers. Because British authors received no royalties from the pirated editions, the publication of American authors, who would have to be paid royalties under American law, was a more expensive proposition. Moreover, while many British authors were well known internationally and therefore easy to market, most American authors were unknown and had yet to prove themselves.

But if such policies had drawbacks as well as positive consequences on the development of a writing and full-fledged publishing community in the United States, in Canada authors and publishers were working under at least double jeopardy. First, Canadians were forced by the Imperial Copyright Act to import British books, thereby incurring both high costs and untimely delays. They were in violation of copyright if they imported cheap American editions. Second, for a Canadian writer wishing to be published, choosing a Canadian publisher could expose his or her works to piracy in both the United States and Great Britain (Richardson, in Parker, p. 81).

However, such laws did not last forever. A prolonged storm of protest eventually brought an amendment to the Imperial Act, known as the Foreign Reprints Act of 1847. It "permitted the importation and sale of pirated British copyright works" (Parker, p. 107) within the British Empire on payment of a 12 1/2 percent customs duty to compensate the British authors (Gundy, 1965, pp. 13–14). This gave Canadians what they wanted—cheap editions of British authors. But in the long run, the effect of the act was "an actual surrender of the Canadian market to the American publisher at an agreed price" (Collins, in Gundy, 1965, p. 36). The reason for this was that it laid the groundwork for importation rather than creating a basis for publishing within the country. The Americans, on the other hand, went on pirating British works and not paying duty.

Early Printing, Bookselling, and Educational Publishing in Canada

Such inauspicious beginnings help to explain the slow development of a Canadian writing and publishing community. However, while explaining the constraints within which Canadian writing and publishing operated, they do not address the printing, writing, publishing, and bookselling activity that did take place.

There are two distinct streams to the development of publishing in Canada. The first involved the printing industry; the second, bookselling. In the background lurks the need for education materials to which both streams responded.

The printing press was brought to Canada in 1751 first by the British and later in 1764 by the French as "an adjunct to the military and civil authorities, to uphold law, order, and good government through the dissemination of official newspapers and proclamations" (Parker, pp. 24–25). In colonial days, government patronage was the key to survival for the printer as printing services were contracted out. Involved as they were with the distribution of information that profoundly affected the political and social life of the colony, there was considerable temptation for printers to comment upon it. It was not long before printers felt the conflict between the desire for freedom of expression and the desire to maintain government contracts. In due course, as a result of individual legal judgements in Canada and other judgements made in Britain and the United States, the right to both undertake government printing and engage in free expression was won.

Somewhat later, in the early nineteenth century, bookstores operating in the English tradition of both selling and publishing books became firmly established in Canada. The booksellers were mainly interested in importing volumes to sell to a public eager to keep in touch with the motherland and the flow of ideas. Only on rare occasions and with considerable prodding did booksellers enter into publishing ventures themselves. Their ability to break even on such ventures was rarer still, even after they were able to claim copyright. The Canadian market was plainly not well enough organized nor big enough to provide satisfactory returns on their investment.

Books were usually published by subscription to ensure the printing costs were covered. This meant the author or bookseller or publisher would have to secure enough advance orders for a book before it would be published. If interest was insufficient, the book would not be published. The subscription process sometimes involved co-publishing as well, and a "group of booksellers collected advances on a work for which they each agreed to take a certain number of copies and whose names would then appear on the title-page" (Parker, pp. 13–14).

As a result, Canadian book publishing became an exception. It was not the preferred medium to address to issues of the day—that position belonged to newspapers. Nor was it the vehicle for short stories or for new writers—that belonged to periodicals. Nor was it the preferred commodity of the retail booksellers. Better known, more marketable titles and authors could be imported from American and British publishers to be sold in Canada. Even the precursor to the modern, home-grown blockbuster failed to earn its publisher, Joseph Howe, a profit. *The Clockmaker*, by Thomas Chandler Haliburton, was published by Howe in 1836. Howe later told Haliburton: "It brought you reputation—plates—books—the means of earning thousands, a handsome sum in subsequent arrangements with Bentley [in London], and it brought me about £35" (Joseph Howe Papers, in Parker, p. 62).

The third piece of the Canadian book publishing history puzzle is to be found in educational publishing. Early nineteenth-century schools were established along denominational lines, and at the time, most textbooks were imported, either from the United States, or from Britain. Disputes over funding and the use of American textbooks for British subjects arose almost simultaneously. Following the immigration of a great number of loyalists into Ontario, many of whom brought with them American schoolbooks, concerns over the dominance of the American products intensified.

In the early 1840s, strong dissatisfaction was expressed in Upper Canada with the strident republican and anti-British tone of American textbooks. A solution was eventually engineered whereby the Commissioners of National Education in Ireland gave their copyrights to colonial printers and booksellers. These commissioners were English appointees, and they had ensured that the schoolbooks were designed specifically to promote loyalty to the Empire and to combat Irish nationalism by excluding any material on Irish culture. In addition, these texts were inexpensive, non-denominational, and designed for the various school grades (Parker, pp. 117–18).

These Irish texts remained in use, with one revision, from 1846 to 1883. When they were finally retired from use due to old age, American texts "enjoyed something of a revival, although they were given a tinge of the maple leaf to make them viable" (Eustace, 1972, p. 42). Toward the end of the nineteenth century, however, the government of Upper Canada moved to limit the number of authorized textbooks in use. As publishers fought to get a piece of the relatively small Upper Canadian market, they met with competition from large catalogue-based, mail-order companies with presses (such as Eaton's). Thus, textbook *publishing* was minimal and could best be described as textbook *manufacturing* as publishers competed with large printers for business. This competition "inhibited the development both of educational departments in publishing houses capable of generating new Canadian books, and of manufacturing facilities geared specifically to the needs of book production" (Eustace, p. 44).

Until the 1930s, schools in the other provinces relied on either the Ontario texts or imports from Britain or the United States. In 1937, revision of curricula in Ontario led to a revision of schoolbook policy as well. None of the texts that were now needed were available in Canada since Canadian publishers had been discouraged from creative educational publishing for so long. A surge of American text imports began, many through agency-representation arrangements with Canadian publishers. American textbooks established themselves and paved the way for the branch-plant manufacture of textbooks. Once established, branch-plant publishing dominated the Canadian school learning-materials market until the present day.

An Overview and Some Exceptions

This rather bleak picture of the development of indigenous publishing was not entirely universal. However, exceptions to the general picture were few. One of the few involved the activities of the Belford brothers. During the 1870s, the Belfords issued cheap reprints of popular American authors, paid no royalties, and sold them by mail to American readers, just as the Americans had been doing in Canada for years. The Belfords' activities, referred to as the "Canadian invasion," greatly upset the Americans. Their activities also helped to encourage a "regularization" of trade between Canada and the United States. Canadian houses became "authorized exclusive agents" for British and American publishers and concentrated their activity on importing, with a resulting decline in original Canadian publishing (Gundy, 1972, p. 5).

Another of the few exceptions to the general pattern involved the Methodist Church publishing house, under the direction of Reverend William Briggs. It became a good outlet for Canadian writers but, as agency publishing brought greater rewards at lesser risk, the amount of indigenous publishing dwindled. As H. Pearson Gundy has described the situation, "The House had taken on a large number of important foreign agencies which provided each year roaring sales of best-sellers from New York and London. . . . If agency titles could be had with little or no risk, why waste time and money on Canadian ventures" (Gundy, 1972, p. 19).

The sales levels and the attitudes of opinion makers encouraged imports. In 1865, J.M. Trout, a contributor to the Toronto Board of Trade reports on the Booksellers and Stationers' Section, wrote with approval: "British publishers have found out at length that the Canadian trade is worth cultivating, and they have been willing to make such terms with our buyers as enable them to offer books at, and in some cases below, English established prices" (Trout, in Parker, p. 138).

By the early twentieth century, all Canadian trade-book publishing houses were exclusive agents for other British and American publishers, whose lists of books they contracted to stock and sell. The majority of these exclusive agents were branch plants of foreign publishers (Gundy, 1972, pp. 22–23). Under this market regime, when a Canadian branch office of a British publisher did not exist, Canadian rights for British works were often awarded to American branch plants or to exclusive agents as part of a North American rights package. Canadian firms were relegated to importing books and applying a markup while their American cousins imported rights and printed and published generally cheaper editions in the United States, often exporting them to Canada.

TOWARD THE MODERN ERA

Between the turn of the century and the late sixties, there have been good times and bad for the Canadian book publishing industry. For example, during the First World War, in the heightened spirit of patriotism, Christmas sales of Canadian war books broke previous records, and publishers and booksellers "found it hard to keep up with the demand" (Gundy, 1972, p. 25). (American and British war books were also in demand.) In the 1920s, nationalistic fervour continued and Lorne Pierce of the Ryerson Press led a Canadian literary revival. (This featured a Canadian anthology, an author series, schoolbooks, and reading tours.) It seemed that "at last Canadian publishers were prepared to make a great sacrifice to see that Canadian writers had a chance" (Pierce, in Gundy, 1972, p. 27).

However, the Depression changed all that. Retrenchment in staff, salaries, and manuscripts was typical. Firms focused more clearly on lowest-risk ventures in order to hedge their chances for survival. Original Canadian publishing slumped, and publishers relied more and more upon promoting sales of the most popular British and American books.

In a delightful paper on The Macmillan Company, making good use of the Macmillan archives now housed at McMaster University, David Young cites the letters of Hugh Eayrs to provide some insight into the position of publishers during the 1930s.

In comparison to his contemporaries, Eayrs was a committed Canadian publisher. Upon assuming the presidency of Macmillan in 1921, Eayrs set aside a fund for "the publication of good books by Canadians, whether they are likely to be successful ventures or not" (Young, 1990, p. 5). By 1938, Eayrs was well aware of the difficulty in maintaining that commitment when almost none of his Canadian books were breaking even. He wrote to George Brett, president of The Macmillan Company in New York:

> You have enough people in this country . . . to put into New York or London. You have about six or seven million. . . . That is why the average novel sells, with luck two hundred and fifty copies in Canada. . . . How on earth, then, is it possible for Canadian publishers to contemplate setting up the average book? (Young, 1990, p. 5).

In his letters to authors, he was no less blunt. Of one he asked for guarantees about the sales prospects of his book. To another he wrote: "Although the material is excellent of its kind . . . I do not think we can find a constituency for it, at all events a large enough one, in these difficult and depressed days to make the financial venture practicable" (Young, 1990, p. 5). In seeking the co-operation of his New York and London colleagues within Macmillan, a pattern was set up—manufacture the books in those centres and import them into Canada—that hardly differed from the exclusive agency distribution of books published elsewhere by other companies.

In the mid-thirties, the company experienced a significant upturn in sales. This upturn was partly as a result of the takeoff of the American advertising industry, which catapulted the sales of blockbusters to new heights. The increased sales allowed for 24 Canadian titles in the spring list of 1934 and 12 in the fall list as compared with an average of 12 over previous lists. Sales continued to increase in that year and throughout the rest of the thirties. Ironically, these increased sales had little to do with the publication of Canadian material. Eayrs's letters tell the story:

> . . . good as last year's sales were, this year up to August the 15th has outstripped them by nearly thirty per cent, and we are still going strong. Thanks to *Gone with the Wind*, the new Huxley, the new Priestley, and so on . . .

> . . . we have done many books in the Canadian General Literature field and have been astonishingly unsuccessful with most of them . . . . We are, therefore, shortening up very drastically on the number of purely domestic items in the general literature field (Young, 1990, pp. 10, 11).

Whether we like to accept the constraints Eayrs set for himself, no one else was able to make the economics of publishing Canadian authors for Canadian audiences work either. In limited areas, that is, in educational and legal publishing, there was a certain level of Canadian activity.

EDUCATIONAL PUBLISHING AND THE MODERN ERA

The years following the Second World War intensified the rout of Canadian publishers that had emerged in 1937. As soldiers returned, the baby boom began, and the educational market expanded dramatically. Canadian publishers found themselves out of touch with the centres of educational innovation and thought in the United States and therefore were unable to meet the emerging demands of the market (Lorimer, 1984). Major increases in sales outside Ontario of American-produced schoolbooks, in combination with the Ontario requirement for Canadian manufacture, led many U.S. publishers to abandon their (Canadian-owned) exclusive agents and join their compatriots in setting up branch plants in Ontario. Within a few years, American-owned branch plants had captured approximately 50 percent of the schoolbook market and in so doing captured much of the profitable publishing in Canada.

The implication of this shift from Canadian agents to branch plants meant that the economic base in the form of cross-subsidization of Canadian-authored trade books by sales of educational books was cut back severely. Again repeating the pattern identified by Eayrs in the late thirties, while markets were expanding, sales of Canadian-authored books were constricting, essentially because they were not being published.

In the late sixties, this situation began to change rather dramatically. As the baby boom—a large population that had been catered to by an expanding and increasingly wealthy, industrializing society—reached the age of political and cultural awareness, it found in the book publishing industry a dearth of ideas, sentiments, attitudes, and opinions on Canadian public issues.

Their solution was not only to take control of the presses but also to demand of governments that they provide the necessary infrastructure for fostering Canadian writing and publishing. They achieved partial success. First the federal government and then every provincial government but one put into place policies supportive of writing and/or book publishing. The publishers called for measures to allow them to compete as businesses with foreign producers. Whether by price subsidies, by guaranteed loans, through copyright law, or by direct support of writers, the publishers asked for mechanisms to counteract the advantages of foreign producers and foreign-owned branch plants with their large markets, access to capital, free access to the Canadian market, and copyright protection.

The policies put in place have been only partially successful. They have, arguably, maintained a respectable flow of Canadian-authored books—in one or two years encouraging a level of production that may even have seemed excessive. However, they have not succeeded in producing an industry with anything near normal wages to its workers nor profit levels allowing for stability, expansion, and growth even in established firms.

Recent events such as the signing of the Free Trade Agreement and changes in federal policy with respect to the publishing industry have the potential to produce major changes in the book publishing scene in Canada. We will end this paper with a review of those changes.

THE BAIE COMEAU AGREEMENT AND THE FREE TRADE DEAL

The policies that have been put in place by various governments in Canada are of two basic types: industrial and cultural. Until 1992, their level of funding was approximately $13 million annually. Industrial policies are meant to build the industry, to produce a profitable, competitive book publishing industry able to bring forward Canadian authors and titles to domestic and international markets. Cultural policies extend the principle of support for artistic and cultural work for which the regimen of the market is inappropriate. The rationale for such policies is to support writing that makes an original contribution to the concerns of Canadians. The models used to justify support speak of "merit goods" and market failure. Such terms represent a way of admitting the failure of economic models to deal with the obvious value of artistic and cultural production while not admitting absolute failure of these models to account for cultural activities.

Cultural policies have remained steady in their orientation, at times falling far short in resources to do an adequate job, but then later catching up. Publishers may receive grants either for individual projects or based on the number of books they have published in the previous year. The type of book is taken into account—for instance, poetry, novels, children's books—and the average deficit the industry incurs in publishing each type. In addition, professional excellence is judged. The proceedings are conducted by a jury of peers. From time to time, the granting process has been accused of excessive subjectivity in allocating grants to individual publishers, but on the whole it has performed a useful function.

Industrial policies have held a far less steady course. At first directed at encouraging the development of a heterogeneous industry in size, location, and orientation, they have resulted in at least two very different policies. First was a program of sales bonuses that rewarded the prosperous. The size of the grant a publisher received was based on the dollar volume of sales. This program was changed quickly when its effects became obvious. It allowed the big to get bigger and encouraged publishers to pursue a high dollar volume of sales and ignore all else. A second, more recent policy encourages innovation and involvement in educational publishing. The administering Department of Communications has become directly involved in the publishing process by setting up a grant review committee to search for innovative plans, especially ones that are oriented primarily to taking the applicant into the educational market, a market that has been traditionally more profitable than the trade market, i.e., selling books through bookstores.

On January 28, 1992, industrial support policy began to change. The Minister of Communications announced a new $140 million, five-year plan increasing overall support to the industry by 260%. As of this writing, while funding is in place, the overall focus of the program is yet to be determined, with the exception of some concrete proposals on foreign ownership discussed below.

The exact terms of the new grant program will be negotiated between government and industry in the context of the primacy of the Mulroney government's central goal to enhance economic activity. To a lesser extent the impact of both industrial and cultural policies will be taken into account. The impact has been as follows. In spite of industrial policies capturing the lion's share of the resources, a stable and profitable industry or industry sector has not emerged. The entire Canadian-owned sector depends on a combination of federal and provincial grants. On the cultural side, a Canadian, fiction and non-fiction writing community has emerged that is recognized nationally and internationally.

Further, the new program will play into a growing schizm in the industry that is sometimes visible and other times papered over. The few larger players focused on growth and profit are looking for more for themselves. They will use these funds to a) acquire the backlists of their smaller colleagues, b) attempt to increase international sales, and c) gain oligopolistic control of the Canadian trade market and industrial support programs. The many smaller players waver between a) selling out for a decent price, and b) continuing to fight on for a culturally-oriented heterogeneous industry in terms of firm size, location, and genre orientation. The most likely scenario seems to be the creation of sufficiently large profits for all firms to allow all to stay in business if they wish, while giving the large firms sufficient profits to buy out the small. The government will then step back and let the industry shake itself out over five years.

That shake-out will also be influenced by an ownership policy that has been called the Baie Comeau policy and the announced changes that are part of the new package. The Baie Comeau policy was introduced by the Mulroney Conservatives in 1985 to increase, through company purchases by Canadians, the market share of Canadian-owned companies. The policy requires that any foreigner who acquires a book publishing company divest him/her/itself of that company within two years. Although such a policy is potentially an extremely powerful mechanism to patriate the industry, it turns out that few Canadians are ready purchasers and few foreign conglomerates, when they buy up smaller multinational companies, are willing to put their newly acquired Canadian branch plants up for sale.

The proposed policy weakens the formal requirement of the Investment Canada Act that foreign investment in the book publishing and distribution sector be compatible with national cultural policies and be of net benefit to Canada and the Canadian-controlled sector. New businesses in publishing will be limited to, at minimum, joint ventures controlled by Canadians. Existing Canadian-controlled businesses will not be permitted to be sold to non-Canadians except under defined, extraordinary circumstances. However, the purchase of businesses located in Canada will be now permitted, subject to a net benefit test designed to enhance the Canadian-owned sector.

These policies exist beside long-standing copyright law and recent changes to copyright that increase the ability of writers to claim recompense for their intellectual property. At a formal level, copyright law exists to encourage writers to create works of benefit to society. At another level, copyright law allows publishers to protect their investment in a single manuscript, encouraging them to distribute it as widely as possible with the assurance that it will not have to compete with other editions. At yet another level, according to Altbach (1987), copyright law provides the means for dominant producers to hinder the development of publishing industries in countries to which they export. Current changes in copyright law, such as requiring royalty payments to be paid to an author for photocopying his or her work, while ostensibly empowering writers, undoubtedly increase the power of publishers from dominant countries to become global publishers and to share in a more thorough collection of royalties and other payments for use. In the main and in the longer term, this favours neither Canadian writers nor Canadian publishers who are not major global players.

A third element of the current book publishing scene in Canada involves the Free Trade Agreement that Canada has signed with the United States. The principle behind the agreement is to provide businesses and professionals with equal access to each other's markets. Certain limited exceptions are built into the agreement, including some concerned with cultural industries. For example, the Baie Comeau principle is preserved. In addition, Section 19 of the Income Tax Act is preserved; section 19 is derived from Bill C-58, and disallows as a business expense for Canadian businesses advertising in foreign-owned media products destined for Canada.

Exceptions not in keeping with the basic principles of an overall agreement often come under scrutiny, and moves to "rationalize" them are sometimes initiated before the ink dries on the papers of the agreement. This is exactly what is happening to the cultural industries exemptions in the Free Trade Agreement. Michigan Congressman John Dingell has already inserted into Congressional records a ten-page denunciation of Baie Comeau. Actually, this is the first of a series of responses derived from a White House document called "Statement of Administrative Action." It notes: "The administration would be mindful of the importance of discouraging if possible the exercise and reliance on 2005.1(the Baie Comeau commitment) by the Government of Canada" (Crooks, 1989, p. 28). The proposed changes in the policy are a move in the direction favoured by the Americans.

However, there is another level of influence that results from the North American Free Trade Agreement. The fundamental principles of the agreement are to encourage free trade. However, significantly, they apply only to certain countries, presently Canada and the United States. In parallel with this agreement, the Europeans are forming a trading area within which goods and services can pass freely—but only among countries in the European community. Similar moves are being made in Asia.

The formation of these limited free trade areas may lead to the development of policies aimed at insulating certain activities from the full discipline of the marketplace. Indeed, such a policy has been formulated in what is termed the European Directive on Broadcasting. Its actual title is "Television without Frontiers." According to this directive, television programs made in Europe will flow freely among European nations provided they meet minimal conditions on amount of advertising time, tobacco advertisements, and activities of sponsors (*Cable and Satellite Europe*, 1989). Other programs, notably those made by Americans, will be impeded. As Jack Valenti, head of the Motion Picture Association of America, has noted:

> The principal issue that is absorbing me right now is the European Community's broadcast directive which aims to impose a majority quota on all non-EC material that comes into the European Community television marketplace—which, of course, means an impediment and a barrier to a free marketplace insofar as American programs are concerned. The President of the United States, the Secretary of State, the Secretary of Commerce and the United States Trade Representative have all been supportive. They have made it clear to the chancellories of Europe that the imposition of this quota is an intolerable thing to the United States (*Canadian Communication Reports*, pp. 2, 3).

The objections that are being mounted by the Americans underscore a paradox that is not immediately apparent in movements toward the establishment of limited free-trade areas. Global corporations such as Rupert Murdoch's News Corporation, the Thomson Corporation, Time/Warner, Hachette, Bertelsmann, and Gulf + Western may be fighting *for* limited free trade to maintain access to the Canadian market but they may be fighting *against* the formation of free-trade blocs to protect their global operations. Currently, in the movie industry, a major lobby is being mounted to maintain the worldwide dominance American producers now have over theatre screens.

Yet another factor of considerable influence is the identities of the major players. The most powerful are mega corporations such as the ones mentioned above. At the same time, they are individually powerful and can and do threaten and cajole governments; some, such as Murdoch and Maxwell, are set on high growth curves and are as vulnerable as Third World countries are to changes in interest rates, changes in costs, and market downturns. Maxwell lost and regained his empire once and Murdoch has been overextended in his debts from time to time (*Financial Post*, 1990). Whether the present mega corporations and their business practices will survive over the long term is difficult to predict. The death of Robert Maxwell has been especially revealing.

At another level, and often involving subsidiaries of these mega corporations, are the individual multinational corporations and their branch plants. After seeing that domestic publishers have been able to develop Canadian authors and Canadian writing, the branch plants are creaming off the best of the Canadian authors and attempting to market them both in Canada and in international markets. To win these authors away from their former publishers they must simply outbid them, something not too difficult in an undercapitalized industry. But undercapitalized or not, the Canadian-owned sector has two things working for it. First is an ability to maximize sales in the domestic market. Second is an ability, on the whole, to estimate sales accurately. Outbidding has thus led into overbidding. Overbidding leads to the printing of too many copies. Such overproduction leads to higher remainder sales and a lessened ability to predict title sales. These factors have been jeopardizing both the Canadian-owned and foreign-owned sectors. The branch plants win when they can bring authors to a waiting international market. The branch plants may also win over the medium term by forcing some Canadian firms into bankruptcy, thereby lessening the bidders in the game. But having achieved that, who is left to develop new authors?

Other policy shifts in Canada are also playing a role. What makes it difficult to assess their influence is that they are apparently contradictory in effect if not intention. Therefore, their long-term status is in doubt. First, the federal government is withdrawing postal subsidies and replacing them with direct subsidies for a net saving of $110 million or 50 percent. (Part of the saving is achieved through a cessation of subsidies to foreign distribution.) For a government trying to eliminate subsidies, this is interesting and suggests that if the same government remains in power for very long, these new subsidies will not be long in disappearing. While affecting book publishers, especially small publishers and those outside major cities, the greatest significance of these changes is on the periodical publishing industry. Without postal subsidies or an adequate replacement, greater than half the industry is vulnerable to being simply wiped out.

In contradiction to the potentially negative consequences of the withdrawal of postal subsidies, a policy to prevent libraries and bookstores from buying from U.S. wholesalers is being mooted as a way of strengthening the book publishing industry. While this would serve the interest of those publishers who were agents for foreign imports, it does nothing for Canadian writing and publishing. Moreover, a "buy Canadian" policy will increase costs and cause inordinate delays in delivery outside of Toronto and Montreal.

The final factor that plays into the future of the publishing industry is the state of the writing community in Canada. There is no doubt that as a result of the energies of writers, publishers, book sellers, librarians, and the attitudes of the reading public, Canadian writing has come of age over the past two decades and has been recognized internationally. In recent years Canadians have been nominated for and have won a number of international prizes. Recently *Solomon Gursky Was Here*, a book by Mordecai Richler not short-listed for the Governor General's Award, was short-listed for the internationally more prestigious Booker Prize. Margaret Atwood and Robertson Davies have also been up for the Booker. In 1979 Antonine Maillet won the equally prestigious Prix Goncourt for *Pélagie-La-Charrette* and both Alice Munro and Mavis Gallant have won praise for their short stories.

Each of the above factors could have considerable consequence. It is tempting to concentrate on one and predict the future on the basis of how it might be expected to play itself out. The problem is that major changes can occur quite suddenly. It would appear that Canadian writing and the Canadian writing community are not going to disappear overnight. Somehow they will be served. And, no doubt, they will be served by new publishers, by established Canadian-owned publishers, and by foreign-owned branch plants. As Lorimer (1990) has argued elsewhere, the sooner the notion is forgotten—that industrial support policies can lead to the establishment of a profitable and stable Canadian-owned industry able and willing to publish culturally important books—the better. Private enterprise is not in business to perform a public, cultural service. The more serious any company gets about the bottom line, the less cultural can be its commitments unless, of course, there is regulation. Government support for cultural publishing is here to stay no matter what the make-up of the industry. Without government support, cultural publishing in Canada is finished, as are theatre companies, ballet companies, opera houses, symphony orchestras, and a host of other facilitating mechanisms for making public the creativity and culture of Canadians.

NOTES

1. This extract is taken from Gundy, H.P. (1965). *Book publishing and publishers in Canada before 1900*, p. 22.

REFERENCES

Altbach, P. (1987). Knowledge enigma: The context of copyright in the third world. In *The Knowledge Context*. Albany, NY: SUNY Press.

Cable and Satellite Europe. (1989, November, pp. 17–25).

Canadian Communications Reports. (1989, December 31). 16 (24).

Crooks, H. (1989, March). Vacuuming the crumbs: the politics of film production. *Canadian Forum*.

Eustace, C.J. (1972). Developments in Canadian book production and design. Royal Commission on Book Publishing: *Background Papers*. Toronto: Queen's Printer and Publisher.

Financial Post. (1990, October 16). p. B1.

Gundy, H.P. (1965). *Book publishing and publishers in Canada before 1900*. Toronto: The Bibliographical Society of Canada.

Gundy, H.P. (1972). The development of trade book publishing in Canada. Royal Commission on Book Publishing: *Background Papers*. Toronto: Queen's Printer and Publisher.

Lorimer, R. (1984). *The nation in the school*s. Toronto: OISE.

Lorimer, R. (1990, May). *Discourse and reality: The Canadian debate on ownership in communications*. Paper given in Dublin at the annual meeting of the International Communications Association.

Parker, G.L. (1985). *The beginnings of the book trade in Canada*. Toronto: University of Toronto Press.

Young, D. (1990, June). *The Macmillan Company of Canada and the Canadian book publishing industry during the 1930s*. Paper given in Victoria at the annual meeting of the Canadian Communications Association.

THE RAVELLED SLEEVE:
ADVERTISING POLICY IN CANADA

Stephen Kline and William Leiss

Not too long ago, Dallas Smythe called advertising the "blind spot" in our understanding of communication because no one gave it serious attention (Smythe, 1977). Today, however, a quick survey of social controversies in the 1980s reveals that advertising has emerged as a high-profile arena of Canadian communications policy. Restrictions on the language on commercial signage and bans on advertising to children in Quebec were but two very prominent cases heard by the Supreme Court that have had wide-ranging repercussions for Canadians. Our courts, broadcast enterprises, and regulatory agencies have recently been preoccupied with advertising issues, including the regulation of tobacco and alcohol advertising, the sexual explicitness of condom marketing, comparative advertising, the packaging and claims made by food and drug manufacturers, the increasing commercialization of children's television, the potential offence given by advertising's gender and ethnic representations, the permissible uses for and funding of government advertising, the role of and limits on partisan advertising in elections, and the restraints appropriate for controversial corporate and advocacy advertising campaigns. It is clear that the roles advertising plays in Canadian society, and the questions concerning the best policy framework for its regulation, are now firmly placed in public view.

In spite of this, Canada has contributed very little of substance to the debate about advertising and culture. As a field of academic enquiry, advertising has tended to be situated in one of two camps: either it was researched as part of the pragmatics of marketing or blithely chastened by ideological critics as the mechanism of manipulating consumer demand or offending public taste. Unfortunately neither of these perspectives took advertising seriously as an important socio-cultural enterprise, nor studied in detail the part it plays within the system of communication. As a consequence, very little is understood about advertising as an arena of cultural and communication policy. Although major public debates have taken place about impartiality and journalism, about ownership and control of media organizations, about violence and sexism in television programming, and about Canadian content in programming and the arts, not much new has been added to the description of the cultural role of advertising since McLuhan diagnosed it as the folklore of modernity (McLuhan, 1951).

Recent cultural-historical theory, however, has refocused our attention on the emergence of the high-intensity marketplace as a significant cultural institution. The historical evidence indicates that advertising's role has changed since the first half of this century when advertising served primarily as a means of introducing new products, conveying information about their use, and generally promoting a system for marketing national branded goods. Advertising agencies are now established as the institutional bridge between our economy and our culture because they have developed and practised a type of communication strategy favoured by manufacturers, governments, political parties, and social advocates as a means of influencing public opinion. As we have noted in our study of modern advertising:

> The primary field of content in modern advertising is contemporary culture itself, and advertising is a contested discourse precisely for this reason. Advertising is more than a mechanism for communicating product information to individuals: it is a cultural system (Leiss et al., 1990, p. 352).

But advertising is not a cultural system in the same sense as organic myths and folklore that simply "reflect" the national culture are. Advertising is purposefully designed as persuasive communication. It is part of what Andrew Wernick called "promotional culture": as a cultural practice, advertising depends upon enormous corporate resources being diverted to the production of these condensed and oft-repeated vignettes about the ways of achieving satisfaction in contemporary life. This concentration of corporate and government resources was essential historically in building the commercial media system and in shaping the broader relationship between programming and audiences that this system cultivates (Wernick, 1988, pp. 180–210).

Of the many cultural practices through which we constitute and interpret ourselves as a nation, advertising has emerged as an influential channel because its messages are neither trivial nor meaningless. Indeed, advertising is becoming more controversial because it increasingly strives to engage our most private and psychologically significant experiences of daily life—our bonds with the world of goods and with each other through them.

Advertising as a cultural practice stands, therefore, at the apex of a unique institutional sub-system that continues to exert its influence on our society in a number of important ways: as the visible dimension of marketing strategy, advertising obviously does play an increasingly important role in the marketplace battles of market expansion and positioning within a global market; as the economic engine of broadcast enterprise, advertising has important consequences for the program decision making, quality, and performance of commercial media; and as an organizational, research, and communicative practice in its own right, advertising is becoming a model for social communication among public relations, political, and social advocacy practitioners. In defining policy for advertising as a form of social communication, it is important also to take account of advertising's historical impact and institutional locus:

1. It has helped to shape the economic framework of market society, enhancing the power of large-scale corporate entities that have the resources to undertake strategic communications.

2. It has created a highly concentrated and increasingly narrowly owned group of agencies (what Innis might have called an oligopoly of knowledge) that are experts in the practices, techniques, and methods of contemporary persuasive communications, including the audience research upon which they are based.

3. It has radically reordered the economics and audience bases of all communications media (including in our own competitive mixed broadcasting situation the CBC and educational networks), creating a cultural role for media (entertainment, pleasure) that favours large-scale concentrated private ownership of media.

4. In harnessing enormous creative resources, it has emerged as a cultural form in its own right, which has in turn helped to shape many of the contemporary practices of communication and socialization in our society, leaving its imprint on the content of programming (especially sports and movies); on program formats such as rock video or children's cartoons; and more broadly on communications strategy in general, such as the way governments plan their services and political parties conduct election campaigns.

Advertising is a contentious socio-cultural innovation not only because its imagery provides us with important cultural information, but also because it is becoming a vital means for co-ordinating the interests of business, government, and media. We suspect it is necessary to appreciate the complexity of this cultural sub-system if we are to broach the question of policies and regulation.

Because advertising is at the centre of an increasing number of contentious communication policy debates in Canada, the analysis of advertising can tell us something about ourselves as Canadians and the unique way we try to deal with those difficult unresolved tensions between a market economy and democratic culture. The Canadian case is particularly interesting not only because we live in the shadow cast by the American economy and media industries, but because our history has been one with a strong public sector and government involvement in cultural policy and communication. In this essay, we will examine three cases of advertising policy making in order to indicate the problems facing current Canadian approaches to regulating the role of advertising in our society.

THE CANADIAN FRAMEWORK FOR ADVERTISING POLICY

Canadian advertising has emerged as the focal point of the market's mediation between the spheres of production and consumption. There is, in fact, no single rationale for the regulation of advertising in Canada. Rather, a set of loosely connected policy debates has emerged, each with its own scope, institutional mandates, organizational actors, and regulatory traditions. Implicitly, there exist several co-extensive regulatory fields pertaining to advertising, including several important pieces of legislation and attendant government activities that regulate business and consumer practices (Combines, Food and Drug, and Consumer Protection); a host of judicial decisions; the CRTC and its hearings, monitoring, and guidelines; the CBC and other media organizations; and a number of industry self-regulatory guidelines and bodies (CAB, CAF, ACA) (Singer, 1986). In this regard, advertising has encountered three different sets of social policy rationales related to its mediation between business, media, and culture—those connected with business and its fair practice, those connected with the operation of a democratic media system, and those related to the social relations engendered by the consumer culture. Advertising professionals and their associations (especially in the United States) have often reacted to suggestions of a connection between "larger" social issues and their own creative activities with a mixture of contempt, wariness, and surprise. Many in the advertising sector itself resent the imposition of restraints on advertising communication, regarding what they say as simply a matter of the rights of commercial free speech—that is, the right of any organization to buy commercial time in the public media to advocate whatever they wish. When threatened with bans or new restrictions, advertisers in the United States like to compare their situation to that of censorship of the arts or news media (Leiss et al., 1990, p. 354). The implication of this interpretation of commercial speech is that it indemnifies advertisers against all restraints, in all media for all products.

Yet in Canada, this notion of the "rights" of commercial speech have generally been tempered by an appreciation of the importance of decorum and restraint within the business sector. Brian Philcox, director of the Canadian Advertising Foundation, acknowledged this in his public defence of the newly won constitutional protection of commercial free speech in Canada: "Commercial free speech does not come without constraints, however. Corporations must operate within the ethical standards of honesty and good taste our society demands. . . . Commercial free speech simply means the right to inform the consumer of what is for sale. It is also the right of the consumer to be informed. At no time does an advertiser have licence to misinform. Let's not forget that advertising, along with all other facets of marketing communication, is a deeply rooted part of our cultural heritage" (Philcox, 1989). Such comments are common from those in the advertising industry to justify the mechanism of industry self-regulation as the basis for a Canadian policy for advertising.

The case for self-restraint is often made on the grounds that one limitation on commercial speech widely accepted by the advertising industry concerns the deception or misleading of the consumer. Deception in advertising (as opposed to puffery or misinformation) is a very real temptation in product advertising as the recent exposé of Volvo's "monster truck" demonstration ad revealed. But not only does outright deception violate conceptions of fair business practice, it is bad for the whole advertising business. As Alan Rae of the Canadian Advertising Foundation (CAF) has stated, both government regulation and industry self-regulation are accepted "as ways of attaining one or two common goals—to protect the consumer and ethical business against false, misleading or even unfair advertising" (Look What the Winds, 1986).

CANADIAN DEBATES ABOUT THE ADVERTISING OF ALCOHOL PRODUCTS

Accepting these limitations is necessary to prevent one exploitive or unscrupulous advertiser from gaining a short-term advantage in the market by making unsubstantiated claims (and thus helping to maintain advertising as a legitimate and tax-deductible business activity). Complaints mechanisms are the accepted means for identifying and dealing with false and deceptive advertising; as Rae notes, "The fact that in recent years complaints received by CAF deal more with social issues indicates that the battle against deceptive advertising is increasingly successful" (Look What the Winds, 1986). This is certainly true, for recently the debates about advertising have gone well beyond the issue of deceptive product claims to the social use of the product itself. And industry self-regulation has been much less successful when it comes to the issue of social use.

Consumption impinges directly upon some very sensitive and important areas of contemporary life, and this has forced Canadians to also consider advertising's proper place in influencing social values and behaviour. To do so, advocacy groups have been re-examining the definition of false and misleading advertising practices. The definition of unfair or misleading, for example, turns out to be a much more controversial matter, given the fact that contemporary advertising communicates its ideas with imagery as well as language and rarely makes claims concerning the performance, utility, or pricing of a product. Even in the Volvo ad, it was the unseen reinforcement of the car and the editing in of a hand-rolled monster truck tire, that made the ad deceptive (the controversy had nothing to do with *stated* claims). Similarly, it has been repeatedly suggested by both the anti-cigarette and anti-alcohol lobbies that cigarette and alcohol advertising encourage young people to take up these habits because the advertising is "youth oriented" in its choice of models, stylistic devices, and references to the symbols of youth subcultures—or simply because these advertisements are placed in media venues that have high proportions of youths in their audiences.

The case of advertising for alcoholic beverage products is particularly instructive, not only because it is one of the longest-running battles of advertising regulation, but also because the attempts to regulate it have revealed natural divisions between the interests of different advertisers (beer versus spirit alcohol), particularly in these advertisers' relationships with the various media. In the wake of Prohibition in the 1920s, the Canadian government had restricted all advertising for alcoholic beverages. After December 1942, however, the spirit beverage producers were allowed, like many other advertisers during the Second World War, to engage in corporate and public service advertisements under the War Time Alcoholic Beverage Order. This order was rescinded in 1947, and thereafter broadcast and print ads were permitted, provided that they were acceptable to the provincial governments who generally defined very restrictive practices for alcoholic beverage advertising. (The spirit alcohol producers voluntarily accepted a ban on the advertising of their products in the broadcast media later on.)

Under pressure from manufacturers and broadcasters, in November 1963 the Canadian government opened up the question of alcohol advertising further by issuing a set of "General Guidelines" for the advertising of beer and wine, which, among other things, stated that the ads could not present drinking as a necessary part of social activity or as a status symbol. Advertisers could not show their product, except incidentally during the manufacturing process, and could include no family scenes, minors, glasses, bottles, or people engaged in consumption of alcohol. A pouring sound could not be used as a sound effect.

These guidelines were liberalized slightly over the next two decades to allow the showing of bottles and "pouring" sound effects. But the guidelines appeared cumbersome and unnecessary to many in the advertising industry, while public interest groups became more vocal and irritated not only by the alcoholic beverage industry's "youth" focus, but also by the fact that beer companies advertised heavily on television with a "lifestyle" emphasis that made drinking an accepted part of everyday life. In 1986, the CRTC decided to reconsider the question of beer and wine advertising, including the controversial limitation on showing people consuming alcoholic products in the ads. The CRTC invited broadcast and advertising groups to draft a new self-regulatory code.

But this attempt to find a compromise concerning the guidelines for alcoholic beverage advertising collapsed under the weight of a number of competing views and interests within industry, advertising, and broadcasting groups concerning the rationale and consequences of such guidelines. Spirit alcohol producers felt that their products had equal rights to advertise in the broadcast media. Some sectors of the broadcast industry, however, were worried that loosening regulations would lead to a backlash that could result in a broader ban, including beer and wine, and the loss of the considerable revenues this brought to some stations. Certain print media also stood to lose considerable advertising revenue if spirit advertising moved to the broadcast media. Meanwhile, advocacy groups argued that alcohol advertising restrictions should be strengthened and demanded more honest informational messages and support for educational messages about moderate drinking from broadcasters and manufacturers.

In support of their position that the advertising industry should be self-regulated in their creation of alcohol product ads, the Association of Canadian Advertisers and the Institute of Canadian Advertising argued that it was the excessive restrictions and meddling by regulators that was responsible for the preponderance of lifestyle advertising that so many critics find offensive in TV beer and wine commercials. "Advertisers should be allowed to show 'slice of life' scenes with consumption of these beverages as they happen under normal, real life, appropriate conditions," they argued (Mehr, 1986). This position was interesting because it implicitly acknowledged that there is distortion or falsification in beer advertising's representation of life, in the sense that beer ads do not depict life "realistically" or show their products in "normal real-life" situations. The advertisers blamed this distortion on the regulations and implied it would disappear under self-regulation.

To many this argument appears specious. The beer advertisers' failure to represent life "as it is," they claim, derives not from regulations but from the inherent tendency of marketing communication to target specific audiences, to communicate through typifications, and generally to concentrate on positive or idealized associations. In its depiction of lifestyles, happiness, leisure, and the good life, beer and wine advertising is little different than that of many other products. Moreover, many people do not believe that alcoholic beverage advertisers wish to talk honestly and truthfully about the use of their products or the consequences of that use. Indeed, if they were required by the guidelines to always be honest, realistic, and authentic in their representations of the social consumption of beer and wine, they would no doubt find this restriction even more onerous. The point is, that to execute their marketing strategies, beer advertisers wanted to be unfettered in their access to media and in their depiction of the social relations of consumption.

Besides, if the issue is really one of deception, then why should the Canadian Association of Broadcasters be an active participant in this self-regulatory process? The obvious answer is that television and radio have proved effective in mustering audiences that attracted beer advertising to sports and music programming: Beer is continually among the most heavily-advertised products on Canadian television. The Addiction Research Foundation therefore objected strongly in its brief to the CRTC's invitation to allow the CAB to get involved with establishing the code for alcohol advertising, arguing, "The Canadian Association of Broadcasters benefits financially from alcohol advertising; therefore, it has an unavoidable conflict of interest in the development or enforcement of a Code of Ethics specific to the advertising of alcoholic beverages" (Addiction Research Foundation, 1986). Meanwhile, given their continuing sensitivity to the public concern about beer advertising, and no doubt hoping to forestall a threat to this important source of revenue, the Brewers Association of Canada in 1987 launched a high-profile advertising campaign of its own against drinking and driving and irresponsible drinking, in general.

Public debates concerning alcohol advertising are made more complex by an intersection of agencies that merges the interests of media, the beer companies, and the advertising agencies. In this broader sectoral interest, the 1972 U.S. broadcasting ban on spirit alcohol advertising led to a voluntary agreement among Canadian broadcasters to restrict the advertising of distilled spirit products to the print media (mainly magazines). What often gets overlooked in such self-regulatory concessions is the convergence between certain media and advertiser interests, which in turn shape advertising policy. The CRTC ban on broadcast spirit advertising in 1974 meant this potential pool of revenue was lost to radio and television stations, but the benefit was that broader impending bans were forestalled.

Broadcaster and advertising agency lobbies have been especially sensitive to the threat of further bans. In Canada, when the Department of National Health and Welfare announced a ban on tobacco advertising for all media in 1989, Bob Foss of the Association of Canadian Advertisers made the policy links between different advertising sectors a central argument in his rationale for taking the issue to court: "What will be next? We know there are many places people would like to see it [an ad ban]. Numerous products have been targets, like tobacco and children's toys and alcoholic beverages. . . . We're afraid [an ad ban] could come about if a precedent is set" (Strauss, 1989).

Both advertising agencies and media can lose significant revenue because of advertising restrictions and bans, but the consequences of public controversy, once it is roused by regulatory hearings, can be unpredictable. The spirit advertising agreement that was written into CRTC guidelines and sustained until 1990 was challenged when spirit alcohol advertisers once again asked the CRTC for the "equal right" to advertise their products on television and radio. The CRTC began holding hearings on this subject in October 1990, and a number of health advocacy groups used this occasion to argue for a total ban on all alcoholic product advertising. The distillers countered this argument with their own views that beer is as dangerous as spirits and that advertising does not increase consumption. Bill Allen of the CRTC announced that the commission could go either way: open the airwaves to distillers or call for another round of public comments on the banning of all alcohol advertising ("CRTC urged to ban," 1990).

Overall, the long-standing debate about alcohol advertising well illustrates how in the absence of a comprehensive communication policy, advertising regulation in Canada has emerged through haphazard policy, self-regulation, and intense arguments among interest groups. But what often gets overlooked in these proceedings is that advertising regulation affects the structure of the media industries. This was the lesson of the infamous Bill C-58, which tried to keep the Canadian magazine industry alive with the withdrawal of tax benefits to Canadian advertisers who placed their ads in U.S. magazines that were distributed in Canada but had little Canadian content. Although the contribution of this legislation to Canadian culture has been questioned, the significance of this policy may lie in its recognition of the difficulty of regulating trans-border flows in communications, particularly advertising, in a market dominated by multinationals and branch plants.

And the situation of media industries is made more complex by the fact that Canadians predominantly read American magazines and watch American television. How effective can Canadian advertising bans (or any other media policy) be if they don't extend to imported media or account for trans-border communication? The question of the channels through which Canadians are exposed to beer and spirit advertising is a crucial one. The experience of the previous ban is instructive. In the wake of the ban on broadcast spirit advertising, magazines with the right demographic profiles (for example, *Maclean's* and limited-circulation magazines) have become increasingly dependent on spirit alcohol advertising (and tobacco advertising before that ban). These magazines are now vulnerable to total bans and also to legislation that might substantially shift spirit advertising back into television. The irony of the situation is that some Canadian publications might have an even tougher time competing with U.S. counterparts if the distillers win the argument. Meanwhile, Canadian television stations are unlikely to benefit from trans-border revenues (e.g., from American distillers using Canadian TV stations to circumvent their own ban).

THE BAN ON TOBACCO MARKETING

An important argument about advertising's role is invoked in the discussion of bans on product advertising, and this argument has been featured in the recent contentions over cigarettes. When bans are threatened or put in place where product use has a health risk or adverse social impact, advertisers are quick to protest the innocence of their craft in stimulating demand for those products. Alcohol product manufacturers, for example, maintain that their advertising is designed solely for brand switching: "Marketers can only promote a brand that fulfills a consumer demand. . . . The sole objective of advertising is to gain brand share at the expense of the competition" (Mehr, 1986).

Similarly, during the last few years tobacco advertising has provoked intense controversy, with many groups calling for either further restrictions on it or a total ban.

Until recently in North America, restrictions on the content and placement of tobacco advertising—for example, its exclusion from radio and television—were the result of voluntary agreements between governments and the industry. However, there is now considerable discussion in the United States about legislating a complete prohibition against tobacco advertising. In Canada, such a prohibition came into effect at the beginning of 1989, a noteworthy event, since—at least in western societies—it is highly unusual for a government to institute a total ban on the advertising of a product that can be sold legally.

The federal government's Bill C-51 became law on June 28, 1988, through the Tobacco Products Control Act, "an act to prohibit the advertising and promotion and respecting the labelling and monitoring of tobacco products." Section 3 defines the purposes of the Act as follows:

(a) to protect the health of Canadians in the light of conclusive evidence implicating tobacco use in the incidence of numerous debilitating and fatal diseases;

(b) to protect young persons and others, to the extent that is reasonable in a free and democratic society, from the inducements to use tobacco products and consequent dependence on them; and

(c) to enhance public awareness of the hazards of tobacco use by ensuring the effective communication of pertinent information to consumers of tobacco products.

Section 4 states: "No person shall advertise any tobacco product offered for sale in Canada"; this includes advertisements by anyone in Canada that are placed in foreign publications or broadcasts for the purpose of promoting tobacco products specifically in Canada, but Section 4 also contains a blanket exemption for the contents of foreign media distributed in Canada.

The ban became effective January 1, 1989, for magazines and newspapers, while the prevailing voluntary ban on broadcasting ads became mandatory on the same date. Outdoor ads were banned as of January 1, 1991, with a provision for gradually reducing expenditures on the same beginning in 1989. Retail signs are banned as of January 1, 1993, but only brand-name store signs in existence at the beginning of 1988 can continue until that date. Promotional sponsorships of cultural or sporting events were also banned as of the beginning of 1989, excluding contractual arrangements that were in place on the date (January 25, 1988) when the final version of Bill C-51 was introduced in the House of Commons. However, no product logos or cigarette depictions are allowed in publicity for events, and monetary expenditures for the same are frozen at 1987 levels. Other provisions in the Tobacco Products Control Act include bans on free distribution of product samples; on rebates, contests, prizes, etc.; and on use of cigarette trademarks or brand names on non-tobacco goods such as clothing.

Section 9 of the Act requires a health-effects warning (to be defined by regulation), including a list of toxic constituents in the products and the smoke produced by burning them, and gives authority for the requirement of an informational insert for product packages. Thus, the passage of the Tobacco Products Control Act marks the first time in Canada that the health-hazard warnings appearing on tobacco packages have the force of law. The new set of warnings, which now must be placed prominently on the front of tobacco packages, appeared toward the end of 1989, replacing voluntary practices in effect since 1971, under which a single English and French text ("Warning: Health and Welfare Canada advises that danger to health increases with amount smoked—avoid inhaling") appeared, in small print, on the side panel of cigarette packages.

Section 9(3) of the Act states: "This section does not affect any obligation of a distributor, at common law or under any Act of Parliament or of a provincial legislature, to warn purchasers of tobacco products of the health effects of those products." Thus, the Act attempts to prevent tobacco firms from using the hazard-warning requirement as a defence against civil liability claims. Finally, the Tobacco Products Control Act contains elaborate stipulations on reporting by manufacturers to the Minister of National Health and Welfare on such matters as sales, product constituents (including prescriptions on testing methods), and controlled expenditures (e.g., for sponsorships).

Almost immediately upon passage of the Act, Canadian tobacco manufacturers— Rothmans, Benson & Hedges, RJR-Macdonald, and Imperial Tobacco—filed lawsuits against the federal government, claiming, among other things, that the prohibition on advertising and promotion in the Act is a violation of the Charter of Rights and Freedoms in the Canadian Constitution, which contains protections for freedom of speech and expression similar to those guaranteed in the First Amendment to the U.S. Constitution. The first of the tobacco cases opened in Quebec Superior Court in October 1989. The court ruled in the tobacco company's favour, but the decision will ultimately be made in the Canadian Supreme Court.

Advertising is sometimes called "commercial free speech," in order to distinguish it from "political speech," which encompasses all comments on social and political issues made by individuals and organizations. Thus, the two main issues to be decided by the courts are: (1) whether commercial speech is entitled to exactly the same kind of protection, as a fundamental freedom, as is political speech; and (2) if not, what restrictions on commercial speech are "reasonable" in a "free and democratic society." In 1988, the Supreme Court of Canada upheld a Quebec law that forbids advertising directly to children, on the grounds that children, being more at risk from influence by the persuasive techniques of advertisers, are entitled to special protection. In other words, the government could restrict or ban commercial speech directed at this particular audience, because children could be presumed to be incapable of "discounting" the persuasive force of advertising messages. (Here, as in the case of tobacco advertising, it is important to note that the prohibitions apply only to Canadian promotional productions, and that Canadian audiences continue to be exposed to such advertising in the U.S. media, both print and electronic, that reach them.)

In the case of tobacco product advertising, the federal government's legislation is based on its understanding of the very serious health risks incurred by users of tobacco products. The government's position may be stated as follows: Even though the effects of advertising and other promotional activities cannot be identified with precision— because human behaviour is complex, and there are so many influences (such as peer approval) on a person's attitudes and behaviour—advertising must be presumed to have *some* persuasive effect on consumers. These presumed effects are helping to encourage persons to begin using tobacco products; encouraging them to continue doing so, even when tobacco users become aware of the associated health risks; and, finally, promoting the erroneous belief that switching to brands that are lower in tar and nicotine content will significantly reduce those health risks. Due to such effects, consumption of tobacco products and the consequent health risks are higher than they would be if people were not exposed to promotional activities (including advertising) on behalf of tobacco products.

In responding to the government's position, the tobacco industry has made three basic points. First, selling tobacco products remains a legal activity, and it is therefore unfair and unwarranted to ban outright promotional activities on their behalf. Second, there are many other products, such as alcoholic beverages and motor vehicles (especially off-road vehicles and motorcycles), whose use and misuse give rise to serious health risks, and yet the government has not imposed a total advertising and promotion ban on these product groups. Third, it is not the intention of tobacco-product marketing to attempt to persuade non-users to begin using their products; rather, tobacco-product advertising is aimed at encouraging existing smokers to switch brands, either among competing manufacturers or among product lines by the same manufacturer. From this perspective, the government's prohibition will not, therefore, have the desired effect of lowering health risks. Nor does it recognize the difficulties posed for Canadian publications, which already have trouble competing with those American magazines that cross the border fattened with American cigarette ads. If the Canadian government's position is to be consistent on the relationship between advertising and demand, some argue, then it must extend the ban to all tobacco advertising in Canada.

CHILDREN'S ADVERTISING

This same issue of trans-border communication is crucial for understanding the current debates about Canadian regulation of children's advertising and the capacity of young consumers to "defend themselves" against the persuasive force of advertising. "The long-standing rationale for regulatory codes for children's advertising is based on the principle that children are incapable of identifying advertising as commercial persuasion, and moreover, do not have the experience and conceptual abilities to evaluate advertisements" (Roberts, 1983). This argument has been at the heart of repeated attempts to restrict or ban advertising to children. In 1978, FTC staff proclaimed:

> It is both unfair and deceptive, within the meaning of Section 5 of the Federal Trade Commission (FTC) act, to address advertising for any product to young children who are still too young to understand the selling purpose of, or otherwise comprehend or evaluate, the advertising. If it is unfair and deceptive to seek to bypass the defenses which adults are presumed to have when they are aware that advertising is being directed at them, then it is unfair and deceptive to advertise to children in whom these defenses do not yet even exist.

This FTC paper articulated the widely accepted notion that children's advertising had to be restricted because of the special vulnerability of children.

This principle was recently confirmed as providing reasonable grounds for limiting broadcast advertising for children in Quebec, where a ban on advertising directed at children under age thirteen has been in place since 1976. The ban was upheld recently in a Canadian Supreme Court (1989) ruling as a reasonable limitation on commercial speech, because it accords with consumer protection legislation that strives to "protect a group that is most vulnerable to commercial manipulation." The court goes on to state that "in sum, the evidence sustains the reasonableness of the legislature's conclusion that a ban on commercial advertising directed to children was the minimal impairment of free expression consistent with the pressing and substantial goal of protecting children against manipulation through such advertising."

For this reason, in 1974 the Federal Communication Commission (FCC) limited Saturday-morning network television to nine and one-half minutes of advertising per broadcast hour. But in 1980, after intensive hearings, the FCC reversed this ruling, reasoning in its suspension of guidelines that market forces and industry self-regulation would prevent the "over-commercialization" of media. The regulatory agency assumed that both the limited demand for children's advertising and self-regulatory codes established for children's broadcasting would suffice to restrain children's advertisers.

Contrary to this expectation, expenditure on children's marketing increased dramatically between 1982 and 1987 in the United States, particularly among toy advertisers, who not only became the leading children's advertisers but also used the de facto deregulation implied by the suspension of children's guidelines to launch product-based animated programs, dubbed the "30-minute commercial." The controversy subsequently led the U.S. Court of Appeals to reverse and remand to the FCC its order eliminating commercial time guidelines in 1987. In doing so, the court questioned why "the commission has suddenly embraced what had theretofore been an unthinkable bureaucratic conclusion" that the market did, in fact, operate to restrain the commercial content of children's television.

The mechanism of deregulating commercial time proved ironic in its effects on children's programming, for it was associated with the general industry deregulation taking place in the 1980s. The next result was the production of new opportunities for children's merchandising, which decreased the role of network broadcasters in children's advertising while increasing the intensity of marketing communication initiatives. By using syndications of television stations in impromptu networks, toy-marketing consortia were able both to compete with network children's programming and to short-circuit the broadcaster-based guidelines for the self-regulation of children's advertising that had been developed independently of the FCC. For example, the broadcast industry codes restricted the use of children's TV heroes in advertisements and required that children's advertisements not take advantage of children's inability to distinguish fantasy from reality, or advertising from programming. Many of the advertisements for character toys, however, use scenes from the animated TV series interspersed with images of children playing with their character toys—in one ad, for example, a young boy is shrunk, climbs into a toy plane, and flies off into a GI Joe program (Kline, 1989). By reorganizing the economic basis of children's television in the United States, toy marketers have been able to circumvent the system of self-regulation set up by network broadcasters. The syndicates encouraged the production of low-cost tied-in programs subsidized by the toy manufacturers.

These changes in American children's advertising came to Canada through satellite and cable. These "30-minute commercials" starred a toy character and were often accompanied by advertising campaigns that violated the Canadian Advertising Standards Council's code for children's ads. This code states in its preamble that because children sometimes do not distinguish between fantasy and reality, "advertisements should respect and not abuse the power of the child's imagination . . . or stimulate unreasonable expectations of product or premium performance." The code has a number of important provisions including the provision that advertising must not exaggerate service, product, or premium characteristics such as performance, speed, size, colour durability, etc. (1b); also "puppets, persons and characters (including cartoon characters), well-known to children or featured on children's programs, must not be used to endorse or personally promote products" (4a); "advertising must not encourage a range of values that are inconsistent with the moral, ethical or legal standards of Canadian society" (8a). Yet, for all these well-stated intentions, this code has no authority over either the character toy programs or the advertisements that were both fanciful and sometimes violent and that promoted them because the signal is redirected through satellite or cable. In Quebec, it was found that even French-speaking children preferred to watch American programs on cable rather than the low-budget programs that were offered by Canadian networks who must operate under the advertising ban.

And although Canadian broadcasters were at first reluctant to run these 30-minute commercials, in order to attract children's advertising, they were forced to find cheap programming that could compete with the popular fare offered on cable. Moreover, the toy industry found it hard to understand why they should place ads with Canadian stations who were forced to vet their ads through the standards council when they could reach larger audiences of Canadian children by advertising on American border stations carried into Canadian markets by cable. So while the CBC gradually left the arena of children's programming, several Canadian stations did run these subsidized programs, but regulation worked against Canadian programmers who might want to produce for Canadian children's television.

The impossibility of this situation obviously also struck the members of the Advertising Standards Council, so that by 1990 they approved a Teenage Ninja Turtle ad that not only used a cartoon character, cut back and forth between animated sequences and children's play sets, but ended with the invocation to "reach out and crush somebody." Susan Birk of the Council explained that the committee felt this incitement to violence did not violate Canadian moral or legal standards because it was said in humour. The "Turtle" who speaks this line in the ad is thought to be smiling. Obviously, those hoping to find a way of producing commercially viable Canadian children's television are not.

BACK TO THE FUTURE

Given the complexity of advertising's social role, the major problem that confronts policy making is the danger of oversimplification: advertising is a policy issue that ties economic, media, and cultural questions into a tight weave, and only a framework of analysis able to recognize the complexity of advertising's cultural and institutional location will be adequate for addressing the future. Based on past, often well-intentioned, attempts to deal with the cultural issues engendered in advertising, one must conclude that Canada's record is not a good one. Canadians see tobacco ads in the American magazines they read, they see American beer ads during the television they watch, and their children (even in Quebec) watch "30-minute commercials" and ads that don't meet Canadian standards, thanks to cable and satellite technologies. Although the regulatory mechanisms are diverse and multi-layered, their mandate and effectiveness are increasingly being called into question by both industry and advocacy groups. Canadian policy appears to be darning the ravelled sleeve without understanding the pattern of the weave: the situation will get no simpler as three new challenges confront advertising policy makers.

The first dilemma awaiting policy makers derives from advertising's success as a form of communication. Advertising is a discursive practice that has emerged from an enormous investment of capital and creative resources: many regard its 30-second visions of life as the most interesting and creative feature of television. Marketers have pioneered ways of compressing and presenting ideas, as well as ways of engaging audiences and producing evocative messages, which are now becoming the standard for effective communication in all spheres. Increasingly, messages about social issues including public health, political programs, and corporate relations are adopting the approaches, techniques, and forms of expression from marketing, bringing with them a whole range of social policy matters into the debates about advertising and communication strategies. These questions are already beginning to emerge on the agenda of bodies such as the Federal Commission on Electoral Reform, for example, about limits on spending and negative advertising, because the reality is that advertising strategies have already changed the nature of election campaigns. Similarly, a number of hard-hitting and potentially offensive social marketing campaigns have raised the issue of how we deal with controversial subjects in advertising.

The second challenge that will increasingly confront advertising in the future is the environmental crisis. When the invisible costs of environmental damage become factored into the market, the tax write-offs granted to corporations who promote consumption, growth, and environmental degradation will look less justifiable. The issues that are invoked by taking the environmental crisis seriously go far beyond "green" consumerism to how we educate the public about the consequences of industrial and consumer practices that lie at the heart of the relationship between production and consumption. Recent controversial advertising campaigns such as those of Tetra Pak, the B.C. Council of Forest Industries, and the Pacific Logging Congress indicate the extent to which advertising is already playing a significant role in public discussion about the environment. Decisions about how to achieve ecologically sustainable social practices will in part come down to persuasive communication and who can afford access to media. The very question of whether the public debate about environmental solutions can be conducted in our commercial entertainment media is not a trivial one.

The last and greatest challenge arises from the cultural conflicts of a global marketplace. The rapid globalization of marketing networks and the introduction of market economics into communist cultures is but one arena in which some very complex questions must be addressed, not only about the necessity of advertising for the management of consumer demand, but more fundamentally about the role of advertising in democratic media systems and in the development of the consumer culture. Are commercial media systems the only "democratic" solution for financing an "independent" press? Is advertising, as conducted in the developed west, destined to become an international cultural practice? There is growing concern that acceptance of the "free market" as an economic institution should not imply the acceptance of American marketing communication as a cultural reality.

We suspect that current trends in global markets will intensify the controversies over advertising as the key link between production and cultural autonomy and force many nations to rethink advertising's social role and responsibilities within the changing global communication context. In spite of Canada's unique situation, which has forced us to wrestle with the issues of social marketing, government advertising, environmental advocacy, and cultural identity in a market society for far longer than most nations have, there is no indication yet that Canadian public policy can deal effectively with these matters. Canada has a unique history with regard to advertising regulation. A succession of issues in health promotion, social marketing, governmental and political advertising, and environmental and social advocacy advertising have forced successive governments to wrestle with the question of advertising's role in a democratic market society. Yet, as the Quebec Superior Court's recent overturning of the tobacco advertising ban (a decision now being appealed by the government) indicates, Canadian public policy making has yet to develop either a more comprehensive conception of advertising's cultural role or the legislative tools to deal effectively with these as matters of public policy. Without this understanding, Canada seems poorly placed to deal with the challenges that lie ahead.

REFERENCES

Note: In addition to new materials, this essay draws freely upon Chapter 12, "Issue in social policy," in W. Leiss, S. Kline, and S. Jhally, (1990), *Social Communication in Advertising*, 2nd ed. Toronto: Nelson Canada, by permission of the publishers.

Addiction Research Foundation. (1986). *Response to CRTC Public Notice No. 1986–68.*

CRTC urged to ban alcohol ads. (1990, October 26). *Globe and Mail.*

Kline, S. (1989). Limits to the imagination. In *Cultural Politics and Contemporary America.* (Eds., Angus, I., & Jhally, S.). New York: Routledge.

Leiss, W., Kline, S., & Jhally, S. (1990). *Social communication in advertising.* 2nd ed. Toronto: Nelson Canada.

Look what the winds will blow in. (1986, January 13). *Marketing.*

McLuhan, M. (1951). *The mechanical bride: Folklore of industrial man.* New York: Vanguard Press.

Mehr, M. (1986, June 2). CRTC pondering codes for booze advertising: CAB awaits verdict on self-regulation. *Marketing.*

Philcox, B. (1989, January 16). The public has a right to know what's for sale. *Globe and Mail.*

Roberts, D. (1983). Children and commercials: Issues, evidence, interventions. In *Rx Television: Enhancing the Preventative Impact of TV*. (Eds., Sprafkin, J., Swift, C., & Hess, R.). New York: Hawthorne Press.

Singer, B. (1986). *Advertising and society*. Don Mills, ON: Addison-Wesley.

Smythe, D. (1977). Communications: Blindspot of western Marxism. *Canadian Journal of Social and Political Theory, 1* (3).

Strauss, M. (1989, September 25). Tobacco firms start challenge of ad-ban law. *Globe and Mail,* p. B1.

Wernick, A. (1988). Promotional culture. *Canadian Journal of Social and Political Theory, 12* (1–2).

SUGGESTED READINGS

"Globalization" year. (1986, January 13). *Marketing.*

Holbrook, M.B. (1987, July). Mirror, mirror, on the wall, what's unfair in the reflections on advertising? *Journal of Marketing, 51* (3), 95–103.

Kline, S. (1988, November). The theatre of consumption: On comparing U.S. and Japanese advertising. *Canadian Journal of Social and Political Theory.*

Leiss, W. (1976). *The limits to satisfaction*. Toronto: University of Toronto Press.

Leiss, W., Kline, S., & Jhally, S. (1986). *Social communication in advertising*. Toronto: Methuen.

Pollay, R.W. (1985, March). Images of ourselves: The good life in twentieth century advertising. *Journal of Consumer Research 11* (4): 887–897.

Pollay, R.W. (1977, July). On the value of reflections in "The Distorted Mirror." *Journal of Marketing 51* (3): 104–110.

Supra-national forces conspiring against advertisers: WFA president. (1986, June 9). *Marketing.*

COMING SOON TO A STATION NEAR YOU?
THE CRTC POLICY ON SEX-ROLE STEREOTYPING

Linda Trimble

[If] Royal Commissions, Task Forces, and reports could change the world, Canada would be a paradise on earth. Even after all that effort [on sex-role stereotyping] over almost ten years, we still have plenty of sexist advertising.

Doris Anderson, 1990

The Canadian women's movement has been attacking the image of women in broadcasting for many years. In the 1970s, feminists protested the stereotypical portrayals of women on radio and television. The women's movement viewed the mass media as a malleable agent of social change and asked government to require the broadcast industry to promote egalitarian and progressive images of women. In 1979, the federal government addressed some of the concerns of the women's movement, including the gender portrayal issue. The Canadian Radio-television and Telecommunications Commission (CRTC) was asked to create a task force to draft antisex-role stereotyping guidelines and decide on a method for their implementation. This paper describes the reasons for the anti-sex-role stereotyping initiative and analyzes the Task Force process, which settled on industry self-regulation as a means of dealing with the problem. The subsequent CRTC policy on sex-role stereotyping in the broadcast media is examined and the effectiveness of the self-regulatory process is evaluated.

ATTACKING THE IMAGE

Canadian women have been criticizing their depiction in the broadcast media since the early years of radio programming.[1] During the 1970s, women's groups began to protest in earnest. They argued that media images of women seriously constrained their integration into the public sphere of business and government. Women's groups were supported in their attack on the mass media by a body of academic research on television content and its effects that found that women were poorly represented and stereotypically portrayed and that these portrayals helped reinforce traditional attitudes about gender roles.

Sex-role stereotypes are rigid and oversimplified generalizations of masculinity and femininity based on the assumption that males and females, by virtue of their sex, possess distinct psychological traits and characteristics (Basow, 1984, pp. 4–5). Stereotypes are manifested in broadcasting by portrayals of men and women that differ in the portrayal of their appearance, abilities, personality, power, occupation, and status. Content analyses conducted in the United States and Canada in the 1960s and 1970s showed very clearly that television images painted stereotypical portraits of women and men (Seegar & Wheeler, 1973; Busby, 1974; Courtney & Whipple, 1974; Tedesco, 1974; Turow, 1974; McNeil, 1975; Cantor, 1977; Caron, 1978; Greenberg, 1980).

According to television programming and advertising, women were young, attractive, married with children, working in the home or in "pink-collar" occupations. Women's attitudes and activities were focused on the home and family. Femininity was equated with dependence, nurturance, the performance of menial tasks, emotional volatility, and relative powerlessness. Males were portrayed as young to middle-aged (usually older than the women), generally attractive, independent, career-focused professionals. Men were in control of the action, wielding the power outside the home. Masculinity was stereotyped as strong, active, authoritative, powerful (to an extreme of violence), and rational. Moreover, broadcast programming and advertising implied that men were more important, as there were many more of them. Male characters generally outnumbered female characters by a ratio of three to one.

In the mid-1970s, Canadian feminists began to lobby the government and the CRTC. Women's groups identified three problems with broadcasting: the unrepresentative and stereotypical portrayal of women; the underemployment of women by the broadcasting industry; and the industry's derisive treatment of the women's movement (McDonald, 1980; NAC, 1974). Consider the following examples of offensive portrayals:

> Our suggestion for "Most Offensive Commercial" is the one in which Nonnie Griffith points her chest at the audience and says, "My Harry thinks my full figure is a knockout!" It ends with "Harry" cupping his hand and grunting, "Eh?"

> Another complaint is about that toothpaste. . . . To refresh your memory—the man talks to his son as they stand back to back. He calls his wife and says angrily, "As long as I am paying his dental bill, he has to use such and such in his toothpaste!" The poor little mousey wife comes out of the kitchen and says, "Relax, dear, he uses such and such!"

> I object most strongly to the TV advertisement for (a department store), which I saw on Sunday, 5 January 1980. The advertisement depicts a woman in an open car being approached by a motorcycle policeman. She is shown to be disorganized, cannot find her driver's licence in her purse, bursts into tears, and passes the (facial tissue) to the cop. The policeman consoles her, tells her to relax and to go shopping at (a department store). My objection is directed to the not-so-subtle message that women (blonde) are disorganized, weepy, and wheedle their way out of trouble with tears. . . .

> I feel obliged to write to complain about a particular advertisement. . . . The commercial was for (a food product). . . . It showed a very worn-out lady rushing home after a hard day and in a panic because her family expected supper shortly. (Food product) to the rescue!!! Meanwhile healthy-looking dad and kids of approximate ages seven and ten, also very healthy looking, are just sitting around the table. I didn't see a piano tied to their asses so why couldn't one of them help prepare the meal?

> News coverage of feminist issues is treated as a joke, made to look subversive, or shown in such a fashion as to make the advocates look asinine. . . . The feminist movement has been sensationalized, demoralized, misinterpreted, and ignored by the news media . . .

> We would like to see women employed as announcers on the national news on both networks and also as foreign correspondents (CRTC, 1982).

Lobbying took two forms. Informal protests included letters of complaint and telephone calls and articles in feminist publications. Formal protests included interventions at network licence renewal hearings. Women's groups appeared at the CBC's network licence renewal hearings in 1974 and 1978 and at the CTV's hearing in 1978 (NAC, 1974; NAC, 1978).

TUNING IN: CREATION OF THE CRTC TASK FORCE

In 1979, the government of Canada drafted a "plan of action" to raise the status of women (Status of Women, 1979). The plan, called *Towards Equality for Women*, identified specific areas within federal jurisdiction for government action and included a proposal to address the concerns of women with respect to sex-role stereotyping in the broadcast media. The CRTC was asked to assist the broadcasting and advertising industries in developing guidelines for the elimination of sex-role stereotyping and the Department of Communications was instructed to form a monitoring group that would publish its findings and thereby "empower the public to bring pressure on broadcasters and advertisers" (Status of Women, 1979, p. 28). Nevertheless, in April 1979, the Minister of Communications, Jeanne Sauvé, delegated responsibility for all aspects of the initiative to the CRTC. She asked the Commission to form a task force representing industry and women's groups.

The Commission did so, albeit reluctantly. There were several reasons for its hesitance. First, the request represented a government directive to an "independent" regulator and was construed as interference in the Commission's regulatory agenda.[2] Second, some commissioners and high-level staff were "dead set against" the Task Force, as they felt it would lead the Commission down a slippery slope toward censorship of broadcasting content.[3] Also, senior staff did not believe that the pursuit of gender equality in broadcasting was within the CRTC's legislative mandate.[4]

Although other commissioners and staff felt the Task Force was important, their support could not compensate for the fact that the sex-role stereotyping initiative was antithetical to the CRTC's "managerial" approach to regulation. This approach emphasized management of industry structure and avoidance of interference in programming content (Salter, 1986, p. 5) and was adopted in response to the Commission's escalating administrative burden and its new responsibility for telecommunications (Johnston, 1980, p. 29). At the time of the Minister's request, the Commission was facing the demand for the licensing of pay television as well as coping with the rapidly expanding cable television industry.

The Commission's reluctance to take on this issue was illustrated by its approach to the Task Force; it was constituted as an independent study group and all of the CRTC appointees to the Task Force were part-time members of the Commission. The six public representatives were selected by the Minister of Communications and included the President of the National Action Committee on the Status of Women (NAC), Lynn McDonald; Stella Baudot of la Fédération des Femmes du Québec; Beth Percival of the P.E.I. Advisory Council on the Status of Women; Sylvia Spring of Vancouver Status of Women; and the editor of *Homemaker's* magazine, Jane Hughes. Industry representatives were chosen by industry groups in consultation with the CRTC and included CBC's Co-ordinator, Portrayal of Women in Programming, four representatives of the private broadcasting industry, and four representatives of the advertising industry.[5]

The Task Force was expected to write a set of guidelines for the portrayal of women in broadcasting and to decide upon the best method for enacting the guidelines: industry self-regulation, CRTC regulation, or government legislation (CRTC, 1982, p. 96). It became clear from the first meeting that these goals would be difficult to achieve as both sides held widely divergent perceptions, beliefs, and objectives. The public representatives said advertising and programming were strongly sex-typed, thus playing a significant role in maintaining the discriminatory environment against women in Canadian society. Representatives such as Lynn McDonald believed that the tendency of the broadcasting media to overlook or trivialize the women's movement and its concerns severely compromised the ability of the movement to pursue its political agenda.[6] The solution was twofold, said the public members of the Task Force: equal employment of women within the industry and regulation of advertising and programming content. However, the former was ruled out from the very beginning, as the CRTC does not have the legislative authority to regulate employment practices within the broadcasting industry.

Private broadcasting and advertising representatives on the Task Force expressed incredulity with the public members' request for regulations. While the CBC, which had sex-role stereotyping programs in place, maintained that the problem was being dealt with, the private industry's initial stance was to deny the existence of a problem. This stand-off between the public members and the private industry groups led to considerable animosity and even a resignation.[7] The industry felt public representatives were not reflecting the views of Canadian women. The Association of Canadian Advertisers, for instance, said most Canadian women did *not* feel insulted by the portrayal of women on the airwaves and that the public members of the Task Force represented a "singular feminist" point of view (*Financial Post*, February 16, 1980, p. 14).

This perceptual impasse was breached in part by a series of public meetings held early in 1980. The public response clearly indicated that many Canadians were aware of and disturbed by the existence of sex-role stereotyping in the broadcast media (CRTC, 1982, pp. 10–28). The advertising representatives in particular were quick to see the implications of consumer dissatisfaction and began in the spring of 1980 to formulate a proposal for industry self-regulation.[8] This proposal, along with agreement that there was a legitimate concern among the public about sex-role stereotyping and that the problem required action, allowed the Task Force to proceed, although members still disagreed about essential issues. On the one hand, the public members contended that sex-role stereotyping could best be dealt with by means of regulations imposed and enforced by the CRTC.[9] On the other hand, the industry wanted the problem to be addressed internally. Regulations would represent unreasonable levels of interference in program content, said industry groups (*Financial Post*, April 5, 1980).

The compromise was industry self-regulation. The three industry groups (the CBC, the Advertising Advisory Board, and the Canadian Association of Broadcasters) each developed self-regulatory guidelines and plans for their implementation. (See Appendix I for texts of the guidelines.) Although the public representatives originally expected the Task Force to produce a set of regulations to be administered by the CRTC, they felt compelled to compromise in light of the insistence by other Task Force members that self-regulation be given a chance. Public members requested a two-year trial period of self-regulation after which the CRTC would assess its effectiveness, and the Commission agreed (CRTC, 1982, pp. 72–77).

VOLUNTARY INDUSTRY SELF-REGULATION

The two-year trial period involved implementation of the industry plans, which had been ratified by the Task Force as a whole. This period represented a process of voluntary industry self-regulation, as there were no CRTC penalties that could be applied to those who breached the guidelines. Each segment of the industry formulated its own guidelines and plan of action for self-regulation. The latter entailed industry education and "sensitization" (making members aware of the guidelines and of public concerns), and mechanisms for evaluating public complaints (CRTC, 1986a). Material was distributed, seminars held, and complaints were received and tabulated.

The CBC's Office of the Portrayal of Women implemented CBC policies on gender portrayal and the Co-ordinator distributed documents and communicated with management (CBC, 1984). The CAB's Standing Committee on Sex-Role Stereotyping circulated information about the Task Force and co-ordinated regional seminars in conjunction with the advertising industry (CRTC, 1986a, pp. 30–64). The Advertising Advisory Board (AAB) produced a video entitled "Women Say the Darndest Things" and distributed the advertising guidelines to advertisers and their agencies (CRTC, 1986a, pp. 65–78).

The public representatives were also active during the trial self-regulatory period. A national lobby group, MediaWatch, was created to educate the public and act as a thorn in the side of the industry and the CRTC. MediaWatch developed a one-step complaint form that facilitated public complaints, conducted a monitoring study of television and radio programming and advertising, produced a video on sexism in the media called "Images of Women," and lobbied the federal government for changes to the Broadcasting Act.

In September 1983, the CRTC put out a public notice requesting all licensees to submit a report detailing their sex-role stereotyping initiatives. Licensees were asked to respond by September 1, 1984, but the deadline was extended to September 30, 1984. Only 66 percent of eligible stations responded by January 31, 1985 (CRTC, 1986b, p. 7). The CRTC outlined few parameters for reporting, and responses ranged from that of a co-operative radio station in Vancouver, which stated that it had been aware of the issue of sex-role stereotyping since its inception and had drafted programming policies designed to avoid stereotyping, to replies of stations that refused to implement any aspect of industry plans for self-regulation (CRTC, 1986a, pp. 51–63).

CRTC POLICY MAKING

The Commission's role at the end of the self-regulatory period was to assess the efficacy of self-regulation and to render a policy decision based on this evaluation. The amount of time the CRTC took to come to a decision indicates that it was a difficult one. The self-regulatory period ended in September 1985. Public hearings were held in Vancouver, Hull, and Montreal in April 1986 (CRTC, 1986c; CRTC, 1986d; CRTC, 1986e). Finally, on December 22, 1986, the Commission released its policy decision (CRTC, 1986b).

The Commission was faced with a dilemma. In a climate of deregulation, the CRTC was pressured by women's groups to flex its regulatory muscle. Women's groups, led by MediaWatch, were unanimous in stating that self-regulation had been ineffective and that stricter measures were required (CRTC, 1986c; CRTC, 1986d; CRTC, 1986e; King, 1987). Yet the Commission was hesitant to invoke regulations. There was great concern about exercising undue influence and interference in a manner that threatened freedom of expression (CRTC, 1986c, pp. 249–50; CRTC, 1986e, p. 30). Some commissioners believed that if the CRTC regulated in the area of gender equality, the Commission would be expected to take responsibility for the portrayal of all minority groups identified by the Charter of Rights and Freedoms (CRTC, 1986e, pp. 174–75). Also, regulations must be written in precise language so that the Commission can take offenders to court; the sex-role stereotyping guidelines were much too vague to serve as regulations.

The actual evaluation of voluntary self-regulation was also difficult because the CRTC did not successfully monitor progress and measure change. When the period of self-regulation began, the CRTC Internal Committee on Sex-Role Stereotyping announced that it would be conducting a monitoring program, and this generated considerable concern on the part of some CRTC commissioners and the private broadcasting and advertising industries. One of the three CRTC members who had refused to approve the report of the Task Force told the *Globe and Mail*, in confidence, that he was opposed to the recommendation that the CRTC monitor the industry: "It's insidious and the principle is dangerous," he said "Big Sister will be watching the media" (*Globe and Mail*, November 22, 1982).

The CRTC decided to undertake a comprehensive content analysis of programming and advertising at the *end* of the self-regulatory period, thus precluding ongoing analysis and any measurement of change (CRTC, 1985). The CRTC commissioned ERIN Research to conduct content analyses in 1985, then released a report summarizing the

TABLE 1
Proportion of Women and Men in Broadcast Material, 1984
CRTC Benchmark Data

Type of Broadcast Material	% Female	% Male
ENGLISH TELEVISION PROGRAMMING		
Characters in children's cartoons *	16	74
Characters in adult drama	41	59
Program staff in news and public affairs	29	71
Persons interviewed in news and public affairs	21	79
FRENCH TELEVISION PROGRAMMING		
Characters in children's cartoons *	16	61
Characters in adult drama	37	63
Program staff in news and public affairs	32	68
Persons interviewed in news and public affairs	21	79
TELEVISION ADVERTISING		
Characters in English television ads	43	57
Characters in French television ads	46	54
Voice-overs in English television ads	11	89
Voice-overs in French television ads	18	82
RADIO PROGRAMMING		
Announcers on English radio programming	12	88
Announcers on French radio programming	14	86
Persons interviewed in English newscasts	14	86
Persons interviewed in French newscasts	14	86
RADIO ADVERTISING		
Characters in English radio ads	38	62
Characters in French radio ads	44	56
Voice-overs in English radio ads	9	91
Voice-overs in French radio ads	14	86

* Some cartoon characters do not have a clearly identifiable sex, thus the sum of females and males is less than 100 percent.

Source: Canadian Radio-television and Telecommunications Commission, *Sex-role stereotyping in the broadcast media: a report on industry self-regulation.* Ottawa.

effort of the industry and the research results (CRTC, 1986a). The ERIN data, which measured the industry as a whole, not individual broadcasters or networks, indicated that women were still under-represented on the airwaves, in all areas of television and radio programming and advertising (see Table 1). Particular problem areas included television news and public affairs, children's shows on television, and radio programming and advertising.

The CRTC data also showed that women and men were portrayed differently, especially on English television programming and advertising, and radio programming (CRTC, 1986g). As the ERIN Research report summarized:

> In television news, for example, women are generally interviewed in a non-expert capacity while men are generally interviewed in the role of expert. In television drama, women are more often associated with home and family roles and men with paid employment roles. In television and radio advertising, men are more often cast as salespersons or experts while women are more often portrayed as consumers (CRTC, 1986a, p. 109).

In other words, gender roles were still strongly stereotyped on Canadian radio and television. Both CRTC staff and ERIN Research analyzed the data and both concluded that none of the CAB and only one of the AAB guidelines had been met to any reasonable degree (CRTC, 1986f; CRTC, 1986g).

During the 1986 evaluation hearings, industry groups argued that considerable progress had been made. In particular, they cited a new awareness of the issue and stated that this was all that could *reasonably* be expected after a two-year period (CRTC, 1986c, pp. 180, 395–96). The CAB said the ERIN study did not measure "sensitization" and thus overlooked the progress made by the industry (CRTC, 1986e, p. 343). Industry groups also focused on employment, arguing that the proportion of female employees had increased since 1982 (CRTC, 1986e, pp. 342, 347, 500, 522). In general, industry organizations said progress had been made behind the camera or microphone, and the results would be evident on the airwaves in the future. Finally, the industry spoke out strongly against mandatory measures (CRTC, 1986c, pp. 266, 315, 371, 422; CRTC, 1986d, p. 275).

In its policy statement, the Commission agreed that the industry did demonstrate sensitivity and commitment to the sex-role stereotyping problem, noting however that this commitment declined at the end of the self-regulatory period and was revitalized only during the hearings (CRTC, 1986b, p. 36). Because the Commission found that awareness and "sensitivity" did not result in measurable progress, it decided to add some "teeth" to the implementation process (CRTC, 1986b, pp. 43–44). Adherence to the sex-role stereotyping guidelines was made a condition of licence (CRTC, 1986b, p. 52).

MANDATORY SELF-REGULATION

By imposing a condition of licence, the Commission was ostensibly saying to the industry, "We've got the teeth necessary to make self-regulation effective." However, in reality, the teeth are like ill-fitting dentures that sit in a glass of water because the user finds it more expedient to go without. Clearly the Commission could not apply the condition, as its own data showed that the guidelines were not being met. Also, the condition of licence represented an anomaly for a Commission that was moving toward deregulation. Finally, the response of the CAB directly challenged the policy.

The imposition of the condition went against the grain of the CRTC's deregulatory approach, which began in 1984 and was clearly evident at the time of the sex-role stereotyping decision. In fact, shortly after the sex-role stereotyping policy was announced, the CRTC stated its intention to "streamline" its regulatory procedures (CRTC, 1987, p. 9). The Commission invited the industry to formulate standards that would take the place of CRTC regulations and would be administered by the industry. The sex-role stereotyping policy stood in clear contrast to this deregulatory trend.

In fact, the CAB challenged the condition of licence on that ground. In its response to the CRTC's call for self-regulation, the CAB stated that it "wholeheartedly supported . . . [the] objective of moving from a regulatory to a supervisory mode of operation" (CAB, 1987, p. 1). However, self-regulation must be purely voluntary, said the CAB. By imposing self-regulatory standards as a condition of licence, the CRTC was pursuing a contradictory strategy that could put both the CRTC and the CAB in an insecure legal position:

> [W]e have been advised that, in the event of a ruling of any governing body charged with surveillance of compliance to the standards leading to a disciplinary action by the CRTC on a broadcaster such as to cause the licensee financial loss, the governing body (the Association) could be subject to substantial civil liability (CAB, 1987, p. 2).

The CAB concluded its response to the Commission's notice by stating that it would not co-operate with the CRTC unless the self-regulatory process was purely voluntary: "[I]n those cases where compliance to a standard is made compulsory by the CRTC through conditions of licence on the industry or on individual licensees, the CAB will withdraw from any voluntary administration and enforcement of such standard" (CAB, 1987, p. 2). In fact, the CAB did not officially act on its threat to withdraw from the sex-role stereotyping initiative. It did attempt to rewrite the guidelines in consultation with women's groups, as was requested in the CRTC policy statement.[10] Yet all other aspects of the sex-role stereotyping plan were abandoned while the CAB lobbied for CRTC adoption of its Broadcast Council proposal.

In its response to the CRTC's call for industry self-regulation, the CAB proposed the creation of a Broadcast Standards Council, which would be composed of a national and five regional bodies, each including public representatives. The Council would enforce the standards by requiring stations found to be in violation of a code provision to broadcast the Council's decision. The CAB said the Council would administer various voluntary codes, including the sex-role stereotyping guidelines, when removed from the condition of licence of CAB member stations. The CAB suggested in its proposal that the CRTC remove the condition when the Council is established and public service announcements have been running on all stations for 60 days (see CAB, 1988).

The Commission did accept the CAB's proposal, despite the protests of MediaWatch, but did not agree to a blanket lifting of the condition. In September 1988, the CRTC issued a public notice (CRTC, 1988, p. 159) stating that, once the Council is set up, member stations that are broadcasting public service announcements and that have previously supplied satisfactory reports on sex-role stereotyping to the Commission can apply to the CRTC to have the condition of licence lifted.

While these critical decisions about policy implementation were being made, licensing decisions proceeded on the basis of the CRTC policy statement. The evidence indicates that the Commission has not had the staff or the political will necessary to use the condition effectively. While a condition of licence is a blunt instrument—rarely does the Commission use its licensing powers to enforce compliance with regulations or conditions—the Commission has other more subtle tools at its disposal. The CRTC can require broadcasters to supply detailed information about compliance on licence renewal forms and at renewal hearings, and it can monitor licensees.[11] In other words, it can make it very clear to licensees that the Commission is concerned about the issue and is willing to scrutinize their actions and make the renewal process uncomfortable for those who show an unwillingness to comply.

The Commission has done none of the above. Licensees are asked a few vague questions on licence renewal forms.[12] Individual station monitoring is not conducted. The last round of television licence renewals clearly indicate that the Commission is unwilling to assess industry actions in any depth. Individual television stations were renewed *en masse* in the fall of 1988, and an analysis of the renewal hearings found that few if any questions on sex-role stereotyping were addressed to licensees (usually only one), that the question asked was of an extremely general nature, that follow-up questions usually were not asked, and that the Commission was satisfied with assurances that the licensee had some sort of mechanism in place to educate staff or monitor programming and advertising.[13]

COMING SOON TO A STATION NEAR YOU?
EVALUATING THE CRTC POLICY

In 1989, the Commission concluded that the sex-role stereotyping initiative had shown success. In its public notice evaluating the 1988 television renewals, the Commission said, "In the last decade important progress has been made to eliminate the most offensive forms of sex-role stereotyping and to ensure that women have equal access to all sectors of the television industry" (CRTC, 1989, p. 27). The CRTC cited five reasons for this conclusion. First, few interventions raised sex-role stereotyping as an issue during the hearing process. Second, MediaWatch "reported good relationships with most broadcasters." Third, "all stations now report internal mechanisms to review and resolve public concerns or complaints and most licensees have formed internal committees to handle such matters or pre-screen programs and commercials." Fourth, many licensees reported increased representation of women on staff. Finally, although some licensees indicated a condition of licence is no longer necessary, all said they would adhere to the CAB guidelines.

The Commission's statement implies that the women's movement is satisfied with the implementation of the policy. This is not the case: MediaWatch is opposed to the Broadcast Council model, and the removal of the condition of licence. MediaWatch stated that "[t]here is at present no evidence to substantiate an improvement in the broadcasting environment that would support a . . . roll-back of the condition of licence" (MediaWatch, 1989, p. 5).

While it is correct to say that few interventions addressed the issue of sex-role stereotyping, this overlooks the fact that MediaWatch was in a state of organizational flux at the time. It was undertaking a thorough re-evaluation of goals and strategies and thus concentrating on organizational renewal rather than lobbying and participation in CRTC hearings (MediaWatch, 1988). As a result of this renewal, MediaWatch gradually shifted from its anti-self-regulation stance and eventually decided to work with broadcasters and advertisers to create effective educational programs. This was apparent in Manitoba MediaWatch's strategy during the television renewals. The Manitoba group was one of the few branches that participated in the hearing process, and it supported the renewals of two Winnipeg stations because these stations had been receptive to collaboration with MediaWatch.[14] It is on this basis that the CRTC concluded that the relations between industry and MediaWatch were now of a "positive" nature.

The other points made by the Commission (that mechanisms were in place to implement sex-role stereotyping initiatives, that more women were employed by the television industry, and that all stations said they would adhere to the guidelines) are important indications that processes are in place, but these points do not address the fundamental question: has the representation and portrayal of women improved? Individual station compliance with the guidelines has not been assessed by the Commission, thus the effectiveness of the policy in achieving the original goals has not been addressed.

Results from the 1988 content analysis, which replicated the 1984 study conducted by the CRTC, indicate that the CRTC had been prematurely optimistic about the success of its policy. The Commission took a very long time to produce the data; the report was originally scheduled for release in January 1990, but analysis of the data was suspended for several months in the fall of 1989 and, as a result, the report was not issued until December 1990. The results are clear and conclusive; the four-year period of industry self-regulation was "characterized much more by stability than change"(CRTC, 1990, p. 7). The CRTC found that women are under-represented in almost every area of Canadian broadcasting (see Table 2).

The data show one area that reflects a general increase in participation by women — program staff. The number of female news announcers and women staff in information programs has risen, but the numbers are still well below the 50 percent mark. The number of women radio announcers has also increased significantly, but even so, women represent only about one-quarter of announcers on radio. Some areas point to increases in gender differences; for instance, there has been a statistically significant drop in women as characters on radio advertising and women were mentioned less often in radio programming. Many of the areas of low representation have not changed; female characters are still grossly under-represented in children's cartoons and women are virtually non-existent in sports programming.

TABLE 2
Proportion of Women and Men in Broadcast Material, 1984 and 1988
CRTC **Benchmark Data**

Type of Broadcast Material	ENGLISH % Female		FRENCH % Female	
	1984	1988	1984	1988
TELEVISION PROGRAMMING				
Children's cartoons	16	24	21	22
Children's hosted programs: Staff	43	35	50	57
Children's hosted programs: Guests	33	36	60	47
Drama (adult)	41	39	37	35
News announcers	31	39	36	45
News reporters	26	28	20	27
News interviewees	21	22	21	27
Sports programming: Staff	2	2	1	8
Sports programming: Interviewees	4	5	0	12
Information programs other than news, sports: Staff	35	41	35	40
Information programs other than news, sports: Interviewees	48	49	36	48
Variety	27	25	36	36
Rock videos	30	30	—	—
TELEVISION ADVERTISING				
Voice-overs	13	14	22	23
Characters	43	41	46	47
RADIO PROGRAMMING				
Announcers	12	22	14	23
News: Reporters	25	25	17	14
News: Interviewees	14	12	14	11
News: People mentioned in news items	10	7	8	8
Non-news programming: Interviewees	22	24	30	24
Non-news programming: People mentioned	22	18	20	17
RADIO ADVERTISING				
Voice-overs	10	14	14	19
Characters	38	24	44	29

Source: Canadian Radio-television and Telecommunications Commission. *The portrayal of gender in Canadian broadcasting: Summary report, 1984–1988*. Ottawa.

The 1988 ERIN research findings pointed to little change in role portrayals. For example, ERIN's analysis of English and French television drama found that, in both 1988 and 1984, women appeared more often than men in roles traditionally associated with women (in family settings, in child-care roles, and as performing household tasks). In English-language drama, the gender difference actually *increased* in two roles: home management and supporting or helping others. There has been no statistically significant change in the portrayal of male roles on English and French TV drama, as men still appear more often in paid employment roles and are more likely to be shown as having staff in paid work settings and committing acts of physical violence. This pattern of gender role portrayal was also found in children's cartoons.

The most frequently used sentence in the report is "There is not a statistically significant difference between the 1984 and 1988 samples." Although there are a few areas where the representation of women has increased, women and men continue to be portrayed in different roles and settings and are shown to have different capabilities and attributes. According to the method employed by the CRTC in 1986 to assess compliance with the anti-sex-role stereotyping guidelines (which used 40 percent as a preliminary target for the representation of women), women are reasonably well represented in only four areas: as staff on English and French information programs (other than news and sports); as interviewees on these information programs; as news announcers on French-language news; and as characters in English and French television advertisements.

The Commission has not indicated how it will interpret these data but has asked for public input so that it can review the policy and contemplate further "CRTC initiatives" (CRTC, 1990, p. 114). Apparently the use of industry self-regulation is not being questioned, as the CRTC has stated quite clearly that the review of the sex-role stereotyping policy will *not* address the issue of the Broadcast Standards Council. This is like reviewing broadcasting policy without discussing the CRTC! In any case, the Commission will be in the same position it was in during the 1986 review process. Women's groups will argue that the condition of licence must be forcefully applied, broadcasters will say change takes time, and the Commission will be forced to find an agreeable compromise.

CONCLUSIONS

The CRTC Task Force initiated a dialogue between feminists and the broadcasting and advertising industries and this led to awareness of the problem on the part of industry groups. Unfortunately, once the members of the Task Force agreed on a set of recommendations, the meetings were discontinued. The conflict-ridden relationship between industry groups and the public representatives continued in the absence of a forum for airing views and managing the conflict. They stopped talking to one another and channelled views through the Commission.

In a sense, the CRTC set up a "no-win" situation for itself as regulator. By granting the industry voluntary self-regulation and by conceding to the public representatives that this was a trial only, the Commission exacerbated the underlying conflict. Each side began the evaluation phase determined to prove the other wrong. The public representatives and MediaWatch attempted to prove that self-regulation was ineffective, and the private industry groups mustered arguments against mandatory self-regulation and CRTC regulation. MediaWatch in particular was in the position of critical outsider; it had no role to play in the implementation of voluntary industry regulation and as such had no stake in the effective implementation of the policy.

Industry self-regulation can follow a voluntary or a mandatory model. The CRTC tried to compromise between the two and in doing so failed to send a clear message to industry and women's groups. Moreover, the Commission ultimately chose a mandatory approach that it was unwilling (and perhaps unable) to implement. When the condition of licence was imposed, the industry groups recognized that the CRTC's sword was made of papier-mâché and were able to call the Commission's bluff.

The CRTC is now in a difficult position. It has declared, by approving the Broadcast Council proposal and by commending television stations on their progress, that industry self-regulation is working. Yet results from the 1988 content analysis indicate that this is not the case. Besides being embarrassing for the Commission, the data illustrate a need for a change in policy. Because of the new Broadcasting Act, the CRTC will be compelled to seek better results, for the Act requires the CRTC to regulate in the interests of the following goal: "The Canadian broadcasting system should . . . serve the needs and interests of and reflect the circumstances and aspirations of Canadian men, women and children, including equal rights . . ." (Bill C-40: Sec. 3, d(iii). This Act will require the Commission to take a clear stand on gender stereotyping. Thus far, the CRTC has taken a muddled and indecisive approach to the implementation of a potentially effective policy instrument. If the Commission is going to watch over industry self-regulation, then it will have to show the industry that the condition of licence is made of stronger stuff.

How can the CRTC make the condition of licence work? It can, in consultation with the industry and the public, choose specific indicators of change, such as the representation of women on news and public affairs programming, sports programming, advertising voice-overs, and children's programming. Each licensee could be asked to measure its current performance on these indicators and set targets for improvement. The Commission could conduct monitoring of stations up for licence renewal, again according to the specific criteria set by the individual licensee. This would not require additional staff as the CRTC person assigned to the licensee could easily check these areas as part of monitoring for adherence to Canadian content regulations and the "code for kids" (which limits the number of commercials aired during children's programming).

The condition of licence as it now stands is being violated by each and every broadcaster in Canada and is little more than a symbolic measure. To achieve the goals of the sex-role stereotyping policy, the CRTC must evaluate television and radio stations according to how well they encourage a more equitable and positive portrayal of women. There may be fewer TV homemakers agonizing over how fluffy their rice is but the problem of sex-role stereotyping is far from solved. Consider the following ads, shown in 1990:

The ad opens with a slow pan up a woman's body which starts at her ankles and pauses on her hips, with the following phrase pulsing in the background: "Devil with the blue dress on" . . .

This ad begins by juxtaposing a shot of a woman's breasts with the lyric, "You're built like a car" (MediaWatch, 1990).

What is being "sold" here?[15]

NOTES

The research for this project was assisted by a Social Sciences and Humanities Research Council Doctoral Fellowship, as well as by the Department of Political Science at Queen's University. I wish to thank John Meisel, Ed Black, and three anonymous reviewers for their helpful comments.

1. For instance, see submissions by women's groups such as the National Council of Women to the Royal Commission on National Development in the Arts, Letters, and Sciences (1941–1951) and to the 1955 Royal Commission on Broadcasting.

2. Interview with CRTC staff members Monica Auer and Sjef Frenken (Hull, February 17, 1988).

3. Interview with former CRTC Chair, John Meisel (Kingston, November 26, 1987).

4. *Ibid.*

5. Industry representatives were as follows: Dorienne Wilson-Smillie of CBC, replaced by Louise Imbeault; Marge Anthony of the CTV Network; Claud Blain of TVA, later replaced by Jean-Paul Ladouceur; Edward Billo of the CAB and Ernie Steele, President of the CAB; Suzanne Keeler of the Advertising Advisory Board; Camille Bachand of the Publicité Club de Montréal; Michael Kennerly of the Association of Canadian Advertisers; Keith McKerracher of the Institute of Canadian Advertising, later replaced by David Morley of the Grocery Products Manufacturers of Canada.

6. Interview with Lynn McDonald (Toronto, May 14, 1988).

7. The representative of the Institute of Canadian Advertising, Keith McKerracher, resigned from the Task Force on February 7, 1980, due to the initial confrontations between the industry and the public members.

8. Interview with Michael Kennerly (Toronto, February 23, 1989).

9. Interview with Sylvia Spring (Hull, February 14, 1988).

10. This process was begun in April 1987. It took three and a half years for the CAB to rewrite the guidelines to the satisfaction of the CRTC.

11. The Commission does this to enforce the only other blanket condition of licence, adherence to the CAB Code regarding broadcast advertising to children. During the 1988 television licence renewals, the Commission conducted monitoring and found instances of failure to adhere to the Code. In its public notice (CRTC, 1989, p. 27), the Commission announced that it would increase its monitoring and discuss its concerns with broadcasters.

12. Television licensees are asked whether they "accept, as a condition of licence, to adhere to the industry code on sex-role stereotyping, as amended from time to time." Television stations are also asked to "specify the mechanisms you propose to introduce to avoid sex-role stereotyping" and are queried about complaints. Radio licensees are asked only whether they undertake to "adhere to the CAB *voluntary code* on sex-role stereotyping." (Emphasis added.) See CRTC, Television and Radio Licence Renewal Forms, Part II (January 1988).

13. CRTC, Transcripts of Public Hearings: See for instance, Edmonton, November 17, 1988; Vancouver, October 26, 1988; Vancouver, October 27, 1988; Hull, November 22, 1988; and Winnipeg, October 12, 1988.

14. MediaWatch Intervention re: Renewal of the Licence of CBC Television, October 12, 1988; and MediaWatch Intervention re: Renewal of the Licence of CKND Television, October 12, 1988.

15. Beer. According to a vice-president with the company that produced the ads, "Ninety percent of my target group get their primary inspiration between their knees and their nipples." (See the *MediaWatch Bulletin*, Winter 1990, p. 4.)

REFERENCES

Anderson D. (1990). Women and the media: Acceptance speech for the Dodi Robb award. *MediaWatch Bulletin*, 4 (2), 4–5.

Basow, S. (1984). *Sex-role stereotypes: Traditions and alternatives*. Monterey, CA: Brooks/Cole.

Busby, L. (1974). Defining the sex-role standard in commercial network television programs directed toward children. *Journalism Quarterly, 51*, 690–96.

Canada. Status of Women. (1979). *Towards equality for women*. Ottawa.

Canadian Association of Broadcasters. (1987). *Response to CRTC PN 1987-9*. Ottawa.

Canadian Association of Broadcasters. (1988). *The Canadian broadcast standards council*. Ottawa.

Canadian Broadcasting Corporation. (1984). *Portrayal of women in programming*. Ottawa.

Canadian Radio-television and Telecommunications Commission. (1982). *Images of women: Report of the task force on sex-role stereotyping in the broadcast media*. Ottawa.

Canadian Radio-television and Telecommunications Commission. (1985). *The portrayal of sex roles in programming and advertising in Canadian television and radio: Summary report*. Ottawa.

Canadian Radio-television and Telecommunications Commission. (1986a). *Sex-role stereotyping in the broadcast media: A report on industry self-regulation*. Ottawa.

Canadian Radio-television and Telecommunications Commission. (1986b). *Sex-role stereotyping in the broadcast media: CRTC policy statement*. Ottawa.

Canadian Radio-television and Telecommunications Commission. (1986c, April 6–7). *Transcripts of proceedings from the public hearing on sex-role stereotyping in the broadcast media*. (Vancouver.) Ottawa.

Canadian Radio-television and Telecommunications Commission. (1986d, April 20–21). *Transcripts of proceedings from the public hearing on sex-role stereotyping in the broadcast media*. (Montreal.) Ottawa.

Canadian Radio-television and Telecommunications Commission. (1986e, April 27–29). *Transcripts of proceedings from the public hearing on sex-role stereotyping in the broadcast media*. (Hull.) Ottawa.

Canadian Radio-television and Telecommunications Commission. (1986f). *Staff comments on the results obtained by the ERIN content analyses on sex-role portrayal.* Ottawa.

Canadian Radio-television and Telecommunications Commission. (1986g). *Statistical analysis of CAB and AAB guidelines as a basis for assessing industry compliance.* Prepared by ERIN Research, Erin, Ontario. Ottawa.

Canadian Radio-television and Telecommunications Commission. (1987). *Public notice.* Ottawa.

Canadian Radio-television and Telecommunications Commission. (1988). *Public notice.* Ottawa.

Canadian Radio-television and Telecommunications Commission. (1989). *Public notice.* Ottawa.

Canadian Radio-television and Telecommunications Commission. (1990). *The portrayal of gender in Canadian broadcasting: Summary report, 1984–1988.* Ottawa.

Cantor, M.G. (1977). Women and public broadcasting. *Journal of Communication, 27,* 14–19.

Caron, M. (1978). *Sex stereotyping in Canadian television.* Ph.D. Thesis, Department of Psychology, University of Regina.

Courtney, A., & Whipple, T. (1974). Women in TV commercials. *Journal of Communication, 24,* 110–118.

Financial Post. (1980, February 16). p. 14.

Financial Post. (1980, Apr. 15).

Globe and Mail. (1982, November 22).

Greenberg, B.S. (1980). *Life on television: Content analyses of U.S. TV drama.* Norwood, NJ: Ablex.

Johnston, C. (1980). *The Canadian Radio-television and Telecommunications Commission: A study of administrative procedure in the CRTC.* Ottawa: Law Reform Commission of Canada.

King, L. (1987). *Broadcasting policy for Canadian women.* MediaWatch: Prepared for the "Adjusting the Image" Conference on Broadcasting Policy, Ottawa.

McDonald, L. (1980). The silenced majority: Women and Canadian broadcasting. *Status of Women News, 6* (2).

McNeil, J.C. (1975). Feminism, femininity and the television series: A content analysis. *Journal of Broadcasting, 19,* 259–269.

MediaWatch. (1988). *Inside Story 4.*

MediaWatch. (1989). *MediaWatch Bulletin 3.*

MediaWatch. (1990). *MediaWatch Bulletin 3* (2).

National Action Committee on the Status of Women. (1974, Winter). *Status of Women News,* 23–25.

National Action Committee on the Status of Women. (1978, December). *Status of Women News,* 3.

Salter, L. (1986). *Issues in broadcasting.* Report to the Caplan-Sauvageau Task Force on Broadcasting, Ottawa.

Seegar, J.F., & Wheeler, P. (1973). World of work on TV: Ethnic and sex representation in TV drama. *Journal of Broadcasting 17,* 201–214.

Tedesco, N. (1974). Patterns in prime time. *Journal of Communication, 24,* 119–124.

Turow, J. (1974). Advising and ordering: Daytime, prime time. *Journal of Communication, 24,* 138–141.

SUGGESTED READINGS

Alliance of Canadian Television and Radio Artists, ACTRA. (1986). *Gender portrayal in CTV network news and information programming, 1986,* Erin, ON: ERIN Research.

Canadian Advertising Advisory Board. (1977). *Women and advertising: Today's messages— yesterday's images?* Toronto: Report of the Task Force on Women and Advertising, 1977.

Canadian Association of Broadcasters. (1984). *Sex-role stereotyping information kit.* Ottawa.

Canadian Association of Broadcasters. (1986). Sex-role stereotyping in the broadcast media. Submission with respect to notice of public hearing CRTC 1986–89. Ottawa.

Canadian Broadcasting Corporation. (1984). *Report on the action taken by the Canadian Broadcasting Corporation further to the report of the task force on sex-role stereotyping in the broadcast media (Images of women).* Ottawa.

Canadian Broadcasting Corporation. (1987). *Trends in the portrayal of people on CBC television, 1977–1987.* Erin, ON: ERIN Research.

APPENDIX

A. CBC POLICY ON THE PORTRAYAL OF WOMEN IN PROGRAMMING

"The CBC accepts as part of its mandate the need to reflect in its programming the role of women in Canadian society and to examine its social and political consequences. The CBC believes that its programming should also contribute to the understanding of issues affecting women.

In applying this policy, CBC programming should:

1. avoid the use of demeaning sexual stereotypes and sexist language;
2. reflect women and their interests in the reporting and discussion of current events;
3. recognize the full participation of women in Canadian society;
4. seek women's opinions on the full range of public issues."

B. ADVERTISING INDUSTRY (AAB) GUIDELINES*

1. Advertising should recognize the changing roles of men and women in today's society and reflect a broad range of occupations for all.
2. Advertising should reflect a contemporary family structure showing men, women, and children as supportive participants in home management and household tasks, and equally as beneficiaries of the positive attributes of family life.
3. Advertising, in keeping with the nature of the market and the product, should reflect the wide spectrum of Canadian life, portraying men and women of various ages, backgrounds, and appearances, actively pursuing a wide range of interests — sports, hobbies, business — as well as home-centred activities.
4. Advertising should reflect the realities of life in terms of the intellectual and emotional equality of the sexes by showing men and women as comparably capable, resourceful, self-confident, intelligent, imaginative, and independent.
5. Advertising should emphasize the positive, personal benefits derived from products or services and avoid portraying any excessive dependence on or excessive need for them.
6. Advertising should not exploit women or men purely for attention-getting purposes. Their presence should be relevant to the advertised product.
7. Advertising should, without going to artificial extremes, employ inclusive, non-sexist terms, for example, "hours" or "working hours" rather than "man hours"; "synthetic" rather than "man-made"; "business executives" rather than "businessmen" or "business-woman."
8. Advertising should portray men and women as users, buyers, and decision makers, both for "big-ticket" items and major services as well as for smaller items.
9. Advertising should reflect a greater use of women, both as voice-overs and as experts and authorities.

* These guidelines, which were in place during the two-year trial period, have since been revised.

C. BROADCASTING INDUSTRY (CAB) GUIDELINES*

1. Broadcast programming should reflect an awareness of and sensitivity to the problems related to sex-role stereotyping.
2. Broadcasters should recognize the changing interaction of men and women in today's society.
3. Broadcasting should reflect a contemporary family structure, showing all persons as equal supporting participants in home management and household tasks, and as equal beneficiaries of the positive attributes of family life.
4. Broadcasters should reflect the wide spectrum of Canadian life, portraying people of various ages, backgrounds, and appearances actively pursuing a wide range of interests.
5. Broadcasters should refrain from the exploitation of men and women and should reflect the intellectual and emotional equality of both sexes in programming.

6. Broadcasters should exercise their best efforts to use language of an inclusive nature in their programming, by avoiding whenever possible expressions that relate only to one gender.
7. Broadcasting should reflect a realistic balance in the use of men and women as voice-overs and as experts and authorities.
8. Broadcasters should attempt to increase the visibility and involvement of women in broadcasting, both on and off the air.
9. Broadcasters should exercise sensitivity to and be aware of the problem of sex-role stereotyping in the acquisition of programming material or rights.
10. Broadcasters should support the voluntary initiatives of the advertising industry in relation to the issue of sex-role stereotyping, to the Advertising Advisory Board, and wherever possible, broadcasters should co-operate with locally organized and nationally conducted campaigns of the Advertising Advisory Board (AAB).

* These are the old guidelines, which were in place between 1982 and 1990. The CRTC accepted a revised version in the fall of 1990.

PART II

MEDIA POWER
AND NATIONAL IDENTITY

CANADIAN BROADCASTING, CANADIAN NATIONHOOD: TWO CONCEPTS, TWO SOLITUDES, AND GREAT EXPECTATIONS

Marc Raboy

As social institutions subject to the tensions and pressures that characterize a given society at any point in time, mass communication systems provide a good indication of how a society sees itself and where it perceives it is headed. This has been particularly true in the case of Canadian broadcasting, whose evolution over the past 60 years has closely parallelled the continuing debate over Canadian nationhood.[1]

Various combinations of political and economic factors have come into play in the federal government's attempts to develop a policy on broadcasting since the late 1920s, but the national question has never been far from the heart of the matter. In this respect, the following characteristics are important to bear in mind:

1. Despite often vigorous claims from the provinces, especially Quebec, broadcasting has been staked out and maintained as an area of exclusive federal jurisdiction.

2. Despite the centralist, unitary nature of the system's governing policy framework, broadcasting services have developed along parallel lines in English and in French.

3. Despite the system's formal autonomy, Ottawa has tended to view broadcasting as an extension of the state—particularly in ascribing to the Canadian Broadcasting Corporation a role in the promotion of national unity.

As this combination of contradictions might lead one to believe, broadcasting in Canada has been seen not only as a means of communication, but as an object of struggle, a contested terrain.

Looking at the evolution of Canadian broadcasting from its inception in the 1920s up to the recent Meech Lake debates can thus tell us a good deal about the nature of our constitutional and national dilemma.

1928–1945: CREATING A SYSTEM . . . AND ITS PROBLEMS

Although broadcasting in Canada actually began in 1919, the basic framework of the Canadian broadcasting system was laid out by the Royal Commission on Radio Broadcasting (chaired by Sir John Aird), which reported in 1929. Remarkably, the central issues in Canadian broadcasting today are essentially the same as they were at that time.

The Aird Commission recommended wholesale nationalization of the then largely commercial radio system and creation of a national publicly owned monopoly to operate all broadcasting in Canada on a basis of public service for the information, enlightenment, and entertainment of the Canadian people. Even before its report was tabled, however, the Quebec government of Louis-Alexandre Taschereau passed legislation authorizing Quebec to erect and operate its own radio station, as well as produce programs for broadcast by existing commercial stations.

Before acting on the recommendations, Ottawa asked the Supreme Court to determine whether jurisdiction over broadcasting lay with the Dominion or the provinces, and in 1931 the Court ruled in Ottawa's favour. An appeal to the Judicial Committee of the Privy Council in London took another year to resolve, and so it was only in 1932 that Ottawa had a clear signal to legislate.

The Canadian Radio Broadcasting Act of 1932 created a national public broadcaster, the Canadian Radio Broadcasting Commission, which had the additional responsibilities of regulating the activities of the private broadcasters. (This double mandate would be transferred to the CRBC's successor, the Canadian Broadcasting Corporation, by the legislative reform of 1936.)

Aird had proposed that control of broadcasting be overseen by assistant commissioners in each of the provinces, but this interesting recommendation was not retained by the legislator. The CRBC, meanwhile, set out to create a national radio service in English and in French: a single service, using both languages alternately, so that the same programs were broadcast in both English and French. Or, to put it another way, the CRBC took the approach that there was only one radio audience in Canada, made up of members of two different language groups.

In its submission to the Royal Commission on Bilingualism and Biculturalism some 30 years later, the CBC reflected on this aspect of its pre-history:

> [This] alternative was tried in the mid-thirties as being the simpler in practice and more feasible in view of the limited human, technical and financial resources then available. Obviously, such an alternative was only workable as long as the program needs of both groups could be met by a single network. With the passage of time and the development of broadcasting techniques and resources, the demands of each group for a more complete service continued to grow, presenting the Corporation with a situation which could only be met adequately by duplicate networks, English and French. These the Corporation proceeded to establish and the pattern then adopted has prevailed to the present.

> Needless to say, the transition was not as simple and orderly as
> the foregoing would suggest . . . (CBC, 1964, p. 5).

Indeed, it was not. The most important factor in compelling the CRBC to move away
from a single service using two languages to "parallel services" in each language as
early as 1934 was the absolute, militant refusal of anglophone communities in the
Maritimes, Ontario, and Western Canada to accept the presence of French on the air.
This has been documented in the memoirs of Canadian radio pioneers such as E.A.
Corbett, Hector Charlesworth, and Austin Weir, according to whom French programming on national radio sparked "a queer mixture of prejudice, bigotry and fear" (Weir,
1965, p. 151).

By 1941, separation of the two services was complete—although the original CBC
news service, created to meet the demands of covering the Second World War,
operated bilingually. Paradoxically, yet to be expected, the institution of separate
services was welcomed by French-Canadian nationalists, who had feared becoming
the marginalized minority within a single, nominally bilingual service. The French
network achieved a degree of administrative autonomy because of "the need for
national unity raised by the war," but no sooner was it in place than it became the
focus of a national crisis (Lamarche, 1960, pp. 6–15).

In January 1942 the government announced it would hold a plebiscite on conscription. In the ensuing campaign, the Quebec-based Ligue pour la défense du Canada, a
broad front of political and social leaders opposed to conscription, sought to use the
public airwaves in order to urge their fellow citizens to vote no. The CBC, by order of
the government, denied the No voice access to its stations. The opponents of conscription were able to promote their cause by purchasing paid advertising on commercial
stations, however, resulting in another paradox: the identification of "public" broadcasting as an oppressive agent of centralized federalism, and of French-Canadian
entrepreneurial capital as a progressive force (Laurendeau, 1962).

1945–1963: CONSOLIDATING THE SYSTEM . . .
AND THE SYNDROME

Citing the educational nature of broadcasting as "a powerful medium of publicity and
intellectual and moral training," the government of Quebec under Maurice Duplessis
claimed that Quebec had the constitutional authority to create a provincial broadcasting
service and passed legislation setting up Radio-Québec in 1945 (Quebec, 1945, c. 56).
Duplessis's legislation was never put into effect, after C.D. Howe announced in the
House of Commons that, "since broadcasting is the sole responsibility of the Dominion
government, broadcasting licences shall not be issued to other governments or corporations owned by other governments" (House of Commons, 1946, p. 1167).

Meanwhile, outside Quebec the "parallel services" of public broadcasting were
developing unequally. While the CBC's English-language radio service extended from
coast to coast by 1938, the same could not be said for French-language service even in
the 1950s. The Royal Commission on National Development in the Arts, Letters, and

Sciences (the Massey Commission) reported in 1951 that French-speaking communities outside Quebec were still poorly served by the CBC: "It has been pointed out to us repeatedly in different parts of Canada that the French-speaking Canadian listener does not receive a broadcasting service equal to that intended for his English-speaking neighbor" (Massey Commission, 1951, p. 297). Six years later, the Royal Commission on Broadcasting (the Fowler Commission) found that many parts of Canada were still unserved in French and suggested that this was more than a question of available resources: "It remains a moot question, however, whether Canada has yet reached the stage of complete national maturity where the introduction of French on the airwaves of Ontario . . . would not be regarded by a substantial majority as an intolerable intrusion rather than the cultural complement that in truth it would be" (Fowler Commission, 1957, p. 242).

The Conservative government elected in 1957 sought to build up the commercial side of Canadian broadcasting and paid little attention to its role in the complexities of the evolving national dilemma. This was most apparent in its response to the historic Radio-Canada producers' strike of 1958–59, which saw, among other things, the rise to political prominence of René Lévesque. Gérard Pelletier has pointed out that much of the problem was attributable to the fact that the French network executives in Montreal lacked the authority to negotiate on behalf of the corporation, while the head office in Ottawa did not bother to take it seriously. The strike paralyzed French-language television for 68 days (there was only one available Canadian channel in each language at the time) and became a symbol of the historic inequality of French and English Canada (Pelletier, 1983).

1963–1980: National Unity and Struggles for Power

By the time the Liberals returned to power in 1963, the situation had changed. In fact, early in its mandate the Pearson government publicly identified cultural policy in general and broadcasting in particular as strategic weapons in its struggle against the rising and increasingly radical nationalist movement in Quebec. In the House of Commons on November 13, 1964, Secretary of State Maurice Lamontagne announced the government's intention to rationalize and centralize the activities of all federal cultural agencies under the jurisdiction of his office and to create a Cabinet committee on cultural affairs. Under the new policy, the national broadcasting service, the CBC, would play a central role:

> The CBC is one of Canada's most vital and essential institutions at this crucial moment of our history. The CBC must become a living and daily testimony of the Canadian identity, a faithful reflection of our two main cultures and a powerful element of understanding, moderation, and unity in our country. If it performs these national tasks with efficiency, its occasional mistakes will be easily forgotten; if it fails in that mission, its other achievements will not compensate for that failure (House of Commons, 1964–65, p. 10084).

This was the clearest enunciation of the CBC's mission, in the government's eyes, since the war. It became clearer still during the next few years. At parliamentary committee hearings in 1966, Liberal backbenchers from Quebec and Radio-Canada middle-management executives sparred over their respective views of the CBC's role vis-à-vis the emerging question of "separatism." When a new broadcasting act was introduced in October 1967, it contained a clause that read as follows: "The national broadcasting service [CBC] should . . . contribute to the development of national unity and provide for a continuing expression of Canadian identity" (Broadcasting Act, 1967–68, c. 25, article 3.g.iv).

In the House, Secretary of State Judy LaMarsh said the national unity clause was "perhaps the most important feature of the CBC's mandate in the new bill" (House of Commons, 1967–68, p. 3754). This was the first time that Parliament had tried to spell out the goals and purposes of the CBC, she told the parliamentary committee: "[The CBC] is the instrument which Parliament has chosen with respect to broadcasting. Parliament is now, in this bill, saying to the instrument that this is one of its purposes, and as long as that purpose is there, to help weld the country together, Parliament is prepared to raise taxes from the people to keep it going. . . . I do not think there is very much more time for public broadcasting to prove itself, to prove to Canadians it is worthwhile spending the money on" (Standing Committee on Broadcasting, 1967–68, pp. 13, 54).

After some vigorous debate, the broadcasting act passed, with the controversial clause intact. The NDP's R.W. Prittie expressed the fear of a witch hunt. Gérard Pelletier admitted he had doubts about it "lead[ing] some people to believe that it is not a matter of promotion but of propaganda" (House of Commons, 1967–68, p. 6017). And an important observation on the implications of the clause came from Conservative MP David MacDonald:

> When we begin to move into areas such as . . . national unity, we are
> in effect moving away from the concept of public broadcasting
> toward the idea of state broadcasting whereby the broadcasting
> system of the country becomes an extension of the state (House of
> Commons, 1967–68, p. 6025).

Radio-Canada's interpretation of its mandate to promote national unity led to bizarre incidents such as keeping its cameras trained on the parade at the 1968 Saint-Jean Baptiste Day celebrations in Montreal, while police and demonstrators fought a bloody battle on the sidelines. During the October Crisis of 1970, the federal Cabinet closely oversaw what was and was not broadcast by Radio-Canada, and a few months later a string of management "supervisors" appeared in the corporation's newsrooms, with no apparent function other than political surveillance (Raboy, 1990, pp. 204–08). The former head of Radio-Canada news and public affairs, Marc Thibault, remembers one official whose job was to monitor all news programs and count the number of times the word *québécois* was used.[2]

The situation culminated with Prime Minister Trudeau's instruction to the federal regulatory agency, the Canadian Radio-television and Telecommunications Commission, to inquire into CBC news coverage in the wake of the election of the Parti Québécois in Quebec in November 1976:

> Doubts have been expressed as to whether the English and French television networks of [the CBC] generally, and in particular their public affairs, information and news programming, are fulfilling the mandate of the Corporation . . . (CRTC, 1977, p. v).

The CRTC dutifully investigated and reported, in July 1977, that the CBC had indeed failed "to contribute to the development of national unity"—but not in the sense anticipated by the Prime Minister. The problem was not a bias in favour of separatist politics, it said, but deficient representation of Canada's "two solitudes" to one another. In English and in French, the CBC did not pay adequate attention to the regions of Canada; it was too centralized and aloof, too influenced by commercial pressures, too bureaucratic. "In the modern world," reported the CRTC, "political and economic developments tend to centralize; cultural developments, on the other hand, tend to be regional, arising in much more sharply delimited areas" (CRTC, 1977, p. 9).

The 1977 CRTC inquiry appears to have been a turning point in the Liberal government's view of the role of media in Canada's constitutional struggle. By year's end, it had created a new agency, the Canadian Unity Information Office, and strategy for containment of the pressures of national fragmentation thereafter flowed through there. Political expectations of the CBC diminished, and in the important run-up to the Quebec referendum of 1980, the Corporation was left to establish and carry out an internal policy of news coverage according to rigorous journalistic standards and the principle of "the public's right to be informed" (CBC, 1979, pp. 377–424). Ultimately, the referendum campaign was covered by CBC as a straight news event, while the government sought to mobilize its constituency directly, particularly through advertising (Johnson, 1983, pp. 6–12; Stark, 1983).

The role of the CBC aside, political struggles surrounding the national question continued to mark the evolution of Canadian broadcasting in the 1960s and 1970s.

From 1968 on, renewed demands from Quebec for constitutional powers in broadcasting highlighted the constitutional debates of the day and marked the evolution of communications in Canada. In its brief to the Constitutional Conference convened by Lester Pearson in February 1968, Quebec claimed the right to play the role of a national state in matters pertaining to language and culture, including broadcasting. As instruments of education and culture, radio and television rightfully belong under provincial jurisdiction, the Quebec brief argued. The court ruling of 1932 was "unacceptable"; federal agencies such as the CBC should be made to reflect the "bicultural reality" of Canada; jurisdiction over broadcasting should not be the exclusive domain of the federal government (Johnson, 1968).

In the coming months, debate focused on the question of "educational broadcasting." The new Broadcasting Act stated that "facilities should be provided within the Canadian broadcasting system for educational broadcasting" (Broadcasting Act, 1968, c. 25, article s.2.i). As we saw earlier, federal policy explicitly excluded provincial governments or their agencies from holding broadcasting licences. Yet education was clearly under provincial jurisdiction. Who then would have control over educational broadcasting? Returning to Quebec from the Constitutional Conference, Johnson declared that his government had decided to apply Duplessis's 1945 law establishing Radio-Québec (Johnson, 1968, p. 3). The move was enough to upset Ottawa's design.

By the end of 1969, Ottawa and the provinces had settled on a definition of educational broadcasting under which, in the 1970s, provincial public broadcasting agencies would begin operating in four provinces.

The growing complexity of communications in the late 1960s prompted Ottawa to create the Department of Communications in April 1969. Determined to match Ottawa move for move, Quebec created its own Ministère des communications six months later. In the early 1970s, negotiating a strong role for Quebec in communications policy became one of the hallmarks of Robert Bourassa's program for achieving "cultural sovereignty." In a series of policy statements authored by communications minister Jean-Paul L'Allier, Quebec proposed "to promote and maintain a *québécois* system of communications" (Quebec, 1971), and to become "master craftsman of communications policy on its territory" (Quebec, 1973).

The cornerstone of Quebec's policy was to be the Régie des services publics, the regulatory authority for utilities falling under the province's jurisdiction. L'Allier saw the Régie becoming a Quebec equivalent to the CRTC, extending its activities to areas such as cable television—which, Quebec argued, were not covered by the Privy Council decision of 1932. In 1973, the Régie began to subject the 160 cable companies then operating in Quebec to its own regulation as well as that of the CRTC, and within a year the inevitable occurred: in applications to serve a community near Rimouski, the Régie and the CRTC awarded licences to two different applicants. It took until November 1977 for the Supreme Court to decide the Dionne-d'Auteuil case in favour of the CRTC, ruling that Ottawa had exclusive jurisdiction over cable (Supreme Court, 1978, pp. 191–210). Oddly enough, the Court split neatly along national lines, the three judges from Quebec dissenting from the majority opinion. As constitutional scholar Gil Rémillard put it: "On the strictly legal level, both options were defensible. The decision was based on the judges' different conceptions of Canadian federalism" (Rémillard, 1980, p. 349).

Under the Parti Québécois government, Quebec did not directly engage with Ottawa over communications policy. The PQ carried over the policy thrust of the Bourassa government but basically abdicated its responsibility for communications because of its lack of power under the existing system. In the view of communications minister Louis O'Neill, political sovereignty was the only solution to Quebec's communications problems (Quebec, 1977, p. B-2095). Paradoxically, the PQ was thus a lot less aggressive than its predecessors in seeking concrete gains from Ottawa in this area. It concentrated instead on developing the programs and policies begun by Union Nationale and Liberal governments: Radio-Québec, now a full-fledged broadcaster, and the particular Quebec form of participatory communication known as "community" media.

1980–1990: POST-NATIONALISM AND THE TRIUMPH OF THE MARKET

Both in Ottawa and Quebec, communication policy took on a new—yet strangely similar—shape after the referendum of 1980.

In Ottawa, as we saw earlier, the view of the CBC as the centrepiece of Canadian cultural policy had begun to shift as of the late 1970s. With the referendum out of the way, the entire cultural sphere took on a distinctly economic vocation. In July 1980, the arts and culture branch of the Department of the Secretary of State and ministerial responsibility for culture were transferred to the industry-oriented Department of Communications (DOC). Communications minister Francis Fox told the parliamentary committee that the diffusion of culture would henceforth depend increasingly on its industrial base and the DOC would be concentrating on the growth of "cultural industries" (Standing Committee, 1980–83, p. 2–9).

The new orientation was underwritten by the Federal Cultural Policy Review Committee (Applebaum-Hébert) that reported in 1982 and was spelled out in detail in a series of policy statements signed by Fox in 1983–84 (Department of Communications, 1983a). Since then, federal policy has been marked notably by a gradual withdrawal of fiscal responsibility for public service broadcasting (CBC budget cuts), privatization of television production (through the Telefilm fund), and the introduction of a wide range of new commercial cable-delivered television signals (pay-TV and non-discretionary subscriber-funded specialty services). In generic terms, the 1980s marked a shift from the political to the economic, and the eclipse of the traditional socio-cultural objectives of broadcasting in Canada.

The new approach in Quebec was strangely similar as, in the post-referendum era, Quebec appeared to lose interest in the socio-cultural possibilities of communications altogether and placed its emphasis on industrial development. Ottawa and Quebec thus found themselves on the same wavelength, as the PQ discourse on communications became increasingly economistic, and its policy industrially oriented during its second mandate. Quebec communications minister Jean-François Bertrand signalled the new situation in June 1981: PQ communications policy would be based on economic development and not on making jurisdictional demands from Ottawa (Quebec, 1981, pp. B326-29). Indeed, Quebec under the PQ seemed determined to outpace Ottawa in shifting the accent in communications from the cultural and political to the industrial and economic spheres (Quebec, 1982, 1983).

So the Quebec referendum changed not only the underlying basis for both Ottawa's and Quebec's strategy in communications and shifted the emphasis from the political and socio-cultural to the economic and the industrial, it also changed the nature of jurisdictional conflict between Quebec and Ottawa — competition over control of cultural development could change to collaboration in the name of economic development (Tremblay, 1988, pp. 57–87). But such collaboration was not possible while the Liberals were in office in Ottawa, given the rigidity of their historic claim to exclusive jurisdiction over communications. It had to await the election of the Conservatives in 1984.

The most generous thing one can say about the new Conservative government's broadcasting policy is that it had none. In general, the government's early initiatives with respect to broadcasting coincided with its general thrust toward reduced public spending and expanding the role of the private sector in the Canadian economy (Caplan-Sauvageau Task Force, 1986). But broadcasting and communications generally quickly emerged as one of the sectors on the cutting edge of the government's plan for "national reconciliation" after the institutionalized antagonism of the Trudeau years.

Brian Mulroney's choice of Marcel Masse to be his Minister of Communications was an astute one in this regard. Masse was not only a loyal Tory, but a reputed Quebec nationalist who had been involved with the Union Nationale government of the late 1960s in its battle for more provincial power through agencies such as Radio-Québec. He was the ideal minister for thawing relations with Quebec while applying broad government policy to communications.

Tendering the olive branch to Quebec was not only an effective manoeuvre in the government's thrust toward national reconciliation; it was also an early move to deflect criticism from its attitude toward national public broadcasting. In an interview with *Le Devoir* in December 1984, Masse said:

> The Conservative Party applies its theories in every sector, in communications as elsewhere. . . . The state is an important tool in economic affairs as in cultural affairs, but we are not about to have a culture of the state. . . . We are going to have a culture of Canadians. We have insisted, to the exclusion of everything else, that the defence of Canadian culture was the CBC's responsibility. We have insisted on this until everyone else wound up believing they had no responsibility. Perhaps it is time to redress the balance. Canadian culture belongs to the Canadian people, and it is up to them, through all their institutions, to see that it flourishes (Descoteaux, 1984).

In the same interview, Masse added that he saw provincial broadcasters as positive instruments for regional cultural development, not as usurpers of federal authority (the standard Liberal view).

Elsewhere, while his government administered crippling surgery to the CBC budget, Masse was fond of reminding audiences of the previous government's attitude toward public broadcasting: "We're not the ones who threatened to put the key in the door of the CBC because we didn't like its news coverage," he told a meeting of Quebec journalists in Montreal.[3]

On February 1, 1985, Masse and Quebec communications minister Jean-François Bertrand signed an agreement on communications enterprises development under which they jointly provided $40 million in seed money to stimulate research and job creation by Quebec-based communications firms. The industrial thrust of the accord was self-evident, aiming at technical innovation and support for the production, development, and marketing of communications goods and services, especially in export markets (Canada/Quebec, 1985b; Tremblay, 1988).

It was the first-ever communications agreement between Ottawa and Quebec since they had created their respective communications ministries a few months apart in 1969. Masse and Bertrand also announced the setting-up of a permanent joint committee, chaired by their two deputy ministers, to pursue further areas of collaboration. This committee has functioned successfully ever since, making communications one field where Ottawa and Quebec actually function *d'égal à égal*.[4]

The committee's first effort produced an important report "The Future of French-Language Television," made public in May 1985 (Canada/Quebec, 1985a). The report's central recommendation was crucial to the developing federal policy with respect to broadcasting, as well as strangely premonitory. It proposed "that the special nature of the French-language television system be recognized within the Canadian broadcasting system, and that government policies and regulations be adapted accordingly."[5] Such a proposal would recognize, for the first time, the historic reality of parallel development of Canadian broadcasting since the 1930s. It would also mark a major shift in Ottawa's official attitude that there is but one policy for Canadian broadcasting, not two.

Specifically, the report proposed the following areas as requiring distinct policy approaches:

1. Radio-Canada should be allowed to evolve separately (*pouvoir connaître une évolution distincte*) from the CBC.

2. The roles to be played by public and private networks in the evolution of the French-language system should not be assumed to be the same as in the English.

3. A policy on French-language cable TV should be developed to protect emerging French-language specialty services against the massive influx of services in English and to foster their introduction by ensuring more favourable financing arrangements.

4. Private television stations should increase their investment in French programming.

5. Public television networks should make greater use of independent production houses, and government funding agencies should increase their support for program creation outside the system.

6. Public and private television networks should work together to maximize audience penetration and combat audience erosion by English-language stations.

7. The status of Quebec community television organizations should be clarified, funding sources increased, and experience used to promote development outside Quebec.

8. Delivery of French signals to under-served areas should be promoted.

In addition, the report proposed general ongoing consultation between Ottawa and Quebec. A "harmonization" agreement for the development of French-language television was signed soon thereafter (Canada/Quebec, 1986). Since then, areas of federal-provincial collaboration have included working groups on cable television, children's advertising, and computer software (Tremblay, 1988, p. 83), and the idea of tailoring policy to meet the distinct needs of different markets has been reflected notably in CRTC decisions (CRTC, 1987) and the policies of the Telefilm fund.[6]

Quebec public opinion welcomed the new distribution of resources in communications, which was seen as a move away from the traditional approach of massive, and exclusive, federal involvement in cultural affairs (Bissonette, 1985). This, it was recalled, had begun as a kind of benevolent state intervention in the 1950s in the wake of the Massey report, only to be transformed into a strategic weapon for the promotion of national unity under the Pearson and, particularly, the Trudeau governments.

The Mulroney government's first term in office was marked by a series of formal initiatives with respect to broadcasting policy: a comprehensive review by the Task Force on Broadcasting Policy (Caplan-Sauvageau Task Force, 1986), lengthy hearings and a report by the parliamentary Standing Committee on Communications and Culture (1988a), a ministerial policy statement (Communications Canada, 1988), and, finally, a new broadcasting act (Broadcasting Act, Bill C-40, 1991).

The first stage of this process took the form of a ministerial task force headed by Gerald Caplan and Florian Sauvageau. Its terms of reference, announced in April 1985, were to propose "an industrial and cultural strategy to govern the future evolution of the Canadian broadcasting system through the remainder of this century," taking into account "the need for fiscal restraint, increased reliance on private sector initiatives and federal-provincial co-operation."

The Caplan-Sauvageau Task Force welcomed the proposals of the federal-provincial committee on French-language television (p. 157), and reiterated many of its key proposals. It proposed "that the distinctive character of Quebec broadcasting be recognized both in itself and as the nucleus of French-language broadcasting throughout Canada" (p. 223). French- and English-language services within the CBC should be recognized as serving "distinct societies" and be allowed to take "different approaches to meeting the objectives assigned to public broadcasting" (p. 217). The CBC's French network budgets should be reviewed "to establish hourly production costs that reflect the role assigned to the French network in the new television environment" (p. 253). As for the CBC's national unity mandate, the task force found it "inappropriate for any broadcaster, public or private. . . . It suggests constrained attachment to a political order rather than free expression in the pursuit of a national culture broadly defined" (pp. 283–84). The task force proposed to replace it with "a more socially oriented provision, for example, that the service contribute to the development of national consciousness" (p. 285).

The parliamentary committee that studied the Caplan-Sauvageau recommendations in 1986–88 made two pertinent proposals of its own. One concerned making the law reflect the CRTC practice of "tak[ing] into consideration the distinctive characters of French and English broadcasting when implementing broadcasting policy" (Standing Committee on Communications and Culture, 1988a, p. 418). The other extended an important task force proposal, specifying that the budget for CBC production costs be established "so that the quality of the Canadian programs of the English and French networks would be comparable" (Standing Committee on Communications and Culture, 1988a, p. 363).

The government's position was formalized in the policy statement *Canadian Voices, Canadian Choices*, signed by Flora MacDonald and made public a few days after the report of the parliamentary committee in June 1988. Here it was recognized that

> [t]he problems and challenges for English-language broadcasting and French-language broadcasting are not the same . . . [and that] these differences between the English and French broadcasting environments necessarily require different policy approaches for each (Communications Canada, 1988, pp. 6–7).

The legislation tabled at the same time (Bill C-136, 1988) featured a half-dozen clauses referring to the linguistic duality of the system. The key clause, article 3.1.b., specified that "English- and French-language broadcasting, while sharing common aspects, operate under different conditions and may have different requirements." The CBC's mandate was changed to read that "the programming provided by the Canadian Broadcasting Corporation should . . . contribute to shared national consciousness and identity" (article 3.1.k.iv). An amendment to this article introduced at third reading added that it should "strive to be of equivalent quality in English and in French" as well (Broadcasting Act, Bill C-136, 1988).

Bill C-136 died in the Senate on September 30, 1988, as Parliament was dissolved for the national elections (Raboy, 1990, pp. 329–34). It was reintroduced virtually intact, however, as Bill C-40 in October 1989. This bill had an even more bizarre itinerary, especially insofar as the aspects that interest us here are concerned.

In retrospect, one of the interesting aspects of the policy evolution between 1985–88 was just how little controversy was provoked by issues with constitutional implications.[7] In spite of an unprecedented outpouring of public discussion and production of official policy documents (Raboy, 1989, pp. 70–75), there was almost no contradictory debate surrounding the questions we have been discussing here. The opposition political parties were especially silent[8]—particularly in view of how vocal they had been on these questions in the past and would soon be again.

The situation changed suddenly when Bill C-40 went to legislative committee in January 1990. The minister was now once again Marcel Masse. He reiterated the general thrust of the legislation as it had been expressed in Flora MacDonald's policy statement of June 1988:

> The new proposed legislation recognizes the distinct character of francophone audiences. It is clear that English- and French-language broadcasting differ in their operations and in their needs . . . (House of Commons, 1990a, p. 11).

Masse then explained the rewording of the CBC's national unity mandate, in terms borrowed from Caplan-Sauvageau:

> I have removed from the CBC its obligation to promote Canadian unity because it is, first, maintaining this political value artificially, and second, it was a constraint on freedom of expression. This obligation also opens the door to an intolerable interference. In removing it, we will rather place greater emphasis on the capacity of Canadians to recognize each other through their values (House of Commons, 1990a, p. 11).

The issue was picked up by the NDP's Ian Waddell: "[Y]ou are now "Meeching" [the CBC]; you are now applying the doctrine of the Meech Lake agreement to this."

Waddell asked Masse to explain what he meant by the CBC's old mandate "maintaining this political value artificially."

Masse: A public broadcaster must reflect society, its sociological aspects as well as its cultural aspects. It is not a propaganda instrument. To become the promoter of one aspect of our reality might easily produce consequences that would limit freedom of expression. You may be too young to remember the time when Liberal governments, before our time, asked the CBC to report on the number of separatists who worked at or did not work at promoting Canadian unity. We lived through those times. They certainly were not the most conducive to freedom of expression in our country.

Waddell: The intolerable interference with the CBC was when the [Liberal] government of the day issued directions that it did not want separatists in the CBC. That is what you mean by intolerable. Is that why you are changing?

Masse: Do you support the government in issuing a directive to Radio-Canada in a sense like that?

Waddell: Yes, yes, yes.

Masse: Do you support that?

Waddell: I believe in Canada. I believe in national unity.

Masse: Do you believe in it to the degree that you want to muzzle *la liberté d'expression* in this country?

Waddell: *Je ne suis pas séparatiste, monsieur le ministre. Êtes-vous séparatiste?* (House of Commons, 1990a, pp. 17–18)

The reader will understand if I abandon the narrative at this point, although the discussion continued through several more exchanges of a similar nature.

In subsequent hearing meetings, Liberal and NDP committee members sought to draw out the views of prominent parties with respect to the national unity mandate—although not a single intervenor raised the question on his or her own steam.

Under questioning from Liberal member John Harvard on February 15, broadcasting historian and former CBC producer Frank W. Peers, appearing for the Friends of Canadian Broadcasting, stated:

I tend to think the wording in the existing act, whereby the CBC is asked in effect to promote national unity, can be a source of difficulty for a public broadcaster which is expected to reflect opinions from all elements of the population (House of Commons, 1990d, p. 29).

The head of the CRTC, Keith Spicer, responding to a question from Waddell, stated on February 22:

> I would agree with the government on this one. I think the words "national unity" had a historic value at the time. . . . I think this new wording is probably more appropriate to the times we live in (House of Commons, 1990e, pp. 17–18).

The CBC's designated chairman Patrick Watson, responding to Liberal member Sheila Finestone, stated on March 12:

> I felt at the time of the passage of the previous law in 1968 that the introduction of the requirement to promote national unity was inappropriate and verged on requiring of the CBC that it become an instrument of propaganda. . . . [T]here is a widely held feeling [within the CBC] that the real obligation of this corporation, of this institution, is to reflect realities (House of Commons, 1990f, p. 6).

So, as in 1968, there was no apparent sign of a public interest (or indeed, of public interest) in the CBC's national unity mandate. It was strictly an affair of politicians (House of Commons, 1990d, pp. 69–84). When Bill C-40 returned to the House for third reading, the government voted down two opposition amendments on the question, one by Sheila Finestone proposing a return to the *status quo ante* ("contribute to the development of national unity and provide for a continuing expression of Canadian identity"), and a hybrid proposal by Ian Waddell ("contribute to national unity, shared national consciousness and identity") (House of Commons, 1990c).

The Commons finally adopted the new Broadcasting Act on December 5, 1990—just as the CBC president was announcing draconian cuts in staff and services that would eliminate public broadcasting at the local level (Winsor, 1990; Caplan, 1990). The combination of cynicism and irony evident in this coincidence stood as a reminder that its ministers' lofty pronouncements on the socio-cultural importance of broadcasting notwithstanding, the Conservative government's lack of support for public broadcasting demonstrated its view of broadcasting as just another business.

CONCLUSION

The distant and recent history I have just outlined is of interest to communications and constitutional scholars alike. For communications scholars, it shows how media systems, institutions, services, and policies evolve according to the political and economic agendas of the surrounding society and its elites. For constitutional scholars, it shows the strategic importance of the media system and pertaining policy issues to the evolving constitutional context.

Aside from what it tells us about media, this history is rich in illustration about governments' conception of media—and of the link between their constitutional agendas and their overall agendas.

Most of the time, Canadian politicians have tended to see broadcasting as an instrument of nation building and have thus been quick to blame broadcasting for failing to contribute to national unity. The blame is misplaced and the expectation unreasonable.

As a forum of public discussion, a mirror of social life, a system in which problems of jurisdiction, allocation of resources, and other areas of conflict are played out, Canadian broadcasting has reflected the lack of consensus about the fundamental nature of Canadian nationhood.

In this sense, it is a microcosm of Canadian society, and of the quintessential Canadian dilemma of how to accommodate divergent socio-cultural demands within a "national" framework when the question of "nationhood" remains unresolved.

NOTES

1. The reader desiring more historical detail is referred to Marc Raboy, (1990), *Missed opportunities: The story of Canada's broadcasting policy*, Montreal and Kingston: McGill-Queen's University Press, from which most of the material in this paper is drawn.

2. This was related by Marc Thibault in comments at the National Archives of Canada conference, "Beyond the Printed Word," Ottawa, October 1988.

3. Comments to a meeting of the Federation professionelle des journalistes du Québec, Montreal, December 10, 1984.

4. This view was expressed to the author in these words by a senior official of the Ministère des Communications de Québec (MCQ) in June 1990, a few days before the collapse of the Meech Lake Accord.

5. (Federal-Provincial Committee, 1985) The French version read: ". . . que le système télévisuel francophone soit reconnu comme une entité spécifique du système Canadien et qu'en conséquence des politiques distinctes lui soient appliquées" (p. 10). According to the MCQ official referred to in note 4, "C'était Meech avant la lettre"—it was a precursor to Meech.

6. However, the functioning of the Telefilm fund is now being contested by Quebec. See, for example, "Les coproductions avec la France vont bien . . . mais en anglais," *Le Devoir* (Paule des Rivières), October 22, 1990.

7. A rare exception came from newspaper columnist William Johnson, for whom Bill C-136 stood for the "Meeching" of Canada. By reflecting "the view that Quebec is a distinct society," he wrote, the bill would "break the national coherence of the CBC" (William Johnson (1988, September 21), "'Meeching' of Canada takes another step forward." *Montreal Gazette*.

8. According to a research project in progress at Laval University, no Liberal or NDP intervention before the Task Force, the parliamentary committee, or the legislative committee hearings on Bill C-136 addressed the question of the distinct society or the CBC's national unity mandate (personal files).

REFERENCES

Aird Commission. See Canada. Royal Commission on Radio Broadcasting. (1929).

Bissonette, L. (1985, March 23). L'envers du décor. *Le Devoir*.

Canada. Communications Canada. (1988). *Canadian voices, Canadian choices: A new broadcasting policy for Canada*. Ottawa.

Canada. Department of Communications. (1983a). *Building for the future: Towards a distinctive CBC*. Ottawa.

Canada. Department of Communications. (1983b). *Towards a new national broadcasting policy*. Ottawa.

Canada. Department of Communications. (1984). T*he national film and video policy*. Ottawa.

Canada. Federal Cultural Policy Review Committee. (1982). *Report*. Ottawa.

Canada. Parliament. House of Commons. Bill C-40, 34th Parliament, second session, first reading, October 12, 1989.

Canada. Parliament. House of Commons. *Debates*. 1946.

Canada. Parliament. House of Commons. *Debates*. 1964–65.

Canada. Parliament. House of Commons. *Debates*. 1967–68.

Canada. Parliament. House of Commons. Legislative Committee on Bill C-40. *Minutes*. January 31, 1990a.

Canada. Parliament. House of Commons. Legislative Committee on Bill C-40. *Minutes*. March 15, 1990b.

Canada. Parliament. House of Commons. Legislative Committee on Bill C-40. *Minutes*. February 15, 1990d.

Canada. Parliament. House of Commons. Legislative Committee on Bill C-40. *Minutes*. February 22, 1990e.

Canada. Parliament. House of Commons. Legislative Committee on Bill C-40. *Minutes*. March 12, 1990f.

Canada. Parliament. House of Commons. Order Paper and Notice Paper No. 170. 34th Parliament, second session. April 23, 1990c.

Canada. Parliament. House of Commons. Standing Committee on Broadcasting, Film and Assistance to the Arts. *Minutes*. 1967–68.

Canada. Parliament. House of Commons. Standing Committee on Communications and Culture. *Minutes*. 1980–83.

Canada. Parliament. House of Commons. Standing Committee on Communications and Culture. *A broadcasting policy for Canada*. 1988a.

Canada. Parliament. House of Commons. Standing Committee on Communications and Culture. *Sixth Report* (recommendation 65). 1988b.

Canada. Parliament. House of Commons. Unpassed Bills. Broadcasting Act, Bill C-136, first reading, June 23, 1988a.

Canada. Parliament. House of Commons. Unpassed Bills. Broadcasting Act, Bill C-136, third reading, September 28, 1988b.

Canada. Parliament. *Statutes*. Broadcasting Act. 1968. Ottawa.

Canada. Royal Commission on Broadcasting (Fowler Commission). (1957). *Report*. Ottawa.

Canada. Royal Commission on National Development in the Arts, Letters and Sciences (Massey Commission). (1951). *Report*. Ottawa.

Canada. Royal Commission on Radio Broadcasting (Aird Commission). (1929). *Report*. Ottawa.

Canada. Task Force on Broadcasting Policy (Caplan-Sauvageau Task Force). (1986). *Report*.

Canada. Task Force on Program Review. (1986). *An introduction to the process of program review*.

Canada/Quebec. (1985a). Federal-Provincial Committee. *The future of French-language television*. Ottawa and Quebec.

Canada/Quebec. (1985b). *Canada-Quebec subsidiary agreement on communications enterprises development 1984–1990*. Ottawa and Quebec.

Canada/Quebec. (1986). Canada-Quebec memorandum of understanding on the development of the French-language television system. Ottawa and Quebec.

Canadian Broadcasting Corporation. (1964). *Submission to the Royal Commission on Bilingualism and Biculturalism*. Ottawa.

Canadian Broadcasting Corporation. (1979). *The CBC—A perspective*. Ottawa.

Canadian Radio-television and Telecommunications Commission. (1977). Committee of Inquiry into the National Broadcasting Service. *Report*. Ottawa.

Canadian Radio-television and Telecommunications Commission. (1987). *More Canadian programming choices*. Ottawa.

Caplan, G. (1990, December 8). CBC cutbacks tear another hole in fabric of national unity. *Montreal Gazette*.

Caplan-Sauvageau Task Force. See Canada. Task Force on Broadcasting Policy. (1986).

Descoteaux, B. (1984, December 20). Marcel Masse: Radio-Canada prend trop de place dans le budget culturel. *Le Devoir*.

Fowler Commission. See Canada. Royal Commission on Broadcasting. (1957).

Johnson, A.W. (1983, March). The Re-Canadianization of broadcasting. *Policy Options, 4*.

Johnson, D. (1968, February 5–7). *Ce que veut le Quebec*. Brief submitted by Daniel Johnson to the Constitutional Conference, first meeting. Ottawa.

Lamarche, Gérard. (1960, Summer). Radio-Canada et sa mission française. *Canadian Communication, 1*.

Laurendeau, André. (1962). *La crise de la conscription*. Montreal: Éditions du Jour.

Massey Commission. See Canada. Royal Commission on National Development in the Arts, Letters and Sciences. (1951).

Pelletier, Gérard. (1983). *Les années d'impatience (1950–1960)*. Montreal: Stanké.

Quebec. Legislative Assembly. (1963). *Journal des débats*.

Quebec. Ministère des communications du Québec. (1971). *Pour une politique québécoise des communications*. Quebec.

Quebec. Ministère des communications du Québec. (1973). *Le Québec, Maître d'oeuvre de la politique des communications sur son territoire.* Quebec.

Quebec. Ministère des communications du Québec. (1982). *Bâtir l'avenir.* Quebec.

Quebec. Ministère des communications du Québec. (1983). *Le Québec et les communications: Un futur simple?* Quebec.

Quebec. National Assembly. (1977). *Journal des débats.*

Quebec. National Assembly. (1981). *Journal des débats.*

Quebec. Statutes. (1945). Loi autorisant la création d'un service de radio-diffusion provinciale.

Raboy, M. (1989). Two steps forward, three steps back: Canadian broadcasting policy from Caplan-Sauvageau to Bill C-136. *Canadian Journal of Communications, 14.*

Raboy, M. (1990). *Missed opportunities: The story of Canada's broadcasting policy.* Montreal and Kingston: McGill-Queen's University Press.

Rémillard, G. (1980). *Le fédéralisme Canadien: Eléments constitutionnels de formation et d'évolution.* Montreal: Québec-Amérique.

Stark, F. (1983). Persuasion, propaganda, and public policy. Paper to the fourth annual conference of the Canadian Communication Association, Vancouver.

Supreme Court of Canada. (1978). *Supreme Court Reports, Volume 2.* Ottawa.

Tremblay, G. (1988, Summer). La politique québécquoise en matière de communication (1966–1986): de l'affirmation autonomiste à la coopération fédérale-provinciale. *Communication information, 9.*

Weir, A.E. (1965). *The struggle for national broadcasting in Canada.* Toronto: McClelland and Stewart.

Winsor, H. (1990, December 6). Drops in funds cited in CBC cuts. *Globe and Mail.*

DEFENDING THE CULTURAL FRONTIER: CANADIAN TELEVISION AND CONTINENTAL INTEGRATION[1]

David Taras

In 1932, Graham Spry argued that Canadians faced harsh choices in broadcasting: "It is a choice between commercial interests and the people's interests. It is a choice between the State and the United States" (Raboy, 1990, p. 40). Spry's judgement has been echoed by virtually every government-sponsored commission on broadcasting from Sir John Aird's royal commission of 1929 through to the Task Force on Broadcasting Policy that reported in 1986. In each and every case, there was a strong insistence that a vigorous public broadcasting system was an essential bulwark against the onslaught of American cultural values, the only guarantee that Canada's cultural integrity could be preserved. In these documents, public broadcasting is viewed as one of the country's great nation-building projects on a scale comparable to the National Policy of 1879 or the establishment by Ottawa of a web of social programs in the 1950s and 1960s. The building of the communications grid that linked the country together through broadcasting signals, satellites, and electronic messages was an act of exceptional will constructed in resistance to powerful continental forces. The publicly financed Canadian Broadcasting Corporation (CBC), created in 1936, was seen as the "spinal column" that linked culture and the state; the CBC sensory system reached across the country's vast expanses creating common bonds and experiences (CBC, 1985, p. 19).

Marc Raboy, one of Canada's leading communications scholars, contends that during the 1980s Canadian governments and regulators largely abandoned the public interest in broadcasting in favour of pursuing economic goals (Applebaum-Hébert Committee, 1982). The licensing of additional private networks, a host of independent stations, and new service channels, as well as a pay-TV option and the permitting of the widespread use of satellite receiving dishes, has been with an eye to improving the lot of commercial stakeholders. At the same time, the CBC has been ravaged by severe budget cuts that have jeopardized its ability to fulfil its basic mandate. To Raboy, the wounds were self-inflicted. If Canadians are inundated by American television to a far greater degree than ever before, and see little of their own reflection on TV, then it is Ottawa's narrow conception of the public interest that is to blame. Governments lost interest in dealing with the agonizing problem of how to reflect a disparate country to itself.

Part of the problem lies in a lack of consensus among elites about the nature of Canada itself. The incoherence of Canadian broadcasting mirrors the general confusion over Canadian identity. In a *Devoir* editorial written in response to the report of the Massey Commission of 1951, André Laurendeau, one of the champions of Quebec nationalism during his day, criticized the "cultural crusade" that was about to be undertaken:

> What dike can be built to defend against this irresistible tidal wave? Only that of a Canadian national culture—that is to say, a myth, a phantom, the shadow of a shadow. There is not one Canadian national culture. There are two: one English and one French (Raboy, 1990, p. 110).

There is also more than a single cultural rhythm in English-speaking Canada. For instance, British Columbia, which faces the Pacific and is increasingly tied to Asia, has a different outlook and sensibility and different interests than Ontario, which is wedged in the centre of the continent and from which British Columbia is separated by thousands of miles.

Northrop Frye believes that true culture has a "vegetable" quality because it can flourish only in "a small region and a restricted locale" (Frye, 1982, p. 62). Artists are nurtured by their unique experiences and surroundings. He argues that it is erroneous to suggest that there are pan-Canadian writers; there are prairie writers, west coast writers, Montreal writers, etc. The playwright Michel Tremblay once described his attitude toward the environment that inspired and sustained him: "I write for myself and for Montreal."

One of the characteristics of Canadian television is that its structure of national networks and centralized production does not allow for the adequate reflection of local cultures. These cultures see neither their own reflection nor an accurate reflection of the country as a whole. The great exception is Quebec, where the CBC's French-language arm, Radio-Canada, has been a key catalyst in the emergence of a vibrant Quebec culture. On television as in so much of Canadian life, however, Quebec speaks only to itself.

A.W. Johnson, a former president of the CBC, has described the difficulty of trying to reach across the cultural divides of English and French:

> We produced some of Michel Tremblay's plays in English; *La Belle Soeur* was the first one. The audiences turned us off in droves. All the predictions of the thoughtful broadcasters were true. All the predictions of the thoughtful political scientists were true. The appetite in English Canada for learning about a totally different culture within the bosom of their own country was small. I came away from the experience chastened, not a pessimist but more realistic than I came in. You have to create an appetite for knowing about one another over a period of time and probably it is going to occur first in the area of popular culture; French-Canadian singers,

> comedians, hockey games, and symbolic things such as covering the
> Olympics. The symbols are so important.[2]

Unfortunately, it is precisely in the area of popular culture that Canadian television is weakest and American television the most appealing. The careful nurturing of cultural appetites, of a common cultural landscape, is all but impossible when broadcasting has become as much a vehicle for the transmission of American culture as it has for Canadian culture. American dominance is now so great that Canadians have become not only "strangers in television's land of the imagination" but strangers to themselves.

This article will examine the pressures and conditions that have led to the Americanization of Canada's airwaves. A society's information network, its ability to communicate within its own cultural boundaries is, as Karl Deutsch has pointed out, the "foundations of nationality." As Deutsch has put it, "The community which permits a common history to be experienced as common, is a community of complementary habits and facilities of communication. It requires, so to speak, equipment for a job. This job consists in the storage, recall, transmission, recombination, and reapplication of relatively wide ranges of information . . ." (Deutsch, 1953, p. 96). Yet there is now a diminished cultural space available to Canadians on television. Basic information about significant Canadian issues, ideas, and events may no longer be reaching important segments of the Canadian public; a vital connection in maintaining a distinct national identity may be in the process of being severed.

According to a British scholar, Richard Collins, the term "Canadianization" is used in Europe to describe the power of new information technologies to "damage polity and culture, destabilizing one and debasing the other" (Collins, 1990, p. ix). With the advent of satellites and cable, videos and VCRS, the cultural frontier is almost impossible to defend. These new technologies are, to paraphrase Collins, "the Trojan horses of continentalism" (Collins, 1990, p. 121).

DEFENCES ALONG THE TELEVISION FRONTIER

Although it is difficult to determine the exact nature of television's influence on the cultural preferences of Canadians, there is evidence to suggest that television has become an "imposing authority" (Iyengar & Kinder, 1987, p. 133). Television may not have the capacity to shape opinions directly but it can tell viewers what is and is not important; it can set the public agenda. It has the power to reorder priorities and legitimize people and institutions. It establishes frameworks for seeing the world around us. As the American media scholar Todd Gitlin has written about the power of the media, "They name the world's parts, they certify reality as reality" (Gitlin, 1980, p. 2).

Television has certainly played a critical role in the formation of Canadian cultural identity. Canadians watch an average of three and a half hours of television per day; roughly nine years out of an average lifetime are spent watching TV. Watching television consumes over half of all leisure time (Starowicz, 1985). The television set has become the centre of the home. For many people, the TV is a companion from early in the morning to late at night. The Task Force Report on Broadcasting Policy released in

1986 claimed that "the CBC is not only the major instrument of Canadian culture, but also of culture in Canada" (Caplan-Sauvageau Task Force, 1986, p. 683). A single television program can be viewed by more people in a single evening than will watch the top grossing Canadian films during an entire year. One episode of a major series can draw a larger audience on a single night than the number of people who will attend all of Canadian theatre annually (Caplan-Sauvageau Task Force, 1986, p. 683). The report of the Fowler Committee on Broadcasting issued in 1965 recognized television's role as a creator and mirror of cultural identity. It proclaimed a bold vision:

> When we declare that broadcasting should be a major instrument for the development of a distinctive Canadian culture, we use that most abused word "culture" in its broadest and original meaning. It is the reflection of life itself, in all its variety—its beauty and ugliness; its significant artistic achievements and its unimportant daily occurrences; its big people and its little people; its important and often inscrutable messages, and its light insignificant interests; its great opinions and its amusing anecdotes; tragedy and comedy, laughter and tears, criticism, irony, satire, and sheer fun and amusement—are all essential.

> To reflect a nation's culture—and to help create it—a broadcasting system must not minister solely to the comfort of the people. Its guiding principle cannot be to give the people what they want. . . . One of the essential tasks of a broadcasting system is to stir up the minds and emotions of the people, and occasionally to make large numbers of them acutely uncomfortable. (Fowler Committee, 1965, p. 4).

In its finest moments, Canadian television has lived up to this ideal.

It can be argued that Canadians play only a minor role and have been reduced to "bit players" within their own television system. The 1986 Task Force Report on Broadcasting Policy revealed that out of roughly 52 000 hours of English-language programming received by Canadian audiences each year, only 370 hours were Canadian drama (Caplan-Sauvageau Task Force, 1986, p. 691). Approximately 90 percent of all dramatic presentations on French-language TV were foreign, mostly American. During the 1989–90 season, the CBC had but seven hours of Canadian drama in prime time each week compared to three hours and two hours respectively for the privately owned CTV and Global networks (Cuff, May 1990). The avalanche of American programming is now so great that Canadian children spend more time watching American television than they will spend in a Canadian school (Starowicz, 1985).

The American domination of Canada's airwaves has occurred in spite of the fact that the Canadian government through its regulatory arm, the Canadian Radio-television and Telecommunications Commission (CRTC), has instituted measures to insure a significant degree of Canadian programming. The CBC and its French-language component, Radio-Canada, the four private networks, and the dozen or so independent stations are obligated to have 60 percent Canadian-content programming throughout their broadcast day. Privately owned networks are allowed as a general rule to reduce their Canadian-content obligations to 50 percent during prime time, which is defined as six p.m. to midnight. The Much Music channel, which shows rock videos, and The Sports Network, which are Canadian-owned specialty services available through basic cable subscriptions, provide 10 and 18 percent Canadian-content programming respectively (Raboy, 1990, p. 319). A program is considered Canadian if its producer is a Canadian citizen and it can score at least six out of ten points based on the number of Canadians employed in key creative positions. If a show airs during prime time and achieves ten out of ten in the scoring system, then the network that buys the program can claim a bonus of 150 percent in "Can-con" time credits.

In hearings on the licence-renewal applications of 75 TV stations in 1989, the CRTC made increased expenditures on Canadian productions a condition of licence renewal. Under the get-tough policy, stations were pressed to commit roughly $2 billion on Canadian productions during the 1989–94 period.

Canadian programs, however, tend to be confined to a "ghetto" within network schedules. Indeed, program schedules can be compared to a sandwich; Canadian shows are the bread but American shows are the meat. The bread consists of the supper-hour newscasts that are shown at between six and seven o'clock and the news and the current affairs programs telecast at the end of the evening. The heart of prime time, the seven-to-ten time slots, belongs to American programming. American shows are the main "breadwinners" for the commercial networks; they pull the largest audiences and bring in the lion's share of advertising revenue. Profits largely depend on buying the right American shows, betting which new series will emerge as the season's hits.

To make matters worse, Canadian TV schedules are constrained if not almost entirely dictated by American schedules. Under a practice known as "simultaneous substitution," Canadian cable operators replace American commercials with Canadian commercials when the same show appears at the same time on both Canadian and American channels. According to the 1991 Task Force Report on the Economic Status of Canadian Television, simultaneous substitution during simulcasting was worth almost $100 million to the industry in 1990 alone (Task Force, The Economic Status of Canadian Television, 1991, p. 81). In order to give this extra boost to Canadian advertisers, stations tend to match the American schedules, making sure that programs air at the same time in both countries.

THE FORCES OF CHANGE

Although Canadians have long been under the sway of American popular culture— what historian Paul Rutherford calls "the culture of bubble gum and baseball and Hollywood"—the pace of envelopment seems to have accelerated because of the power of television (Rutherford, 1990, p. 13). Structural changes that have taken place in broadcasting in the last ten to fifteen years have enhanced the influence of American television in Canada. New economies of scale in television production, the changing circumstances of the CBC, and the advent of technologies such as satellite, cable, and video have all contributed to an enlarged American presence and a diminished Canadian presence on television.

The economies of scale enjoyed by the U.S. television industry has given it enormous advantages over its Canadian competitors. Costs are absorbed within the large U.S. domestic market so that shows can be sold abroad at prices that undercut those of foreign television productions. Discount prices make buying American shows almost irresistible (Hoskins, Mirus, & Rozeboom, 1989). The cold economic reality is that it costs far less to purchase an American series "off the shelf" than to produce an equivalent Canadian series. Canadian networks can buy a U.S. show for $50 000 to $75 000—5 to 6 percent of the cost of production per episode. The cost per episode of producing a popular American dramatic series is between $1 million and $1.5 million. These series are loaded with what those in the industry call "production value": highly paid actors and creative personnel, elaborate sets and wardrobes, and the most expensive film and sound quality. The saying in Hollywood is that "all the money is on the screen" (Miller, 1990, p. 46). According to Mark Crispin Miller, the large production companies have an interest in paying exorbitant salaries and in inflating the costs of production. The object is to drive the less wealthy competitors out of the market (Miller, 1990, p. 8). The recession of the early 1990s, however, has forced the U.S. networks and production houses to cut costs and produce less expensive shows.

Canadian producers are, of course, hard pressed to compete against Hollywood's production juggernaut. What makes Canadians competitive at all is the existence of the Broadcast Development Fund operated by the federal government through Telefilm Canada. The fund acts as a "pump-priming" mechanism whereby Ottawa matches the money raised for projects by producers; in some circumstances, the Fund can provide up to 70 percent of the budget for French-language productions and 49 percent for English productions. Financial assistance for TV programs is in the form of equity participation. Without this fund, commercial successes such as "Danger Bay," "Lance et Compte," "Les Filles de Caleb," "E.N.G.," "Street Legal," or "Road To Avonlea" would have been impossible. Even with the Fund, Canadian producers must sell their programs abroad to make money as only about 30 percent of their costs can be recouped in the Canadian market.

The CBC, which depends on an annual grant from Parliament for roughly 80 percent of its budget, has particular difficulty competing against glitzy high-voltage American entertainment shows. With the federal government engulfed in debt, the CBC's budget will have been cut, according to projections in the 1990 federal budget, by an estimated one-third during the period from 1984 to 1994. It is doubtful whether the CBC will be able to fulfil even its basic mandate in the 1990s, let alone launch a new generation of mass-market entertainment programming that can compete with Hollywood.

The CBC's mandate is to provide a balanced service, one that can appeal to a variety of audiences and tastes. It must be all things to all people. Indeed, clause I(1) of section 3 of the Broadcasting Act of 1991 instructs the CBC to produce programming that is "varied and comprehensive, providing a balance of information, enlightenment and entertainment for men, women and children of all ages, interests and tastes" (The House of Commons, 1990, p. 4). The CBC has explained its mandate to provide balanced programming this way: "The CBC has varied audiences with varied interests requiring varied television genres. While drama is one element of the service the CBC must provide, so too are magazine programs, talk shows, variety and quiz programs, fine arts programs, conservative programs, bolder programs, big-budget as well as low-budget programs, informative, entertaining, educational programs, some for the young, some for the old, etc. It is in this diversity that the Corporation provides a homogeneous whole that, taken overall, reflects its absolute uniqueness as a public broadcaster" (Task Force, The Economic Status of Canadian Television, 1991, p. 128). So unlike its competitors, who aim their programs at audiences that are the most desired by advertisers (up-scale viewers with disposable income), the CBC must offer a full menu of choices: cultural events, children's programming, serious current affairs documentaries, in-depth coverage of important state occasions and national events, as well as dramatic programs designed to appeal to a mass audience. Even its dramatic programs have a different texture. Although the CBC presents its share of fantasy, schlock, and thrills, its view of life is less sugar-coated than that of the American networks. According to critics, dramatic programs have tended to have a slower pace, greater character development, more realism, and less violence than do their Hollywood counterparts (Wolfe, 1985). The enormously popular "Anne of Green Gables" is typical of the tone and pace of CBC drama. News and current affairs programs tend to be sombre and emotionally demanding with few whimsical moments or light touches.

The CBC has become, as a consequence of its mandate, an invaluable cultural resource but its mandate also prevents it from being as profitable as its rivals. It is caught in a tension between its obligations to serve a series of minority audiences and its need to capture a mass audience. A survey conducted for the CRTC in November 1990 revealed widespread dissatisfaction with the CBC. Canadians rated all other networks and services as more appealing than the CBC with PBS, the U.S. public broadcaster, favoured over the CBC by a three-to-one margin (CBC queries, 1991).

The CBC has also had to shoulder the weight of serving such a vast country, one that spans a quarter of the world's time zones. The Corporation maintains production facilities in all major centres and reaches areas of sparse population that are too uneconomical to be of interest to the private networks. In order to achieve the political goal of making minority language populations at home everywhere in the country, it operates an English-language TV station in Quebec City and French-language stations in Western Canada. The northern service links remote communities across the great expanse of the Arctic and sub-Arctic regions, broadcasting in at least a dozen Native languages. In addition, the CBC must co-ordinate a constellation of different networks, channels, and services. It operates English- and French-language TV networks, four radio networks—mono and stereo—in both languages, a twenty-four-hour all-news channel on television, a channel to televise the proceedings of the House of Commons, and Radio Canada International.

It is not only the CBC, however, that is reeling under a financial strain. Private networks and ownership groups are also facing considerable financial difficulty. The recession of the early 1990s and increased competition for scarcer advertising dollars has deeply shaken the industry. Moreover, as networks and ownership groups have had to compete against each other to buy the hot American shows, the prices for these programs have soared. The Canadian Association of Broadcasters has estimated that as a result of bidding wars, the average annual cost of foreign programs rose by 21.9

percent between 1988 and 1989. The cost of buying the popular sitcom "Cheers" shot up by 40 percent in a single year (Task Force, The Economic Status of Canadian Television, 1991, pp. 37–39). Yet the lure of American programs remains undiminished. American shows have increased in profitability to the extent that for each hour of Canadian entertainment that is produced by CTV, it claims it loses $5 million in profits (Task Force, The Economic Status of Canadian Television, 1991, p. 39).

The advent of new technologies has also played a role in diminishing the Canadian identity on television. Satellite, cable, and video cassette recorders have transformed the television landscape, allowing viewers to exercise a measure of sovereignty and to gain some control from the networks. Viewers now have a vastly increased number of choices available to them and are liberated from network programming schedules. But at the same time, the audience has been splintered and fractured into narrow segments, fuelling an intense competition among the networks for ever-smaller segments of viewers. Canadian television networks face "the brutality of the glutted marketplace" (Raboy, 1990, p. 250).

During the 1960s, Canadian viewers were able to watch only the CBC, CTV, and the three American networks. Canadian television was thus assured of a sizable viewership. By 1990, Canadian viewers had access to as many as 40 channels, depending on where they were in the country and how much they were willing to spend for cable and pay-TV services. Next to Belgium, Canada is the world's most cabled country with 76 percent of available households subscribing (McPhail & McPhail, 1990, p. 189). Cable operators predict a "100-channel universe" by the year 2000, and some cable systems in the United States already carry more than 100 channels. Canadians who own satellite receiving dishes, of which there are more than 250 000 in the country, can draw as many as 115 channels, including signals from as far away as Mexico and the Caribbean. A host of direct broadcast satellite services (DBS) will come on stream in the early 1990s. The SkyPix satellite package offering as many as 70 pay-per-view channels will be launched in 1991, and Rupert Murdoch's 108-channel Sky Cable will have the capacity to reach most Canadian centres by 1993. More powerful satellites and smaller, less costly receiving dishes could allow DBS to challenge and perhaps overrun cable by the turn of the century. DBS services have been called the "death stars" because of the threat that they pose to Canadian television.

Because of these developments, the concept of the audience has changed. The economics of television now revolve around "narrow-casting," that is, capturing a specialized audience that has a desirable demographic profile—the affluent sports fan, the hard-pressed business executive who wants business news, or aficionados of films or culture—to attract advertisers who wish to target a particular market niche. Profits are made by offering viewers "boutique" rather than "department store" television.

To make matters more complex, studies in the United States have found that more than half of those under 34 years of age routinely watch at least two programs at the same time, flicking back and forth during lulls in the action (Stackhouse, 1990). The problem, as Peter Herndorf once put it, is that with so much competition, the CBC might go from being a national voice to a "national whisper" (Vipond, 1989, p. 150).

Video cassette recorders, which can be found in over 70 percent of Canadian homes, have also restructured television viewing (Einsiedel & Green, 1988). They have given audiences the capacity to free themselves from television schedules and from the commercials that are the bread and butter of the television system. Once having recorded a program, viewers can "zap" commercials entirely or "zip" through them quickly. In practice, however, video cassette recorders have become movie machines. Movies are either rented from video stores, borrowed from libraries, or recorded from television. Almost invariably, the movies that are watched are American. The video revolution is controlled by a tight web of foreign producers and distributors and has helped to marginalize Canadian films within the Canadian domestic market.

THE DIMINISHED WORLD OF CANADIAN TELEVISION

The great difficulty for Canadian television is that these new technologies are overwhelming national boundaries. Although it can be argued that these technologies, and particularly satellite, have the capacity to foster a more powerful domestic communications system, in the Canadian case the linkages seem to have been weakened. First, attempts to regulate the Canadian media are almost meaningless in the face of so much foreign programming. Ottawa has virtually no control over most of the programming and advertising to which Canadians are exposed. The problem has been made worse by the sweeping deregulation that took place in the United States in the 1980s. As Keith Spicer, chairman of the CRTC, has described the dilemma facing Canadian regulators, "The CRTC could become a little bit like King Canute holding back the waves. The Berlin Wall has fallen. . . . We cannot erect a new electronic Berlin Wall" (Geddes, 1990).

Second, the flood of American images and messages is now so great that it might be preventing basic information about Canadian developments from reaching large numbers of Canadians. There is simply too much competition, too many voices, too much media clutter for some smothering of Canadian messages not to be occurring. After almost two years of intensive media coverage, and a clamorous debate among the country's political and business leaders, public opinion polls revealed that a majority of Canadians knew little about the Free Trade Agreement that Canada had negotiated with the United States. Similarly, most Canadians were unfamiliar with the contents of the Meech Lake Constitutional Accord despite the saturation coverage by the national media that took place in spring 1990 (*Globe and Mail*, 1990). A survey taken in Alberta in December 1990 found that a substantial majority of those polled had not heard of the two commissions charged with identifying new constitutional options for Canada and Quebec, the Spicer Commission and the Bélanger-Campeau Commission. Both commissions had received extensive news coverage (Geddes, 1991). There is now an astonishing level of illiteracy on almost all public policy issues despite or perhaps because of the fact that Canadians are watching more television than ever before.

Brian Stewart contends that of all the new developments that have taken place, it is pay-TV that poses the greatest threat to the CBC (1983, pp. 17–40). Canadian cable operators offer pay-TV packages that consist almost entirely of American specialty channels: news, arts and entertainment, films, children's programming, rock videos, etc. The CBC's clientele is drawn from the same group of older, more affluent, and better educated viewers that are the most likely to subscribe to pay-TV. Pay-TV cuts directly into the CBC's core constituency. The advent of pay-per-view services will only exacerbate the problem. Having all but lost the battle for the mass entertainment audience, the CBC is facing competition for its audience for current affairs and cultural programming. During the Persian Gulf War, for instance, many Canadians chose to get their news from CNN rather than from "The National" or Newsworld.

The widening spectrum of choices and the splintering of the audience has also brought fundamental changes to television production. As the battle for audiences and hence advertisers has intensified—the goal being to grab and hold viewers so that they don't click to another channel—producers have developed production techniques based on bombarding the audience with jolts. Jolts are rapid bursts of activity that are designed to keep audiences riveted. Violence, insults, gags, sexual encounters, or aggressive suspenseful actions are part of a continual barrage of jolts. Morris Wolfe describes the logic that lies behind the jolts-per-minute technique: "[I]f a long time goes by without a jolt of verbal or physical or emotional violence on the screen, or if the picture doesn't change quickly enough as a result of a jolt of rapid editing or camera movement, or movement by people or objects within the frame, or if the soundtrack doesn't have enough decibels, viewers will switch to a channel or a program that gives them more of those things" (Wolfe, 1985, p. 13). Jolts production methods infuse virtually every aspect of American television. In situation comedies, jokes are told in rapid-fire succession. In soap operas, sexual behaviours occur at a frenetic pace; one study counted an average of 20.7 sexual encounters per hour during the 1987 season of "Days Of Our Lives" (Lowry & Towles, 1989). News stories are shorter, punchier, and more dramatic than they were fifteen or twenty years ago (Adatto, 1990). Commercials that were a minute long in the 1970s are now only fifteen seconds. There is even talk about moving to a seven-second commercial.

The long-term effects on viewers of being constantly bombarded by television jolts has yet to be conclusively determined. Some scholars believe that a severe distorting effect occurs when information is presented in "bite-sized" pieces, as is the case in television newscasts. The public actually receives little useful information. Patterson and McClure found in their study that "since the nightly news is too brief to treat fully the complexity of modern politics, too visual to present effectively most events, and too entertainment-minded to tell viewers much worth knowing, most network newscasts are neither very educational nor very powerful communicators" (Patterson & McClure, 1976, p. 90). Another school of opinion argues that television is essentially a passive medium. The constant barrage of visual sensations tranquillizes viewers, making them less reactive, less caring, less arousable. Absorbing so many shocks renders the viewer inactive. A third perspective is that our nervous systems are being hyperstimulated by the incessant stream of jolts to which we are exposed. As a result, our attention spans, our ability to relax and even to cope are being severely strained. Hyperactivity on TV contributes to an increased impatience with the pace of everyday life.

The particular effect of jolts production methods on Canadian television is difficult to determine. Canadian producers have had to adapt to market conditions dictated by audiences that have become conditioned to jolts. Not only do Canadian productions have to compete for Canadian viewers against high-voltage U.S. programs but they must sell in the U.S. market in order to be profitable. The problem, according to

Richard Collins, was that Canadian shows frequently suffered from a "cultural discount"; they had too much Canadian content to be attractive to international audiences. The cultural elites' insistence that television reflect Canadian values and preoccupations proved to be an economic handicap, preventing the penetration of the American market by Canadian shows that is the precondition for the emergence of a more economically viable domestic television industry (Collins, 1990, pp. 248–49).

There is evidence, however, that Canadian programming has taken a sharp turn toward the American model. According to television critic John Haslett Cuff, "Shows such as 'Danger Bay,' 'My Secret Identity,' 'Night Heat,' 'E.N.G.,' 'Neon Rider,' 'Street Legal' are arguably American in everything but cast, crew, and locale. It's significant that the success of the 'officially Canadian' television shows is measured by each product's ability to mimic the cosmetic look, facile emotions, easy violence, and hyper-thyroid syncopation of the American shows" (Cuff, October, 1990). While Cuff may be exaggerating, the danger of an increasingly American look is there. A recent ad for the CBC's hit series "Street Legal" announced, "The Heat is on The Street" and showed a couple locked in a steamy embrace. The ad might well be seen as a metaphor for what may happen to Canadian television if it embraces the Hollywood model.

TELEVISION AND THE CANADIAN STATE

Richard Collins has argued that the separation of state from culture that has occurred in Canada is a natural, even an advanced, development. The old idea of the nation-state does not apply to Canada because "Canada is better understood as a pre-echo of a post-national condition," a new kind of political formation (Collins, 1990, pp. 248–49). There can be little congruency between economic, political, and cultural domains in a world where global economics, political egalitarianism, and cultural diversity have become the dominant realities. Rather than seeing Canada as battered, weak, and emasculated because of the relentless assault of American television, Collins views "Canadianization" as inevitable, a development that is about to sweep through Europe and will even affect the United States. Indeed, one might suggest that a "decoupling" of state and culture is now well underway in the United States; Sony has acquired Columbia Pictures; Matsushita has bought MCA/Universal; Thomson of Canada is the second-largest owner of newspapers; Pathé, an Italian corporation, owns MGM; the German giant Bertelsmann controls RCA records and Doubleday books; and a British firm, Saatchi and Saatchi, is the largest player on Madison Avenue. Ironically, the same economic forces that allowed the United States to produce a global mass entertainment culture may now be threatening genuine American culture.

Collins's assumption that a state does not have to be sustained by a national culture seems to fly in the face of some of the painful realities of the Canadian situation, for example, the degree to which Canadian identity has been eroded by the flood of American images and values. It's not just that state and culture are becoming uncoupled. It's that in Canada both state and culture are now jeopardized.

According to John Meisel, one of Canada's foremost scholars and a former chairman of the CRTC, "Inside every Canadian, whether she or he knows it or not, there is, in fact, an American. The magnitude and effect of this American presence in us varies considerably from person to person but it is ubiquitous and inescapable" (Meisel, 1986, p. 152). Meisel argues that there is a mass/elite dichotomy. Those who are better educated and enjoy a higher standard of living tend to be more knowledgeable about and receptive to Canadian culture. Canadian culture has a high-brow quality that appeals only to a minority. As a consequence, "the more low-brow an American cultural activity, the wider its appeal in Canada" (Meisel, 1986, p. 156). It can be argued that American music and sports, fashions and lifestyles, celebrities and slang have been woven into the Canadian cultural fabric and prevent the emergence of widely accepted Canadian alternatives. A recent survey of Ontario university students found that they admired George Washington, the first U.S. president, by a margin of three to one over Canada's first prime minister, John A. Macdonald. They preferred the American political system to the Canadian and some 74 percent thought that Canada would join the United States in their lifetimes (Finlay, 1988).

The level of ignorance about Canada's history and institutions should be a cause of great concern. A survey conducted for the Bronfman Foundation in 1991 found that fewer than six out of ten Canadians knew the name of Canada's first prime minister or the date of Confederation. More than half couldn't name a Canadian artist and 30 percent couldn't name a Canadian writer. Only 41 percent could identify the Leader of the Opposition, Jean Chrétien (Canada's first, 1991).

The inability of Canadian television to reflect English- and French-speaking Canadians to each other or to cultivate the "vegetable gardens" of local and regional cultures may have damaged Canada's prospects for survival. To create a television system that could accomplish these tasks would have taken extraordinary acts of will and imagination and a sizable commitment of resources. Instead, recent Canadian governments have chosen to see broadcasting as an economic tool rather than an instrument for nation building. As a consequence, cultural fences are almost impossible to maintain. The problem for Canada is that, to paraphrase the American poet Robert Frost, "Good neighbours require good fences."

NOTES

1. Parts of this article are taken from a paper first presented at a conference, Small National Cultures versus the United States, sponsored by the Netherlands Association of American Studies, Middleburg, The Netherlands, June 1990. Another version was presented at a conference, The Nation State versus Continental Integration: Europe and North America Compared, held at the University of Augsburg, Germany, December 1990.

2. Taken from David Taras's interview with A.W. Johnson in Ottawa, August 21, 1990.

REFERENCES

Adatto, K. (1990, May 28). The incredible shrinking sound bite. *The New Republic,* pp. 20–23.

Applebaum-Hébert Committee. See Canada. Federal Cultural Policy Review Committee (1982).

Canada. Committee on Broadcasting (Fowler Committee). (1965). *Report.* Ottawa.

Canada. Federal Cultural Policy Review Committee (Applebaum-Hébert Committee). (1982). *Report.* Ottawa.

Canada. Parliament. *Statutes*. Broadcasting Act. 1991.

Canada. Task Force on Broadcasting Policy (Caplan-Sauvageau Task Force). (1986). *Report*. Ottawa.

Canada. Task Force, The Economic Status of Canadian Television. (1991). *Report*. Ottawa.

Canada's first PM? Sir John A. Who. (1991, April 1). *Calgary Herald*, p. A1.

Canadian Broadcasting Corporation (1985, December). *Let's do it. Report*. Ottawa.

Caplan-Sauvageau Task Force. See Canada. Task Force on Broadcasting Policy. (1986).

CBC queries results of survey. (1991, February 20). *Globe and Mail*, p. A11.

Collins, R. (1990). *Culture, communication and national identity*. Toronto: University of Toronto Press.

Cuff, J.H. (1990, May 19). Cancon could use a rewrite, but it has kept the Yanks at bay. *Globe and Mail*, p. C3.

Cuff, J.H. (1990, October 11). Taking it to the sheets. *Globe and Mail*, p. A9.

Deutsch, K. (1953). *Nationalism and social communication*. Cambridge, Massachusetts: MIT Press.

Einsiedel, E., & Green, S. (1988, Spring). VCRs in Canada: Usage patterns and policy implications. *Canadian Journal of Communications*.

Finlay, R.J. (1988, July 14). Uneasy on the campus. *Globe and Mail*, p. A7.

Frye, N. (1982). *Divisions on a ground*. Toronto: Anansi.

Geddes, A. (1990, September 8). Spicer predicts end of Canadian quotas. *Calgary Herald*, p. E2.

Geddes, A. (1991, February 22). Albertans give unity a shrug and a ho hum. *Calgary Herald*, p. A1.

Gitlin, T. (1980). *The whole world is watching*. Berkeley: University of California Press.

Gitlin, T. (1990). Down the tubes. In *Seeing Through Movies* (Ed., Miller, M.C.). New York: Pantheon.

Hoskins, C., Mirus R,. & Rozeboom, W. (1989, Spring). U.S. television programs in the international market: Unfair pricing? *Journal of Communication*, 55–75.

Iyengar, S., & Kinder, D. (1987). *News that matters: Television and American opinion*. Chicago: University of Chicago Press.

Lowry, D., & Towles, D. (1989, Spring). Soap opera's portrayals of sex, contraception, and sexually transmitted diseases. *Journal of Communication*, 76–83.

McPhail, T., & McPhail, B. (1990). *Communication: The Canadian experience*. Toronto: Copp Clark Pitman.

Meisel, J. (1986). Escaping extinction: Cultural defence of an undefended border. In *Southern Exposure: Canadian Perspectives on the United States* (Ed., Flaherty, D., & McKercher, W.). Toronto: McGraw-Hill Ryerson.

Miller, M.C. (1990). The big picture. In *Seeing Through Movies*. (Ed., Miller, M.C.). New York: Pantheon.

Patterson, T., & McClure, R. (1976). *The unseeing eye: The myth of television power in national elections.* New York: Putnam.

Raboy, M. (1990). *Missed opportunities: The story of Canada's broadcasting policy.* Montreal: McGill-Queen's University Press.

Rutherford, P. (1990). *When television was young: Primetime Canada 1952–1967.* Toronto: University of Toronto Press.

Stackhouse, J. (1990, May). Izzyvision. *Report on Business Magazine,* p.8.

Starowicz, M. (1985). *Open skies: The struggle for Canada's airwaves.* The Atkinson Lecture at Ryerson Polytechnical Institute.

Stewart, B.W. (1983). Canadian social system and Canadian broadcasting audiences. In *Communications in Canadian Society* (Ed., Singer, B.). Toronto: Addison-Wesley.

The Globe and Mail–CBC News Poll. (1990, July 9). *Globe and Mail,* p. A4.

Vipond, M. (1989). *The mass media in Canada.* Toronto: James Lorimer.

Wolfe, M. (1985). *Jolts: The TV wasteland and the Canadian oasis.* Toronto: James Lorimer.

CANADA'S QUEST FOR "CULTURAL SOVEREIGNTY": PROTECTION, PROMOTION, AND POPULAR CULTURE

John Herd Thompson

In the introductory "letter" in his polemic, *Why We Act Like Canadians*, Pierre Berton lectures Sam, his fictitious American correspondent, on the definition of the enigmatic word "culture":

> As for culture we [Canadians and Americans] don't even speak the same language. You [Americans] think of culture in terms of opera, ballet, and classical music. To us [Canadians] it covers everything from Stompin' Tom Connors to "Hockey Night in Canada." What is merely "industry" to you is culture to us. Books, magazines, movies, radio, television—all culture. Anne Murray is culture. . . . *Maclean's Magazine* is culture. The government subsidizes them all, in one way or another, because all are genuine Canadian artifacts, distinct and unique, something that nobody else has—the ingredients of our national mucilage (Berton, 1987, p. 9).

"Sam" should be forgiven any confusion. Culture, writes Raymond Williams, "is one of the two or three most complicated words in the English language" (Williams, 1983, p. 87). Nowhere is the word more complicated than in the cultural relationship between Canada and the United States. "Culture" has a number of distinct and incompatible meanings, and those of us who presume to talk about it should at least attempt to define how we're using it. Neither Berton, Sam, nor I is using the word in its "anthropological" sense—as an independent and abstract noun meaning "a given people's particular set of preferences, predispositions, attitudes, goals, its particular way of perceiving, feeling, thinking, and reacting to objective reality" (Gagne, 1972, p. 526). The culture in the quotation and in this paper is "the independent and abstract noun which describes the works and practices of intellectual and especially artistic activity" (Williams, 1983, p. 90). Berton is accusing Sam of seeing culture only in terms of "culchah": the "high culture" of painting, sculpture, literature, music, opera, ballet of Europe, adopted by the bourgeoisie of North America to differentiate itself from the masses. What Berton is celebrating as Canada's "national mucilage" is the "mass" or "popular" culture[1] Canadians consume as the product of their subsidized cultural industries. In this context, "cultural sovereignty" is the power of a sovereign government to control the operation of cultural industries.[2]

For almost a century, Canadian governments have attempted to assert this "cultural sovereignty"—and to control the allegedly deleterious effects of American newspapers, popular fiction, magazines, comic books; motion pictures and now videotapes; radio and eventually television and the associated recording industry. Canadians now routinely use the term "cultural imperialism" to describe these effects; an American sociologist has recently suggested that "cultural diffusion" would be more appropriate (Smith, forthcoming, pp. 13–15). However we choose to describe it (until very recently, Canadians have favoured aquatic metaphors: flood, tidal wave, deluge, torrent, swamp), no one would deny the widespread presence of American popular culture in Canada. Although every nation-state on the planet is penetrated by American mass media to some degree (during the Gulf War, CNN became the principal source of news in Moscow and Beijing, as well as Ottawa), Canada's situation has been and remains unique. The explanations for this situation are familiar and may be quickly summarized. First, Canada's exposure to American mass culture is not mediated by language; 70 percent of its population shares a language with America. Second, English Canadians have had no long history of national existence upon which to build a national identity; like Americans, they trace their ideological roots back to seventeenth-century Britain. These two characteristics Canada shares with Australia and New Zealand. The critical difference is that Canadian exposure to U.S. mass culture is not mediated by distance. Eighty percent of the Canadian population lives within 100 kilometres of the U.S. border. American comics, magazines, and the "McNews" of *USA Today* can be bought on the street corners, American radio and television signals picked up off the air.

Canadian cultural nationalists have long had statistics at their fingertips to demonstrate the consequences of this proximity. Rick Salutin's litany in the anti-free-trade anthology *If You Love This Country* can serve to illustrate their case:

> Only 3 to 5 percent of all theatrical screen time in Canada goes to Canadian films; 97 percent of profits from films shown in Canada go out of the country, 95 percent to the United States; 95 percent of English-language TV drama is non-Canadian; Canadian-owned publishers have only 20 percent of the book market, though they publish 80 percent of Canadian titles; 77 percent of the magazines sold here are foreign; 85 percent of record and tape sales are non-Canadian; . . . Canadian plays are the *alternative* theatre here . . . (Salutin, 1987, pp. 205–6).

Allowing for the appearance of new technologies, similar figures could be provided for any decade back to the 1920s. To a Canadian cultural nationalist, these numbers add up to the conclusion that "the overall extent of Canadian cultural domination [by the United States] is effectively unparalleled" (Parker, 1988, p. 34).

This explains why Canada has been in quest of "cultural sovereignty" almost as long as America has been exporting popular culture. Prodded by a nationalist intelligentsia concerned with creating a Canadian national identity, and by Canadian cultural industries seeking the same sheltered market enjoyed by other Canadian manufacturers, successive governments have groped for policies to cope with American mass culture. The invariable first step has been investigation. From Aird to Massey to Applebaum-Hébert, royal commissions, task forces, and special committees have filled library shelves with weighty reports. The legislation that sometimes followed (governments rarely enacted the prescriptions of investigators without substantially diluting them) falls into two broad categories: attempts to protect Canadian cultural industries with regulatory or tariff barriers, and attempts to promote indigenous Canadian mass culture through subsidies to individual artists or government-sponsored creation of a cultural infrastructure. Policies were not always clear cut; protectionist and promotional solutions were sometimes applied alternately or even simultaneously.

The most unambiguously protective cultural legislation has been Canadian policy toward American periodicals. The protracted battle between the Canadian government and *Time* is the most intensively studied case, (Litvak & Maule, 1974 and 1980, pp. 70–90) but magazines were first identified as a problem during the 1920s. In 1925, each of four American magazines had larger circulations than the leading Canadian magazine, then—as now—*Maclean's*, and *Saturday Evening Post* rubbed salt into the circulatory wounds of its Canadian competitors by (truthfully) billing itself as "Canada's best-selling magazine." The subsequent campaign against American magazines illustrates the typical alignment of forces behind campaigns for cultural sovereignty. It combined publishing entrepreneurs seeking an advantage against their American competitors with a nationalist intelligentsia that argued that American mass culture was "a menace to Canadian ideals and to the moral development of the youth of this country." It was difficult to accuse *Saturday Evening Post* or *Ladies Home Journal* of immoral influence, so the target became "pulp" magazines imported from the United States, with titles like *Black Mask*, *Dime Detective*, and *Spicy Adventure*, "the offscourings of the moral sewers of human life, . . . a putrid flood of undisguised filth." Aroused Canadians demanded that something be done "to dam this trash flowing over the border." In 1930, the Bennett Conservatives obliged the Magazine Publishers' Association of Canada with a tariff that quickly had the desired effect: by the mid-1930s, Canadian circulation was up 65 percent and that of American magazines down an equal amount (Vipond, 1977).

Legislation to promote alternative Canadian mass cultural industries has been a more typical response than protection. The first direct subsidy to a mass cultural industry was made in 1903, when the Canadian government provided Canadian Associated Press, a newspaper wire service, with an annual grant of $60 000 to distribute news from Britain that had been overlooked by American-based Associated Press, from whose wires all Canadian dailies received their European news.[3] The King Liberal government evaded demands for a magazine tariff in the 1920s, by offering Canadian publishers a tax incentive, a "drawback" on the import duties they paid on special grades of papers.

But what became the most characteristic Canadian promotional response to the conundrum of "cultural sovereignty" was the creation of a publicly financed infrastructure (Smith, 1990), the approach adopted in filmmaking and broadcasting during the 1930s. After competition from Hollywood suffocated the infant Canadian film industry in its cradle, the Canadian government rejected the quota solution used in Britain and Australia in favour of a Canadian Government Motion Picture Bureau (later the National Film Board) charged with production of documentaries rather than feature films.[4] The Canadian Radio Broadcasting Commission, which became the Canadian Broadcasting Corporation in 1936, marks the most visible difference between the cultural industries of Canada and the United States: Canada has a publicly owned and publicly financed radio and television broadcasting system and the United States does not. The creation of the CBC was an outspoken assertion of "cultural sovereignty." "Britannia rules the waves—shall Columbia rule the wavelengths?" was the slogan of the Canadian Radio League, a national lobby group of the early 1930s that rallied more extensive popular support for public broadcasting than any "cultural sovereignty" cause, before or since. As Graham Spry, a League spokesperson, put it to one of those ubiquitous parliamentary committees, "The question is, the State or the United States!" (Prang, 1965). The Broadcasting Act of 1968 requires all radio and television stations, public and private, to "safeguard, enrich and strengthen the cultural, political, social and economic framework of Canada"—to be an ingredient, in other words, of Berton's "national mucilage."

Cultural promotion has given Canada cultural industries that are substantially non-market driven, whereas in America, the market rules. Even with the severe budget cutbacks imposed on the CBC in recent years, Ottawa spends more on culture, broadly defined, than Washington does, to serve a Canadian population one-tenth that of the United States.[5]

Because they don't "speak the same language" with regard to culture, Americans have never taken Canadian complaints of American cultural domination seriously. There has never been any conscious government-business conspiracy to push the products of American popular culture northward on unwilling readers, listeners, and viewers; therefore any cultural influence exerted upon Canada is understood as passive and probably benevolent. There is no understanding of, let alone sympathy for, Canadian policies to achieve cultural sovereignty. When Parliament first discussed restricting the circulation of American magazines in 1923, the New York *Times* held up Holland, Switzerland, and Belgium as small nations that had survived next to large ones: "These examples from Europe ought to convince the Canadians that they are not in danger of cultural extinction" (Canadian culture, 1923). Americans have also viewed Canadian cultural policies through what Roger Frank Swanson has called a "first amendment optic," the belief that any interference with the free flow of ideas is inherently wrong (Swanson, 1977, p. 56). "We have learned better," said the same New York *Times* editorial, and "the Canadians, too, may learn that they will gain nothing by giving their own publications virtual freedom from competition." If Canada went ahead with its plan to ban the importation of U.S. magazines, the *Times* suggested "an agreeable form of reciprocity. As Canada bootlegs rum to us, we could bootleg literature to Canada."

These American beliefs are not simply rationalizations, but "well entrenched and held largely without cynicism" (Fairbairn, 1989). John Meisel has observed, however, "that this ideological position often miraculously coincides with crass self-serving economic interests" (Meisel, 1986, p. 165). The historical and contemporary importance of this economic interest is easily calculated. Although Canada has a much smaller population than America's other trading partners, it has been and remains the most important single export market for American popular culture. These products are not unsalable surpluses being "dumped" at fire-sale prices; prices are in fact traditionally "slightly higher in Canada." The most recent figures reflect long-standing trends, again allowing for technological change in the cultural industries. In 1989, Canadians bought 39.9 percent of all the American books and 78 percent of all the American magazines sold abroad—more than $1.4 billion U.S. worth.[6] Canada is the second-largest absolute consumer of American movies and by far the largest per capita consumer, returning 1989 rental fees of $152.5 million U.S. (U.S. Department of Commerce, 1991, p. 32). Recorded music sales return about $80 million U.S., but the Department of Commerce notes that this neglects the "large proportion of pre-recorded music sold [which] is manufactured by subsidiaries of U.S. companies" (U.S. Department of Commerce, 1991, pp. 32–34). Sales of television programs earn an estimated $125 million Cdn. (Fairbairn, 1989, p. 76). These are figures for gross earnings from cultural industry exports, but there has traditionally been a very large percentage profit on cultural exports to Canada; once a cultural product has been produced, the marginal cost of exporting it to Canada is minimal, for the linguistic and geographic reasons discussed above. Asked in 1975 why his magazine was struggling to preserve its Canadian operation, a *Time* executive replied, "They don't call Canada the candy store for nothing" (*BusinessWeek*, October 20, 1975, p. 52).

Neither American cultural industries nor the United States government has been prepared to see the "candy store" closed. Not all of Canada's "cultural sovereignty" policies are perceived as equally threatening, however. There has been a pattern to American reactions that may be summarized as follows: Canadian cultural protectionism has usually drawn an immediate response, but Canadian attempts to promote domestic mass culture (and domestic high culture, for that matter) have usually been ignored because these attempts have never seriously threatened the profits of the U.S. firms exporting cultural products. The documentary niche chosen by the NFB represented no threat to the major Hollywood studios' production of feature films. Nor was the demonstration effect of Canadian cultural public enterprise feared by American private business. Corporate America showed a great deal more hostility to Ontario's system of public electric power generation than it did to public film production or broadcasting. Cultural promotion, in its public enterprise form, was not only unthreatening; its effects could even be positive. CBC television, for example, has spent millions to buy programs from U.S. networks; in the supreme example of this irony, American football first came to Canadian screens via the CBC! (Rutherford, 1990, p. 131).

If the general pattern of the U.S. response has been predictable, the precise stratagems employed by business and government or the two acting in concert have not. American entertainment companies have not always needed Washington to help them counter Canadian cultural sovereignty policies that threaten their interests. If they have a Canadian subsidiary, American cultural exporters can make their case directly, as *Time* did to dissuade the Diefenbaker government from discriminatory tax changes (Diefenbaker, 1976, pp. 308–10). Even if they don't, they can lobby the Canadian government. In 1947, faced with an impending quota law and the possibility that the NFB would begin feature film production, the Motion Picture Association of America sold the Canadian government on the so-called "Canadian Co-operation Program," a transparent flim-flam that promised to display Canada to the world through the work of Hollywood studios. Producers were to be "encouraged" to use Canadian locations whenever appropriate, Canadian news in the newsreels was to be increased, and scriptwriters promised that Canada would be mentioned as frequently as possible in the dialogue of features made in Hollywood! The wonder is not that the plan achieved no results, for Hollywood did not intend it to, but that this bizarre scheme took in such otherwise hard-headed Canadians as C.D. Howe and Donald Gordon.[7]

When the U.S. government intercedes on behalf of an American cultural industry, it is for the same reasons that it acts when any U.S. economic interest is threatened: because the firms concerned are domestically important and can bring pressure to bear on Washington. This is not "calculated subversion" on the American part; the goal is to enhance export earnings, just as it would be with any other industry. In addition, as Roger Swanson points out, "Washington is not a monolith." Aggrieved American cultural industries can work through the White House, the legislative branches, or through the State or Commerce departments (Swanson, 1977, p. 64). The balance of trade in the products of mass cultural industries is so heavily in favour of the United States that it is impossible to retaliate by cutting off mass cultural imports from Canada. When Bill C-58 devastated the advertising income of U.S. border television stations, a proposal to block Canadian exports of film, videotapes, and sound recordings was quickly discarded as useless. Threatened (or actual) retaliation takes place in another trading sector. The twenty-year campaign to defend *Time* and *Reader's Digest* featured alleged threats by the Department of Defense to cancel aircraft purchasing contracts, to block the 1965 Auto Pact, and to impose quotas on oil imports from Western Canada (Litvak & Maule, 1974).

The pace and intensity of Canadian action and thus of American reaction quickened in the mid-1960s. Standing guard against foreign direct investment and the snares of NATO and NORAD was no longer sufficient, John Kenneth Galbraith warned the 1968 Couchiching conference:

> Economic autonomy as a whole is rather unimportant. . . . If I were a practising, as distinct from an advisory Canadian, I would be much more concerned about maintaining the cultural integrity of the broadcasting system, and making sure that Canada has an active book publishing industry, films, newspapers [and] magazines. . . . These are the things that count (Bowles et al., 1973, pp. 88–89).

Canadian governments accepted Galbraith's advice. There was a flurry of investigation with findings similar to those of previous investigations. And when action followed, it became more difficult to distinguish in policy terms where promotion left off and protection began. The Broadcasting Act of 1968 not only demanded that "programming should be of a high standard," and be "predominantly Canadian in content and character"; it also required that the programming be produced "using predominantly Canadian creative and other resources." The legislative record is too long to describe in detail, but the most important steps must be summarized briefly. In broadcasting, the first was the imposition of quotas for Canadian content on both radio and television, and the creation of the Canadian Radio and Television Commission (now the CRTC) to enforce them. When cable transmission systems were established, Canadian cable companies were allowed to retransmit American signals without paying royalties to the originating stations. In the spirit of "Catch-22," Canadian stations have the privilege of "simultaneous substitution"; they can "bump" from cable distribution U.S. stations that are carrying the same program at the same time. To Canadian filmmakers demanding the protection of a quota, the government offered promotion through the Canadian Film Development Corporation (now Telefilm), which granted public funds for film (and now television) production, and through the Capital Cost Allowance program, which permitted a 100 percent tax credit for investment in a Canadian feature film. In all cultural industries, the Liberal government of Pierre Trudeau applied the regulations restricting foreign investment with particular rigour, but within this already restricted cultural sector, book publishing companies received special care. Canadian magazines were protected by tariffs prohibiting the entry of American competitors with more than 5 percent Canadian advertising, and mail subscriptions were promoted through postal subsidies. The most dramatic of the new policies as far as the Canadian-American relationship was concerned was Bill C-58, a 1976 amendment to the Income Tax Act that denied deductions for advertising costs to Canadian advertisers who attempted to reach their domestic market via U.S. radio and TV stations or periodicals. It was this "Maclean-Hunter monopoly bill" that eliminated *Time Canada* and launched *Maclean's* as English-Canada's news weekly.

Have these policies worked? Canadian cultural sovereignists grumble that, for radio and television, "Canadian content . . . continues to be very loosely defined" (Audley, 1983, p. 257). But if not strictly defined, the content regulations are strictly enforced, so that in terms of the quantity of Canadian mass cultural production, the record is uneven, but on the whole impressive. The most obvious broadcasting failure is English-Canadian television drama, which is almost non-existent. The best example of success is recorded music. The combination of a protective tariff on imported tapes and LPs and the promotion of Canadian content regulations for airplay have launched both a domestic industry and the individual careers of the Stompin' Tom Connerses and Anne Murrays celebrated in Berton's quotation. There is room for scepticism about the quality of the popular culture government policy is promoting and protecting. Critics lampoon the "reel estate boom" of the late 1970s created by the tax credits and CFDC dollars, or sniff haughtily at "filling the airwaves with undistinguished rock-and-roll—acceptable as long as it is played by a band from Sudbury or Winnipeg, but not if it comes from Des Moines" (Chenoweth, 1980; Pullen, 1988, p. 888). The cultural sovereignist responses to such comments range from denial to a defensive "sure, it's junk, but at least it's *our* junk."

Arguing that these policies have established "cultural sovereignty" would require a leap of faith that not even a cultural bureaucrat from the Canadian Secretary of State could make. But the fact that the ultimate goal remains elusive is never accepted by their supporters as a reason for eliminating the policies. As John Hutcheson puts it,

> Notwithstanding this very large gap between the stated aims of broadcast policy and the reality of broadcast performance, the Government of Canada and some provincial governments are responsible for the maintenance of such Canadian programming, as there is still a matter of vital concern to Canadian producers, writers, technicians and performers as well as those interested in the accessibility of Canadian culture. . . . The pattern is repeated in one Canadian cultural industry after another. Canadian production holds only a minor share of the market, but what little there is [is] a consequence of some form of government support, whether subsidy, regulation or tax incentive" (Hutcheson, 1987, p. 109, 111).

American response to these new cultural policies of the 1970s had evolved a long way from the bemused paternalism with which the New York *Times* lectured Canada in the 1920s. As an academic commentator observed at a Can-Am conference in 1976, "There are indications that U.S. tolerance levels are not as high as they were a few years ago" (Swanson, 1977, p. 63). This puts the case in the mildest terms possible; what are referred to as "irritants" by professional trade negotiators are festering sores to the members of Congress who speak for the U.S. cultural exporters afflicted by them.

The Canada-U.S. Free Trade Agreement has healed some of these sores but broken others open. Canada's negotiators claimed that culture had been kept off the negotiating table and had been formally exempted from the final agreement; Canadian critics of the FTA denied both these contentions.[8] The FTA is in fact ambiguous. Article 2005, paragraph 1, says that "cultural industries are exempt from the provisions of this agreement," with the exception of certain specifically enumerated concessions by Canada: the recording industry is not exempt, and the 11.8 percent Canadian tariff must be eliminated; royalties must be paid to American broadcasters for signals retransmitted on Canadian cable systems. This general exemption in paragraph 1, however, is followed by paragraph 2, which says that "notwithstanding any other provision of the agreement, a Party may take measures of equivalent commercial effect in response to action that would have been inconsistent with this agreement but for paragraph 1." In other words, if Canadian cultural sovereignty legislation is exempted from the FTA, so is the American right to retaliate exempted. The Canadian government's claim that Canada's cultural legislation has any privileged position in the FTA is specious; the most generous interpretation would be that the FTA restores the cultural *status quo ante bellum*: Canada can keep the policies it already has, but the United States has the power to retaliate against them in any sector it wishes. Testifying before the House Ways and Means Committee last March 12, U.S. Trade Ambassador Carla Hills said exactly that: "We didn't give it up in the Canadian agreement. . . . What we did was agree to disagree. We maintain our rights to bring cases against Canada. . . . Canada has maintained its right to disagree with us" (Reuter Transcripts, 1991).

Since negotiating the FTA, however, Canada has made three significant cultural concessions not formally required by the agreement. When Canadian cultural sovereignists charged that secret undertakings had been reached to water down old policies and shelve proposed new ones, Flora MacDonald dismissed this as nonsense. "Canada's right to determine its own culture has been respected in every way," she promised in *Quill & Quire,* the trade magazine of the Canadian publishing industry (*Quill & Quire,* 1988, p. 82). MacDonald's promises didn't survive the November federal election— nor did MacDonald, for that matter. Three of the specific promises she made in her *Quill & Quire* article have already been broken: on postal rates, foreign ownership in the publishing industry, and film policy.

A preliminary version of the agreement called for Canada to equalize postal rates for American magazines. This clause was removed, but the Canadian government has in effect begun to carry out what the FTA had not required it to do. A $220 million Cdn indirect subsidy was first translated into a vaguely defined $110 million Cdn program to begin in March 1990, but the new program was cut by $45 million Cdn before it was introduced (Godfrey, 1990).

The second major Conservative cultural casualty has been the film distribution policy proposed by Secretary of State Flora MacDonald, a policy that went beyond the creation of pop culture to require that Canadian companies control the means to disseminate what they created. But once the legislation had been reworked by cabinet it was, in Jeffrey Simpson's words, "lights, camera, *in*action" in Ottawa (Simpson, 1988). "The minister has gone in with a tiger of a policy," wrote Susan Crean, "and come out with kitty litter" (Crean, 1988, p. 31). The American campaign against the bill was carried out very visibly. "The most important person in the Canadian film industry," wrote Allan Fotheringham, "is a squat little man who lives in Washington. Jack Valenti, the rich lobbyist for the Hollywood interests who has R. Reagan's ear, . . . through Washington-via-Sussex Drive pressures has emasculated Flora MacDonald's brave but futile attempt to guard Canadian film interests" (Fotheringham, 1988). Valenti appeared on CBC radio and before the Empire Club to defend his point of view: if a traditionally co-operative country like Canada challenged the distribution systems of major studios, he argued, it would have what he called a "viral contagion" effect in other countries. A redrafted film distribution bill has been described as "a feeble shadow of what was recommended" by Daniel Weinzweig of the National Association of Canadian Distributors (Godfrey, 1990). Even in its new form, however, there can be no guarantee that the legislation will not be a cause for compensation under Article 2005, paragraph 2.

In book publishing, the Canadian government has backed off from its so-called "Baie Comeau policy" on foreign takeovers, a policy that required that companies up for sale be offered to Canadian purchasers and that used the traditional device of state ownership of the company as a final alternative to a takeover. The government main-tains that the policy remains in force, but "actions speak louder than words," complained publisher Malcolm Lester after New American Library of Canada van-ished into the maw of Penguin. "If cultural matters are exempt from the Free Trade Agreement," Lester asked, "why does the government appear to be caving in to U.S. pressure?" (Fineprint, 1988). Fifteen months later, a representative of the Association of Canadian Publishers wrote a requiem on the demise of Lester & Orpen Dennys,

Malcolm Lester's publishing house: "The government's so-called Baie Comeau Policy to expand Canadian control of the industry has been timorously and inconsistently applied. And a package of new measures . . . has been languishing on Masse's desk for weeks without getting to Cabinet" (MacSkimming, 1991). This is the Conservative government's "Cultural Development Fund," a new promotional cultural policy to be administered by the Federal Business Development Bank which will presumably invest $33 million over five years in the publishing, film, and recording industries (McLennan, 1990). Originally promised to be in operation by April 1991, Marcel Masse's "long-awaited cultural industries assistance package" remains just that—long awaited (*Globe and Mail*, 1991). Were it implemented, it could certainly be claimed to be in violation of the FTA and become the subject for retaliation or demands for compensation.

The government's changes of course on film distribution and book publishing are examples of the sort of dispute-avoidance strategies that will be necessary to make the FTA work as intended. The real significance of the FTA for Canada's cultural industries is that America was once indifferent to cultural promotion and accordingly left cultural promotion activities alone; today, all is all negotiable. Canada has conceded the United States definition of culture, that culture is a business like any other, and that any action to restrain it, even those grandparented in the FTA, calls for retaliation or compensation. This is not to say that America ever comprehended or accepted Canada's understanding, but now Canada has lost that understanding of culture, even as a tool of mystification. Susan Crean's corollary that "from here on in, the business definition of culture will prevail in Canada too" (Crean, 1988) does not necessarily follow, but the Mulroney Conservative government has made no secret of its distaste for state enterprise in general. The FTA is part of their attempt (similar to the one going on in Mexico) to make Canada a more market-driven society. The severe cuts in the budget for public broadcasting, and the quiet retreat from the cultural policies just described, suggest that, so long as the Conservatives are in office, Canada will move toward the market-driven model of mass cultural industries that prevails in the United States. This is not, however, to say that the Conservatives have used the FTA as a way to deliberately sabotage Canada's cultural industries and undermine the nationalist intelligentsia that has so heartily opposed them and their trade policy. Even if they have watered down Baie Comeau, Tory policies like that on investment in the book publishing industry still infuriate Americans such as Representative John Dingell, a Michigan Democrat who has pressed the administration to "urge the Canadian government to do away with the policy altogether."[9]

What are the implications of the prospective Canada-United States-Mexico North American Free Trade Agreement (NAFTA) negotiations for Canadian cultural industries? At first glance, there shouldn't be any, and that is the official Canadian government position. There is no significant cultural industry trade between Mexico and Canada, and even between Mexico and the United States, trade in the products of cultural industries is small, much smaller than that between the United States and Canada.[10] If trade increases, it may be Mexico that benefits, with sales to the Spanish-speaking market in the United States. The real significance of the trilateral NAFTA negotiations for Canadian cultural sovereignty policies is that they will rip the bandages off the "festering sores" left from FTA-1. As I explained above, the Canada-U.S. FTA did not remove all the "irritants" in the area of cultural industries, and senators and representatives have good job security and long memories. As *Globe* correspondent Jennifer Lewington put it, "Some irritants, especially in the cultural area, are political time bombs with an uncertain fuse" (Lewington, 1989). President Bush's January biennial report on the FTA singled out "Canadian actions to enforce the investment restrictions in the cultural sectors" as "irritants," reminded Congress of the compensation Article 2005, and promised further negotiations (U.S. Congress, 1991, pp. 32–33). The administration is attempting to persuade the Senate and the House to grant it the "fast track" negotiating authority so important to legislation of the Canada-U.S. FTA. One of Carla Hills's most consistently effective sales pitches is the argument that renewed negotiations will mean new opportunities to resolve the question of Canadian cultural sovereignty legislation in America's favour.[11] The promise to deal severely with "offensive" Canadian legislation such as Bill C-58 is being held up to a wary Congress as an inducement to get involved with free-trade negotiations with Mexico![12]

There is a notion that Mexicans and Canadians might co-operate to "counterbalance" the United States, both in the negotiating process and within the agreement, that each country might lend its support to the other to prevent the United States from goring its "sacred cows." That such co-operation would take place seems implausible, that it would be effective even less likely. During his recent visit to Canada, President Salinas dismissed out of hand a reporter's suggestion that cultural issues could pose a problem. Americans share this opinion. Asked in a Congressional committee hearing if she could "assure us that the agreement [with Mexico] will not restrict the trade in American products under the guise of so-called cultural protection," Carla Hills replied confidently that "we don't anticipate a problem with the North American Free Trade Agreement with Mexico; that has not been a position that Mexico has taken."[13]

Of course, there are many Mexicans who worry about their "cultural sovereignty" if NAFTA becomes a reality (Ellison, 1991). But available evidence suggests that Mexicans neither understand the Canadian point of view on this issue nor sympathize with Canada on it. "Canada should be the fifty-first U.S. state," a young Mexican told a *Globe and Mail* reporter in February 1991. "Canada is so lacking in its own culture that it had to steal hockey and the Stanley Cup from the United States to have something to call its own[!]" (Drohan, 1991).

NOTES

1. "Mass" culture is the better descriptive term, because, again as Raymond Williams notes, popular culture is not a culture created by "the people," and the term itself was not bestowed upon this form of culture "by *the people*, but by others, and it still carries two older senses: inferior kinds of work; and work deliberately setting out to win favour."

2. Given an anthropological definition of culture, "cultural sovereignty" would be absurd: "a nation doesn't possess a culture as one possesses property, a nation *is* its culture." Michael Bergman, (February 1988), "Free trade: Trick-or-treaty?" *Cinema Canada, 149*, 14–15, cited in Barbara Fairbairn, (1989), "The implications of free trade for television broadcasting in Canada," *Canadian Issues/Themes canadiens, XII*, 80.

3. John A. Schultz, (1980), "Whose news: The struggle for wire service distribution, 1900–1920," *ARCS, 10*, 27–35. The subsidy failed to accomplish its purpose; according to Schultz, "CAP cables consisted mainly of society news and rarely averaged more than 500 or 600 words daily." The experiment was ended in 1910.

4. Peter Morris, (1978), *Embattled shadows: A history of Canadian cinema, 1895–1939*, (Montreal, McGill-Queen's University Press), pp. 175–195. The governments of Ontario and British Columbia had short-lived and less successful civil service movie companies. British Columbia went so far as to require theatre owners to show these documentaries; the government was unable, however, to persuade moviegoers to actually watch them!

5. The budget President Bush presented to Congress for the 1991–92 fiscal year allotted $833 million U.S. to "Culture, Arts, and Humanities." (*New York Times*, 1991, February 4, p. 8). Note that in the United States, high culture is not governed entirely by market forces, but most patronage comes from private philanthropists, not the state.

6. U.S. Department of Commerce, International Trade Administration, *U.S. Industrial Outlook* (Washington, 1991), 26–2, 26–9. The next largest customer for both is Britain, which purchases 8 percent of U.S. book exports and 5 percent of U.S. magazine exports.

7. The project is described in "Canadian co-operation, Hollywood style," Chapter 4 of Pierre Berton's *Hollywood's Canada: The Americanization of Our National Image*. (Toronto, McClelland and Stewart, 1975), pp. 167–200.

8. The best-argued example is Susan Crean's, (1988, May), "Reading between the lies: Culture and the Free Trade Agreement," *This Magazine, 22* (2), 29–33.

9. Dingell speaks for Gulf and Western Inc., which ran afoul of the policy through its acquisition of Ginn & Co. and has refused to go. Jennifer Lewington, (1989, March 18), "Ottawa book policy target of attack by quiet Congress veteran," *Globe and Mail*.

10. Using magazines as an (admittedly language- and education-biased) example, Canada takes in 78 percent of U.S. magazine exports and Mexico 3 percent. *U.S. Industrial Outlook* (Washington, 1991), 26-6.

11. See her testimony before the Senate Finance Committee, February 21, 1991, and before the House Ways and Means Committee, March 12, 1991.

12. The *Globe's* Bronwyn Drainie has issued apocalyptic predictions that Telefilm, allegedly a target on Jack Valenti's list, will be among the free trade fallen. "Round two: Knockout?" *Globe and Mail*, (1990, March 30), p. C3.

13. See Hills's testimony before the Senate Finance Committee, February 21, 1991, and before the House Ways and Means Committee, March 12, 1991.

REFERENCES

Audley, P. (1983). *Canada's cultural industries: Broadcasting, publishing, records and film.* Toronto: James Lorimer.

Berton, P. (1987). *Why we act like Canadians: A personal exploration of our national character.* Markham, Ontario: Penguin/McClelland and Stewart.

Bowles, R.P., et al. (1973). *Canada and the U.S.: Continental partners or wary neighbours.* Scarborough: Prentice-Hall.

Business Week. (1975, October 20). p. 52

Canadian culture. (1923, March 7). *New York Times.*

Chenoweth, D. (1980, March 21). Does the quantity equal the quality? *Montreal Gazette.*

Crean, S. (1988, May). Reading between the lies: Culture and the Free Trade Agreement. *This Magazine, 22* (2), 29–30.

Diefenbaker, J. (1976). *One Canada: Memoirs of the Rt. Hon. John G. Diefenbaker.* Toronto: Macmillan.

Drohan, M. (1991, February 9). Here we go again. *Globe and Mail,* p. D1.

Ellison, K. (1991, April 17). Free-trade pact raises cultural concerns. *Raleigh News and Observer,* p. 22A.

Fairbairn, B. (1989). The implications of free trade for television broadcasting in Canada. *Canadian Issues/Themes canadiens, XII, 80–81.*

Fine print in trade pact turns good news to bad. (1988, September 16). *Globe and Mail.*

Fotheringham, A. (1988, July 11). The trouble with thinking aloud. *Maclean's.*

Gagne, R. (1972). French Canada: The interrelationship between culture, language and personality. In *Canadian History since Confederation* (Eds., Hodgins, B., & Page, R.). Georgetown, Ontario: Irwin-Dorsey Ltd.

Globe and Mail. (1991, March 29). p.B2.

Godfrey, S. (1990, January 20). Is culture truly excluded from free trade? *Globe and Mail,* p. C1, C3.

Hutcheson, J. (1987). Culture and free trade. In *The Future on the Table: Canada and the Free Trade Issue* (Ed., Henderson, M.D.). Toronto: Masterpress.

Lewington, J. (1989, March 18). Ottawa book policy . . . *Globe and Mail.*

Litvak, I.A., & Maule, C.J. (1974). *Cultural sovereignty: The Time and Reader's Digest case in Canada.* New York: Praeger.

Litvak, I.A., & Maule, C.J. (1980). Bill C-58 and the regulation of periodicals in Canada. *International Journal, 36.*

MacSkimming, R. (1991, January 16). Does the political will exist to save the publishing industry? *Globe and Mail,* p. A11.

McLennan, H. (1990, July 5). New cultural development fund. *Globe and Mail,* p. A7.

Meisel, J. (1986). Escaping extinction: Cultural defence of an undefended border. In *Southern exposure: Canadian Perspectives on the United States.* (Ed., Flaherty, D.H.). Toronto: McGraw-Hill Ryerson.

Parker, I. (1988, February/March). The free trade challenge. *Canadian Forum.*

Prang, M. (1965). The origins of public broadcasting in Canada. *Canadian Historical Review, XLVI* (1) p. 9–31.

Pullen, C. (1988, Winter). Culture, free trade, and two nations. *Queen's Quarterly, 95* (4).

Quill & Quire. (1988, September). *54* (9).

Reuter Transcripts. (1991, March 12).

Rutherford, P. (1990). *When television was young: Primetime Canada, 1952–1967*. Toronto: University of Toronto Press.

Salutin, R. (1987). Keep Canadian culture off the table—Who's kidding who. In *If You Love this Country*. (Ed., LaPierre, L.). Toronto: McClelland and Stewart.

Simpson, J. (1988, May 11). Lights, camera, inaction. *Globe and Mail,* p. A7.

Smith, A. (1990, October). Canadian culture, the Canadian state, and the new continentalism. *Canadian-American Public Policy, 3*, pp. 10–20.

Smith, J. (Forthcoming). Canada's television, entertainment, and national culture dilemma reconsidered—Real or spurious?

Swanson, R.F. (1977). Canadian cultural nationalism and the U.S. public interest. *Canadian Cultural Nationalism* (Ed. Murray, J.L.). New York: CIIA/Council on Foreign Relations by NYU Press.

U.S. Congress. (1991). 102d Congress, 1st Session, House Document 102-36. Washington.

U.S. Department of Commerce, International Trade Administration. (1991). *U.S. Industrial Outlook*. Washington.

Vipond, M. (1977, March). Canadian nationalism and the plight of Canadian magazines in the 1920s. *Canadian Historical Review, LVIII* (1), 43–63.

Williams, R. (1983). *Keywords: A vocabulary of culture and society*. London: Fontana Paperbacks.

BROADCASTING AND NATIVE NORTHERNERS

Gail Guthrie Valaskakis

O n September 20, 1990, the Canadian Radio-television and Telecommunications Commission (CRTC) issued the Northern Broadcasting Policy (NBP). The new policy provides a definition of and expanded recognition for aboriginal broadcasting. Even within the current context of extensive cutbacks in Native communications, this policy statement represents a landmark in the development of northern communications and reflects Canada's long-standing interest in issues of culture and in communications technologies. But the development of Native communications is the result, in equal measure, of the insight and determination of aboriginal peoples themselves.

Communications technologies have been increasingly recognized as agents of economic centralization, cultural fragmentation, and political control. Within this context of persuasive critical analysis relating communications to cultural imperialism and economic domination (e.g., Schiller, 1976), aboriginal peoples across Canada have demanded access to media in an effort to support Native culture and identity and to build Native communities and institutions. This is evident in the far North, where Inuit and other aboriginal nations have used media in attempting to combat, even reverse, the cultural impact of compelling new communications technologies. As in other countries, the "demand for local programming, and even more, for local programming rooted in tradition . . . is a question of whether one wants one's culture to be overwhelmed and homogenized" (Katz, 1977, p. 116).

Technology and Change: Historical Trends

In the far North, technology and cultural change have been interrelated throughout the last 400 years. The Inuit experience in eastern Canada suggests a definite relationship between cultural change and technological control, including access to and participation in media (Valaskakis, 1979). More recently, questions about indigenous language and culture have been raised in relation to Native broadcasting. These questions arise in the context of Native social change and cultural incorporation, processes that, in the far North, are closely connected to the availability of technology.

Northern social history is an analysis of the relationship between Native and non-Native peoples. This relationship has been defined and cemented through technology, the conditions of its access, and its transfer from a dominant to a marginal people.

Historically, technology has been provided to Native people on a limited and directed basis. The earliest and most continuous form of interaction between Inuit and non-Natives took the form of trading. At first, bells, mirrors, and beads were traded for skins, food, and tools. But when whalers and traders realized the potential of a Native labour force for resource extraction, European technology became an important motivating force. Knives, guns, traps, and boats were exchanged for Inuit goods and services. The influence of this early technology transfer led to clear patterns of social and cultural change in Inuit communities.

Three major trends have been important in establishing the relationship between current communications technology and Inuit culture in modern northern communities. First, non-Natives gained positions of authority by merely possessing the technology and controlling its distribution. Inuit had to respond to the functional superiority of metal knives, guns, and wooden boats. In the eastern Arctic, the authority this conferred upon all non-Natives was reinforced by European navigational skills, the impact of the English language and Christian religion, and a seemingly endless supply of trade goods.

Second, through the directed transfer of technology, non-Natives initiated new criteria for leadership in Inuit society. As the first non-Native agents of change in the far North, whalers designated selected Inuit as "whaling bosses" or contact agents to direct Native activity to serve the economic needs of non-Native institutions. Whaling bosses were the "captain's voice" (Fleming, 1956, p. 75) who engaged Inuit hunters, guides, and other personnel necessary to the whale hunt. These Natives were rewarded for their efforts with technology—guns, ammunition, boats—which, in turn, secured their positions of status in the Inuit community.

Thus, the social structure was altered as European technology was introduced. As Inuit with wooden boats decided where and when to travel and Inuit with guns provided more food for their extended families, leadership began a rudimentary shift toward people with access to technology and authority. Social and cultural change was not extensive during the seasonal activity of the whaling period because Inuit leaders such as *shaman* or *angakok*, respected healers in Inuit society, could easily take on the new role of whaling boss. But this system of contact became the modus operandi used by all the non-Native institutions that penetrated the North. Missionaries established "lay readers" or "catechists" who assisted ministers or themselves propagated the faith. Inuit who became "Christian bosses" could be young or even women but, for obvious reasons, could not be *shaman* or *angakok*. Native catechists tended to spread southern culture along with Christian doctrine and to undermine the most powerful Inuit leaders at the turn of this century, when institutionalized trading entered the North.

Trading companies brought new technology and trade goods. The processes of trapping necessitated changes to old hunting techniques and residence patterns; the processes of trading reinforced non-Native authority and hierarchical interaction. Traders established both camp and district "trading bosses"—individual Inuit who, like "leading Indians" in the fur trade empire to the south, organized Native trading on a local level. They gained their positions on the basis of being able to obtain furs, a criterion that could exclude older, less robust hunters; their status was enhanced by their knowledge of the new technology and trade goods. Post trading eventually established Inuit families who remained in the employ of traders as "post servants" and, as missionaries and traders were joined by police, settlements began to develop in the far North. The Royal Canadian Mounted Police (RCMP), too, engaged contact agents, Inuit guides, and providers who eventually took on the role of Special Constables, that is, employees outside the normal ranks of the force.

With the formation of small northern settlements, the role of contact agent led to new activities and functions that demanded new skills: interaction skills. These were acquired, used, and diffused through families whose access to authority established them as "people of the whites" (Vallee, 1967, p. 110). "People of the land" could be distinguished from "people of the whites" (ibid., p. 140), who had adopted more Euro-Canadian language and custom through their association with non-Native institutions. Conflicting authority figures became absorbed in a new, plural society that distinguished between those who were contact agents and those who were not. This distinction "was instrumental in eroding or eliminating the process of local decision-making, except in those matters well outside the white man's interest" (Phillips, 1967, p. 80). At the same time, pluralism began to fragment the consensual basis of Inuit cultural and social action.

A third aspect of technology is related to contact. Beginning with the explorer Martin Frobisher, non-Natives traded goods for certain Inuit information. This exchange was formalized through the broad authority of the non-Native institutions that moved North. As new technologies became essential to Inuit lifestyle, information became a commodity that, like skills and products, Inuit exchanged for material goods. The importance that information acquired is related in Archibald Fleming's (1956, pp. 153–54) account of a contact agent for an American whaler who was killed by other Inuit for revealing how many pelts they intended to trade with a second whaler. Information about the Inuit was used to control residence, credit, and trading. At the same time, Inuit access to information was restricted through the introduction of Inuit literacy, paradoxically a process that reinforced the development of two separate non-complementary communication systems: one within the Inuit community, another within the non-Native community.

Missionaries introduced syllabic and roman orthography systems for writing the Native languages in the late 1800s. By 1910, probably 98 percent of Inuit in the Eastern Arctic were literate in Inuktitut (Graburn, 1979, p. 204). But three different orthographies in Canada and six across the greater North maintained dialect differences and regionalization among Inuit whose language was basically similar. Because Inuit did not become functionally literate in English, written information did not allow Native adaptation of their own institutions or participation in those brought North. Prior to 1972, only nine secular books and four periodicals were published in Inuktitut and, according to Jenness, oral tradition in the form of storytelling was no longer evident by 1924 (Mayes, 1972). Information between Inuit and non-Natives passed through contact agents, or community "go-betweens."

As a result of this historical process, technology and communication during the first half of the twentieth century played a vital role in Inuit cultural and social change. This process contributed to the economic and political dependency of Inuit people. It was equally important in contributing to the acculturation of Inuit within a model that can best be described as "cultural replacement." Inuit culture became associated with the communication medium over which Inuit maintained control: syllabic writing. Since this technique for writing the Inuit language was limited largely to Christian communication, secular documents of Inuit culture and society did not appear in the post-contact period. Inuit wrote no historical documents, no community policies, no precedents in law, no educational materials. In Harold Innis's (1950) terminology, non-Natives established an English-language "monopoly of knowledge" as they moved southern institutions to the North. Non-Native authority defined public process in northern communities; non-Native control of information and technology excluded Inuit from participating in the cultural and social change fundamental to adaptation and development. Southern institutions stood at the political centre of northern settlements (Brody, 1975, p. 39), and

> [m]ost of the important sources of messages are not natives of the Arctic, and . . . most messages flow into the region from outside. . . . The political and social position of the senders determines their authority. . . and decision-makers of the most important channels of information are almost exclusively white, and located outside the Arctic (Mayes, 1972, p. 84).

During the past two decades, Inuit participation in northern social and cultural adaptation has changed considerably, primarily as a result of the organization and action of Native people themselves.

EARLY MEDIA TECHNOLOGY

Native people began establishing aboriginal organizations across Canada on both a regional and a national basis in the late 1960s and early 1970s, a period when the federal government's interest in communications extended to issues of northern development, Native acculturation, and national unity. Like the historical role of the continental railroad, satellites could provide information to alleviate the cultural and linguistic differences that characterize the country. As Arthur Kroker (1984, p. 9) suggests, the satellite programs illustrate "the degree to which Canadian experience has been shaped by the spread of communication technologies." In the early 1970s, Inuit became increasingly aware of the role early media played in reinforcing, even expanding, the southern cultural values and the economic and political control initiated by earlier technologies. Radio was established in the far North in the late 1920s, just as airplanes began to provide easy access to the Arctic. In the eastern Arctic, radio reception was often poor, but agencies were still quick to recognize the advantage of shortwave for communication over distance. By the early 1930s, trading posts, missions, and police posts were equipped with high-frequency radios. Small radio networks were established, primarily to communicate the directives of southern agencies. New interaction patterns removed much of the localized authority of post managers and, as Innis (1950) would suspect, placed Inuit under the increasing control of southern bureaucracies.

The role that radio played in the development of the RCMP suggests the relationship between early communications technologies and the increasing marginalization of Inuit. In 1927, three radio stations were established in the eastern Arctic, to which RCMP constables were attached in an advisory capacity (Steele, 1936, p. 287). For the following three years, the RCMP restructured the agency and centralized the control of Arctic detachments "for greater administrative convenience" (Kelly & Kelly, 1973, p. 171). Prior to 1934, the MacKenzie and western Arctic posts were controlled from Edmonton; detachments on the west side of Hudson Bay reported to Winnipeg; and the Eastern Arctic posts were under the jurisdiction of Montreal. With increased air access and communication through radio, all the Arctic detachments were integrated into "G" Division, with headquarters in Ottawa.

Although high-frequency radio solidified the interests of southern institutions, broadcast radio, which was appreciated and welcomed by non-Native northerners by the mid-1930s, provided little information for Inuit. The first Inuktitut program was not broadcast until 1960, two years after the formation of the CBC Northern Service. As late as 1972, only 17 percent of CBC's shortwave service was broadcast in the Inuit language although most Inuit did not speak English (Mayes, 1972). Moreover, Canadian broadcasting was limited in the eastern Arctic before the introduction of satellites. Nigel Wilford (1986) describes listening to the radio in Pangnirtung, Baffin Island:

> I remember listening to Radio Moscow, Radio Peking, Voice of America, the BBC and sometimes on a clear night if the wind was blowing in the right direction, the Northern Service of the CBC.

When television was introduced in the North, Inuit were not consulted. They were equally removed from decisions on television availability or programming. In 1967, "Frontier Package" television began in the first of eighteen Arctic communities, mainly in the western Arctic. These four-hour videotape packages of southern programming were sent North primarily for the transient, non-Native population. Relayed videotapes contained no Native-language programming, a pattern that extended into the 1970s.

MODERN COMMUNICATION TECHNOLOGIES

The modern era of Canadian aboriginal communications really began in 1969, when the Honourable Jean Chrétien, then Minister of Indian Affairs, released a White Paper on Indian policy. In its intention to change the status of Indian people, this governmental position paper ushered in a new era of Native action. As they unified against the Paper's assimilationist implications, aboriginal nations realized that they lacked communication channels to inform their people or receive feedback from them. With the White Paper, several provincial Native organizations began communication branches. Some of these became Native communications societies when the Department of the Secretary of State program was established in the mid-1970s.

The far North was also drawn into communications issues in 1969 when the Telesat Canada Bill proposed the first geostationary satellite system in the world as a "Northern vision for the 1970s" (Kenny, 1971 (1), p. 20). Although the Anik system was clearly a welcome response to the conditions of northern distance and isolation, it was a mixed blessing for Native northerners. Inuit, who were never consulted in the discussions that led to the satellite program, knew that the introduction of earlier media played a forceful role in maintaining the authority of non-Native institutions and in restricting Native access to information in their communities. Satellite television posed new threats to their language and culture "by parachuting telephone, radio, and live television simultaneously into a region that is culturally different from that of the producers of both the technology hardware and software" (Roth, 1982, p. 3). And the South-North structure of the broadcasting system threatened to increase southern domination, making Native northerners even more marginal to the political and economic reality of southern Canada. This prospect seemed all the more probable when Cabinet refused the CBC's 1969 request for a northern programming budget, the first of CBC Northern Service's many attempts to meet the media needs of Native northerners. At the same time, the communication needs of Native northerners expressed here in the words of Peter Inukshuk of Inukjuaq, northern Quebec, were widely recognized among Inuit:

> We need information, masses of it. We need it in our own language.
> . . . We need to have that information spread throughout our communities. . . . This has to happen fast. If it doesn't, we will vanish as a people. Our future is at stake (*The Northerners*, 1974, p. 112).

NATIVE COMMUNICATIONS PROJECTS

In 1971, the first government-sponsored communication project took place in the North, involving both Indian and Inuit communities. The federal Department of Communications sponsored a three-year northern pilot project in community radio in Big Trout Lake, Ontario, and the Keewatin Community of Baker Lake. This was the forerunner of the Wawata Native Communications Society in northern Ontario and, in some ways, of the Baker Lake Production Centre of the Inuit Broadcasting Corporation. In 1971, too, a community video project was mounted in La Ronge, Saskatchewan. This project reinforced the National Film Board's interest in the relationship between film and video and social change. On a small-scale basis, these media could provide regional communication to increase Inuit participation in northern communities. Inuit films could be televised, allowing Inuit the first opportunity to "see themselves" on broadcast media. In 1972, the National Film Board began the Cape Dorset film workshop in Baffin Island. This led to the Iqualiut film workshop, which, begun in 1974, became Nunatsiakmiut a year later.

A second phase of Native communications developments began in 1973. In that year, the Anik satellite system became operational and Cabinet approved funding for CBC's Accelerated Coverage Plan (ACP), providing radio and television to Canadian communities with populations of 500 or more. Monies were allocated for hardware, but not for production; little of the programming available through the ACP was relevant to northern Native people:

> The Accelerated Coverage Plan was originally intended to provide intra-provincial distribution of services, but many of the transmitters installed relayed local and regional news programming which is not relevant to the viewers in the area. For instance, viewers in Baker Lake receive the volleyball scores from the Avalon Peninsula, viewers in Dryden, Ontario, hear about municipal gatherings in Winnipeg, and viewers in Old Crow in the Yukon watch the crocuses blooming in Vancouver in mid-winter (Department of Communications Canada, 1983, p. 15).

In 1973, too, Cabinet approved funding for the Native Communications Program (NCP). While the first Native communication societies incorporated in Alberta, Nova Scotia, Ontario, and elsewhere, Inuit in northern Quebec protested the CBC's plan to extend television service to the North without Inuktitut programming, or even relevant northern programming.

By the mid-1970s then, the players in the development of Native communications were all in place: politicized Native organizations, a framework and funding for Native communication societies, government-sponsored local media projects, and initial northern broadcasting policy statements.

With the establishment of Native communication societies, several groups began developing media programming, broadcasting agreements, and newspapers. In British Columbia, Ontario, and northern Quebec, media priorities included community radio and "trail" radio—communication for people travelling on the land to hunt and fish or camp. As communication societies continued to develop in response to regional needs, satellite experiments became a new focus of aboriginal action.

In 1975, the Alberta Native Communication Society mounted the Hermes satellite project called Ironstar and in 1977, Tagramiut Nipingat Inc. (TNI) began the Naalakvik 1 project, which linked the Hermes and Anik A satellites to produce an interactive, or "two-way" radio network in eight northern Quebec communities. Between 1978 and 1981, TNI and the Inuit Tapirisat of Canada participated in Anik B satellite experiments, using interactive audio and direct video, which included the first direct, North-to-North television programming through satellite uplinks. These efforts led to the formation in 1981 of the Inuit Broadcasting Corporation (IBC), the first Native-language television network in North America. In the same year, the CRTC expanded the availability of Native broadcasting by licensing undertakings of Indian communication societies in the western Northwest Territories and the Yukon.

But Native communities also had to contend with an increasing array of southern media. CanCom, a pay-TV package of American and Canadian television and radio stations, was also licensed in 1981. In addition, southern commercial television became widely available across the North. Native communities received television on satellite dishes, and video playback units became common in Native homes. Within this context of diverse and competing media, the Inuit Broadcasting Corporation has become a flagship of northern Native television.

The Development of Inuit Broadcasting

Inuit television is the result of northern Native people's resolve to participate in the social transformation of their world. Inuit acted to gain access to this compelling and pervasive medium "to strengthen the social, cultural, and linguistic fabric of Inuit life" (IBC, 1982, p. ii). Amid commercial television spanning the range from "All in the Family" to "Cheers," "Sesame Street," and the national news, which Rosemarie Kuptana (1982, p. 5), then president of IBC, labelled "a cultural assault" because it reflects southern interests and values, Inuit television represented

> a means of cultural expression through drama, documentary, current
> affairs, news entertainment and the arts. . . . We want to preserve part
> of ourselves—our language, our social habits, our survival skills.
> And we want to do it in the context that is most comfortable for us:
> an Inuit system which can link the old and new Inuit (1982, pp. vi, v).

The opportunity to develop such a system was forged through satellite-access experiments and smaller-scale communications projects. The most important of these with regard to television were the Inukshuk and the Nalaakvik II experimental satellite projects.

The three-year Inukshuk Project used the Anik B Communications Program to experiment with Inuktitut television broadcasting in the Baffin, Keewatin, and Central Arctic regions of the Northwest Territories. This project linked six communities in regions with different time zones and dialects through one-way video transmission from Iqaliut, and two-way audio among all six communities. The project established regional production facilities, trained staff and, for eight months during 1980–81, broadcast Inuktitut television on both a local and a network basis. A significant amount of the 323.7 hours of network programming broadcast during the experiment was devoted to public affairs, current issues, and education, areas of particular relevance to Inuit cultural stability and social participation (Valaskakis, Robbins, & Wilson, 1984, p. 304). In northern Quebec, where TNI operated a similar Anik B experiment linking five communities, Inuit broadcasting expanded with production facilities, training, and regional television broadcasting. By the time the two Anik B projects led to the formation of the Inuit Broadcasting Corporation in the summer of 1981, Inuit broadcasting had attained considerable experience, expertise, and credibility. At the same time, Canadian communications policy reflected increasing concern with issues of national pluralism and cultural sovereignty. Native broadcasting took on new importance as the country became more aware of the threat to Canadian cultural sovereignty posed by U.S. satellites. In the early 1980s, recognition of the relationship between broadcasting and the cultural and linguistic integrity of aboriginal peoples began to be reflected in regulatory policy.

In 1980, the CRTC issued the report of the Therrien Commission on the Extension of Service (CRTC, 1980). Reflecting the deliberations of the first CRTC Commission to hold northern hearings and to include an Inuk commissioner, the Therrien report asserted that government had a responsibility to assure broadcasting that supported aboriginal languages and cultures. As Native people gained a "special place in cultural policy" (Applebaum-Hébert Committee, 1982, p. 11), the Therrien report became the basis for the federal government's first Northern Broadcasting Policy, issued in 1983. The five basic principles of this policy recognized the communication needs of north-erners, especially Native northerners, for whom it specified widespread participation in all aspects of media programming, in regulatory decision making, and in broadcasting distribution on the basis of "fair access" and "consultation" (Canada, 1983, p. 2).

The implementation of these principles led to the Northern Native Broadcast Access Program (NNBAP), begun in 1983 with $13.4 million a year to fund the production of regional, Native radio, and television programming through the thirteen northern com-munication societies. Funding for the NNBAP was cut to $11.1 million in 1990–91; and funding for the Native Communications Program sponsoring Native newspapers and radio among southern groups, and for the National Aboriginal Communications Society was eliminated altogether. The Inuit Broadcasting Corporation and the twelve other northern production groups are working to raise monies from other sources, but given the limited resources of Native people themselves, the NNBAP will remain the primary funding source for the production and distribution of northern Native media. The elimi-nation of the Native Communications Program and the reduction of funding for the Northern Native Broadcast Access Program are severe setbacks for all Native media. However, Native communication societies continue to play central roles in defining the nature and extent of Native broadcasting, a process that has had important implications for the very definition of aboriginal culture.

ISSUES OF NATIVE CULTURE AND LANGUAGE

The Northern Broadcast Access Program was approved as a vehicle to promote aborig-inal cultures and aboriginal languages. This is reflected in the production guidelines for the program, which target five hours of television and twenty hours of radio per week in Native languages. An Irish study on broadcasting and "the Lesser Used Languages of the European Community" (Alcock & O'Brien, 1980) suggests that this amount of programming is the minimum exposure needed to maintain a minority lan-guage. On a broader level, the Irish study raises the more basic and political issue of what is meant by "native culture"; assumptions about aboriginal culture and language relate to the values and codes that are instrumental in the daily lives of Native peoples today. These issues raise questions about the notion of culture itself and the role of media in cultural expression.

> Culture is individuality and collectivity. It is an expression of being, of vitality, of assertiveness, of confidence and of pride in a way of life. Culture grows by the vitality and dynamism of society. Cultural industries grow, not only from commercial viability, but because they are able to express the cultural good of the societies in which they emanate (Bergman, 1985, p. 9).

Culture is, at the most basic level, a patterned response to environment based on selected values. It is rooted in shared social practices and experiences—the context of social relations—which are maintained through communication. For Inuit, the dynamic nature of culture and the process of northern social history have contributed to a re-definition of "traditional" culture. Hugh Brody (1975) has written that eastern Arctic Inuit consider as "traditional," square dancing, the mouth harp and accordion, trapping, the Christian church, syllabic writing, and other aspects of culture that they have incorporated since European contact. These activities and even the institution of the church can be considered part of the culture of the "Inummariit" or "real Inuit" (Brody, 1975, p. 144), largely older Inuit who demonstrate skill and control on the land, where they continue to hunt and trap on a regular basis. Nathan Elberg (1984) observed that, based on his fieldwork in a northern Quebec community, the concept of "real Inuit" is causing problems for the identity and self-esteem of younger Inuit, who are far less adept at hunting and trapping, far less knowledgeable about the land. Elberg suggests that the stories of urban difficulties told by young Inuit are "as significant in understanding the life of contemporary Inuit as some of the older stories about cold and anguish collected in earlier decades are to an understanding of the culture of those times" (Elberg, 1984, p. 6). He believes that "it is time that the people in southern Canada stopped evaluating the authenticity of contemporary Inuit according to the standards (should I say clichés) for previous generations of Inuit" (p. 9) and concludes with a comment from a young Inuk:

> It's like if you have Inuit as primitive people of the past, cavemen sort of deal. . . . That can be one definition of Inuk. . . . The definition of Inuit today should be an Inuk with a Honda, living in a house designed by a non-Inuk. But the Inuit of today is obviously not the same as *quallunaak* culture. . . . We are aware of people going to the moon and we're using speedboats and things like that but still we are saying, "We are Inuit." And some people are saying that we are too much of space men, not enough stone-age men. In that way, mixed up (pp. 9–10).

As non-Natives associate "traditional" Inuit activities with precontact behaviour, young Inuit experience the cultural struggle related to the concepts of "traditional" and "real" Inuit. At the same time, assimilation characterized by the control patterns of earlier Euro-Canadian contact has been encouraged by satellite access to southern broadcasting. Cultural incorporation and adaptation are important factors in defining the Native cultures and languages that are basic to daily life in contemporary Native communities. These processes also relate to the media products that reinforce Native languages and cultures. Recognizing this has challenged broadcasting policy and programs to defer to Native nations in determining the cultural or linguistic definition and relevance of indigenous media products.

Inuit broadcasting spans a range that is similar to southern programming: public affairs, documentaries, news, drama, and children's programming. But local broadcasting may also reflect the communality of radio or television bingo, the creativity of local rock bands, or the particular involvement of municipal elections. And on both local and regional levels, Inuit programming goes far beyond "traditional" cultural content, which can reflect the "quaintness of culture: the preservation of Native traits, colourful customs, folk-dances, and songs" (Bergman, 1985, p. 9). The difference between southern network programming and Inuit television is suggested in the following discussion of "Oagik," IBC's regular current events/news program:

> "Oagik" may look western. It even adheres to several characteristics applied to southern news. But it does it on its own terms. Its programs focus on items of geographic or psychological proximity to its audience (the Inuit and issues important to them). It is concerned with timeliness (but that can mean something that happens within weeks, not minutes and hours). Significance plays a major role in the "Oagik's" staff story selection (but what is significant can range from the rescue of a snowy owl, and an examination of an eight-legged caribou fetus, as well as the Nunavut Constitutional forums discussing the possibility of quasi-independence within Canada, and alcoholism and environmental issues). Visuals are important [to] "Oagik" (but the visual style is different) (Madden, 1990, p. 14).

Inuit have resisted the communication policy and program guidelines that framed the provision of services within the boundaries of "traditional" culture rather than the broader context of access to Native information. Narrowly defined, cultural broadcasting runs the risk of becoming a vehicle for the continued marginalization of the Native people themselves.

PERSPECTIVES ON MEDIA IMPACT

Considerable research has been done on the impact of southern broadcast media in northern Native communities. Even before satellite television was pervasive, Coldevin (1977) began collecting data on the attitudes of Inuit adolescent viewers. His "hard-data" approach differed from the longitudinal fieldwork of Grantzberg, Steinbring, and Hamer (1977) on the cultural role of television among the northern Cree. But both studies documented Native cultural dislocation resulting from the prevalence of southern television viewing.

The interpretative framework for these and the many studies that followed focused on the relationship between television images and information, and Native cultures. Television was understood not as a successful force for Native modernization, but as "an alien socialization agent" (Coldevin, 1977), carrying disruptive cultural images (Grantzberg, 1982; Wilson, 1981; Caron, 1977; O'Connell 1977). The benefits of electronic media were associated with community-level communication (Dicks, 1977; Hudson, 1977; Salter, 1976) rather than attitude change, motivation, and skills to encourage acculturation. Analysis emphasized the historical role of earlier agents of change in Native communities and the expansion of media as a factor in southern control of the North (Mayes, 1972; Valaskakis, 1979). More recent studies have considered the longer-term role of southern media impact (Coldevin & Wilson, 1985) and the role of Native communications projects in northern participatory development (Valaskakis, Robbins, & Wilson, 1984).

No long-term research has been conducted on the impact of Native media in Native communities. But Kate Madden (1990) has begun to analyze Inuit cultural expression in IBC programming; and Native communication societies under the NNBAP have surveyed respective audience viewing patterns and preferences. This research indicates that in many northern areas, Native language use is widespread, especially among the old who often do not speak or understand a second language. As a result, "a high percentage of respondents from all regions tend to listen to or watch Native-language and Native-oriented programming when it is available" (Hudson, 1985, p. 4). The surveys suggest, too, a strong interest in extending Native-language programming and in providing programming that will reach the young, the majority population in most Native communities. This is consistent with the decade-long Inuit lobbying effort to add aboriginal language broadcasting rights to the English and French rights entrenched in the Broadcasting Act.

Equally important to our understanding of Native nations today is the fact that language is intimately but not uniquely associated with culture. In some northern regions such as the eastern Arctic, 95.2 percent of the Inuit population speak Inuktitut (Valaskakis & Wilson, 1985, p. 10). On the other hand, a large percentage of Inuit in Labrador and Indians in the Yukon and British Columbia do not speak their Native language on a regular and daily basis. An analysis of the 1981 census data indicates that English is replacing aboriginal languages in southern regions, especially among the young. The study found that the retention rate for Native languages is higher for Native people the further north they live and the older they are, but concludes that, in general, the retention rate of Native languages is decreasing (Jarvin n.d., p. 13). This suggests a special role for Native media. Working to increase the interest and ability of young speakers, broadcasters may help to slow the growing generation gap between young and old, and the relative isolation of unilingual elders. But at the same time, Native media must respond to the changing cultural and linguistic realities of northern communities, and they must compete with southern media programming. Native cultural products need not be produced exclusively in Native languages. Their importance lies in the reflection of Native perspectives and the extension of community achieved in shared expression, shared information. This position is recognized in the 1990 Native Broadcasting Policy, which defines a Native undertaking not in relation to "the preservation of aboriginal languages and cultures" as proposed by commercial broadcasters, but in relation to Native ownership and control, Native target audience and Native-oriented programming (CRTC, 1990, pp. 6–7).

CONCLUSION

In the two decades during which Native communications has developed, satellites have become a critical force in Canadian broadcasting; they have been joined by fibre optics in the development of telephone and data transmission. Newer satellites have greatly enlarged capacities, and current regulatory policy allows Telesat Canada to distribute communications services directly rather than through common carriers. Debate continues over the definition, role, and mandate of public broadcasting and "narrowcast" or specialty broadcasting services in Canada. And as telecommunications encourages shifts in interaction, control, and culture, aboriginal broadcasting increases in both vulnerability and importance.

The Native Broadcasting Policy and the Northern Native Broadcast Access Program represent a framework for the development of northern communications in Canada. Ironically, in the 1990s this framework is being both strengthened through the provision of a dedicated satellite channel to extend distribution and weakened through cutbacks to production funding for Native broadcasting. At the same time, Native northerners have demonstrated the efficacy of their position as a "first service" and full partner in the regional broadcasting system. The communication services that Native media provide are basic to aboriginal access and participation in the cultural and political realities of northern life. Native northerners will continue to struggle with marginality and unsettling notions of culture and language related to historical patterns of control and the changing nature of Native communities. Native broadcasting will play an increasingly important role in the far North as Canada responds to the threats and promises of new communications technologies.

In the words of George Henry of Northern Native Broadcasting Yukon, "Media consumption without the ability to answer back is the most colonized situation possible" (National Aboriginal Communication Society, 1987). There can be little doubt about the increased tendency of Native people to "answer back."

REFERENCES

Alcock, A., & O'Brien T., (1980, June). *Policies to support radio and television broadcasting in the lesser used languages of the European Community*. Northern Ireland: The University of Ulster.

Applebaum-Hébert Committee. See Canada. Federal Cultural Policy Review Committee. (1982).

Bergman, M. (1985). The impact of free trade on Canadian cultural industries. *Cinema Canada*.

Brody, H. (1975). *The people's land: Eskimos and whites in the eastern Arctic*. Harmondsworth, England: Penguin.

Canada. Department of Communications. (1983). *Northern broadcasting*. Discussion Paper. Ottawa.

Canada. Federal Cultural Policy Review Committee (Applebaum-Hébert Committee). (1982). *Summary of Briefs and Hearings*. Ottawa.

Canada. (1983). *The Northern broadcasting policy*. Federal Government News Release. Ottawa.

Canadian Radio-television and Telecommunications Commission. (1980). The 1980s: A decade of diversity: Broadcasting satellites and pay-TV. *Report of the Committee on Extension of Service to Northern and Remote Communities*. Ottawa.

Canadian Radio-television and Telecommunications Commission. (1990, September 20). *Native Broadcasting Policy*.

Caron, A. (1977, June). The impact of television on Inuit children's cultural "Images." Paper presented at the annual meeting of the International Communication Association, Berlin.

Coldevin, G.O. (1977, Autumn). Anik I and isolation: Television in the lives of Canadian Eskimos. *Journal of Communication, 27*, (4).

Coldevin, G.O., & Wilson, T.C. (1985, September). Effects of a decade of satellite television in the Canadian Arctic. *Journal of Cross-Cultural Psychology, 16*, (3).

Dicks, D.J. (1977, Autumn). From dog sled to dial phone. *Journal of Communication, 27*, (4).

Elberg, N. (1984, October). In search of real Inuit. Paper delivered at the 4th Etudes Inuit Studies Conference. Montreal: Concordia University.

Fleming, A. (1956). *Archibald the Arctic*. New York: Appleton-Century-Crofts.

Graburn, N.H.H. (1979). *Eskimos without igloos*. Boston: Little, Brown and Co.

Grantzberg, G. (1982, Winter). Television as storyteller: The Algonkion Indians of central Canada. *Journal of Communication, 32*, (1).

Grantzberg, G., Steinbring, J., & Hamer, J. (1977, Autumn). New magic for old: TV in Cree culture. *Journal of Communication, 27* (4).

Hudson, H. (1977). *Northern airwaves: A study of the CBC Northern Service*. Ottawa: Keewatin Communication Studies Institute.

Hudson, H. (1985). *The need for Native broadcasting in northern Canada: A review of research*. Ottawa: Department of the Secretary of State.

Innis, H.A. (1950). *Empire and communications*. Toronto: University of Toronto Press.

Inuit Broadcasting Corporation. (1982, August). Discussion Paper. Ottawa.

Jarvin, G.K. (n.d.). *Changes in language use among native peoples of Canada*. Ottawa: Department of Secretary of State.

Katz, E. (1977, Spring). Can authentic cultures survive new media? *Journal of Communication, 27*, (2).

Kelly, N., & Kelly, W. (1973). *The Royal Canadian Mounted Police: A century of history*. Edmonton: Hurtig.

Kenny, G.I. (1971). *Communications study: Man in the north project. Parts I and II*. Montreal: Arctic Institute of North America.

Kroker, A. (1984). *Technology and the Canadian mind*. Montreal: New World Perspectives.

Kuptana, R. (1982, November 30). Brief to the CRTC Ottawa: Inuit Broadcasting Corporation.

Madden, K. (1990, June). *The Inuit Broadcasting Corporation: Developing video to sustain cultural integrity*. Paper delivered at the annual meeting of the International Communication Association, Dublin.

Mayes, R.G. (1972). *Mass communication and Eskimo adaptation in the Canadian Arctic*. M.A. Thesis. Montreal: McGill University.

National Aboriginal Communication Society. (1987). Sharing a dream. Video directed by Jeff Bear.

The Northerners. (1974). (Taqramiut) Les Septentroinaux. La Macaza, Quebec: Northern Quebec Inuit Association.

O'Connell, S. (1977, Autumn). Television and the Canadian Eskimo: The human perspective. *Journal of Communication, 27,* (4).

Phillips, R.A.J. (1967). *Canada's north.* Toronto: Macmillan.

Roth, L. (1982). *The role of Canadian projects and Inuit participation in the formation of a communication policy for the north.* M.A. Thesis. Montreal: McGill University.

Salter, L. (1976). *Community radio—Five years later—Concept and development in review.* Speech prepared for the Canadian Broadcasting League Conference. Halifax: St. Mary's University, August 12.

Schiller, H.I. (1976). *Communication and cultural domination.* White Plains, NY: M.E. Sharpe.

Steele, H. (1936). *Policing the north: The story of the conquest of the Arctic by the Royal Canadian (formerly North-West) Mounted Police.* London: Jarrolds.

Valaskakis, G. (1979). *A communication analysis of interaction patterns: Southern Baffin, eastern Arctic.* Ph.D. Dissertation. Montreal: McGill University.

Valaskakis, G. (1987). From smoke signals to satellite. *The Native Canadian.* Vancouver.

Valaskakis, G., & Wilson, T. (1985). *The Inuit Broadcasting Corporation: A survey of viewing behavior and audience preferences among the Inuit of seven communities in the Baffin and Keewatin regions of the Northwest Territories.* Montreal: Concordia University.

Valaskakis, G., Robbins, R., & Wilson, T. (1984). *The Inukshuk Anik B project: An assessment.* Ottawa: Inuit Tapirisat of Canada.

Vallee, F.G. (1967). *Kabloona and Eskimo in the central Keewatin.* Ottawa: St. Paul University.

Wilford, N. (1986). Northwest Territories Pavillion, Expo 86, Vancouver.

Wilson, T.C. (1981). *The role of television in the eastern Arctic: An educational perspective.* M.A. Thesis. Montreal: Concordia University.

PART III

MEDIA POWER
AND SOCIAL CHANGE

TELEVISION: THE SHARED ARENA

Joshua Meyrowitz

In 1950, only 9 percent of U.S. homes owned television sets. Little more than 25 years later, only 2 percent of households were without one. In a remarkably short time, television has taken a central place in our living rooms and in our cultural and political lives. On average, a U.S. household can now receive 30 channels; only 7 percent of homes receive six or fewer stations. Some 95 percent of homes own a colour TV, 63 percent own two or more sets, and 64 percent own a video cassette recorder.

Television is the most popular of the popular media. Indeed, if Nielsen research and other studies are correct, there are few things that Americans do more than they watch television. On average, each household has a TV on almost 50 hours a week. Forty percent of households eat dinner with the set on. Individually, Americans watch an average of 30 hours a week. We begin peering at TV through the bars of cribs and continue looking at it through the cataracts of old age.

Plato saw an important relationship between shared, simultaneous experience and a sense of social and political interconnectedness. Plato thought that his Republic should consist of no more than 5000 citizens because that was the maximum number of people who could fit in an arena and simultaneously hear the voice of one person. Television is now our largest shared arena. During the average minute of a typical evening, nearly a hundred million Americans are tuned in. While a book can usually win a place on the lists of the top 50 fiction or non-fiction bestsellers for the *year* with 115 000 hardcover sales, a prime-time network program with fewer than 15 million viewers for *each episode* is generally considered a failure.

Even the biggest bestsellers reach only a fraction of the audience that will watch a similar program on television. It took 40 years for *Gone with the Wind* to sell 21 million copies; 55 million people watched the first half of the movie on television in a single evening. The television mini-series "Roots" was watched, in part or whole, by approximately 130 million people in only eight days. Even with the help of the television promotion, fewer than 5 million copies of *Roots* sold in eight years.

The television arena, like a street corner or a marketplace, serves as an environment for us to monitor but not necessarily identify with. Reading a newspaper requires an investment of money and reading effort, and at least some minimal identification with its style and editorial policy. We have to reach out for it and embrace it—both literally and metaphorically. But with television, we simply sit back and let the images wash over us. While we usually select reading material that clearly reflects our own self-image, with TV we often feel we are passively observing what other people are like.

Most of us would feel uncomfortable stopping at a local store to pick up the current issue of a publication titled *Transvestite Times* or *Male Strippers' Review*, or a magazine on incest, child abuse, or adultery. But millions of viewers feel quite comfortable sharing their homes with transvestites, male strippers, and victims and perpetrators of incest, or almost anyone else who appears on "Donahue," "Oprah," or "Geraldo." Ironically, our personal dissociation with TV content allows for the most widespread sharing of similar experience in the history of civilization.

In the 1950s, many intellectuals were embarrassed to admit that they owned a television set, let alone that they spent any valuable time watching it. But the massive saturation of television into virtually every U.S. home now imbues the activity of watching television with multiple layers of social significance. One can watch popular programs not merely to see the program but to see what others are watching. To watch television may not be to stare into the eyes of America, but it is to look over its shoulder and see what Americans see. Watching television—with its often distorted versions of reality—does not allow us to keep our finger on the pulse of the nation so much as it allows us to keep our finger on the pulse the nation is keeping its finger on. With television, it somehow makes sense for a viewer to watch the tube avidly while exclaiming, "My God, I can't believe people watch this stuff!"

Even though many people watch it alone, television is capable of giving each isolated viewer a sense of connection with the outside world and with all the other people who are watching. During major television events—whether fictional or non-fictional—such as the final episode of "M*A*S*H" or the explosion of the *Challenger*, one is likely to find that more than one out of every two people one sees on the street the next day has had a similar experience the night before. Regardless of specific content, then, television often serves a social function similar to the weather: No one takes responsibility for it, often it is quite bad, but nearly everyone pays attention to it and sees it as a basis of common experience and conversational topics. Perhaps this is why even pay cable households spend more than half their viewing time watching "regular" network programming and why the most frequent use of VCRs is for time shifting of programs broadcast by network-affiliated stations.

For many people, someone or something that does not appear on television does not fully exist in the social sense. The Watergate scandals became "real" not when the *Washington Post* reported the stories but when network television news reported that the *Washington Post* reported the stories. Similarly, civil rights and anti-Vietnam War protests became social realities not when demonstrators took to the streets but when the protests were viewed on television. And although most of our early presidents were seen by only a few of the voters of their day, it is now impossible to imagine a serious candidate who would not visit us all on TV. And so it is that politicians, salespeople, protestors, and terrorists all design their messages in the hope of capturing the television eye.

Too Close to the Set

Despite its ubiquity, the impact of television is not yet seen very clearly. For one thing, most of us watch television too closely—not in the way that mothers warn their children about, but in the sense of evaluating television primarily on the basis of whether we like or don't like its programs. Even scholars tend to reduce the impact of television to its past and current programming and to the motives of the institutions that control it. The overwhelming majority of television research and criticism has focused on the nature of the programs, their imitative or persuasive power, their aesthetic value or bankruptcy, the range of meanings that viewers can draw from them, or their underlying economic and political purposes.

These are important but insufficient questions. The effects of a new communication technology cannot be understood fully by looking only at the medium's typical content and patterns of control. To see the limits of such an approach, we need only to consider what its use in the fifteenth and sixteenth centuries would have revealed about the impact of the printing press, then spreading through western culture. A content/institutionalized approach to printing probably would have led observers to conclude that books had two major effects: 1. the fostering of religion (most early books were religious in content) and 2. the strengthening of central religious and monarchal authorities (who controlled much of what was printed). The underlying, but ultimately more significant, long-term effects of the printing press—such as the growth of individual thinking and science and the spread of nationalism and constitutional systems—would remain invisible.

This is not to suggest that the short-term, surface effects are inconsequential. Just look at William Carter. He printed a pro-Catholic pamphlet in England in 1584 and was promptly hanged. Similarly, our current information environment is choked and narrowed by the way television is controlled.

The television business is not structured to deliver quality programming to viewers but rather to deliver viewers to advertisers. We are sold to advertisers in lots of a thousand. The real programming on television is the commercial. That is where the time, the money, and the competition are. That is where the most creative television "artists" (if we want to use that term) are working. The TV shows—whether news or entertainment or "infotainment"—are simply the bait.

We are misled when we are told that program ratings are part of an audience-centred, "democratic" process that allows us to "vote" for shows. In fact, we are usually offered choices among advertiser-friendly programs. This is why TV ratings systems rarely ask whether or why we like or dislike a show or what we would like to see instead. Most ratings simply measure how many of what type of people are there for the ads.

Even if networks can draw millions of viewers to a program, the last thing they want to do is put the audience in a mood that does not mix well with consumption of the advertised products. One of the most-watched programs in television history, "The Day After," for example, was an ad failure. After all, what companies would want their products associated with nuclear holocaust? In fact, as one vice-president of the network confided to me, the airing of "The Day After"—as bland a treatment of its subject as it was—almost led to a stockholder suit against ABC because the network could have made more money airing a rerun of a program such as "The Harlem Globetrotters Visit Gilligan's Island."

But to reduce television to a cultural nuisance or to a slickly disguised salesperson, as some analysts do, is to miss what is happening in our culture because of television and how it—not merely through its content but also as a certain form of shared experience—reshapes our attitudes and behaviours.

The effects of new media of communication arise not solely from their content but also from the new ways in which the medium packages and transmits information. Writing and print, for example, were able to foster the rise of individual thinking and science because they literally put information in the hands of individuals and because they allowed for the recording and wide-scale distribution of ideas that were too complicated to memorize (even by the people who came up with them). Even as William Carter swung from the gallows by regal decree, printing was quietly working against its apparent masters, ultimately secularizing the culture and encouraging the overthrow of monarchies. Similarly, the impact of television cannot be reduced to programs that come through the tube or to the institutions that control it. There are effects apart from, and even in opposition to, these forces.

The most significant long-term effects of television may also lie in its manner of packaging and transmitting information and in the ways that it undoes some of the systems of communication supported by print. Television has changed "who knows what about whom" and "who knows what compared to whom." As a result, it has changed the way we grow from childhood to adulthood, altered our sense of appropriate gender behaviour, shifted our perceptions of our political and other leaders, and affected our general sense of "them" and "us."

VIDEO NURSERY

As printing and literacy spread through western culture, literate adults discovered they could increasingly keep secrets from preliterate and semiliterate children. Adults used books to communicate among themselves without children overhearing. Clerics argued for the development of expurgated versions of the classics, and the notion of the innocence of childhood began to take hold, eventually spreading to the lowest classes with the growth of universal education.

Childhood was to be a time of innocence and isolation. Children were protected from the nasty realities of adult life. Unable to read, very young children had no access to the information available in books. Young children were presented with an idealized version of adult life. Children were slowly walked up the ladder of literacy with a new, somewhat less idealized view of adult life presented to them at each step of reading ability.

Television dilutes the innocence of childhood by undermining the system of information control that supported it. Television bypasses the year-by-year slices of knowledge given to children. It presents the same information to adults and to children of all ages. Children may not understand everything they see on television, but they are exposed to many aspects of adult life that their parents (and traditional children's books) would have once protected them from.

Parents often clamour for more and better children's television. But one could argue that there is no such thing as "children's television," at least not in the sense that there is children's literature. Children's literature is the only literature that children can read, and only children read it. In contrast, studies since the early days of television have found that children often prefer to watch programs aimed at adults. And adults often watch programs aimed at children—about a third of the audience for "Pee Wee Herman's Playhouse" is over eighteen.

At some point during the last decade, each of the following has been among the most popular programs in *all* age groups, including ages two to eleven: "Dallas," "The Muppets," "The Dukes of Hazzard," "Love Boat," "The A-Team," "Cheers," "Roseanne," and "The Golden Girls." Thus, children have been avid viewers of adult soap operas, and adults have found pleasure in a children's puppet show.

In both fictional and non-fictional programs, children learn that adults lie, cheat, drink too much, use drugs, and kill and maim each other. But perhaps the most dramatic revelation that television provides to young children is that parents struggle to control children.

Unlike books, television cannot be used easily by adults as a tool to discuss how to raise children. A parental advice book can be used by adults to communicate among themselves about what to tell and not to tell children. But the same conversation on television is usually overheard by thousands of children, who are thereby exposed to the very topics suggested for secrecy and to the "secret of secrecy" itself—the fact that adults are anxious about their parental roles and conspire to keep secrets from children.

Even seemingly innocent programs reveal significant secrets to children. When the first TV generation watched programs such as "Father Knows Best" and "Leave It to Beaver," for example, they learned that parents behaved one way in front of their children and another way when they were alone. In front of their children, the TV parents were calm, cool, and collected, but away from their kids, they were anxious and concerned about their parental behaviour. Because we often reduce the effects of TV to imitation, we forget that while the children *on* such programs were innocent and sheltered, the children *watching* the shows often saw how adults manipulated their behaviours to make it appear to their children that they knew best. This is a view that undermines traditional parental authority by making children less willing to take adult behaviour at face value. It is no wonder, perhaps, that the children who grew up watching "Father Knows Best" became concerned with the "credibility gap"; that is, the difference between what people proclaim publicly and what they say and feel privately.

Subsequent situation comedies, such as "One Day at a Time," shocked many viewers because the parents in the shows revealed their fears and anxieties about parenting in front of their children and because the child characters on the shows were no longer sheltered or innocent. But in terms of what *child* viewers learned about the concerns of parents, there was relatively little new information. The third phase of family shows, including "The Bill Cosby Show" and "Family Ties," offers a compromise between the two earlier family visions: The line between parents and children has been partly re-established, but the children are more sophisticated than early TV children and the parents are both less surefooted in front of their children and less conspiratorial away from them.

In a book culture, control over the flow of information is literally placed in parents' hands. Parents can easily give some books to children and withhold others. Parents can read one book while their children sit in the same room reading another. Television is not so co-operative. Parents often find it difficult to censor their children's viewing without censoring their own, and parents cannot always anticipate what will happen on TV the way they can flip through a book. A father may think he is giving his daughter a lesson in science as they watch the *Challenger* take off, only to discover that he has exposed her instead to adult hubris and tragedy.

Most television programs are accessible to children in a way that most book content is not. The visual/aural form of television allows children to experience many behaviours and events without the skill of decoding written sentences. And it is much simpler for children to wander off "Sesame Street" and slip beyond "Mr. Rogers' Neighborhood" into grown-up television than it is for children to buy or borrow books from a grown-up library or bookstore. Television takes our children across the globe before we as parents even give them permission to cross the street.

As children's innocence declines, children's literature and children's programming have changed as well. Some children's books now discuss sex and drugs and other once-taboo topics, and war and divorce have recently visited "Mr. Rogers' Neighborhood."

This does not mean that adults should abdicate their authority over children or even give up trying to control children's viewing of television. Adults are more experienced and more knowledgeable. But it does mean that the old support system for unquestioned adult authority has been undermined by television. In a television culture, children are more suspicious of adult authority, and many adults feel somewhat exposed, finding it more difficult to pretend to know everything in front of their children. The result is a partial blurring of traditional child and adult roles. Children seem older and more knowledgeable, and adults now reveal to their children the most childish sides of themselves, such as doubts, fears, and anxieties. Thus, we are seeing more adultlike children and more childlike adults, behaviour styles characteristic of preliterate societies.

GENDER BLENDER

Our society once tried to maintain a clear distinction between the male realm and the female realm. The Victorians spoke of the "two spheres": a public, male world of brutal competitions, rationality, and accomplishments; and a private, female world of home, intuition, and childrearing. Men were to suppress their emotions and women were to suppress their competitiveness. The ideal of separate spheres was quite strong in our society when television became the newest home appliance.

Yet even as television situation comedies and other programs featured very traditional gender roles in the two separate spheres, television, as a shared arena, was beginning to break down the distinction between the male and the female, between the public and the private realms. Television close-ups reveal the personal side of public figures and events (we see tears well up in the eyes of a president; we hear male voices crack with emotion) just as most public events have become dramas that are played out in the privacy of our kitchens, living rooms, and bedrooms. Television has exposed even homebound women to most of the parts of the culture that were once considered exclusively male domains—sports, war, business, medicine, law, politics—just as it has made men more aware of the emotional dimensions and consequences of public actions.

When Betty Friedan wrote in *The Feminine Mystique* that women in 1960 felt a "schizophrenic split" between the frilly, carefree image of women in women's magazines and the important events occurring in "the world beyond the home," most of her examples of the latter were unwittingly drawn from the top television news stories of the year. By 1960, television was present in nearly 90 percent of U.S. homes. Similarly, other feminist writers have described changes in the 1960s by writing metaphorically of the "breaking of boundaries" (Gloria Steinem), "a sudden enlargement of our world" (Elizabeth Janeway), and of women having "seen beyond the bucolic peacefulness of the suburbs to the war zone at the perimeter" (Barbara Ehrenreich and Deirdre English). But these writers seem unaware of how closely their metaphors describe the literal experience of adding a television to a suburban household.

The fact that early TV programs generally portrayed active men and passive, obedient women had no more of an imitative effect on women viewers than the innocent child characters on "Father Knows Best" had on child viewers. Television, it is true, suggested to women how society thought they should behave, just as etiquette books had for centuries. But television did something else as well: It allowed women to observe and experience the larger world, including all-male interactions and behaviours. Indeed, there is nothing more frustrating than being exposed constantly to adventures, activities, and places that you are told are reserved for someone else. Television also demystified the male realm, making it and its inhabitants seem neither very special nor very intimidating. No wonder women have since demanded to integrate that realm.

Television's impact has been greatest on women because they have traditionally been more isolated. But men are affected as well, partly because women have demanded changes in their behaviour and partly because television emphasizes those traits traditionally ascribed to women: feelings, appearance, emotion. On television, "glorious victories" and "crushing defeats" are now conveyed through images of blood and limp bodies and the howls of survivors. Television has helped men to become more aware of their emotions and of the fact that emotions cannot be completely buried. Even at televised public hearings, it is hard to ignore the facial expressions, the yawns, the grimaces, the fatigue.

The way men react to public issues is also being subtly feminized. Men used to make fun of women for voting for candidates because of the candidates' appearance rather than their stands on the issues. But recent polls show that millions of men, as well as women, will now vote for a candidate they disagree with on the issues, if they "personally like" the candidate. About a third of Ronald Reagan's votes came from such supporters.

Television is one of the few public arenas in our culture where men routinely wear make-up and are judged as much on their personal appearance and "style" as on their "accomplishments." If it was once thought that women communicated and men accomplished, it is telling that our most successful recent president was dubbed the

"Great Communicator" and was admired for his gentle voice and manner and his moist-eyed emotional appeals.

With television, boys and girls and men and women tend to share a great deal of similar information about themselves and the "other." Through TV close-ups, men and women see, in one month, many more members of the opposite sex at "intimate distance" than members of earlier generations saw in a lifetime. Further, unlike face-to-face interactions, in which the holding of a gaze may be construed as insulting or as an invitation to further intimacy, television allows one to stare and carefully examine the face, body, and movements of the other sex. Television fosters an easy and uninvolved intimacy.

Just as women have become more involved in the public realm, men are becoming more involved in the private realm, especially in the role of fathers. Traditional distinctions cannot be erased in a generation, of course. But dramatic changes have taken place in a remarkably short time. In 1950, only 12 percent of married women with children under six worked; by 1987, 57 percent did. Recent studies also show that men are now more likely to turn down overtime pay or travel and relocation offers in order to spend more time with their families.

In spite of its often sexist content, television, as an environment shared by both sexes, has made the membranes around the male and female realms more permeable. As a result, the nature of those two realms has been blurring. We are witnessing more career-oriented women and more family-oriented men; we are developing more work-oriented homes, and there is increasing pressure to make the public realm more family-oriented.

PRESIDENTIAL PIMPLES

Just as television tends to mute differences between people of different ages and sexes, so does it tend to mute differences between levels of social status. Although television is certainly an important weapon in the arsenal of leaders, it often functions as a double-edged sword. Unlike other media, television not only allows leaders to reach followers, it also allows followers to gain unprecedented access to the close-up appearance and gestures of leaders.

"Leadership" and "authority" are unlike mere power in that they depend on performance and appeal; one cannot lead or be looked up to if one's presence is unknown. Yet, paradoxically, authority is weakened by excess familiarity. Awe survives through "distant visibility" and "mystified presence." One of the peculiar ironies of our age is that most people who step forward into the television limelight and attempt to gain national visibility become too visible, too exposed, and are thereby demystified.

The speaker's platform once lifted politicians up and away from average citizens, both literally and symbolically. In newspaper quotes and reports, the politician—as flesh-and-bones person—was completely absent. And on radio, politicians were disembodied voices. But the television camera now lowers politicians to the level of the common citizen and brings them close for our inspection. In recent years, we have seen our presidents sweat, stammer, and stumble—all in living colour.

Presidential images were once much better protected. Before TV coverage of press conferences, newspapers were not even allowed to quote a president without his explicit permission. As late as the start of the Eisenhower administration, *The New York Times* and other publications had to paraphrase the president's answers to questions. In earlier administrations, journalists had to submit their questions in advance and were forbidden from mentioning which questions the president refused to answer. Presidential advisers frequently corrected presidents' answers during meetings with the press, and such assistance went unreported. In the face of a "crisis," our presidents once had many hours, sometimes even weeks or months, to consult with advisers and to formulate policy statements to be printed in newspapers. Now, standing before the nation, a president is expected to have all relevant information in his mind—without notes and without consultation with advisers. A president must often start a sentence before the end of the sentence is fully formed in his mind. Even a five-second pause for thought can seriously damage a leader's credibility. The apparent inarticulateness of all our recent presidents may be related more to the immediacy of television than to a decline in our leaders' mental abilities.

In language, the titles "president," "governor," and "senator" still call forth respect. But the close-up TV pictures of the persons filling those offices are rarely as impressive. We cannot help but notice the sweat on the brow, the nervous twitch, the bags under the eyes.

Television not only reduces our awe of politicians, it increases politicians' self-doubt and lowers self-esteem. A speaker's nervousness and mistakes usually are politely ignored by live audiences and therefore soon forgotten by the speaker as well. But with videotape, politicians have permanent records of themselves mispeaking or anxiously licking their lips. Television may be a prime cause of the complaints of indecisive leadership and hesitant "followership" that we have heard since the mid-1960s.

In the 1950s, many people were shocked that a genuine hero, Dwight Eisenhower, felt the need to hire a Hollywood actor to help with his television appearances. But now we are much more sophisticated—and more cynical. We know that one cannot simply *be* the president, but that one has to *perform* the role of "president." The new communication arena demands more control on the part of politicians, but it also makes the attempts at control more visible. Many citizens lived through twelve years of FDR's presidency without being aware that his legs were crippled and that he often needed help to stand. But we are now constantly exposed to the ways in which our presidents and presidential candidates attempt to manipulate their images to create certain impressions and effects.

The result is that we no longer experience political performances as naive audiences. We have the perspective of stage hands who are aware of the constructed nature of the drama. Certainly, we prefer a good show to a bad show, but we are not fully taken in by the performances. Rather than being fooled, we are willingly entertained, charmed, courted, and seduced. Ironically, all the recent discussions of how effectively we are being manipulated may only point out how visible and exposed the machinations now are.

I am not suggesting that television has made us a fully informed and aware electorate. Indeed, relatively few Americans realize how selective an image of the world we receive through television news. When the same sort of occurrences take place in El Salvador and in Nicaragua, or in Poland and in Chile, they are often covered in completely different ways, often in keeping with pre-existing news narratives concerning each country. But regardless of the ways in which the content of television news is often moulded, television is having other effects due to its immediacy and visual nature.

Most of our information about other countries once came through the president and State Department, often after careful planning about how to present the information to the public. This allowed the government to appear to be in control of events and always to have a ready response. In many instances, we now experience events at the same moment as our leaders, sometimes before them. The dramatic images of the fall of the Berlin Wall and other changes in Eastern Europe were watched by the president, the secretary of state, and millions of other Americans at the same moment. The immediacy of television often makes leaders appear to be "standing on the sidelines" rather than taking charge or reacting quickly.

Television's accessible, visual nature also works to level authority. Average citizens gain the feeling that they can form their own impressions of Mikhail Gorbachev, Phillippine "People Power," and other people and events without depending on official interpretations. Once formed, the mass perceptions constrain our leaders' presentation of events. Ronald Reagan found he needed to temper his talk of the "Evil Empire" as the public formed a positive perception of Gorbachev. And the televising of Filipinos facing down Marcos's tanks made it difficult for Americans to accept our president's suggestion that the reported results of that country's election should stand because "there was cheating on both sides." President Reagan might have changed the rhetoric on these topics in any case, but the public's direct access to the television images made it appear that Reagan was following rather than leading the nation.

The speed of television affects authority in relation to domestic events as well. The videotape of the attempted assassination of Ronald Reagan aired on television *before* a coded transmission about the event was received by Vice-President Bush aboard his airplane. Several years later, Reagan had no immediate reaction to the *Challenger* explosion, because millions of Americans saw the *Challenger* explode before he had a chance to watch it on videotape. In both cases, the gap between the experience of the event and a unified administration response made the administration appear temporarily impotent.

As our leaders have lost much control over the flow of information—both about themselves and political events—they have mostly given up trying to behave like the imperial leaders of the past. We now have politicians who strive to act more like the person next door, just as our real neighbours seem more worldly and demand to have a greater say in national and international affairs.

SHARED PROBLEMS

The recognition of television as a new shared arena solves a number of mysteries surrounding television viewing, including: why people complain so bitterly about TV content but continue to watch so much of it; why many Americans say they turn to

television for "most" of their news even though the script for an average evening network news broadcast would fill only two columns of the front page of *The New York
Times*; why people who purchase videotape machines often discover that they have little interest in creating "libraries" of their favourite television programs.

The shared nature of the television environment creates many new problems and
concerns over media content. Content that would be appropriate and uncontroversial in
books directed at select audiences often becomes the subject of criticism when
presented on television. When television portrays the dominant and "normal" white,
middle-class culture, minorities and subcultures protest their exclusion. Yet when
television portrays minorities, many members of the majority being to fear that their
insular world is being "invaded." The nature of the portrayal of some groups becomes
a catch-22. If homosexuals are portrayed in a negative and stereotypical manner, for
example, gay rights groups protest. If homosexuals are portrayed as normal people
who simply have a different sexual orientation, however, other viewers object to
television "legitimizing" or "idealizing" homosexual life.

Similarly, television cannot exclusively present content deemed suitable only for
young children because adult viewers demand more mature entertainment and news.
Yet, when truly mature content is placed on television, many parents complain that the
minds of child viewers are being defiled.

Without the segregation of audiences, a program designed for one purpose may
have quite different effects. An informational program for parents on teenage suicide
may not only help some parents prevent a death, it may also encourage a previously
non-suicidal teenager to consider the option. Similarly, a program on how to outwit a
burglar may make some home owners more sophisticated about protecting their homes
against professional criminals at the same time that it makes unsophisticated burglars
more professional.

Even a choice between happy endings and realistic endings becomes controversial
on television. When programs end happily, critics argue that serious issues are
trivialized through 30- or 60-minute formulas for solving major problems. Yet when
realistic endings are presented—a criminal escapes or good people suffer need-
lessly—critics attack television for not presenting young children with the ideals and
values of our culture.

When looked at as a whole, then, it becomes clear that much of the controversy surrounding television programming is not rooted in television content per se but in the
problems inherent in a system that communicates everything to all types of people at
the same time.

As a shared environment, television tends to include some aspect of every facet of
our culture. Fairy tales are followed by gritty portrayals of crime and corruption.
Television preachers share the airwaves with female wrestlers. Poets and prostitutes
appear on the same talk shows. Actors and journalists compete for Nielsen ratings. But
there is little that is new about any of the information that is presented on television;
what *is* new is that formerly segregated social arenas are blurred together. Information
once shared only among people of a certain age, class, race, religion, sex, profession,
or other subgroup of the culture has now been thrown into a shared, public forum—
and few are wholly satisfied with the mishmash.

A substantial part of the social significance of television, therefore, may lie less in what is on television than in the very existence of television as a shared arena. Television provides the largest simultaneous perception of a message that humanity has ever experienced. Through television, Americans often gain a strange sort of communion with each other. In times of crisis—whether an assassination or a disaster—millions of Americans sit in the glow of their TV sets and watch the same material over and over again in an effort, perhaps, to find comfort, see meaning, and feel united with the other faceless viewers.

Even when video cassettes and other activities pull people away from broadcast and cable television, the shared arena is not destroyed. The knowledge of its existence functions in many ways like the knowledge of the "family home" where relatives can spontaneously gather at times of crisis or celebration. The shared arena does not have to be used every day to have a constant psychological presence.

Majority Consciousness

The shared arena of television does not lead to instant physical integration or to social harmony. Indeed, the initial effect is increased social tension. Informational integration heightens the perception of physical, economic, and legal segregation. Television enhances our awareness of all the people we cannot be, the places we cannot go, the things we cannot possess. Through exposure to a wider world, many viewers gain a sense of being unfairly isolated in some pocket of it.

Shared experiences through television encourage members of formerly isolated and distinct groups to demand equal rights and treatment. Today's "minority consciousness," then, is something of a paradox. Many people take renewed pride in their special identity, yet the heightened consciousness develops from the ability to view one's group from the outside; that is, it is the result of no longer being fully *in* the group. The demand for full equality in roles and rights dramatizes the development of a mass "majority," a single large group whose members do not want to accept any arbitrarily imposed distinctions in roles and privileges. The diminutive connotation of the term *minority* does not seem to refer to the small number of people in the group, but rather to the limited degree of access the members feel they have to the larger society. The concept of minority as it is sometimes applied to women—the majority of the population—is meaningless in any other sense.

Ironically, many minority group members express their special desires to dissolve into the mainstream, to know what everyone else knows, to experience what everyone else experiences. When gays, blacks, Hispanics, women, the disabled, and others publicly protest for equal treatment under the law, they are not only saying: "I'm different and I'm proud of it," they are also saying, "I should be treated as if I'm the same as everyone else." As gay politician Harry Britt of San Francisco has said: "We want the same rights to happiness and success as the nongay." In this sense, many minorities proclaim their special identity in the hope of losing at least part of it.

Television makes it seem possible to have integration, but the social mechanisms are not always in place. The potential for gaining access to the male realm, for example, is much greater for some women than for others. The feminist movement has primarily advanced upper- and middle-class women—often through the hiring of lower-class women to clean house and mind children. For many segments of our society, television has raised expectations but provided few new opportunities.

The shared information environment fostered by television also does not lead to the identical behaviour or attitudes among all individuals. Far from it. What is increasingly shared is a similar set of *options*. The choice of dress, hairstyle, speech pattern, profession, and general style of life is no longer as strongly linked as it once was to traditionally defined groups.

Michel Foucault argued convincingly that the membranes around prisons, hospitals, military barracks, factories, and schools thickened over several hundred years leading up to the twentieth century. Foucault described how people were increasingly separated into distant spheres in order to homogenize them into groups with single identities ("students," "workers," "prisoners," "mentally ill," etc.). The individuals within these groups were, in a sense, interchangeable parts. And even the distinct identities of the groups were subsumed under the larger social system of internally consistent, linearly connected, and hierarchically arranged units. While Foucault, observed that modern society segregated people in their "special spheres" in order to homogenize individuals into components of a larger social machine, he did not observe the current, post-modern counter-process. As the membranes around spatially segregated institutions become more informationally permeable, through television and other electronic media, the current trend is toward integration of all groups into a relatively common experiential sphere—with a new recognition of the special needs and idiosyncrasies of individuals. Just as there is now greater sharing of behaviours among people of different ages, different sexes, and different levels of authority, there is also greater variation in the behaviours of people of the same age, same sex, and same level of authority.

A GLOBAL MATRIX

In many instances, the television arena is now international in scope. Over 400 million people in 73 countries watch the Academy Awards; "Live Aid" reach 1.5 billion people in 160 countries; Eastern European countries monitor western television; westerners watched Romanian television as capturing the TV station became the first goal of a revolution; the world watched as Chinese students in Tiananmen Square held English protest signs in front of western TV cameras. The shared arena of television is reinforced through worldwide phone systems, satellites, fax machines, and other electronic media.

But this larger sense of sharing with "everybody" is too wide and diffuse, too quickly changing, too insubstantial. Metaphors aside, it is not possible to experience the whole world as one's neighbourhood or village. Even discounting the numerous political, economic, and cultural barriers that remain, there is a limit to the number of people with whom one can feel truly connected. Electronic sharing leads to a broader, but also a shallower, sense of "us."

The effect of this is both unifying and fractionating. Members of the whole society (and world) are growing more alike, but members of particular families, neighbourhoods, and traditional groups are growing more diverse. On the macro level, the world is becoming more homogeneous, but on the micro level, individuals experience more choice, variety, and idiosyncrasy. We share more experiences with people who are thousands of miles away, even as there is a dilution of the commonality of experience with the people who are in our own houses and neighbourhoods. So the wider sense of connection fostered by electronic media is, ironically, accompanied by a greater retreat to the core of the isolated self. More than ever before, the post-modern era is one in which *everyone* else seems somewhat familiar—and somewhat strange.

As traditional boundaries blur—between regions, between nations, between east and west—there is a rise in factional and ethnic violence within areas that formerly seemed relatively homogeneous. Along with increased hope for world peace, the shared arena may stimulate new types of unrest. As the threat of world war recedes, we are faced with an increase in skirmishes, riots, and terrorism. Whether the era we are now entering will ultimately be viewed as a time of unprecedented unity or a period of unprecedented chaos remains to be seen.

REPRESENTING ORDER

Richard Ericson, Patricia Baranek, and Janet Chan

The eighteenth century was the age for analyzing society as a machine, the nineteenth century was the age for analyzing society as an organism, and the twentieth century is the age for analyzing society as a communications network. Today an understanding of society, and the institutions of which it is comprised, must include analysis of what passes for knowledge and how it is communicated. Harold Innis, Marshall McLuhan, and Raymond Williams are among the prominent scholars who have taught us that effort to see through society and culture must include analysis of public conversations and the ways those conversations are communicated.

In this paper we analyze public conversations about crime, law, and justice, and how they are communicated in the news media. We broaden our previous research in this field (Ericson, Baranek, & Chan, 1987, 1989) methodologically, theoretically, and substantively.

In terms of methodology, we employ content analysis to examine news products in the aggregate. A limitation of our previous studies is that they present a series of case examples but no aggregate view. What is now required is a composite portrait of news products, and it is this mosaic that is crafted in the present volume.

In terms of theory, we explore how and why our public conversations are dominated by talk of crime, law, and justice. In our previous work we demonstrated that news is produced by journalists and sources in power/knowledge relations involving imputations of deviance and efforts at control. In the present work we show that the aggregate product of this activity is representations of order. News of deviance and control represents order through constituting an active discourse about the ordering activities of the people reported on. As such, news perpetually represents order—morality, procedural form, and social hierarchy—in ways that help people to order their daily lives. As an active *agency* of social control, stability, and change, news representations provide people with preferred versions and visions of social order, on the basis of which they take action.

In terms of substance, we focus on how news varies among news outlets that operate within different media and market orientations. In our previous research, we learned that the format constraints of each medium and each market orientation have substantial influence on the practices of journalists and news sources. While detailing the strategies and techniques of journalists and sources in dealing with different medium and market formats, we did not analyze the medium and markets either as a central focus or in terms of aggregate data. "It remains important to study variation among media (not only networks and newspapers but, importantly, wire services, radio, and local television) and among institutions within a single medium" (Gitlin, 1980, p. 302). Are news organizations that operate within the same medium most similar, regardless of their market orientation? Are news organizations with a similar market orientation most similar, regardless of the medium in which they operate?

In this paper, we initially elaborate our theoretical focus on news as a discourse that represents order. We then detail the differences in media and market orientation that inform our subsequent analyses of variation in news of social deviance, law, and justice.

NEWS, LAW, AND ORDER

The news institution focuses upon what is out of place: the deviant, equivocal, and unpredictable. News operatives attend to the more calamitous happenings in other institutions that have proved difficult to classify or that contradict standard expectations in the social structure about rights and the distribution of power. The goal is to provide a set of classifications that are workable in that they establish the normal, reduce equivocality, and increase predictability—that is, to represent order.

News operatives pursue this goal through the use of social and cultural practices that have been well documented (Altheide, 1976; Schlesinger, 1978; Tuchman, 1978; Fishman, 1980; Ericson, Baranek, & Chan, 1987). These practices include the use of formats—media, language, techniques (e.g., dramatization, simplification, personalization)—that make news discourse distinctive, and distinctively a part of common sense. The common-sense knowledge available in the news does not provide instruction on "*how things are*" as much as "*where they fit*" into the order of things (Hartley, 1982; Hall, 1979, p. 325).

In telling stories about where things fit, the news deals with three fundamental aspects of order. First, there is *moral evaluation*: whether something is in or out of order is judged in terms of whether it is good or bad, healthy or unhealthy, normal or abnormal, efficient or inefficient. As such, order is not a neutral concept. Second, order incorporates a conception of *procedure*. Order entails proceeding according to an established sequence or customary procedure. It is a method according to an established sequence or customary procedure. It is a method according to which things are understood to act or events to take place. When things or events do not proceed methodically, visualizations of deviance come to the forefront and procedural strays are identified. Third, order addresses *hierarchy*. Order means class, status, position, rank, and distinctions as to quality (higher and lower orders). It entails differentiation on the basis of special interests, occupation, character, excellence, and so on. News is fundamentally a discourse of morality, procedure, and hierarchy, providing symbolic representations of order in these terms.

Symbols are essential to the quest for order. Humans construct order in the form of symbols that can be referred to, deferred to, and used to accomplish everyday routines. Symbols have the practical "capacity to inspire or to give meaning to individual or collective activity, to delegitimate other activity and to bring to bear the force of social control. In a word, symbols and symbol systems provide an important ordering impulse to social affairs and to the collective views of the world. Thus they are an essential part of the reality of everyday life" (Wuthnow et al., 1984, p. 37).

The act of making symbols, and of remaking them in the practical activities of everyday life, is captured by the word "representing." Humans perpetually represent the world around them in and through the available symbolic forms. Whether it is news discourse in newspapers, radio, and television; scientific discourse in scholarly journals; or legal disclosure in case-law books, there is in common an effort to represent a world in which one's descriptions make sense.

News production involves five interrelated components that together define "representing." The components are visualizing, symbolizing, authorizing, staging, and convincing. Through dramatized descriptions, metaphoric language, and pictures, news depicts events that are called up in the mind (visualized) even while they remain invisible to the eye. News representations are symbolic in the sense that they embody, stand for, or correspond to persons, events, processes, or states of affairs being reported on. News representation involves authorization of who can be a representative or spokesperson of a source organization, of what sources are "authorized knowers" (Tuchman, 1978). In addition, journalists authorize themselves to represent the people, to stand in for citizens in making representations to powerful officials and bureaucracies on their behalf. News also "represents" in the sense of being staged according to standard locations, scripts, props, and actors who are well-rehearsed in news-media formats and fictions (Ericson, Baranek, & Chan, 1987). Through all of the components noted above, news representation involves a process of convincing others, for example, making statements by way of expostulation, remonstrance, or incentive that will "bring the facts home" and thereby influence others. Representing order in the news always combines the five core ingredients of visualizing, symbolizing, authorizing, staging, and convincing.

Representing order entails consideration of the *conditions* necessary for the reproduction of morality, procedural form, and hierarchical relations. Of particular significance is an assessment of the extent to which threats or dangers to hierarchy are absent, for example, levels of crime or public protest. Representing order also addresses the procedures by which threats and dangers are minimized, including especially the rule of law and the police power of the state. Order is "the condition in which laws or usages regulating the public relations of individuals to the community, and the public conduct of members or sections of the community to each other, are maintained and observed; the rule of law or constituted authority; law-abiding state; absence of insurrection, riot, turbulence, unruliness, or crimes of violence" (*Oxford English Dictionary*).

Order thus has legal meaning. Law is a conceptual device for the co-ordination of institutional activities. Law is a kind of "order system" (Weber, 1954, p. 13) that functions to allocate resources (by guaranteeing and protecting relationships, and by intervening to enforce policies and programs); to regulate and resolve conflict (by providing principles and procedures for doing so); and to keep the peace (by establishing rules of behaviour and enforcing violations and sanctions). News discourse is dominated by representations of law and legal relations in these terms. It concentrates on the allocation of resources, the regulation and resolution of conflicts, and peace-keeping. It focuses on procedural improprieties that raise questions of law; it assigns responsibility and thereby specifies who should be controlled by what legal procedures; and it relies upon legal officials and their documents to support the validity of its claims about what needs to be done to keep things in order. Contemporary with the society it reports on, news discourse represents order through a particular obsession with law.

There are many affinities between law and the news media in representing order. Both the law and the news media offer disciplinary and normalizing discourses (Foucault, 1977), intertextually related to each other and to other disciplinary and normalizing institutions and discourses, whether religious, economic, or political. As Goodrich (1986, p. 147) observes, "any common-law text belongs to a wider tradition and community of texts (intertextuality) and the values that such tests espouse. To a very great extent the so-called 'logic of the Common Law' is precisely this tireless elaboration and affirmation of the values of legal community and legal order—the text is as much sermon and an exhortation as it is in any strict sense an exercise of logical subsumption." The legal text combines with others, including the news, to make authoritative imprints of order. With the news media, the law participates actively in the constitution of social order by functioning as "social discourse, as part of a continuing political and administrative dialogue as to the terms and conditions of social life" (ibid, p. 20). As such, news of law serves as an influential vehicle through which the authority system can instruct people on what to *be* as well as what to *do*.

As disciplinary and normalizing discourses, law and news are both fundamentally concerned with *policing*, defined in the original French sense, as a mechanism for the moral health and improvement of the population. Law and news police the major institutions of society in terms of how the classifications, values, and procedures of these institutions fit with the expectations of various evaluators. This policing fosters a perpetual public conversation about what institutional arrangements are most appropriate.

In the process of policing, law and news articulate public morality. Morality is built into the classifications that members use for conducting their routine business. The very act of classification, including disputes about misclassification, involves questions of right and wrong and is therefore loaded with moral content. Morality is embedded in an institution's classification scheme, and it is this scheme that gives, and frames, a sense of justice. In policing classifications, values, and procedures, the law and news offer a sense of justice.

The news media and law also share an affinity in claiming that their policing is in the public interest. The basis of this claim is the appearance of neutrality. The consequence of this claim is that the news media and law are able to accomplish a degree of legitimacy and authority for their own institutions, while also selectively underpinning or undercutting legitimacy and authority of other social institutions.

Moral principles and justifications require publicity (Bok, 1979, p. 96), especially as they are used in quests for legitimacy. Legitimacy is defined in terms of right and just actions. When justice and propriety can be imputed to actions, the legitimacy of those actions is in place. The importance of legitimacy is that it offers stability and order, not only in the narrow sense of preserving the status quo, but also in the sense of ensuring an adaptive capacity to cope with strains or changes in the environment. As Habermas (1975, 1979) states, legitimacy depends on the ability of authorities to make convincing *claims*, arguments that they are acting in accordance with social norms. Hence questions of legitimacy revolve around procedural norms, procedural propriety, and the search for and sanctioning of procedural strays. Especially regarding the legitimacy of the state, this obsession with procedure is expressed in terms of the constitutionality and legality of decisions.

The news-media institution is pivotal to the ability of authorities to make convincing claims. It offers a pervasive and persuasive means by which authorities from various institutions can attempt to obtain wider consent for their moral preferences. Moral authority is always subject to *consent*, and legitimacy is always something that is *granted*. There is institutional space for choice in consenting to a given moral authority and in granting legitimacy, albeit circumscribed by institutional frames and their imprints on reality and morality.

The legal institution is also pivotal to the ability of authorities to make convincing claims. Public conversations about law are not only instrumentally directed at the solution and rationalization of particular problems, but also expressions of authority. Law justifies authority. Perfected, law makes authority appear natural, part of the order of things. Justifications of authority in law invoke not only core cultural values of justice, such as freedom and equality, but also core social institutions, such as the state and its policing apparatuses. Thus legal decisions are taken in the name of the state, the maintenance of particular moral standards, and the interests of the legal institution itself (e.g., the efficient administration of justice or so as not to bring the administration of justice into disrepute).

The news media and law also share affinities in their techniques of policing and moral brokerage. They share an orientation to conflicts that emerge during events, the individualization and personalization of conflicts, procedural form, realism, and precedent.

The news media and law share an event-orientation, examining conflicts as they arise on a specific, case-by-case basis. They both address moral principles deemed applicable to conflicts that emerge during particular events. That is, moral principles are articulated, delineated, sustained, and altered as they are grounded in the particular conflict, rather than summarized and synthesized into abstract concepts and rankings.

The news media and law also deal with moral principles through individualization and personalization. A lot of news consists of moral-character portraits: of demon criminals, of responsible authorities, of crooked politicians, and so on. The emphasis on individual morality is not only a dramatic technique for presenting news stories as serial narratives involving leading actors but also a political means of allocating responsibility for actions and attributing accountability. Moreover, in law enforcement, as in news, personalization combined with an event-orientation "produces the appearance (or collective representation) that troublesome persons rather than troublesome social structures are at fault. This mystifies the social roots of trouble in a society that is structurally unequal" (Pfohl, 1985, p. 353). By individualizing problems on a case-by-case basis, the news and law rule out systemic and structural accounts that might question the authority of cultural values, the state, and the news and legal institutions themselves. As Goodrich (1986, p. 204) observes with respect to law, "It is of the very essence of legal rhetoric that it individualizes the issues before the court. Legal meaning is always to be attached to individual acts and legal explanation is correspondingly biographical and moral rather than sociological and contextualizing."

The emphasis on concrete events and individuals involved in them is linked to another aspect of moral brokerage in both news and law, namely the emphasis on procedures. Both news and law can be described as social discourses of procedural propriety. Both are obsessed with institutional procedures and how they cohere with interests, morality, and accountability. This obsession is in keeping with the decreasing significance of absolute values or tradition in sustaining legitimacy, and the increasing significance of procedural propriety for claims of legitimacy. It is also in keeping with the search for responsibility and accountability, and the attendant emphasis on effects of actions more than on causes. As Wuthnow and associates (1984, p. 222) observe, referring to the work of Habermas on legitimation,

> the legitimacy of the modern state no longer rests on tradition or absolute values, but is rooted in conceptions of proper *procedures*— procedures deemed legitimate if they have been established according to norms of legality and constitutionality and if they conform to certain conceptions of citizenship and representation. They are intended to serve as mechanisms for negotiating policies oriented towards the common good. The modern period is characterized by a relatively high degree of reflection about these procedures. They are not taken for granted as the way things simply must be, but are consciously subjected to scrutiny to determine if they in fact produce desired consequences.

While legal procedures may have been established with reference to tradition or higher morality—God, truth, justice, community, democracy—such reference tends to be expressed rhetorically or is simply silenced in the drone of administrative discourse about procedural propriety.

The event-orientation, personalization, and obsession with procedure in the news are packaged realistically. While news events are staged and performed by actors in social dramas—for example, in news conferences, formally structured interviews, and photo opportunities—they are "naturalized" and presented as unmediated reality. While news is politically and socially constructed, includes elements that are fabricated and fictive, and presents evaluative differences as differences in fact (Ericson, Baranek, & Chan, 1987), it appears as reality. That is, while news is based on the laws of social and moral constructs, it appears as if it is based on the laws of nature.

> The world *is*, naturally and of itself, what the mind-originated conventions of realism say it is . . . a *story* may be fictional, but the way it is related tells it like it is . . . realism requires that it be accepted not as *one* way of seeing, but as *the* way of seeing; realism's reference is not to bourgeois modes of thought but rather to

nature itself. . . . Once the "real" is established as such, it becomes a vehicle for the communication of messages which embody, not our "real" social relationships, but rather cultural mythologies *about* those relationships (Fiske and Hartley, 1978, pp. 161, 165, 170).

Law also operates in the mode of realism. Law "justifies authority and makes it appear natural" (Goodrich, 1986, p. 64) through conventions and techniques similar to those we have identified in the news. While law is politically and socially constructed (McBarnet, 1981), includes aspects that are fictive (Fuller, 1967; Scheppele, 1990), and presents evaluative differences as differences in fact (Goodrich, 1986), its realistic functioning in public culture erases these aspects. It functions as if facts naturally relate to laws without human and organizational mediation. If functions as if it is in pursuit of *the* truth—as if legal truth, and procedures for establishing legal truth, authenticate and guarantee "the whole truth" rather than truth reduced to the genre capacities of the law report. It functions as if legal proof, which is largely a matter of formal procedure, and knowledge, which is largely a matter of the substance of the facts, are the same thing. To paraphrase what Fiske and Hartley are quoted as saying above: a law report may have fictional properties but the way it is related tells it like it is. Even though the law report is limited to its genre capacities, as realism it requires acceptance not as *one* way of seeing but as *the* way of seeing. As realism the law report does not embody real social relationships but cultural mythologies about these relationships.

Presented realistically, the news and the law have the character of precedent, "the repetition of a discourse or way of life and mode of belonging" (Goodrich, 1986, pp. 127–28). Precedent provides a vocabulary for classification of the world, and authority for that classification (Ericson, Baranek, & Chan, 1987, 1989). It is common-sense knowledge about the order of things, a source of comfort about what seems right and real. Through repetitive formulas and ritualized tests, precedent literally "brings home" a familiar discourse that people feel comfortable with and incorporate as a significant part of everyday life. Given all of the affinities between law and news, it is little wonder that the most familiar discourse today is a blend of news, law, and order.

THE REPRESENTATIVES OF ORDER

Order is a verb as well as a noun. As a verb, order connotes *agency*: giving orders or commands that are intended to produce morality, procedural form, and hierarchical relations. It connotes "the *action* of putting or keeping in order; regulation, ordering, control," and bringing "into order or submission to lawful authority; hence, to inflict disciplinary punishment on; to correct, chastise, punish" (*Oxford English Dictionary*). It connotes people in *interaction*, actively seeking to co-ordinate and control each other's actions by identifying strays and responding to them through proper procedures.

News discourse involves journalists engaging sources in representing order through acts of visualizing, symbolizing, authorizing, staging, and convincing. As documented in our previous studies (Ericson, Baranek, & Chan, 1987, 1989), representing is embedded in the micropolitics of power/knowledge struggles between journalists and sources. While news is a highly institutionalized form of knowledge, its institutionalization depends on the power/knowledge struggles of sources and journalists. Social order is reproduced in micro-episodes of conflict (Collins, 1975), including discursive struggles or meaning contests over what is reported (secrecy and publicity) and how it is reported (the ordering and combining of words). And, while "meanings are gained or lost through struggles . . . what is at stake is ultimately quite a lot more than either words or discourses" (Macdonnel, 1986, p. 51).

What is at stake is news as a power resource. The institutions and processes of the news media are entwined with political structures and processes more generally (Garnham, 1986, p. 87). While access to the news depends on the possession of other resources of social, political, and economic power, the news resource itself is used to regulate the control and distribution of these other resources (Golding, Murdock, & Schlesinger, 1986; Ericson, Baranek, & Chan, 1989; H. Schiller, 1989). The very condition of possibility of news as knowledge is in hierarchical roles and the power relations they entail in terms of control of resources. Analytically, the concern is not whether news as knowledge is true or false, but how it enters into power relations and serves to legitimate or to undermine these relations. In summary, sources and journalists do not merely report on politics, they constitute the news media as a political institution. In the representations that emerge from their discursive struggles, they construct the community, including especially its sense of order (Williams, 1961).

As they engage discursive struggles in a particular institution, journalists become part of that institution, including its processes of social control. We have documented this thoroughly in the case of journalistic involvement in the legal institution (Ericson, Baranek, & Chan, 1987, 1989). Journalists are directly involved in the activities of lawmakers and law-enforcers, joining with them as agents of social control. This social-control activity includes surveillance of deviant people and organizations, the identification of procedural strays, recommendations for controlling them, and direct social control through the stigmatic effects of publicity. The legal agencies themselves are included as objects of journalistic surveillance and control. The news-media institution intersects with the legal institution as part of the coercive apparatus as well as the ideological apparatus. "No hard and fast line can be drawn between the mechanisms of hegemony and the mechanisms of coercion; the hold of hegemony rests on elements of coercion, just as the force of coercion over the dominated presupposes and reinforces elements and hegemony" (Gitlin, 1980, p. 253).

Hegemony addresses how superordinates manufacture and sustain support for their dominance over subordinates through dissemination and reproduction of knowledge that favours their interests and how subordinates alternatively accept or contest this knowledge. The "hegemonic" (Williams, 1977) is produced out of transactions between superordinates and subordinates, and entails enormous labour, meets resistance, gets deflected, needs revision, and is never complete. The hegemonic process is at the core of transactions between journalists and sources. "A lived hegemony . . . is never either total or exclusive" (ibid, 112–13), and is "not so much the finished article itself, but the whole process of argument, exchange, debate, consultation and speculation by which it emerges" (Hall, 1979, p. 342).

It is "a lived hegemony" as a process, not as a "finished article," that appears in the news. The news provides a daily barometer of hegemonic processes. Through a focus on conflict and opposition, in and between major social institutions, the news provides "indicative features of what the hegemonic process has in practice had to work to control" (Williams, 1977, pp. 112–13). The central aspect of this focus is reporting claims to authority and challenges to those claims, in the context of conflict over one or more of the following: the stratification of expert knowledge; the stratification of official knowledge; key values such as freedom and equality; rights associated with these values, such as rights to liberty and well-being; and just procedures to achieve these rights, including legal procedures. Daily news about procedural propriety, rights claims, value conflicts, official versus unofficial versions of events, and expert renditions of events testify to hegemonic processes at work. Since there is a high level of conflict and contradiction in the discursive struggles of news production in these terms (Ericson, Baranek, & Chan, 1987, 1989), conflict and contradiction are also evident in daily news.

There are three general categories of participants in the news process. There are news sources, people who make news through their positions of institutional authority or involvement in newsworthy events. There are journalists, people who are mandated by their news organizations to make news in conjunction with authorized sources. There are consumers, people who make news through reading, watching, and listening to it, and locating its meaning in their own lives.

While research on relations between journalists and their sources stresses that "both media and interpersonal interaction . . . [are] part of the same system of 'behaving' or responding to the behaviour of others" (Meyrowitz, 1985, p. x), the point holds for everyone who reads, watches, and/or listens to the mass media. People spend several hours each day exposed to the mass media. Many people spend more time in "mass-mediated" interaction than in direct "live" interaction with other people. The mass media are just about everywhere—not at the level of production, in the sense claimed by some news organizations that their journalists are everywhere to reflect reality (Ericson, Baranek, & Chan, 1987), but in the sense that news broadcasts penetrate all temporal and spatial arrangements in society. Television news appears on video screens in bars, in the home, and in prison cells. Radio news accompanies daily activities such as working, shopping, driving an automobile, riding in an elevator, sitting in a waiting room, and waiting on the telephone for someone to deal with a business or service call.

News messages become part of the repertoire of extrasituational information used to engage in the transactions of everyday life. News words are also deeds, providing links to further action. "Words build bridges to actions, and some people will choose to walk over those bridges" (Wagner-Pacifici, 1986, p. 87). Knowledge derived from the mass media is used along with that obtained from person-to-person interaction and other sources as part of the person's "information system" (Meyrowitz, 1985), on the basis of which further action is taken.

These observations on the interactive nature of mass media suggest that there is substantial overlap among the roles of source, journalist, and consumer. News sources often function as journalists by, for example, submitting news releases that are published or broadcast verbatim, and producing commissioned features or regular slots or columns for news organizations. Sources are also avid news consumers, staying "on top" of the news in order to manage the news in directions that will keep them "on top" of the authority structure of their institution. Journalists often function as news sources by, for example, being interviewed by journalists from other news outlets and writing pieces for publications produced by the organizations they themselves report on. Journalists are also avid news consumers, obtaining most of their ideas for story assignment and angles from previous news stories. News consumers who are not regular news sources often function as news sources by, for example, calling in story ideas, using consumer-complaint columns or action lines, participating in phone-in segments on broadcast media, and being the subjects of "person in the street" segments to show reaction to news stories. News consumers also function as journalists by, for example, writing letters to the editor and participating in popular news formats that allot them air time or column space to express their views.

There is heuristic value to thinking in terms of four broad categories of news sources: spokespersons for government institutions and organizations, spokespersons for institutions and organizations outside of government, individual citizens, and journalists.

The main research focus has been on sources in major institutions, especially those in government, because of their importance as authorized knowers to the mass media, and because of the significance of the news media to them. From the time of the founding of newspapers, governments have recognized the significance of news communication as an organizer of public opinion and as an agency of social control. Governments were active in buying and subsidizing newspapers, and journalists were also "bought" (Burns, 1979, pp. 48–49). Governmental purchases of media power have continued to the present era, including the practices of keeping journalists on retainer (Royal Commission on Newspapers [RCN], 1981a, p. 61), buying advertising (Singer, 1986), and establishing national broadcasting corporations (e.g., the Canadian Broadcasting Corporation and the British Broadcasting Corporation). While direct purchases are giving way to apparently more distant and benign public relations machines, behind this veil of administrative decency contemporary public relations perpetuates the same purpose of being close enough to the mass media to influence what they publicize.

Large corporations and interest groups have also realized the purchasing power of public-relations operations. Private capital is invested in the symbolic politics of news and advertising because sophistication in defending against bad news and trafficking in good news is seen as an essential part of achieving capital gains (Blyskal & Blyskal, 1985; D. Schiller, 1986; H. Schiller, 1989; Garnham, 1986; Ericson, Baranek, & Chan, 1989, chap. 5).

Both government and private-sector organizations are oriented to public relations, including news, because public communications are an essential component of organizational enactment (on organizational enactment, see Weick, 1979, 1983; Meyer & Rowan, 1977; Putnam & Pacanosky, 1983; Rock, 1986, 1988; Manning, 1982, 1988; Ericson, Baranek, & Chan, 1987, 1989). Organizations are first and foremost *images*, "subjective congeries of experience which are bound and located spatially and temporally" (Manning, 1982, p. 13). Thus "most 'objects' in organizations consist of communications, meaning, images, myths and interpretations" (Weick, 1979, p. 156). These objects are used by members to create the ideology of the organization. Ideology gives organizational members their sense of place and power in interorganizational relations, their authoritative position.

"In so far as organizational work reproduces the larger order of authority in society, it reflects the position of the structure of meaning in class and power systems as well. Organizations are sources of hegemonic meanings, and tools by which interests are given shape" (Manning, 1982, p. 131). As such, organizations provide the discourse and the platform on which members can perform their authority. The news media do their part by providing outlets for performances (Meyrowitz, 1985; Ericson, Baranek, & Chan, 1989). An adequate performance depends on variously avoiding news as well as taking part in it. Through both an ability to stay out of the news and an ability to shine when the news searchlight becomes a spotlight on their activities, sources enact their organizations and thereby help to establish their place in the hierarchy of authority. The power to stay out of the news, and alternatively to have access to the news, reflects social structure and hierarchy, and news content in turn communicates knowledge that is hierarchically and differentially distributed.

People appear in the news as individuals when there is no specification of an institutional role and status directly relevant to the story. The individual does not appear in the news as a representative of an organization, or as representative of the public in a statistical sense. Rather, the individual is typically used to make a representation on behalf of "the public," to express what are visualized to be public sentiments about government policy, a calamitous event, an industrial strike, etc. As such, the individual presents the fiction of "the public" that is central to mass democracy.

Journalists function as news sources in authoring texts—working in material that makes the journalist himself or herself the original source of the material (Ericson, Baranek, & Chan, 1987, chap. 7). This source function is evident when the anchor on radio or television news interviews a reporter from his or her own organization. It is also common practice for the anchor or reporter from a broadcast news organization to interview journalists of other news organizations, especially in foreign-news coverage. The Canadian Broadcasting Corporation's "The Journal" uses this format frequently: its experts abroad are often journalists who happen to be posted to the place in question or who reside there permanently and are members of a local news organization. More pervasive are practices related to the use of already published news produced by journalists from other news organizations: the radio-news practice of "ripping and reading" news items from local newspapers; the use of syndicated videotapes, audio-tapes, and print columns; and the use of news-wire material. Journalists function as news sources, both directly and indirectly, with great frequency.

Journalists and their news organizations are key players in hegemonic processes. They do not simply report events, but participate in them and act as protagonists. Journalism is "the art of structuring reality, rather than recording it" (Smith, 1978, p. 168). The media institution affords journalists considerable power as *selectors* of which people can speak in public conversations, as *formulators* of how these people are presented, and as *authors* of knowledge.

As selectors, journalists influence which institutions and which particular spokespersons within institutions will be given access (space with opportunity for favourable representation), given mere coverage (space but with the risk of unfavourable representation), or excluded (no space). Journalists have the power to "certify" the "authorized knowers" (Tuchman, 1978) who serve as regular sources in the eternal recurrence of officially generated news, as well as the "stereotyped persons" who are "accorded a right to parade quickly through the pageant of the news" (Gitlin, 1980, p. 284).

As formulators, journalists control the subtle aspects of source access and coverage. For example, on television, experts are usually presented in half-profile and/or with books or other authoritative signs of their office in the background. Those who are not experts, who represent other people's knowledge (including journalists) or a "vox pop" opinion, are presented full-face and without the authoritative trappings of an office (often on the street). The line of questioning can differ substantially between opposing forces in a major conflict. The difference can be as subtle as addressing a union spokesperson by his first name (*Arthur* Scargill), while using the more distant and deferential prefix of "Mr." for the management perspective (*Mr.* MacGregor) (Tracey, 1984).

As authors, journalists control the representations of sources as outlined above. However, they themselves are subject to substantial control. What appears under the newspaper reporter's byline, and before the broadcast reporter's sign-off, is material framed by the format and *Weltanschauung* of the news organization, media, and vocation of journalism. Nevertheless, journalists do struggle for and obtain considerable autonomy. Reporters actively resist efforts by powerful sources and by editors to censor their material (for notorious examples, see RCN, 1981b), and they have made legal gains by having protection in this regard written into their contracts with management (RCN, 1981c). Newsrooms are characterized by resistance and conflict over control of the news process, not by a conveyer-belt consensus within a smoothly running media machine (Ericson, Baranek, & Chan, 1987). Moreover, as Meyrowitz (1985, p. 324) points out, journalists form the one group in society who are able to use their institutional and organizational resources to control news-media threats to their position as authorized knowers. While sources in all other institutions are vulnerable to having journalists attack their authority—indeed, the greater their formal authority the greater their vulnerability (ibid; Ericson, Baranek, & Chan, 1989)—journalists can use their powers of selection, formatting, and authorship to minimize such threats to themselves.

News consumers are participants in the news process (Ericson, 1991). Ultimately, as McLuhan argued, it is consumers who give media its content. To the extent that news helps them to understand "what is important . . . who is important, where important things happen, when to expect specific things, and why to think about these things" (Robinson & Levy, 1986, p. 45), consumers use the news to represent order in their own lives. They intentionally seek knowledge that will help them with the chores of everyday life (Blumler & McQuail, 1969; Blumler & Katz, 1974; Levy & Windahl, 1985). News influences specific chores: who to vote for; whether to return a microwave oven to the manufacturer because of an announced product defect; whether to avoid certain places because of an announced crime wave. News is also used as entertainment, as a "companion," and as a form of "background noise" to other more pressing activities such as doing the ironing or driving to work (for a review, see Robinson & Levy, 1986).

Specific to our focus on news of social deviance, law, and justice, news is also monitored and used for its lessons in law. Many people learn about law from exposure to television and other media of popular culture, not from direct experience in the legal system (Macauley, 1987). As a social discourse, the law is recognized as valid more through the ways it is "mediated" in popular culture than through its formal procedures or substantive content as construed in legal culture (Mathiesen, 1987; Goodrich, 1986; Macauley, 1987). In popular culture, no one is outside of the law. Law is there as a "normal" part of public conversation in the media, to be represented as well as obeyed. Thus people experience the law not only in terms of constraint, but also as a form of knowledge that allows them to visualize realities, including the authoritative structure of society. As such "law is not a bounded set of norms . . . but part of a distinctive manner of imagining the real" (Geertz, 1983, p. 173).

Consumers are interactive with the news process. This is obvious in the case of regular news sources who are avid users because they need to stay on top of how they are being represented in the news and to produce further material to sustain a reasonable representation. However, people who are not regular sources also interact with news operatives in such forms as letters to the editor; other letters or calls of complaint, correction, or information not intended for publication; the use of consumer action lines or media ombudsmen; and doing "vox pop" interviews. The interactive capacity of the media is perhaps most fully demonstrated in the success of televangelism, which has built empires—including universities, fantasylands, and the largest cable-television network in the United States—out of its techniques of convincing people that they should send in donations along with their letters asking for help, guidance, and prayer (Gardner, 1987; Hoover, 1988).

There is a range of views regarding the participation of the consumer in the news process. Toward one extreme are those who depict the consumer as a mere spectator at the public dramas enacted by journalists and elite authorized knowers, and who argue that this role fosters political indifference among people. For them, the free market of public opinion is as much a fiction as the free market of the economy: the reality is that powerful institutions control the media system to inculcate their messages into the mass consciousness with little effective opportunity to answer back (Adorno & Horkheimer, 1979; D. Schiller, 1986; H. Schiller, 1989). People are not quite relegated to the status of empty vessels waiting to be filled up, but they are depicted as no better than spectators left to cheer the heroes and boo the villains of news melodramas (Wagner-Pacifici, 1986). News is "inert" and it leaves people "inert" because it has "no genuine connection to our lives" and therefore can provide "something to talk about but cannot lead to any meaningful action" (Postman, 1985, pp. 68, 76). Growing tired of echoing news clips and of their own voices, people are discouraged politically and their voices become inactive (Robinson, 1976). In the process, they defer to officials and experts of the administered society who parade before them in the news media.

Toward the other extreme are those who view people as highly active and interactive in their uses of news. These analysts claim that the news media are better in some respects than other media in communicating certain types of knowledge (Berry, 1983); that this knowledge is variously sought and used by different types of people for further action (Blumler & McQuail, 1969; Singer, 1973; Blumler & Katz, 1974; Robinson, 1976; Levy & Windahl, 1985); and that news therefore is an active agency in both participatory and pluralistic politics among groups (Robinson & Levy, 1986, especially pp. 51–54).

Both these positions are correct about the role of news consumers, depending on what group of consumers is being considered, the social and cultural context of that group, and the purposes of group members. A lot of confusion and vacuous debate derive from working with the fiction of the general "public," instead of being specific about which public is using the news in which context and for which purpose. There is a need to classify particular publics within the knowledge structure of society and to delineate differences among them in the making and use of news. "The differential choices of, and responses to, media content predominantly reflect differences in social structure and in the social distribution of opportunity" (McQuail, 1986, p. 135; see also Fiske, 1987, chap. 5).

The question of how people use the news is obviously related to the question of the effects of news content on readers. There is a long tradition of fear that the popular news media, with their penchant for reporting crime, sex, and scandal, have ill effects on ordinary people (Murdock, 1982; Pearson, 1983). In the contemporary period, these fears have been translated into media-effects research, which tries to show that bad news has bad effects on individual behaviour (for reviews, see Rowland, 1983; Gunter, 1987).

Counter to this are more recent cultural theories that bad news has the effect of reproducing consensus about social order. It does so through the ritualistic qualities of social dramas (Gusfield, 1981; Wagner-Pacifici, 1986); through the "politics of signification" in which elite sources maintain a monopoly over the media as a resource in the hegemonic process (Hall et al., 1978; Hall, 1982); and through a reliance on established channels of official discourse, which are already framed to support the status quo (Tuchman, 1978; Fishman, 1980; Altheide & Johnson, 1980).

Both research that argues that bad news has bad behavioural effects and research that argues that bad news reproduces law-and-order ideology in favour of the powerful are too simplistic in their renditions of media effects. The effects of content from all media vary substantially. There is variation according to whether the consumer is directly involved in the story as a source. There is variation according to whether the events are local or distant. There is substantial variation in how people attend to particular news communications, and what they recall. For some people, the news can serve as a vehicle for debunking the hierarchy of authority and have a democratic levelling effect rather than lead them to embrace the authority structure. It can function this way both by showing the faults, foibles, and foul-ups of the powerful and by failing to conceal the staged pseudo-ness of official events and social dramas. The media foster a pluralism in values, morality, and belief systems, and the effect can be a "deinstitutionalization" of stable meanings that have traditionally shored up major social institutions.

REFERENCES

Adorno, T., & Horkheimer, M. (1979). The culture industry: Enlightenment as mass deception. In *Mass Communication and Society* (Eds., Curran, J., et al), Beverly Hills: Sage.

Altheide, D. (1976). *Creating reality: How TV news distorts events*. Beverly Hills: Sage.

Altheide, D., & Johnson, J. (1980). *Bureaucratic progaganda*. Boston: Allyn and Bacon.

Berry, C. (1983). Learning from television news: A critique of the research. *Journal of Broadcasting, 27,* 359–370.

Blumler, J., & Katz, E. (Eds.). (1974). *The uses of mass communications: Current perspectives on gratification research.* Beverly Hills: Sage.

Blumler, J., & McQuail, D. (1969). *Television in politics: Its uses and influence.* Chicago: University of Chicago Press.

Blyskal, J., & Blyskal, B. (1985). *PR: How the public relations industry writes the news.* New York: William Morrow.

Bok, S. (1979). *Lying: Moral choice in public and private life.* New York: Vintage.

Burns, T. (1979). The organization of public opinion. In *Mass Communication and Society.* (Eds., Curran J., et al.). Beverly Hills: Sage, pp. 44–69.

Canada. Royal Commission on Newspapers. (1981a). *The newspaper and public affairs.* Ottawa: Research Studies on the Newspaper Industry.

Canada. Royal Commission on Newspapers. (1981b). *The journalists.* Ottawa: Research Studies on the Newspaper Industry.

Canada. Royal Commission on Newspapers. (1981c). *Labour relations in the newspaper industry.* Ottawa: Research Studies on the Newspaper Industry.

Collins, R. (1975). *Conflict sociology: Toward an exploratory science.* New York: Academic Press.

Ericson, R. (1991). Mass media, crime, law and justice: An institutional approach. *British Journal of Criminology*, forthcoming.

Ericson, R., Baranek, P., & Chan, J. (1987). *Visualizing deviance: A study of news organization.* Toronto: University of Toronto Press; Milton Keynes: Open University Press.

Ericson, R., Baranek, P., & Chan, J. (1989). *Negotiating control: A study of news sources.* Toronto: University of Toronto Press; Milton Keynes: Open University Press.

Fishman, M. (1980). *Manufacturing the news.* Austin: University of Texas Press.

Fiske, J. (1987). *Television culture.* London: Methuen.

Fiske, J., & Hartley, J. (1978). *Reading television.* London: Methuen.

Foucault, M. (1977). *Discipline and punish: The birth of prison.* New York: Pantheon.

Fuller, L. (1967). *Legal fictions.* Stanford: Stanford University Press.

Gardner, M. (1987, August). Giving God a hand. *New York Review of Books*, pp. 17–23.

Garnham, N. (1986). The media and the public sphere. In *Communicating Politics* (Eds., Golding, P., Murdock, G., & Schlesinger, P.). Leicester: Leicester University Press, pp. 37–53.

Geertz, C. (1983). *Local knowledge.* New York: Basic Books.

Gitlin, T. (1980). *The whole world is watching*. Berkeley: University of California Press.

Golding, P., Murdock, G., & Schlesinger, P. (Eds.). (1986). *Communicating politics: Mass communications and the political process*. Leicester: Leicester University Press.

Goodrich, P. (1986). *Reading the law*. Oxford: Blackwell.

Gunter, B. (1987). *Television and the fear of crime*. London: John Libbey.

Gusfield, J. (1981). *The culture of public problems*. Chicago: University of Chicago Press.

Habermas, J. (1975). *Legitimation crisis*. Boston: Beacon.

Habermas, J. (1979). The public sphere. In *Communication and Class Struggle*, Vol. 1 (Ed., Matterlart, A., & Siegelaub, S.). New York: International General.

Hall, S. (1979). Culture, the media, and the "ideological effect." In *Mass Communication and Society* (Eds., Curran, J., et al.). Beverly Hills: Sage, pp. 314–348.

Hall, S. (1982). The rediscovery of ideology: The return of the repressed in media studies. In *Culture, Society and Media* (Eds., Gurevitch, M., et al.). London: Methuen, pp. 56–90.

Hall, S., Crichter, C., Jefferson, T., Clarke, J., & Roberts, B. (1978). *Policing the crisis*. London: Macmillan.

Hartley, J. (1982). *Understanding news*. London: Methuen.

Hoover, S. (1988). *Mass media religion: The social sources of the electronic church*. Beverly Hills: Sage.

Levy, M., & Windahl, S. (1985). The concept of audience activity. In *Media Gratifications Research: Current Perspectives* (Eds., Rosengren, K., et al.). Beverly Hills: Sage.

Macauley, S. (1987). Images of law in everyday life: The lessons of school, entertainment and spectator sport. *Law and Society Review, 21*, 185–218.

Macdonnel, D. (1986). *Theories of discourse*. Oxford: Blackwell.

Manning, P. (1982). Organizational work: Structuration of environment. *British Journal of Sociology, 33*, 118–134.

Manning, P. (1988). *Symbolic communication: Signifying calls and the police response*. Cambridge, MA: MIT Press.

Mathiesen, T. (1987). The eagle and the sun: On panoptical systems and mass media in modern society. In *Transcarceration: Essays in the Sociology of Social Control* (Eds., Lowman, J., et al.). Aldershot: Gower, pp. 59–75.

McBarnet, D. (1981). *Conviction: Law, the state and the construction of justice*. London: Macmillan.

McQuail, D. (1986). Diversity in political communication: Its sources, forms, and future. In *Communicating Politics* (Eds., Golding, P., et al.). Leicester: Leicester University Press, pp. 133–147.

Meyer, J., & Rowan, B. (1977). Institutionalized organizations: Formal structure as myth and ceremony. *American Journal of Sociology, 83*, 340–363.

Meyrowitz, J. (1985). *No sense of place: The impact of electronic media on social behaviour.* New York: Oxford University Press.

Murdock, G. (1982). Disorderly images: Television's presentation of crime and policing. In *Crime, Justice and the Mass Media* (Ed., Sumner, C.). Cambridge: Institute of Criminology, University of Criminology, pp. 104–121.

Pearson, G. (1983). *Hooligan: A history of respectable fears.* London: Macmillan.

Pfohl, S. (1985). *Images of deviance and social control.* New York: McGraw-Hill.

Postman, N. (1985). *Amusing ourselves to death: Public discourse in the age of show business.* New York: Viking.

Putnam, L., & Pacanosky, M. (Eds.). (1983). *Communication and organization.* Beverly Hills: Sage.

Robinson, J. (1976). Interpersonal influences in election campaigns: Two-step flow hypotheses. *Public Opinion Quarterly, 40*, 304–319.

Robinson, J., & Levy, M. (1986). *The main source: Learning from television news.* Beverly Hills: Sage.

Rock, P. (1986). *A view from the shadows.* Oxford: Oxford University Press.

Rock, P. (1988). On the birth of organizations. *Canadian Journal of Sociology, 13*, 359–384.

Rowland, W. (1983). *The politics of TV violence.* Beverly Hills: Sage.

Scheppele, K. (1988). *Legal secrets: Equality and efficiency in the common law.* Chicago: University of Chicago Press.

Schiller, D. (1986). Transformations of news in the U.S. information market. In *Communicating Politics* (Eds., Golding, P., et al.). Leicester: Leicester University Press, pp. 19–36.

Schiller, H. (1989). *Culture, Inc.: The corporate takeover of public expression.* New York: Oxford University Press.

Schlesinger, P. (1978). *Putting reality together: BBC News.* London: Constable.

Singer, B. (1973). *Feedback and society.* Lexington, MA: D.C. Heath.

Singer, B. (1986). *Advertising and society.* Don Mills: Addison-Wesley.

Smith, A. (1978). The long road to objectivity and back again: The kinds of truth we get in journalism. In *Newspaper History* (Eds., Boyle, G., et al.). London: Constable, pp. 152–171.

Tracey, M. (1984, August 28). Does Arthur Scargill have a leg to stand on? — News. *The Sunday Times*, p. 43.

Tuchman, G. (1978). *Making news.* New York: Free Press.

Wagner-Pacifici, R. (1986). *The Moro morality play: Terrorism as social drama.* Chicago: University of Chicago Press.

Weber, M. (1954). *On law and economy in society*. (Max Rheinstein, Trans.). Cambridge, MA: Harvard University Press.

Weick, K. (1979). *The social psychology of organizing*, 2d ed. Reading, MA: Addison-Wesley.

Weick, K. (1983). Organizational communication: toward a research agenda. In *Communication and Organization* (Eds., Putnam, L., & Pacanosky, M.). Beverly Hills: Sage, pp. 13–29.

Williams, R. (1961). *Communications*. Harmondsworth, Middlesex: Penguin.

Williams, R. (1977). *Marxism and literature*. Oxford: Oxford University Press.

Wuthnow, R., Hunter, J., Bergesen, A., & Kurtzweil, E. (1984). *Cultural analysis*. London: Routledge.

CAMPAIGN '88:
TV OVERDOSES ON THE INSIDE DOPE

William Boot

The Bush era is nearly upon us and the shoal of political correspondents is migrating rapidly toward the feeding grounds of a new administration. All eyes are on the future, but I'm going to ask you to cast your mind back several months to October 5, 1988. That evening the networks aired, live from Omaha, the Dan Quayle-Lloyd Bentsen debate. Quayle, you may recall, faltered repeatedly when asked what he would do if he had to take over as president; he spewed out his programmed answers and, after Bentsen hit him with "You're no Jack Kennedy," just seemed to deflate. Even some loyal Republicans were made queasy by his performance—and so, evidently, was the public. By a margin of 51 to 27 percent, 600 people whom ABC polled that night deemed Quayle the loser and about half said he was unfit to assume the presidency.

Curiously enough, here's what some prominent TV commentators told the nation, just after the debate ended but before the poll results were announced, about Quayle's performance:

- "He did a credible job. . . . Most of the time he performed well"—Jeff Greenfield, ABC.

- "The bar over which Senator Dan Quayle had to get was pretty low. It seemed to me that he did that. He was calm. He marshalled his arguments rather well"—Dan Rather, CBS.

- "No one tonight scored a decisive victory"—Tom Brokaw, NBC.

- "No, but I think Dan Quayle did himself a little bit of good . . . If you were undecided . . . I think you might feel that Dan Quayle is not the kind of hopeless lightweight the Democrats have said he is"—John Chancellor, NBC, responding to Brokaw.

What is astonishing is not so much the networks' stretching to be charitable. It's that these were the same news organizations that just a few weeks earlier had been in frenzied pursuit of Quayle, sharply questioning his record and qualifications. They never got satisfactory answers, but, for reasons I'll touch on shortly, they called off the chase.

And this was by no means the only sharp turn of 1988. As I was monitoring the campaign coverage last fall, with a focus on the networks, news organizations often darted in tandem, first one way, then another; they turned suddenly toward George Bush's Dukakis-bashing rhetoric and away from Michael Dukakis's blander message; toward the idea that Bush had locked up the presidency (e.g., ABC ran a lengthy lead story on October 12 showing Bush with a colossal electoral lead, and the *Houston Chronicle* wrote on October 15 of a "growing perception that . . . Bush will be the inevitable victor"), then away from it (e.g., ABC, on October 30, reported that Bush aides were nervous because of an apparent Dukakis surge, and *Time*, on October 31, cited arguments that Dukakis "has the longshot chance to win"), then toward it again (e.g., GOP THOUGHTS TURN TO LANDSLIDE—*Richmond Times-Dispatch*, November 3; *"What might have been* . . . should be the Democrats' song of lamentation for this year's campaign"—*Time*, November 7).

Most intriguingly, they turned away from tough scrutiny of candidates' conduct (Gary Hart and Joe Biden must have wondered why it didn't happen sooner) and toward "inside dope" stories on candidates' strategies for prevailing on the all-important TV screen. This last topic, television, led the networks into a hall of mirrors where they lost their bearings and began darting toward their own reflections. More about this hall of mirrors a little later.

How can one account for all these sudden shifts in direction? Seeking some scholarly insight, I turned to Dr. Richard Rosenblatt. He is an ichthyologist at the Scripps Institution of Oceanography in La Jolla, California, and knows a lot about group behaviour ("schooling") in fish. Why was it, I asked him, that when schools change direction they seem to do so as one organism, each fish turning almost simultaneously? Rosenblatt explained that the creatures are "oriented on one another"—they use their eyes and a special organ sensitive to water movement (the lateral line) to keep tabs on their fellows and copy their every movement reflexively. "If the first fish turns, everybody turns," he said. "Any fish that gets out of the school is vulnerable prey. There's safety in numbers." For those of us who have covered national presidential campaigns, Rosenblatt's account may sound a bit like a job description.

The top ichthyologists of the 1988 campaign were, of course, Bush's men—campaign chiefs James Baker, Lee Atwater, and media guru Roger Ailes. These three were far more effective than Dukakis's team in exploiting the reporters' safety-in-numbers instinct. They used negative reinforcement and other behavioural modification techniques to entice the schooling journalists into their corner. They stirred the water and sprinkled food in just the right way to make the fish turn in useful directions at strategic moments.

Negative reinforcement included the notorious "Huntington massacre," just after the Republican convention, in which reporters clamouring to question Quayle finally were permitted to do so—in his home town, over a live microphone, before a loudly booing pro-Quayle crowd—and were made to look like bullies. After Huntington, reporters faced booing crowds frequently at stops along the Bush-Quayle campaign trail. The pursuit of Quayle slackened, perhaps not coincidentally, and by the time of the debate with Bentsen he was being given the benefit of a great many doubts. (For the record, James Baker denied that Huntington was an anti-press setup.)

Among other techniques employed by Ailes and Baker were tricks perfected by Michael Deaver & Co. in the Reagan campaigns of 1980 and 1984. Here (encapsulated in a sound-bite, as is only fitting) is the Deaver approach—"Read my lips: No access. Daily visuals. Simple message. See Dick clap. See Jane cheer. See Dick and Jane vote Republican." Adhering religiously to that credo, Bush's handlers kept reports at such a distance from the candidate that some resorted to binoculars and megaphones. And at least once a day they cast their bait—carefully staged visuals concocted to exploit TV's hunger for lively pictures. With the bait came a hook, the so-called message of the day, usually a barbed one-liner about Dukakis. With astonishing frequency, the networks bit, the hook was set, and TV was running with the Republican message.

Here's an example of just how well the Republican technique worked:

Labour Day, September 5. NBC's Lisa Myers reports on Bush campaigning in Disneyland. We see Bush surrounded by U.S. Olympic athletes and folks dressed up like Disney cartoon characters. He awards gold medals in the shape of Mickey Mouse heads to the Seoul-bound athletes. Cut to scene of Bush at lectern, with Mickey Mouse dressed in red-white-and-blue Uncle Sam garb standing beside him.

Myers (voice-over): "Sometimes it pays to be vice-president!"

Bush (to athletes): "You're representing the country of the little guy. No matter what the circumstances of your birth and background, you can go anywhere and do anything."

Cut to the Andover-Yale-Skull-and-Bones man, sleeves rolled up, unloading fish at a San Diego cannery. (Myers: "To identify with the little guy.") Then cut to Bush at lectern, San Diego Harbor as a backdrop, firing a salvo at Dukakis: "I wouldn't be surprised if he thinks that a naval exercise is something you find in Jane Fonda's workout book."

Note: No press conference, no access, yet Bush images compliantly mongered, along with the scripted messages: Bush is no elitist but Dukakis is an exotic lefty.

The Dukakis people were simply no match in this contest to reel in "free media." Dukakis's incredible slowness in responding to Bush's attacks left him mauled in the battle of the sound-bites. Ultimately, Dukakis did hit back and even emulated Bush's PR approach to some extent, cutting back on press conferences, staging more events purely to be photographed (e.g., he staged a cross-country trip for the sole purpose of being photographed viewing Yellowstone Park forest fires), and pounding home a simple-minded slogan: "We're on your side." But the Democrat never put himself totally off limits to reporters, even when he was politically wounded. This openness drew some hungry predators, as illustrated rather poignantly by the following case, courtesy of ABC:

October 19. We see the governor in shirt sleeves speaking at an outdoor rally in Illinois. He denounces the Bush people for purveying "garbage . . . political garbage" —referring to a brochure declaring that criminals such as the notorious Massachusetts rapist-on-furlough Willie Horton would be voting for Dukakis.

Cut to scene on a campaign motorcade bus, where we see Dukakis struggling inef-fectually to close his window. It seems that Sam Donaldson and crew have been given access to the candidate's own bus. (That alone would have constituted news had it occurred on the Bush campaign.) Donaldson: "Did you see in the paper that Willie

Horton said if he could vote he would vote for you?" Dukakis (face impassive, eyes averted from Donaldson, still struggling with window): "He can't vote, Sam."

Dukakis had tried to go on the attack at his rally, but by responding to Donaldson he slumped back on the defensive. He had "stepped on his message," as they say in today's politics.

This was a mistake that Roger Ailes had coached Bush to avoid like poison. During Bush's famous foray to Boston Harbor to blast Dukakis as a pollution-coddler, reporters sought to question the vice-president on his own environmental record. Bush brushed them off with a frankness bordering on gall: "We're not taking any questions. . . . We want the message to be on what I got to say later." He felt confident he could get away with it, and he did.

One can't blame Donaldson for asking Dukakis the Willie Horton question. But more broadly speaking, one has to question the perverse pattern of rewarding candidates who refuse to answer questions, while circling the more accessible ones like sharks. Should the networks have been airing Bush's visuals and sound-bites, which were tantamount to free campaign commercials, while he was hiding from reporters?

It isn't as if television was unprepared for the likes of Baker and Ailes in 1988. There had been a great deal of soul-searching in the news business following 1984, when the insulated Reagan team had spun its hallucinations so easily. There were, in fact, some major improvements in 1988. Among other things, the networks seemed to devote a little more airtime to campaign issues of substance such as the deficit; they painstakingly, if sometimes belatedly, corrected misstatements made by the candidates during the debates; by the end of the race, they were even running point-by-point rebuttals of the most egregiously misleading campaign ads. CNN, for its part, transcended television's traditional superficiality, at least for a half-hour a day, with its "Inside Politics '88" program. But these improvements, welcome though they were, came through rather faintly in the daily din of sound-bites and visuals. As Garrick Utley put it in an October 23 NBC "Sunday Today" report on campaign coverage: "It is the candidate's message, visually and verbally, which has the greatest impact."

The most astonishing thing about campaign coverage in 1988 was that so much of it was *about* media manipulation—highly introspective and self-critical. "Is TV doing its job. . . . What is happening here? Is it reporting or a political commercial or both?" asked Utley. Tom Brokaw, in a November 6 special, asked whether the Republican media chieftains had been exploiting the networks. ABC's Ted Koppel devoted a full hour to press performance a day after the election, etc. (Major newspapers also weighed in: TV MANIPULATION IN THE '88 CAMPAIGN, POLITICS GETS THE UPPER HAND—*Boston Globe*, October 24; FRUSTRATED REPORTERS ADD MEGAPHONES, BINOCULARS TO NOTEPADS—*Washington Post*, November 2; etc.)

This news-media hand-wringing ran in cycles: staged events were compliantly aired, then they were exposed as manipulative, then a new round of reports on visuals was aired, and then these, too, were picked apart or derided on the air. Frequently this bizarre cycle was repeated in a single report, with the correspondent mongering a campaign's concocted images but at the same time stressing such terms as "backdrop," "choreographed," and "staged." Consider Brit Hume's October 28 ABC report on a Bush visit to a California Highway Patrol Academy:

We see a police car skidding dramatically in a demonstration of high-speed-chase training. Cut to a watchful Bush. We see patrol cars driving in formation. Cut to Bush. Then cut to new scene of candidate surrounded by cheering uniformed cops, receiving plaque from beefy officer. Officer: "America's number one crimefighter award!" Finally, we hear Bush's attack line: "The [Democratic] leadership, much of it, is a remnant of the sixties, the New Left, those campus radicals. . . ."

Meanwhile, in his voice-over, Hume all but mocks the contrived proceedings: "Bush didn't get to go to Disneyland today, but, given the enthusiasm he's shown for law enforcement in this campaign, he probably thought the place he did go was even better. . . . Bush didn't go on the rides they have here, but he watched with obvious interest and later he got some prizes—a jacket and a cap, which he didn't put on, and a plaque with a billy club on it."

Hume was evidently trying to function as a kind of consumer's warning label (Caution: what you're seeing is a setup), but as an old TV pro he must know that verbal disclaimers of this sort are close to futile. Mark Crispin Miller of Johns Hopkins University said recently (*Sunday Today*, October 23): "A visual image is always going to overwhelm a mere voice that accompanies it—the pictures will win out, and that's something that most adept handlers really understand. I'm afraid not enough TV reporters understand. . . ." Miller later told me, "These correspondents seem to think that their discussion is so articulate that it will erase the effects of the footage." He appears to be right about the impact of visuals. After my first viewing of the Bush-cops broadcast, the main thing that stayed in my mind was not Hume's sarcasm; it was the image of a speeding police car and a quick cut to the vice-president—an almost subliminal linkage between candidate and the forces of justice. "Poppy" Bush and Don Johnson.

On the whole, network correspondents seemed to have few serious objections to taking what they were given each day by the image mongers. CBS's Bob Schieffer told Utley in the *Sunday Today* report: "It is not our business to make the agenda or to make the debate." Lisa Myers of NBC seemed to think that Deaver/Ailes-style campaigning was a pillar of American democracy: "From a reporter's point of view this kind of campaign is frustrating. But from a politician's point of view it's absolutely necessary. Because it's only by hammering away at the same message day after day that the message gets through to the American people." As if sound-bite politics were an institution, something to include in a civics text.

Others in the TV news business made more radical noises, vowing to shake themselves free of the grip of the demon visual. The *New York Times* reported on October 4:

> "If the photo opportunity of the day is simply a visual with no substantive core we should walk away from it," said the NBC news correspondent Andrea Mitchell. . . .

> Brian M. Healy [of] CBS News, said the [Bush] flag factory [event] was really the last straw. "They're going to have to earn their way onto the air," he said.

Brave talk, but of course nothing really changed. On Sunday, October 30, for instance, Bush went to Pennsylvania on a trip laid on at the last minute to demonstrate that he was not complacent about his lead. He performed a few stunts for the camera —catching a football on the tarmac at Andrews Air Force Base, bellowing to crowds through a bullhorn in Pennsylvania, and posing with a Catholic prelate decked out in photogenic red trappings. He said nothing of consequence, even by the special standards of his own campaign, yet he made it onto the networks, getting heavy coverage on ABC. The "substantive core" of ABC's story can be summarized as follows: "George Bush wanted some free TV advertising. We gave it to him." Correspondent Mike von Fremd's only complaint was that Bush, less well-choreographed than usual, "often [had] his back to the cameras."

Often had his back to the cameras? That comment suggests the depths to which TV news had descended—faulting the candidate's competency at manipulating TV news itself. More broadly, it points up the networks' preoccupation with politics as performance, with the mechanics and strategies of political persuasion and all the little details of life in the campaign fishbowl. As Tom Brokaw said self-consciously of the tight circle of politicians, campaign aides, pollsters, and political reporters who run together in a presidential election year: "We kind of speak our own language, live in our own universe, have our own culture." He can say that again—and note the word "we."

After both of the Bush-Dukakis debates (September 25 and October 13), the network correspondents dwelt heavily on the candidates' skills as television actors. In their new role as drama critics, the correspondents seemed to be telling viewers that what was really important was how well a would-be president could project qualities such as:

- Nonchalance, when he was probably quite nervous. ("I think it was [Bush's] body language throughout. He seemed more confident and relaxed. . . . I saw a comparable change in Dukakis, but I thought Bush did it in a more believable way"— NBC's John Chancellor, October 13.)

- Likeability, when it may not come naturally. ("[Dukakis] . . . wanted to show he was a sympathetic figure. He smiled a lot . . . but I'm not sure that in that 90 minutes he came across as anybody's idea of their favourite uncle"—NBC's Chris Wallace, September 25.)

- A mature understanding of TV camera angles. ("I noticed . . . how Dukakis played to the camera. . . . When he answered a question . . . he looked straight into the camera"—ABC's Jim Wooten, September 25.)

You may be thinking that there are other, more important considerations in choosing a president. Well, the networks agreed. They heavily stressed two other vital factors, sound-bites and spin doctors, and virtually made them into household words.

No sooner did each debate end than the networks were harping on which candidate had produced the most memorable bites. After the second debate, for example, NBC's Ken Bode told viewers: "[An] exchange you are liable to see tomorrow on the instant television replays had to do with labels . . . and this is how it looked." (Cut to sound-bites.)

Is it just me, or is there something downright daft about predicting on the air which snippets you are likely to broadcast the next day? Over on CBS, sound-bites kept coming up like King Charles's head when Dan Rather had the floor. "Senator Bradley?" Dan inquired after the September 25 debate. "If you were putting together a campaign commercial for Michael Dukakis and you wanted to use a George Bush sound-bite out of this, what would you use?" He then asked New Hampshire Governor John Sununu: "What Dukakis sound-bite would you use in a George Bush commercial?" A few minutes later, his intensity building, Rather asked Republican pollster David Keene: "Now, Dave, let's turn it around. You're making a George Bush commercial and you're looking for a sound-bite of George Bush. . . . What's his best shot?" etc.

Sadly, two weeks later, shortly after the close of the second Bush-Dukakis debate, a perplexed-sounding Rather broke this news to viewers: "There weren't many, I didn't hear or see many *sound-bites*." But correspondent Bruce Morton jumped to his rescue with a key insight: "One of [Dukakis's] problems in this whole campaign is that his message doesn't sound-bite as easily." Yes, ladies and gentlemen, it's official — "sound-bite" is now a verb.

Then there were the spin doctors, the partisans for each candidate who besieged the press-room after the debates and became another 1988 network obsession. On the one hand, the networks treated them as figures of fun, so predictable and biased that correspondents could not keep straight faces. On the other hand, they were regarded in a strange, convoluted way as campaign soothsayers. If you interpreted correctly what their utterances *really* signified, you had discovered the ultimate inside dope.

Consider this exchange, following the October 13 debate:

Dan Rather (lightheartedly): Their handlers— and don't they have a lot of them?— have been nonstop on what's called spin patrol, descending on the assembled reporters, trying to influence press accounts. Lesley Stahl joins us now from the eye of the spin storm. Lesley?

Stahl (smiling): Frankly, it's getting a bit like a broken record. We're spinning round and round and round and round. . . . All the handlers standing right up next to each other, Republicans and Democrats, with hordes of reporters crowding in to hear a good sound-bite. . . . And standing next to me, Dan, are three reporters who have been spun. . . . This is Mark Nelson, first, of The Dallas Morning News. *. . . Let's ask him first what the Bush spinners are saying.*

Nelson: The Bush people are very happy. They think the vice-president did exactly what he had to do. . . .

Stahl: You gonna write that in your paper tomorrow?

Nelson: I don't know. . . . We don't believe everything we hear from these guys.

Stahl, still in a joking mood, then asks Bob Drogin of the Los Angeles Times *what the Dukakis spinners are saying.*

Drogin (smiling): Even before [the debate] started, one of the Dukakis aides came up to me and said, "In case I don't catch you later, we're elated." And they're trying to keep that up. . . .

At this point, the banter stops as Stahl turns to Linda Breakstone of the Los Angeles Herald Examiner *and asks the touchstone question.*

Stahl: What's the difference between the two spinning teams? Do you feel one side is genuinely more elated than the other?

Breakstone (earnestly): I think the Bush people are happier. They're calmer about their spin. The Dukakis people are a little afraid of their own spin. . . . Lee Atwater [the Bush campaign leader] . . . is very calm about it, secure about it.

The Stahl-Breakstone exchange illustrates one of the real innovations in campaign reporting last year—the quest for what one might call "genuine spin." Through appraisal of the posture, voice, tone, and facial expressions of the spin doctors after a major campaign event, you make a judgement as to which candidate's quacks are lying least. That's the candidate who "won." Oh, I forgot—another criterion is the speed at which the spin doctors reach the press area from the debate arena, as in: "Tonight the Bush people were literally bounding into this room" (Lisa Myers, NBC, October 13). The campaign that wins the post-debate 100-yard dash to the press room also wins the debate. Perhaps the Federal Election Commission should begin testing for steroids in 1992.

Speaking of sports, political reporters assumed a role akin to sportswriters in 1988. This was in keeping with a long tradition of "value-free" political reporting. But in '88 the limitations of that tradition became more painfully apparent than ever before. For much of the race, journalists discussed an unprecedented flood of inaccurate charges and misleading television campaign ads in terms of the effectiveness of a candidate's "game plan." The focus was on strategy, not content or legitimacy—to wit: HOW THE FURLOUGH ISSUE BECAME A STRATAGEM OF THE BUSH FORCES (*Washington Post*, October 28); or, again, "Bush . . . moved early to offset a major potential negative, casting Dukakis as the polluter with his dramatic 'raid' on polluted Boston Harbor . . ." (*Boston Globe*, October 23).

It was not until the Bush camp ran its notoriously inaccurate "tank ad" attacking Dukakis that TV news saw fit to correct the record. The ad—which appropriated footage of an ill-conceived Democratic visual in which Dukakis rode in a tank, grinning goofily—claimed he opposed several weapons that he, in fact, supported. On October 19, ABC ran a point-by-point rebuttal of the Republican ad and other networks followed suit (as did a number of newspapers). By then, unfortunately, several factually dubious Bush ads had been running for weeks, all but unchallenged in the press, among them the "furlough" spot showing prisoners going through a revolving door and implying falsely that, under Dukakis, 268 Willie Horton clones had been released.

Not only were news organizations late in zeroing in on the inaccuracies; they were overly cautious in what they said, bending so far backward to appear balanced and non-partisan that they gave the impression both candidates were equally at fault in the distortion game. The Dukakis camp did claim misleadingly in one ad that Bush had voted to cut Social Security (in fact, he had voted to cut a cost-of-living raise—a cut that would have weakened a pensioner's buying power). But University of Texas professor Kathleen Hall Jamieson, who has written books on the history of campaign advertising and who studied the 1988 TV commercials closely, says the Bush campaign was the more flagrant offender by far, perpetrating the most blatantly distorted TV spots ever aired in a presidential race.

Jamieson told me that, when she was invited to appear on network talk shows ("Good Morning America," "Sunday Morning," etc.) to discuss distorted ads, an equal number of cuts from Bush and Dukakis spots would be shown, giving the false impression that the two sides were "equally sleazy and unfair." Jamieson added, "It was very difficult, given that visual structure, to make the point that Bush's ads were, one, effective and, two, lies, and that Dukakis's ads were, one, ineffective and, two, truthful."

That impression of equal culpability was widely circulated, in print as well as on the air. *Newsweek*, in a cover article illustrated with a Garry Trudeau cartoon showing Dukakis and Bush hurling mud at each other, declared: "There was blame enough to spare for the flying mud" (October 31). In an October 10 report—2 SIDES ESCALATE AIRWAVES WAR OF NEGATIVE ADS—The *New York Times* equated Dukakis's efforts to counter distorted ad attacks ("Do you believe it when George Bush tells you he's going to be the environmentalist president?") with Bush's original attacks.

There are limits to what news organizations can do to correct lies and distortions during a presidential campaign. "Single news segments cannot erase dozens of exposures to a sludge-clotted Boston Harbor," as Jamieson put it. When a candidate fails to carry the burden of rebuttal, as Dukakis failed to do for much of the race, that makes it all the harder for reporters to patrol as accuracy cops, because they might be accused of serving as surrogates for the silent candidate.

Nevertheless, commercial television had a special obligation to counter the distortions. For one thing, commercial TV was the original breeding ground for sound-bite politics. For another, it carried Bush's allegations, unchallenged, to millions of homes. TV's obligation is even more compelling given its role in creating what *The Washington Post's* Lloyd Grove has termed the "perpetual fusion" of news and advertising. News broadcasts have borrowed techniques from TV commercials (shorter bites, quicker cuts, flashier graphics, more attention to camera angles), while campaign commercials have aped the style of news and exploited impressions created on the TV news. All of this causes public confusion—an *Adweek* study in early September showed that a number of viewers mistook news reports for commercials.

Confusion was compounded in 1988 by a proliferation of television news reports about commercials, of commercials inspired by news reports, and of commercials about commercials. Consider Dukakis's "tank" event: in the beginning was a campaign visual, and the visual begat news reports making light of the stunt ("Biff! Bang! Powie!" was how Bruce Morton of CBS summed it up); and these begat a Republican attack commercial ridiculing Dukakis, and the Republican attack commercial begat more news reports, and all of the above begat a Dukakis ad attacking the Republican attack commercial. The Dukakis spot spawned even more news reports. These generally showed the correspondent standing beside a TV set on which could be seen an angry Dukakis, himself standing beside a TV set, on which could be seen footage of Dukakis on the tank in the Republican ad. The paragraph you are now reading is, as nearly as I can calculate, at least four (or is it five?) times removed from the original visual, a phony event to begin with.

There are several things television could have done in 1988 to break us free from this crazy world and restore some reality to the campaign. Initiatives along the following lines might have been especially interesting:

Dan Rather: Seven days after the Labor Day campaign kickoff, and the two presidential candidates are still ducking major issues. Nothing from either on what programs they would cut to fight the deficit. . . . (Cut to end of broadcast.) And that's the way it is, Monday, September 12, the seventh day of general-election waffling by the two major party candidates for president. (This closing line would be repeated daily unless or until the candidates grappled with the substantive issues.)

Peter Jennings: ABC *can report tonight that the major networks have invited George Bush and Michael Dukakis to participate in a series of weekly debates. One on one. Specific topics, starting with the deficit. If one man agrees and the other declines, the first will be given an hour of prime time per week to use in any way he sees fit.*

Tom Brokaw: George Bush spent the day in his campaign cocoon again, avoiding reporters. He appeared as usual at a carefully choreographed event before a friendly audience, in this case an Orthodontists for Bush rally in Sarasota, Florida. You won't be seeing any film of that visit. The reason: NBC *has imposed the following conditions on our campaign coverage: film of candidates' staged events will be shown only on days when they hold press conferences. Bush did not hold one today.*

Of course, in reality, the networks are petrified at the idea of using their maximum power to improve electioneering. (Yes, ABC invited the candidates to debate on the Ted Koppel show, but that was a one-time shot, late in the campaign, on October 25. Dukakis had to submit to Koppel's tough interrogation, solo, for 90 minutes. This in itself might have persuaded Bush to stay off the air, letting his rival be the one to writhe alone.) The networks' fear stems in part from questions about their own identity: Is network TV the playing field on which candidates contend, making it inappropriate for the networks to redraw the boundaries during the game and compelling them to assume a *totally* passive role? Is it a detached interpreter of the campaign, thus *largely* passive? Is it an active player—a character cop, accuracy policeman, arbiter of what the issues should be? Most of the time the networks don't seem to know which role to emphasize and uncertainty breeds weakness. The more passive roles held sway for much of the fall.

In any event, it's all over now and we ended up with George Herbert Walker Bush. Within a short time of inauguration, God willing, he will hold his first press conference as president. I can already imagine the big evening. It is 8:45 and Bush and his wife sit contentedly before a roaring fire in the family living quarters, a dog at their feet. At length Bush yawns, stretches, sets down his teacup, and gets to his feet. "Well, Barbara," he says. "Tension City. I've got to go and feed the fish."

WOMEN AND THE MEDIA IN CANADA: A PROGRESS REPORT

Gertrude J. Robinson

Thou shalt love everything that is beautiful.
Thou shalt speak low but clearly and distinctly.
Thou shalt listen intelligently.
Thou shalt dress well.
Thou shalt be perfectly groomed.
Thou shalt not be awkward.
Thou shalt not be selfish.
Thou shalt not paint thy face.
Thou shalt not use slang.
Thou shalt not worry.

> *From "The Homemaker," a popular* Globe and Mail
> *column of the 1930s, as cited in Sexton, 1990*

Issues of gender and the media are complexly intertwined and their study up to now has been piecemeal.[1] This is because "gender" was previously viewed as a property of individuals. Feminist theory, however, has shown that gender is a principle of *social organization,* which systematically structures all human interactions and power relations (Schneider, 1988, p. 6). Every aspect of a woman's life and career, as well as the description of women by the Canadian media, are therefore affected by gender. This paper will address these interconnections and elucidate the ways in which *social* barriers and media *descriptions* are interrelated. These interrelations will be examined in three areas: women's progress in the media professions, the portrayal of women in the media, and the role of Canadian women lobbyists in fostering progress toward women's equality in the past decades.

WOMEN'S PROGRESS IN THE MEDIA PROFESSIONS: A FOOT IN THE DOOR

If women and men were treated equally in our society, one would expect that they would be about equally represented in different areas of work and in different professions. In most societies, however, social and structural factors make it more difficult for women to gain access to the better types of jobs. Media work is no exception. My 1974 study of women journalists found that women were a minority of about 35 percent in Canada's English-language dailies and that they tended to cluster in the lowest reportorial positions. Roger de la Garde found a similar situation in the French-language dailies (Robinson, 1975, p. 8). This figure compared favourably with the situation in the United States, where women constituted only 23 percent of all journalists. More detailed American data additionally showed that women had a better chance of being employed in the less prestigious print media than in broadcasting. Newsmagazines had 30 percent women journalists; weeklies, 27 percent; dailies, 23 percent; wire services, 13 percent. In radio and TV, the most prestigious sectors, only 10 percent of the employees were women at that time (Bowman, 1974, p. 100). In Canada, of all the media industries, radio and TV, had the lowest representation of women. Only 14 percent of CBC employees were women. Similar distributions were recorded in Quebec, as well as in Europe (Britain, Germany, and Scandinavia), where women were also more prevalent in the print than in the broadcast media (Saint Jean, 1990; Berg, 1975, pp. 19–20; Tunstall, 1971, p. 13; Stockholms Journaliter, 1971, p. 18). The relatively low rate of female employment furthermore indicated that media work was considered one of the more desirable (elite) professions and thus difficult for women to enter. Though three times as many women were working outside the home in the seventies as in the forties, their entry rate into these professions had remained virtually static.

In all media institutions, women and minorities face barriers to access and promotion and receive less pay for work of equal value. Traditionally, women were excluded from media production management positions because it was felt that they belonged in the home, lacked education, were generally troublesome, and needed protection from the danger and shocking sights connected with some assignments (CBC, 1975, pp. 17, 33, 45). These notions also systematically discouraged women from applying for media jobs and produced a situation in which they were promoted more slowly and paid less, in spite of demonstrated competence.

Data collected from 1974 on female CBC producers and editors showed that most of these views had little to do with reality. CBC women were predominantly single, while male editor/producers were overwhelmingly married. In addition, these professional women were generally younger than the men, with 60 percent under 36 in contrast to 60 percent of the men, who were over this age. Interviews revealed that these women had the same job aspirations and willingness to move to another city as did men. Their general educational background also turned out to be virtually indistinguishable from their male counterparts. The only difference was that women generally lacked sufficient technical and electronic training to compete for the top engineering positions in broadcasting (CBC, 1975, pp. 50–52).

Where are we today? Susan Crean answers this question by pointing out that in the nineties, women broadcasters have made it through the door and into the mainstream at the level of production and in management (1987, p. 20). Women are best represented in CBC radio, where they represent 28 percent of the staff and 39 percent of the management (CBC, 1984; CBC, 1986). Among others are Joan Donaldson, former head of Newsworld, CBC's all-news channel, and Trina McQueen, vice-president, CBC news and current affairs. Doubtlessly this is partly the result of Dodi Robb's tireless activities when she was head of the radio department in the 1950s, where she trained many high-profile women such as Barbara Frum (Crean, 1985). In the private radio industry, however, women constitute only 20 percent of the FM labour force and a minuscule 4.5 percent of AM radio producers. Disc jockeys remain just that—a male species. Women are more likely to be traffic and weather reporters and to function as interviewers. Their participation in the management of private stations also remains token at 1 percent (Crean, 1987, p. 20; Toronto Women, 1990).

Even television statistics show improvements. A 1990 study discovered that women now make up 35 percent of the film, video, and television sectors. However, the picture is not so rosy when one looks more closely and sees that women are still virtually excluded from about 80 percent of all job categories. They dominate instead in 6 out of 51 job types: office (accounts, typing, etc.), make-up, script, and wardrobe, and represent 10 percent or less in thirteen categories, among them creative positions (Toronto Women, 1990, p. 10). Once again, the public CBC had a better women's employment record (34 percent) than the private industry, where women are still a negligible 14 percent of the television production staff. Yet, while women have made it through the door, the most visible positions and the top managerial posts still elude them. Ninety-one percent of all experts we see on the screen are men; they are 77 percent of all newsreaders and 70 percent of voice-overs. In addition, while women today hold 28 percent of network TV management positions in the CBC, they are congregated in the bottom two out of nine levels, indicating that the "glass ceiling" is still in place.

This evidence suggests that Canadian society continues to value the male voice and the male presence more highly than the female voice and presence and that this preference is reinforced by the bureaucratic institutions in which we all work. The under-valuation is furthermore manifested by the fact that women broadcasters continue to receive a lower salary, though the degree of this discrepancy depends on a person's position. The general spread lies between 67 percent and 97 percent for an average of 75 percent of male salaries. In the CBC, women are paid a slightly better 86 percent of what men with equal qualifications receive (Toronto Women, 1990).

In the nineties, the problem is no longer getting a foot into the doors of the media professions, but the much more complicated task of keeping a career *going* once it has been started. Private and public attitudes have changed under the impact of the women's movement, so visible barriers to equal access are now prohibited by law. The barriers existing today are therefore "invisible" and are based on actions rather than laws. They are found in attitudes, biases, and presumptions that senior managers, who are frequently in their sixties, continue to harbour concerning women. They are, as Crean puts it, "sins of omission rather than of commission." They consist of opportunities not extended, networks of information not available to women, and the strains of the "double role" that make it virtually impossible for the career woman to spend the same amount of time on job-related outside activities as do her male counterparts. In order to remain competitive, a young career woman must therefore remain unmarried and childless. Although men's roles are also changing, it is still women, more often than men, who are asked to make this sacrifice.

IMAGE AND PORTRAYAL: A GREAT LEAP FORWARD?

If women continue to have difficulties in gaining access to Canada's media industries, one must also expect that women's portrayal and representation, which are so important for identity formation, will also be problematic. Gaye Tuchman et al. (1978) suggested that those media that make the most money from women were also the most likely to pay attention to women and their changed life experiences. In a 1977 study, I found that women's magazines and the women's pages of daily papers were indeed the places where women's novel work experiences were first discussed (Robinson, 1983). As women's magazines began recording women's increasing labour-force participation, newspapers also reacted. Their women's pages, which had covered housewifery, children, and social affairs for decades, slowly shifted content. New stories about health, education, entertainment, and consumer information began to fill these pages. Big city dailies furthermore acknowledged this shift by renaming their women/society pages; they became *Lifestyle* sections.

The more costly broadcast media, in contrast, were initially virtually silent about women's changing lives. Tuchman described this situation in the seventies as the "symbolic annihilation" of women in broadcasting and noted that it was especially virulent in television (Tuchman et al., 1978, p. 7). In a 1978 Montreal CBC programming study, I corroborated this absence. Women and women's issues rarely appeared on nightly news broadcasts. Furthermore, if there was any mention of women-related issues at all, these appeared at the end of the newscast, where these items received very little play. The secondary status of women and women's issues was also symbolized by the fact that women were never consulted on "hard news" (politics, economics) items, but were queried only about family-related matters, or about their entertainment career if they were pop stars (Robinson, 1978, pp. 94–155). This kind of a content treatment indicates that women's views on public affairs were not highly regarded, though their gender was considered useful in selling goods. In television advertising as well as situation comedies of the time, such as "All in the Family," women were viewed as the "second sex" whose minds were presumed to be inferior and who could be used unhesitatingly as the butt of family sitcom jokes.

By the 1990s, the most blatant sexual stereotyping of women has been corrected, though the images that are used to transmit women's reality still leave a lot to be desired. This is because these images are not the result of "transparent snapshots" of reality. Media images are instead "mediated reconstructions," *programs about women*, usually written and directed by male producers and/or directors. Consequently, these programs (including the news) contain stereotypes. These stereotypes are cultural distillations, which present what are considered the most "typical" understandings presently circulating in our society.

Stereotypes concerning women and their capabilities have evolved since the 1950s. The old-fashioned "mother" image of a woman concerned solely with her home, children, and husband, has given way to an image of the "new" woman. She is the Superwoman, alternately portrayed as a young and dynamic mother and a successful career woman. In the latter image, she reconciles the two domains of home and work with seeming ease, giving no hint of the heavy psychic and physical costs this "dual role" imposes. There is also a new image for the older woman, for the print media have transformed the "grandmother" image. The staid, resigned "granny" of twenty years ago is today transformed into the Swinging Fifties Woman. With her grey hair flying, this married woman participates in sports, is her retired executive husband's gracious hostess, and still has energies left over for community work (Saint Jean, 1990, p. 85). There is no hint that most older women are single and that many have to exist below the poverty line.

Though the stereotypes concerning women have changed over the past two decades, there remain troublesome differentiations between the portrayals of women and men. "Gender" continues to be used as a simple interpretive device for subtly symbolizing the superiority of the male half of the population. Tannis MacBeth Williams and her colleagues at the University of British Columbia tried to find out how this secondary status is signalled by looking at the types of roles that males and females play in television programs. To their great surprise, they found that even today, there is still a two-thirds preponderance of males over females. Furthermore, this disproportion has not changed *at all* in U.S. or Canadian programming since the 1950s (1986/90, p. 9). The lack of representation of women is particularly marked in non-dramatic programming, where 73 percent of all programs had a preponderance of males and only 35 percent of programs featured an even mix of both genders (p. 12). These figures unfortunately show no significant improvement even in the CBC, where the English and French networks implemented a "woman-friendly" hiring and promotion campaign at the beginning of the decade. In 1986, in English CBC news and public-affairs programs, only 20 percent of the anchors or hosts were female, only 26 percent of the reporters were female, and only one out of every four on-air interviews featured a female expert (CBC, 1986).

In prime-time drama, women did a bit better: about half of all of these programs had all-male casts (55 percent), while the other half had an even mix or predominance of women characters. Women received the best representation in day-time soaps, where 79 percent of shows had an even mix of female and male roles. This high proportion of women's representation is, however, in the least prestigious program type—the one furthermore designated to attract an all-female audience. We lack studies about whether this high proportion of females will be maintained as soaps move into prime time and play to mixed audiences. Does "Dallas" make a difference?

Women are not only under-represented in virtually all program types, they are additionally portrayed as less powerful, less authoritative, and less knowledgeable. In non-fiction programming, 90 percent of powerful characters are male; in fiction, 81 percent; and in day-time soaps, 73 percent are strong males. Together, these statistics indicate that the stereotypes making up the concept of the "weaker sex" are alive and well even today (MacBeth Williams et al., 1986/90).

A further dimension which the Vancouver researchers looked at was the range of occupations that female and male characters inhabited. Interestingly, here the portrayal of women has made some strides, responding perhaps to the large-scale entry of women into the labour force throughout the past twenty years. Fifty-eight percent of programs portrayed women in predominantly non-traditional or in a mix of traditional and non-traditional occupations. Males, in contrast, were overwhelmingly shown

(98 percent) in traditional male occupations (MacBeth Williams et al., 1986/90, pp. 15–16). Along this dimension, Canadian programming also did much better than U.S.-produced shows, where women were still largely portrayed in traditional occupations. Interestingly, women in news and information programs were more likely to be shown in non-traditional occupations than those in entertainment shows. These women were also closer to their counterparts on the "power/knowledge" dimension, than they were in any dramatic programs. Some men have complained that there is a greater degree of occupational stereotyping of males than females (1986/90, p. 19). The researchers believe that this occurs because cross-sex behaviour is generally more acceptable for North American females than it is for males (Kimball, 1986, p. 8).

A final aspect of "gendered" portrayal that came under scrutiny was the question of the incidence of sexist comments and women's portrayal as sex objects. In our consumer society where sex sells all kinds of products, the portrayal of women as sex objects is institutionally supported by the advertising world. The study shows that women are indeed portrayed as sex objects more frequently than men in programs as well as advertisements. In non–Canadian-produced shows, such portrayal is found in 35 percent of all programs, whereas in Canadian shows, it is only half as prevalent, appearing in 18 percent of all programs. Men, in contrast, are very rarely represented as sex objects (3 percent). However, looking at overall programming, it appears that in almost one-quarter (22 percent) of prime-time programs (many of which are U.S. produced) on seven networks there was one or more blatant portrayal of women as sex objects. This is a staggering amount of reinforcement for learning that it is socially acceptable to use women as objects (MacBeth Williams et al., 1986/90, pp. 22–23). These statistics, too, have remained virtually static over time. There was a better track record covering sexist comments, however. These tend to have virtually disappeared from prime-time programming (13 percent), showing that the complaints of women have been more effective in this domain than in other areas of portrayal.

What might be the effect of having more prominent males than prominent females on television? MacBeth Williams et al. suggest three influences. First, fewer models are provided for female than for male viewers. This may be especially detrimental for girls who are still learning role models. Second, the small numbers of prominent females make it more likely that these portrayals will continue to be stereotyped in the future. Third, the consistent portrayal of more prominent males than females conveys the implicit message that females are less important than males in Canadian society. Counting fewer women on the screen subtly suggests that they count less in society (1986/90, p. 10).

MEDIA ACTIVISM: WHAT HAS IT ACCOMPLISHED?

Doris Anderson, past editor of *Chatelaine* and ex-president of the National Action Committee (NAC), points out that by the 1990s, policy activism and lobbying has resulted in significant gains for women (1990, pp. 24–28). These gains were based on three types of activities that had occurred throughout the past twenty years. The first was the publication of the Royal Commission on the Status of Women Report in 1970, which made 167 recommendations for greater equality between the sexes. This report prepared legislators to focus on the lack of representation of women and minorities in the political and social domains. It also provided a blueprint for developing solutions for "gender"-based inequality by 1975, the UNESCO-designated International Women's Year.

The Royal Commission's report recommendations gave impetus to the establishment of both the women's program in the Department of the Secretary of State (in 1972) and the Advisory Council for the Status of Women (NAC) in 1973. The former funds regional and local women's initiatives such as rape crisis centres, while the latter sponsors research and formulates action programs on behalf of all Canadian women (Anderson, 1990, pp. 22–23). In the 1982 fight for the Charter of Rights, women discovered that although the government had acknowledged their concerns, it continued to overlook their need for legal protection. Continued pressure led to a Royal Commission on employment equity headed by Judge R.S. Abella. The Abella Commission recommended that the federal government set targets for hiring more women and that large contractors of more than 100 employees live up to the same guidelines. The federal Employment Equity Act was passed in 1986 as a result of these initiatives.

In the wake of these developments, two groups of media activists were also persuaded to use legislative avenues to further employment equity and non-sexist representation goals. One was the ACTRA performers' union and the other was MediaWatch, which had started out as a sub-committee of NAC, but became independent in 1983. In the past decade, the Vancouver-based MediaWatch group, with grass-roots support from audience members across the country, mounted an effective campaign against sexist television advertising and programming. In 1987, it demanded mandatory CRTC guidelines against sexism in advertising and program content after the two-year voluntary change period led to no significant improvement (Jeffrey, 1990, pp. 76–78). And in 1988 it joined ACTRA in a "Common Committee" to persuade sympathetic parliamentarians that the time had come to include women in the new broadcasting act that the Conservative government was preparing. The ACTRA-proposed wording for this inclusion was: "The Canadian broadcasting system (iii) should through its programming and its employment opportunities . . . serve the needs and interests and reflect the circumstances and aspirations of Canadian men and women, including equal rights." MediaWatch and professional women's groups argued that employment equity rules could be balanced with "freedom of expression and journalistic, creative and programming independence" which is enjoyed by broadcast undertakings (Jeffrey, 1989, p. 7).

The new Broadcasting Act of 1991, for the first time, formally recognized women as a legitimate constituency with the right to equal employment opportunities and fair representation. This legislative victory was won in spite of the Canadian Radio-television and Telecommunications Commission's reluctance to act against advertisers and broadcasters on behalf of women. Though performance content and advertising performance criteria concerning women are largely unwritten, media professionals can now use employment equity legislation to assure access to media positions.

After two decades of activism, groups concerned with better access to the media and with sexism in portrayal have drawn three conclusions that are generally echoed by concerned women in the United States and Western Europe: first and most important, sustained activism is required to bring about change in women's status in Canadian society. In addition, it has become clear that mandatory quotas and evaluative processes are needed to monitor and ensure that progress continues to be made in the realm of women's employment. Liss Jeffrey furthermore concludes that the women's movement and female activism have given women experience in public life and have sensitized them to the fact that the media constitute an important "symbolic battleground" where women *qua* women must strive to be able to speak in their own voice and define their own realities (Jeffrey, 1990, p. 79).

The Stalled Revolution

The inability of women to make their own voice heard may begin to change in the nineties with the emergence of the economic viability, new audience groupings, and the availability of multiple program choices, channels, and VCR storage. These audience groupings, statistics show, are increasingly determined by age and gender, rather than solely by economic status. Because of the number of available cable channels, the CBC estimates that it is now profitable to program for audience segments as small as 7000 people. The implication is that television, which had previously been a national medium, is now turning into a narrow-casting distribution system, as have magazines before it. Increased audience fragmentation in broadcasting has forced television producers to pay greater attention to those content characteristics that audiences find appealing. The Swedish Broadcasting Corporation found that gender was once again one of the major predictors. The chief criterion audiences look for in all programs is the opportunity to identify with a believable figure. For women, this identification occurs with female as well as male figures, whereas for men, identification is always with a *same-sex* figure. Gender was also important in dramatic format choices. Women preferred stories focusing on the lives and fates of women, portrayed as figures of integrity and importance. Men, in contrast, preferred fast-paced, conflict-based stories centring on contests. Only those programs combining both of these dramatic narrative features appealed to both genders (Abrahamsson, 1988). The Swedish Broadcasting Corporation today maximizes its shrinking audience by providing two very different program types on its two prime-time channels hoping that different family members will tune into different programs in households with two sets, or that the VCR will capture the alternative program.

In spite of the fact that there has been substantial change in women's lives during the past two decades, media and other male-run organizations are changing much more slowly. This resistance reflects what sociologists call the existence of a power "threshold." This report suggests that by 1990 women had gained a foot in the door of print as well as broadcast media and are now poised for takeoff. Yet, the final ascent to the top of the hill of *social equality* in the home and work worlds will be even more difficult to achieve than the *legal* equality gained in the past twenty years. Achieving social equality between women and men fundamentally rearranges established private and public power patterns. For these rearrangements, no road maps are presently available, and the revolution seems stalled.

The broadcast media demonstrate the "stalled revolution" both in their personnel and program policies, where female and male perspectives are not yet valued equally. In fifteen years, women's job participation has increased by only eight percentage points, from 32 percent in 1975 to 40 percent in 1989 and sex-stereotyped job classifications have virtually not shifted at all. At present, 31 percent of all personnel work in non-sex-stereotyped positions, while 45 percent work in male-stereotyped and 24 percent in female-stereotyped positions (Abrahamsson, 1990, p. 7). The data also show that it takes time for women to be trained for new broadcast occupations (technical) and for male supervisory personnel to become sensitized to the presence of gender related biases in beliefs and attitudes.

To get the "stalled revolution" going again may require a new strategy. Though media women have gained access to the male sandbox, they are presently not yet permitted to use their tools. Perhaps what we need to aim for in the twenty-first century is to build a new sandbox in which new tools can be co-operatively designed (Jeffrey, 1990, p. 79).

NOTE

1.   Only a few scattered reports exist on selected aspects of women's relationship to Canadian media, and some of it is generally inaccessible.

REFERENCES

Anderson, D. (1990). Changing goals of women's organizations in Canada: The second wave. In *Women and Power: Canadian and German Experiences* (Eds., Robinson, G.J., & Sixt, D.). Montreal: McGill Studies in Communications/Goethe Institut.

Abrahamsson, U. (1988). *Television in the eyes of the viewer*. Stockholm: Swedish Broadcasting Corporation.

Abrahamsson, U. (1990). *Are we nearing the top of the hill? Notes from a decade of working toward equality in Swedish Broadcasting*. Stockholm: Swedish Broadcasting Corporation.

Berg, E. (1975, Fall). Women in German broadcasting, *EBU Review, 26*, (4).

Bowman, W.W., (1974). *Distaff journalists: Women as a minority group in the news media*. Unpublished Dissertation, Chicago: University of Illinois.

Canadian Broadcasting Corporation. (1975). *Women in the CBC*. Montreal.

Canadian Broadcasting Corporation. (1984). *Portrayal of women in programming: Summary report on the action taken by the CBC on the report of the Task Force on Sex Role Stereotyping in the Broadcast Media*. Ottawa.

Canadian Broadcasting Corporation. (1986). *Portrayal of women in programming: Submission to the CRTC*. Ottawa.

Crean, S. (1985). *Newsworthy: The lives of media women*. Toronto: Stoddard.

Crean, S. (1987, Spring). Piecing the picture together: Women and the media in Canada. *Canadian Women's Studies Journal, 8* (1).

Jeffrey, L. (1990). Women and media in Canada: A question of cultural authority. In *Women and Power: Canadian and German Experiences* (Eds., Robinson, G.J., & Sixt, D.). Montreal: McGill Studies in Communications/Goethe Institut.

Jeffrey, L. (1989, March). Waiting for the results. *SCAN.*

Kimball, M.M. (1986). Television and sex-role attitudes. In *The Impact of Television: A Natural Experiment in Three Communities.* (Ed., MacBeth Williams, L.T.). New York: Academic Press.

MacBeth Williams, T., Travis, L., Phillips, S., Wotherspoon, D., & Furlong, A. (1986/90). *Gender portrayal on North American TV: Continuity and change.* Unpublished report. Vancouver: University of British Columbia (Psychology).

Robinson, G.J. (1975). *Women journalists in Canadian dailies: A social and profession profile.* McGill Working Papers in Communications. Montreal.

Robinson, G. J. (1978). Women, media access and social control. In *Women and the News* (Ed., Keir Epstein, L.). New York: Hastinghouse.

Robinson, G J. (1983, Spring). The media and social change: Thirty years of magazine coverage of women and work. *Atlantis, 8,* (2).

Saint Jean, A. (1990). Les femmes et l'information: une perspective québécoise. In *Women and Power: Canadian and German Experiences* (Eds., Robinson, G.J., & Sixt, D.). McGill Studies in Communications/Goethe Institut.

Schneider, B. E. (1988). Political generations and the contemporary women's movement. *Social Inquiry, 58* (1).

Stockholms Journaliter. (1971). Report on the status of women in journalism. Malmoe.

Toronto Women in Film and Video. (1990). *A statistical profile of women in the Canadian film and television industry.* Project Report with Peat Marwick, Stevenson & Kellogg. Toronto.

Tuchman, G., Kaplan Daniels, A., & Benet, J. (Eds.). (1978). *Hearth and home: Images of women in the mass media.* New York: Oxford University Press.

Tunstall, J. (1971). *Journalists at work.* London: Constable.

Suggested Readings

Robinson, G.J. (1977, Spring). The future of women in the Canadian media. *McGill Journal of Education, 12* (1).

Robinson, G.J., & Sixt, D. (Eds.). (1990). *Women and power: Canadian and German experiences.* Montreal: McGill Working Papers in Communications/Goethe Institut.

Sexton, R. (1990, April 28). Former Globe editor is toasted and roasted. *Globe and Mail.*

Smith, V. (1990, March 24). Women of the press. *Globe and Mail.*

CHILLING EXPRESSION:
OBSCENITY LAW AND THE HALO ZONE

Janice Dickin McGinnis

All law is meant to modify human behaviour. If there were no aspect in a given activity that society wanted individuals to do—or stop doing—there would be no reason for an instrument of force pertaining to that activity. In this way, it can be said that society uses law to freeze in place certain patterns, to set and safeguard standards that it feels a need to rely on in order to carry out the rest of its affairs.

But if law has a freezing effect, it can also be said to have a chilling effect. Sometimes, in their conscientious attempt to obey the law, people fall shorter of the mark than they need. Perhaps the most familiar example of this effect is what traffic police call the "halo zone," that area on the speedometer just below the speed limit into which we drop after spying a squad car. We modify our behaviour to be *sure* we fall within legal boundaries; we don't just obey the law, we cringe.

This chilling effect is felt particularly in areas where the law is vague. When we see the radar trap, we ask ourselves two fairly basic questions: What is the speed limit and how fast am I going? We may have forgotten the speed limit, but we cannot argue that it is not a settled matter and usually sufficiently advertised.

Traffic regulations tend in general to be of a pure and simple nature. They require of us little analysis regarding the legal status of our actions before we either yield or not, wait or walk, slow for the amber or accelerate through the red. This peerless simplicity, however, is not a hallmark of most laws having to do with the more complicated aspects of our lives.

The farther we move from areas of consensus, the vaguer our laws become. Compare, for example, our prohibitions against murder with those against pornography, the subject of this discussion. Both involve moral issues and value judgements. But although prohibition of murder is pretty well a settled matter for us (no matter how much we may argue over proper punishment and proper parameters of justification), sanctions against pornography are anything but. This is so because there is no settled Canadian opinion in this area.

No doubt if we could decide on a range of acceptable conduct in this matter, we could find the words to express it in our statute books and in our case law. Or perhaps vague wording would remain unchallenged because we would all be so satisfied with the outcome. Barring this highly improbable event, we are going to have to learn to live with a certain degree of insistence that people who fundamentally disagree that such a law should even exist must nonetheless comply with it.

Law is, after all, one of the basic tools we use to deal with societal problems, and it cannot refuse to do a job just because it is a difficult one. However, we must in all cases weigh carefully the price of passing laws in areas of uncertainty. Since the general rule could be roughly summed up as "the vaguer the law, the bigger the chill," we must consider carefully whether the actual effect of having contentious laws on the books is worth the risk of chilling activities on the periphery of the specific activity that is meant to be frozen.

THE FEMINIST SCHISM

That the law pertaining to pornography is a contentious area is clear from the vast amount of contention currently surrounding it. In recent years, this issue has made for some exceedingly curious bedfellows. One arm of the feminist movement has allied itself on this one issue with moral fundamentalists, accusing unlike-minded feminists of being, of all things, liberal! This flight from the very political philosophy that has given feminism both birth and sustenance to the bosom of a conservative faction that even anti-pornography feminists disagree with on most any other issue indicates that there is hardly the kind of consensus here that will allow passage of and adherence to a firm law.

To say that the rift in the feminist movement is a bitter one is an understatement. No matter how healthy this realization that nature has not programmed all progressive feminine genes to respond identically to all questions, it cannot be denied that, like all movements that must deal with the basic non-homogeneity of their various components once the pressure is off, the feminist movement is not happy about its loss of solidarity. Both sides would like to think the other will just come around if only the right words can be found. But clearly our desires are not to be fulfilled.

There cannot be said to be a "feminist position" on pornography in Canada or elsewhere. There is instead an anti-pornography movement in which feminists are involved with non-feminists, but for feminist reasons. These feminists gained impetus from a like-minded group in the United States that collected many of its early ideas into *Take Back the Night* (Lederer, 1980), the classic, uncluttered statement of the feminist anti-pornography position. This book was followed five years later in Canada by the classic, uncluttered, feminist anti-censorship statement, *Women Against Censorship* (Burstyn, 1985). Particularly since the emergence of the positions taken in the second book served to illustrate the fact that this is an area of serious contention within the feminist community, there has been a growing literature on the topic, not only in Canada but in the United States, Australia, and the United Kingdom.

Only in the very recent past has the feminist movement accepted this schism as a fact of life. And, no doubt because pornography is such an emotional question for *all* feminists, we are still having a hard time playing fair with the other side. For example, Susan Cole in her 1989 book, *Pornography and the Sex Crisis*, does address the fact that the blanket term "feminists" is inaccurate and does attempt to develop a more use-ful terminology.[1] Her titles are, however, not untinged by her own values and, just as name-calling does in the abortion battle, her titles have their political purposes here as well. Cole announces her decision to call feminists who are "fighting pornography" "anti-pornography feminists" and those who are "fighting censorship" "anti-censorship feminists" (Cole, 1989, p. 9). Although this is better than use of the old blanket desig-nation, it is either an unconscious or a disingenuous failure to see what the real argument is about here.

The fact is that many feminists whom Cole designates anti-censorship are, myself included, at the same time anti-pornography. It is hard not to be against something that makes you squirm in your chair, even as you try to assess it from a careful scholarly perspective, and makes you doubt your relationships with your mates and sons and brothers, not to mention the quasi-stranger in the next office. Pornography does tell terrible lies about women. It also tells terrible lies about men. It is certainly no place to turn to for education on either sex or gender, and its existence within our society is worrisome.

It cannot be said that feminists such as myself are not anti-pornography, nor is it accurate to call us anti-censorship if you are determined to define our purpose as that of "fighting censorship." Actually, we reject the idea of making the censorship of pornography a central issue at all. We accept pornography as only a symptom and fear that concentrating on it will distract our gaze from the root causes of inequality in this society, not only for women but for all less powerful groups.[2] We fear, as Sara Diamond put it fairly early on, that "[c]ensorship won't make general ideas of violence against women go away: it won't make pornography disappear, just move under-ground" (Diamond, 1985, p. 49).

Still, my own tendency is also to call feminists with my approach to the issue "anti-censorship," but to define them as "feminists who reject censorship as a solution." I use this to differentiate us from what I have tended to call "pro-censorship feminists." But, just as Cole's definition does injustice to my side, giving her side the designation "pro-censorship" does injustice as well and I hereby vow to eschew its use. For no other reason than that this group has made pornography its focus, I am willing to grant it full title to the name "anti-pornography." And despite the fact that I am not out on the battle lines trying to quash censorship on an active basis, I accept the name "anti-censorship." I enter the arena that they have constructed only through that door and am content to do battle clothed in their perception of me.

I am battling against the danger posed by passing vague and sweeping laws without full and careful consideration of their effect on our ability to explore and develop our identity. I accept that far-reaching legislation against pornography may indeed have the effect of freezing in place laws that will make it riskier to be a pornographer, but I fear that this will be accomplished only at the expense of chilling expression in general. So far, the legislation suggested has certainly looked likely to have this effect and it is probable, given the vagueness of these laws and our inability to decide precise guidelines here, that a general chill on freedom of expression will be a sidelight of any attempt to draft a new pornography law for Canada.

FAILED PORNOGRAPHY PROPOSALS

Censorship movements tend to be cyclical in nature[3] and Canada's latest phase kicked into gear in response to the increased amount and violence of pornographic literature dating from the 1970s. By the early 1980s, energy was focused against such establishments as Red Hot Video, a chain leasing "hard-core" porn in British Columbia.[4] In response to growing pressure from feminists and fundamentalists alike regarding this and another perceived social problem, the federal (Liberal) government established the Special Committee on Pornography and Prostitution in 1983. After two years of research and public hearings, the Committee set down what it took to be a reflection of Canadian public opinion regarding pornography and prostitution.

The report of the so-called Fraser Committee (Special Committee on Pornography and Prostitution, 1985) recommended a shift of emphasis in the Criminal Code from obscenity to pornography, in particular sexually violent and degrading material and that which involved actual physical harm in the production thereof (Special Committee on Pornography and Prostitution, 1985, Vol. 1, pp. 276–79). Despite its shift of focus from obscenity to pornography—a fundamental demand of the anti-pornography feminists—the report was criticized for not taking a strong enough stand regarding harm claimed to result not just to those used in the production of pornography but that caused to society and particularly to women by the finished product.[5]

The emphasis placed by anti-pornography feminists on direct harm caused by pornography can be explained partly through its role in making the crucial political differentiation between erotica and pornography. But there is also a strict legal reason for this emphasis: harm is required to justify the presence of pornography legislation in the Criminal Code, where they clearly want it located.

Theoretically, acts are not to be designated criminal in this society unless they do harm to someone. For this reason, at least three offences barred by the Criminal Code are open to attack, all of which refer to forms of expression and all of which have been abused. Blasphemy entails oral or written reproach of God; sedition entails advocating treason; and obscenity entails doing acts to corrupt public morals. As constructed and enforced, none requires proof of harm. Neither God, the state, nor morals need actually suffer for one to be found guilty of blasphemous libel (*Criminal Code*, R.S., c. C-34, s. 296), seditious libel (*Criminal Code*, R.S., c. C-34, ss. 59–63), or an offence tending to corrupt moral (*Criminal Code*, R.S., c. C-34, ss. 163–72).

Because of the difficulty of proving actual harm to the targets, what we see is lesser beings putting themselves in the way to draw fire. We therefore see blasphemy laws used to punish those who have challenged the power of a dominant religious organization and sedition to punish those who have challenged the activities of a dominant political faction. In turn, obscenity laws have been put to use against those who have challenged the moral beliefs of a dominant social group. Anti-pornography feminists argue that the dominant group has so far ignored the perspective of women and are demanding that that now be written into the law. I, and many like me, question whether it is ever justifiable to put problematic laws into the hands of anyone. We worry that the chill will be too great.

Perhaps we would feel differently if we could bring ourselves to believe that law could be used to remove the really destructive forces in our society, the cancer that sickens the body politic. But we know that social surgery, no matter what its claims, is blunt and bloody and destructive and, in the end, usually not worth the cost it exacts. That initiatives taken to satisfy the current anti-pornography coalition are open to this effect is clear from the unsatisfactoriness of the two pieces of legislation unsuccessfully proposed so far.

Bill C-114, introduced by the Conservative government shortly after it came to power under Brian Mulroney, directly addresses coalition concerns regarding violence and degradation and provides for higher penalties for kiddie-porn. It attempts to replace the vague term "obscenity" not with the only slightly less vague term "pornography" alone, but with four designations: "degrading pornography," "pornography that shows physical harm," "pornography that shows sexually violent behaviour," and simply "pornography." Each of the categories is laid out in full and is dealt with separately.

Each definition has its own problems in interpretation. For example, under "degrading pornography," the phrase "one person treating himself or another as an animal or object" no doubt raises different images in different minds. But the greatest problem comes with the last category, simply "pornography." This is defined in Bill C-114 as follows:

> "pornography" means any visual matter showing vaginal, anal or
> oral intercourse, ejaculation, sexually violent behaviour, bestiality,
> incest, necrophilia, masturbation or other sexual activity.

It is the phrase "other sexual activity" that is most problematic here. According to the penalties provided, one could serve up to five years' imprisonment for importing, making, printing, publishing, broadcasting, distributing, or possessing for the purpose of distribution—or only two years for selling, renting, offering to sell or rent, receiving for sale or rental, possessing for the purpose of sale or rental or displaying in a way visible to a member of the public in a public place—the representation of a kiss. There is, of course, the usual provision of a defence for "genuine educational or scientific purpose or . . . artistic merit."

Met with criticism and even ridicule, Bill C-114 was allowed to die on the order paper in 1986 and was replaced by a second draft in May 1987. Bill C-54 took a different tack. No doubt stung by accusations of prudery, its drafters attempted to make a clear differentiation between pornography and erotica, the latter defined as

> any visual matter a dominant characteristic of which is the
> depiction, in a sexual content or for the purpose of the sexual
> stimulation of the viewer, of a human sexual organ, a female breast
> or the human anal region.

The new pornography definition aimed at greater certainty through greater length. Although it does not make the error of open-endedness Bill C-114 did with "or other sexual activity," Bill C-54 does ban visual matter depicting lactation or menstruation in a sexual context as well as vaginal, anal, or oral intercourse, therefore still erring on the side of breadth.

Although differentiation of erotica and pornographic depictions may not have been perfectly clear, consequences were clearly enough laid out. "Dealing in pornography" in a variety of ways could get you up to ten years in prison, but erotica was fine so long as you did not purvey it to minors or display it in public without "a prominent warning notice advising the nature of the display therein" or concealed in the proverbial plain brown (here, "opaque") wrapper.

Despite this attempt at sexual enlightenment, Bill C-54 was derided as moralistic in its own turn. As the official organ of the Canadian Association of University Teachers (CAUT) described its fate:

> With the calling of the 1988 federal election, Bill C-54 died on the House of Commons order paper at second reading. One is not hard pressed to conclude that the bill was intended to do so. The government could then pacify its "Moral Majority" wing without actually, in the end, doing anything (CAUT Bulletin, Censorship and academic freedom, 1990, p. 18).

What the CAUT article glosses over in this quote is the fact that the impetus for this legislative urge came not just from what it dismisses as the "Moral Majority" but also from a group on a whole other part of the social, political, and sexual spectrum.

One has only to compare the film *Not a Love Story* produced by the National Film Board in 1981 with *Times and Seasons: Pornography in Canada*, produced by the Church of Jesus Christ of Latter Day Saints in 1986 to see the gulf between radical feminists such as the American Catharine MacKinnon[6] (a big influence on the Canadian movement) and groups such as Canadians for Decency, who clearly see no reason whatsoever to try to differentiate between "good" and "bad" sexual expression.

The 1980s ended with no consensus, continued pressure from both factions of the old coalition, and the old obscenity laws still on the books.

PROBLEMS WITH CURRENT OBSCENITY LAW

This failure of the pornography bills of the 1980s does not leave us with no law in the field. Rather, it leaves us with law from an earlier era that must be bent to our new purposes or, as others hope, serve to hold back the hands of time. Despite—or perhaps it is better to say because of—their antiquated nature, the obscenity laws are capable of giving off quite enough chill in their own right.

Canada inherited its obscenity law from England and wrote it into its first Criminal Code in 1892. The early provisions merely banned obscene materials without including a definition of obscenity. As is usual in such cases, a definition developed through case law to fill the gap. The test for obscenity entered Anglo-Canadian law through the case of *R. v. Hicklin* (1868) LR 3 QB 360, involving a publication purporting to reveal deviant sex practices among Roman Catholic priests. The accused was found not guilty at trial on the grounds that he had not meant to prejudice good morals but rather had meant to undermine the Roman Catholic church.

On appeal, the court ruled that the publication's innocent nature or object was irrelevant in the case of obscenity. According to Chief Justice Cockburn, the proper test was

> whether the tendency of the matter charged as obscenity is to
> deprave and corrupt those whose minds are open to such immoral
> influences, and into whose hands a publication of this sort may fall.[7]

The definition suffered from both elitism and imprecision. In time, it would be replaced by a definition written into the Code itself which, if it suffered less from elitism, failed to cast off entirely the cloak of obscurity. Passed into law in 1959, s. 163(8) of the Code states that

> any publication a dominant characteristic of which is the undue
> exploitation of sex, or of sex and any one or more of the following
> subjects, namely, crime, horror, cruelty and violence, shall be
> deemed to be obscene.

Obscenity cases ever after have exhausted forests of paper and oceans of ink on just the question you would suspect from looking at this section: When does exploitation of sex cross into the realm of the "undue"?

It has been established for quite some time and regularly reaffirmed by our courts that "undueness" is to be judged according to contemporary community standards in Canada.[8] It has also been established and reaffirmed that these are to be community standards of tolerance, not what Canadians think it right for themselves to see but what Canadians would not abide other Canadians seeing (*Towne Cinema Theatres Ltd. v. R., 1985*). Anti-pornography feminists, who after all form a minority in any community, are not happy with this test. They argue that what constitutes the standards of a given community is more likely than not to be established by (usually male) expert witnesses. They argue, for example, in the area of lewd performances, that "the standards of those who do not attend such performances are ignored" (Mahoney, 1985, pp. 77–112).

Feminists are not the only ones who feel their values go unrepresented in the legal arena. Charles Freeman, a record store owner in Florida, was recently convicted under similar U.S. obscenity laws for selling a record by the sexually explicit and violence-celebrating rap music group, 2 Live Crew (Store owner convicted, 1990). Freeman, facing a possible year in prison and/or up to $1000 in fines, argued as passionately as any feminist against the injustice of being judged by a community of which one is not really a part:

> "It doesn't represent my community where E-C Records is!"
> Freeman, who is black, shouted as he left the Fort Lauderdale
> courthouse. "It's unfair. The jury was all white. They don't know
> where E-C Records is. They don't know a goddamned thing about
> the ghetto" (Store owner convicted, 1990).

If feminists and ghetto blacks feel beleaguered, so do those whose job it is to expand a society's horizons through force of imagination.

Even the unamended legislation carries some recognition that some obscenity might have something to be said for it. Subsection 163(3) provides that no person is to be convicted of corrupting public morals if it can be established that "the public good was served by the acts that are alleged to constitute the offence." The test in *R. v. American News Co. Ltd.* (1957), 118 C.C.C. 152 (Ont. C.A.) asks whether the matter charged is "necessary or advantageous to religion or morality, to the administration of justice, the pursuit of science, literature or art, or other objects of general interest."

This is not only a hard standard to meet but probably one that creative members of our society—artists, writers, performers, educators—should strive *not* to meet, given that the whole purpose of their work should be to challenge the stock ideas a society has about itself, not knuckle under to them.

Despite the fact that this defence looks like a concession to these people, the weight of the law is still against them. Once their work is found obscene according to the community standards test, they cannot simply say, "But this work is good for the community whether it appreciates it or not and even perhaps precisely because it does *not* appreciate it." To be eligible for the defence of public good, it is not sufficient that it have merit for "the more sophisticated reader." If it is made available to a public unequipped to grasp either the symbolism or the psychology, the accused cannot rely on the defence of public good (*R. v. Delorme,* 1973).

Even so, the defence is on occasion still floated successfully. A recent U.S. example is the Contemporary Arts Center case in Cincinnati, Ohio.[9] Obscenity charges were laid against the center and its director because of a photographic exhibit entitled "Robert Mapplethorpe: The Perfect Moment." Among 175 photos on display were five depicting graphic sex acts involving men and two showing children with their genitals exposed. One of the factors upon which the jury seems to have based its verdict is the failure of the prosecution to undermine the defence of artistic merit (hence, public good).

While one can only celebrate the finding in the Mapplethorpe case, the existence of this defence means that you also get a lot of puerile arguments made in court on behalf of material that probably doesn't even approach art, let alone possess any artistic merit. In the recent prosecution of a Toronto record company for its involvement in two albums by Victoria's Day-Glo Abortions band, expert witness Dr. Richard Meen, psychiatrist and director of a youth detention centre, argued that the music focused on desperation and alienation, not violence and sexuality.

> Although sex "permeates" the music, "it serves as a vehicle for wide concerns about adolescent life," he said. And the violence pointed out by the Crown in several songs is fantasy rather than reality.
>
> Meen said such music can have a cathartic effect—allowing teenagers and young adults to realize that others are troubled by the same problems that bother them (Rock songs, 1990).

It is nonsense—although in terms of defence strategy, necessary nonsense—to discuss this work in terms of artistic merit and public good. The point is not whether you can find a suitably expert witness who can get you off the hook but whether this sort of material rates this type of attention in the first place. I doubt that Day-Glo Abortions serves the public good but I doubt that it does us much harm either. Societies make music; music doesn't make societies. Eradicating symptoms will not cure but only interfere with attempts to deal with the root cause of our perceived social ills.

A major defect in the public good defence is that it can only be accessed in court. This means that, so long as sweeping obscenity laws are on the books, you can be forced to undergo the monetary and emotional expense of defending work that turns out to have been for the public good all along. We have a defence then that may give you a chance to break free at the last moment but does little to reduce the chill of these laws in general.

Recently, the public good defence has been attacked on constitutional grounds. To demand that the accused have to prove, even according to the lesser standard of "on balance of probabilities" (compared to the standard of proof "beyond a reasonable doubt," usually demanded in criminal law), that the matter involved served the public good has been found to offend the guarantee of presumption of innocence provided by s. 11(d) of the Canadian Charter of Rights and Freedoms (*R. v. Fringe Products Inc., et al.,* 1990). This means that, so long as the accused can raise a reasonable doubt in respect to that defence, the onus passes to the Crown, who must then take on the heavier load of proving that it does *not* serve the public good. While this gives the defendant a fairer shot in the courtroom, it does not address the big issue regarding expression and law.

THE CHILLING EFFECT

The big issue is, of course, the big chill. And criminal obscenity laws, while the best publicized form of censorship, are only the tip of the iceberg. There are many ways expression can be censored by this society. It is done legally through customs restrictions on importation of certain material, postal regulations, municipal by-laws regarding zoning and display, and classification systems such as those policed by our provincial film censorship boards.

Socially, censorship can be accomplished through suasion and ridicule. Illegally, it can be done through terrorism, a tactic adopted by the Wimmen's Fire Brigade, which took credit for bombing three Red Hot Video outlets in British Columbia in 1982 (Cole, 1989, p. 53). Although not yet a factor in Canadian jurisprudence, there is also the possibility of individual civil suits for those who claim to have been directly and personally harmed by pornography.[10] Taxation could be stepped up, much as it has been recently for alcohol and tobacco. Perhaps a separate, non-criminal statute could be used to ban material with a slightly less heavy hand.

Public education might succeed in reducing pornography's panache, again much like the current campaign against alcohol and tobacco. Perhaps organization and protection of pornography workers on the job would go some way to cleaning up material requiring the actual performance of dangerous and/or degrading acts in situations where simulation will not create the images desired. Certainly laws pertaining to assault and employment of minors already exist to back up greater initiatives in this area.

Very recently we have seen expansion of the hate propaganda provisions of the Criminal Code (ss. 318–320) in such a way that they may have implications for pornographers (*R. v. Keegstra,* 1990). On a more insidious level, censorship can be accomplished politically through funding manipulation, such as is currently being practised in the United States by the National Endowment for the Arts.[11] There is also industry regulation such as the old Comics Code out of the 1950s (Dickin McGinnis, 1988, p. 19). And, of course, you can just do it to yourself.

Self-censorship can be seen on one level as simply the attempt of the good citizen to comply with the law. While this may very well be true, we have a right to expect more direction from the law regarding what exactly constitutes compliance. We do not have this with our vague censorship laws. Should we stick a knife into someone, we have a pretty good understanding that we are going to be in trouble with the law—that this is an act that we can say with some confidence is going to put us in a situation where we are going to have to explain our actions.

Relevant limits in terms of obscenity law are not so easy to establish. When I write or paint or photograph a scene that I know to be sexual in nature, I do not necessarily know it to be obscene. It is not comparable to the situation where I know the speed limit but decide to take a chance that there's no cop around. In this case, I really don't know the obscenity limit. Not only that, I *can't* know it until I have tested it in this specific matter.

In other words, I cannot know whether my work is obscene until I have been put on trial for obscenity. Once it has been so deemed, I will not be let off with a warning, now that I know that this particular act is illegal, not to repeat it. Rather, I will be penalized for doing something that, at the time I did it, was not actually illegal.

People then must aim at a standard that is unclear and because it is unclear, they will be forced to fly broad surveillance over their activities to make good and sure they stay out of trouble. This is hardly the best climate for the development of either individual or societal identity. That self-censorship would become a real factor in the current anti-pornography campaign was to be expected. That its effects have been so pervasive is no doubt cheering to many but is clearly unsettling to me.

Not only are "respectable" members of the intellectual community dropping back into the halo zone but so are what have been dubbed the "dirt-for-dirt's sakers" (Herbert, 1974, p. xiv). In fact, it is the respectable who are fighting hardest their urge to cringe. Thus, we have the board of the Calgary Public Library deciding not to comply with reader demands that it cancel subscriptions to the *Canadian Forum* after it ran Andres Serrano's photograph of a crucifix in a glass container of urine, entitled Piss Christ, on its July-August cover (Tousley, 1990). Thus we also have the Canadian Broadcasting Corporation refusing to materially change its "Brave New Waves" program just so it can be broadcast over (American) National Public Radio where it would have to comply with the U.S. Federal Communications Commission ban on language or images referring to "sex or excretion" ("Anti-obscenity," 1990).

It is heartening to see that those charged with managing the intellectual life of our society are, in fact, thinking carefully about how much they will comply. And it is probably not surprising that those who are in it largely for the money will feel they have little to fight for.

Indeed, it is a little difficult to imagine anyone seriously wanting to wind up in court arguing the artistic merits of, for example, Das Damen's record *Das Damen*, advertised in SST Records' recent mail-order catalogue as follows:

> Like four men running on empty, Das Damen breathes fumes and sparks combustion like a four-wheel sex machine. Fill up your mind and check your strawberry-love-oil levels; six songs for six cylinders of molten love rock (Harper's Magazine, 1990, p. 30).

Is this the sort of expression one stands on one's artistic principles for? Clearly not, given the rush by 2 Live Crew to put out a sanitized version of its controversial album "As Nasty as They Wanna Be," entitled hilariously "As Clean as They Wanna Be." Record dealers in Canada and the United States, afraid of sharing the fate of the Florida record store owner referred to above (who, ironically, was convicted while 2 Live Crew successfully challenged its own obscenity charges for a live performance), now have a choice of version to carry (Zimmerman, 1990). Serious scholars will no doubt wish to acquire both for purposes of study and comparison.

SANITIZING PORNOGRAPHY

It is, of course, nonsensical to talk about the bulk of such material in terms of artistic merit. In the case of hard-core pornography with its whips and chains and knives and guns, such talk goes beyond cynicism. Business persons whose main concern is making a buck in a competitive market will not be interested in the defence of public good but rather the test of community standards of tolerance. It is not asked of us to like this stuff or buy it or applaud, it is only asked that we avert our eyes or just stay out of that part of town. What some purveyors of pornography are trying to establish at this point, then, is how much they need do to avoid prosecution in the first place.

In Canada, magazine distributors in particular have taken the initiative in trying to anticipate community standards of tolerance. To this end, the three-person Ontario Advisory Committee (since renamed the Periodical Advisory Committee) was established in 1976 for the purposes of advising distributors what material proposed for distribution meets community standards and what does not. Although the Committee's advice does not keep the distributors entirely out of trouble,[12] it clearly performs a service of value to an industry that, after all, seeks only to traffic in magazines.

That some business interests are not just willing but positively eager to take direction regarding what they can get away with is demonstrated even more clearly by the strange liaison between distributors on the west coast and the British Columbia Periodical Review Board (BCPRB), established in 1984. The Board grew out of a successful attempt to embarrass prominent Vancouver businessman, Jimmy Pattison, newly appointed head of Expo 86. Pattison also headed Mainland Magazine Service, a purveyor of—among other things—porn. Pattison and his colleagues responded by asking that a board, set up to the satisfaction of the very people who had publicized the issue, be constituted to advise distributors on whether material proposed complied with the guidelines on obscenity issued to prosecuting counsel by the office of the British Columbia Attorney General (Ridington, 1989).[13]

According to the chairperson, Jillian Ridington, who says she took the position "because someone was going to take it, and I thought a well-qualified feminist should" (Ridington, 1989, p. 32), the Board is dominated by feminists. Feminists also

> dominate the hiring committee. . . . [G]roups known to have extreme views are not invited to nominate members: a representative of the Canadian Civil Liberties Association or the Pentecostal Church would make consensus in B.C.P.R.B. decision's [sic] impossible (Ridington, 1989, p. 11).

While the politics of these groups would only get in the way of the Board getting on with its task, feminist politics seemingly would not. Besides, it would seem that feminists have a positive duty to act in this area due to special aptitude:

> While it is easy for feminists to distinguish between non-violent pornography and erotica, it may be impossible for legislators and courts to do so (Ridington, 1989, p. 6).

This aptitude is not, however, exercised without cost. Ridington says that three years of spending 25 hours a week reading or thinking about porn gave her an ulcer and aggravated pre-existing arthritis. Other board members have suffered tension headaches, neck kinks, breathing disorders, depression, irritability, anger, and inhibited sexual response. I don't doubt for a moment that that much exposure to porn would have similar effects on me. I just wish I could believe that so much human suffering was worth the end result. But that I cannot do.

Funding for the Board comes—albeit through trusts—from the distributors themselves. We therefore have a situation where anti-pornography feminists not only serve as bedfellows to fundamentalists but as mistresses to pornographers. Board members are charged with the task of alerting the distributors to material that will not get by the community standards test. Board members testify in court as to the acceptability of material passed by them. And despite the tendency of the bulk of this stuff to make the members physically ill, about 70 percent of it receives their seal of approval.

In time, producers of pornography also found they could turn to Board members for counsel. In a chilling passage, Ridington describes one joint initiative of feminists and pornographers regarding an advertisement for a so-called sexual aid that was having a hard time getting into Canada:

> One example was an ad for a large dildo. The advertiser claimed that it would "make any woman say, 'Ouch, it hurts.'" Following consultations with Customs, the ad now reads, "It will give any woman a feeling of total satisfaction." A small step, but progress (Ridington, 1989, p. 17).

I envision a scene where he is shoving that damned thing into her and she says, "Ouch, it hurts," and he says, "But the feminists say it will give you a feeling of total satisfaction."

There is an argument to be made that saying some types of objectification of women are unacceptable is to say, by implication, that others are acceptable. In the case of the cleansed dildo ad, the approval is not just implied but firmly stated and celebrated as, of all things, feminist progress! From the other side of the schism, I protest.

To help the "bad guys" in the porn business order their affairs so as to meet the standards of the "good guys" in the Attorney General's office is not only to risk supporting the pornography business but to support keeping us under the debilitating "protection" of the power structure. To concentrate on eradicating hard-core porn is to risk backhanded approval of soft-core porn. And to concentrate on porn at all is to risk putting a stamp of approval on the myriad other ways women are objectified in this society: through advertising, humour, language, medicine, religion, and law, to name a few.

CONCLUSION

At the same time, to be critical of the campaign against pornography is to risk supporting the pornographers, to risk splitting the feminist movement, and to risk downplaying the offensiveness of this type of material. The production of pornography is big business. In six months in 1980, *Penthouse* alone grossed $8 556 075 in Canada (Assiter, 1989, p. 102). And consumption is on the increase.[14] It worries me.

But what worries me more is that pornography can be used to divert attention from more pressing problems facing women. As Lisa Steele put it years ago in the Burstyn collection:

> Porn is simply the part of women's agenda that they—politicians and others in power—can most easily buy into. They may hedge around equal pay, abortion rights, universal day care, but ask them about porn and they're ready to rewrite the laws tomorrow, so deep is their "concern." And, to be realistic, censorship is the cheapest item on the shopping list of the women's movement (Steele, 1985, p. 61).

But in the long run, censorship is never cheap. It is expensive because it shuts people up. In particular, it shuts people up who have not always had things to say that those in control of a society want to hear. Currently, law shuts up homosexuals whose literature is still regularly stopped at the border by Canada Customs.[15] It also shuts up feminists like filmmaker Bonnie Klein whose exposé of pornography, *Not a Love Story*, had to be subjected to a court hearing before the Ontario Film and Video Appreciation Society could show it to its members (Lacombe, 1988, p. 48). More expensively, it draws our attention away from the really pressing problems within our society.

Is pornography really something worth focusing a great deal of our resources on? The cyclical nature of obscenity campaigns in general indicates that it is something we clearly want to mull over from time to time. Perhaps the current cycle is coming to a close. On January 17, 1991, a few hours after the United States began to bomb Iraq and Kuwait, a jury in Fort Lauderdale, Florida, took only thirteen minutes to acquit the rock group Too Much Joy of charges that it performed an obscene show. The jurors said the thing that took the longest in coming to a consensus was that a couple of people had to go to the bathroom. The jurors said the prosecution was frivolous and a waste of time. The "[j]urors also said they felt foolish sitting in such a trial while war erupted in the Persian Gulf" (Walsh, 1991).

Anti-censorship forces should not take too much joy from this occurrence. The rock group probably did put on an obscene performance. They sang six songs from 2 Live Crew's "Nasty" album (not the "Clean" one) in which the lyrics are often hideously and hurtfully misogynistic, throbbing with macho self-doubt. The jury's decision can be read to say that war is more important than violence against women, an ancient and vicious lie. It can be read as a feminist defeat, which saddens me.

However, I cannot in my heart of hearts find it in me to condemn the outcome of this trial. I cannot find it in me because I fear the effects of vague laws more than I fear the effects of pornography. Making something a legal question by writing it into our statute books does not make it any less of a political question. It may, however, make the political aspects more difficult to confront, and in the long run that will work against society in general as well as feminism in particular. To nurse the type of chill that is given off by obscenity laws is to accept someone else's definition as to the acceptable limits of the halo zone. This does not provide a climate in which anyone can fully examine and develop her identity.

POSTSCRIPT

As this article went to press, the Supreme Court of Canada handed down its decision in *R. v. Butler* (1992) SCJ no. 15 (27 February 1992). There is much that needs to be said about this decision and its implications but for the purposes of this article, its effects can be fairly easily summarized.

In terms of the practical outcome, the decision sent the proprietor of Winnipeg's Exxxtasy video stores back for retrial on 250 counts of possessing obscene materials. At trial, he had been convicted on some counts but acquitted on others, on the simple grounds that the judge found some of the material to be obscene and some not. On appeal initiated by the prosecution, convictions were entered on all counts by the Manitoba Court of Appeal, on the grounds that these materials did not constitute a form of expression protected by the Charter. The Supreme Court took a third tack, finding that the obscenity restrictions do impinge freedom of expression but that they constitute a reasonable and justifiable limit thereon, as allowed under section 1 of the Charter of Rights and Freedoms. This is not an unusual route for the courts to pursue.

What is unusual is that the Supreme Court adjusted the community standards test from one focusing on offense to morals to one acknowledging likelihood of harm. In other words, if the community can be shown to believe that such material causes harm, it fails the test and can be banned whether it can be shown to cause harm or not. Anti-pornography feminists, whose position was argued by the Women's Legal Education Action Fund, have rightly claimed this as a victory, a direct legal recognition of their position. Unable to pressure new legislation, they have succeeded in swaying judicial interpretation of existing law. The implication of this will have to be and will be worked out in Canada's courts. Until that well has run dry we are unlikely to see any direct legislated initiatives in the area of obscenity.

NOTES

I wish to acknowledge the Canada Research Fellowship Programme of the Social Sciences and Humanities Research Council of Canada which funds my work in this and other areas.

1. Compare Cole's definition with the earlier use of the simple term "feminist" in Christine Boyle and Sheila Noonan, (1986), Prostitution and pornography: Beyond formal equality *Dalhousie Law Journal, 10,* 225–265.

2. See, for example, discussion in Alison Assiter, (1989), *Pornography, feminism and the individual,* London: Pluto Press, p. 146.

3. For an earlier Canadian initiative, see Janice Dickin McGinnis, (1988), Bogeymen and the law: Crime comics and pornography, *Ottawa Law Review, 20,* (3).

4. For a case growing out of this, see *R. v. Red Hot Video Ltd.* (1985), 45 C.R. (3rd) 36 (B.C.C.A.).

5. See, for example, Sheila Noonan, Pornography: Preferring the feminist approach of the British Columbia court of appeal to that of the Fraser Committee, a case comment following *R. v. Red Hot Video Ltd.*, supra, n. 8, 36 at 61.

6. See, for example, Catharine A. MacKinnon, (1987), *Feminism unmodified: Discourses on life and law,* (Cambridge: Harvard University Press), Chapter 15: "On collaboration," pp. 198–205.

7. Quoted by Chief Justice Dickson, in *Towne Cinema Theatres Ltd. v. R.* (1985) 45 C.R. (3d) 1 at 12 (S.C.C.).

8. See, for example, *R. v. Prairie Schooner News Ltd. and Powers* (1970) 1 C.C.C. (2d) 251 (Man. C.A.).

9. Widely covered in the media. See report of the verdict in Art gallery and boss cleared of obscenity charges, (1990, October 6), *Calgary Herald*, p. C3.

10. Municipal by-laws to establish this cause of action have been supported by feminist groups in the United States. MacKinnon, (1987), *Feminism unmodified.* Cambridge: Harvard University Press, p. 201.

11. See guarantee that must be signed by grantees certifying that none of the money will be used for materials that "may be considered obscene, including but not limited to depictions of sadomasochism, homoeroticism, the sexual exploitation of children, or individuals engaged in sex acts and which, when taken as a whole, do not have serious literary, artistic, political or scientific value." Reproduced in *Harper's Magazine* (1990, May), p. 30.

12. See *R. v. Regina News Ltd.* (1987) 39 C.C.C. (3d) 170 (Sask. C.A.) where photographs of bound Japanese women published in the December 1984 issue of *Penthouse* were passed by the Committee for distribution but found in excess of community standards by the court.

13. All material regarding the BCPRB comes from Jillian Ridington, (1989), *Confronting pornography: A feminist on the front lines.* Feminist Perspectives, no. 15, Ottawa: Canadian Research Institute for the Advancement of Women. Only quotes are hereafter separately noted.

14. Albeit in a climate where consumption of all consumer products has risen sharply. A.W.B. Simpson, (1983), *Pornography and politics: The Williams Committee in retrospect,* London: Waterloo Press, p. 75.

15. See reference to *Globe and Mail* reportage in *CAUT Bulletin*, (1990, November), Censorship and academic freedom: The Tory years, p. 18.

REFERENCES

Anti-obscenity fervor stings CBC. (1990, August 21). *Calgary Herald*, p. C3.

Assiter, A. (1989). *Pornography, feminism and the individual*. London: Pluto Press.

Burstyn, V. (Ed.). (1985). *Women against censorship*. Vancouver: Douglas and McIntyre.

Canada, Parliament. House of Commons. Bill C-54. *An act to amend the criminal code and customs tariff*. 1st Session, 33rd Parliament, 33–34–35 Eliz II, 1984–85–86.

Canada, Parliament. House of Commons. Bill C-114. *An act to amend the criminal code and other acts in consequence thereof*. 2nd Session, 33rd Parliament, 35–36 Eliz II, 1986–87.

Canada. Special Committee on Pornography and Prostitution. (1985). *Pornography and prostitution in Canada*. 2 volumes. Ottawa.

Censorship and academic freedom: The Tory years. (1990, November). *CAUT Bulletin*.

Cole, S.G. (1989). *Pornography and the sex crisis*. Toronto: Amanita Enterprises.

Diamond, S. (1985). Pornography: Image and reality. In *Women Against Censorship* (Ed. Burstyn, V.). Vancouver: Douglas & McIntyre.

Dickin McGinnis, J. (1988). Bogeymen and the law: Crime comics and pornography. *Ottawa Law Review, 20*.

Harper's Magazine. (1990, August), p. 30.

Herbert, A.P. (1974). Introduction to St. John-Stevas, N., *Obscenity and the Law*. New York: da Capo Press.

Lacombe, D. (1988). *Ideology and public policy: The case against pornography*. Toronto: Garamond Press.

Lederer, L. (Ed.). (1980). *Take back the night: Women on pornography*. New York: William Morrow.

Mahoney, K.E. (1985). Obscenity, morals and the law: Challenging basic assumptions. In *Justice Beyond Orwell* (Eds., Abella, R.S., & Rothman, M.L.). Montreal: Les Éditions Yvon Blais.

Ridington, J. (1989). Confronting pornography: A feminist on the front lines. *Feminist Perspectives, 15*. Ottawa: Canadian Research Institute for the Advancement of Women.

Rock songs could be beneficial, witness tells obscenity trial. (1990, November 8). *Calgary Herald*, p. A16.

R. v. American News Co. Ltd. (1957), 118 C.C.C. 152 (Ont. C.A.).

R. v. Delorme (1973), 15 C.C.C. (2d) 350 (Que. C.A.).

R. v. Fringe Products Inc. et al. (1990), 53 C.C.C.. (3d) 422 (Ont. Dist. Ct.).

R. v. Keegstra, [1990] S.C.R. 131

Steele, L. (1985). A capital idea: Gendering in the mass media. In *Women Against Censorship* (Ed., Burstyn, V.). Vancouver: Douglas & McIntyre.

Store owner convicted for selling rap album. (1990, October 4). *Calgary Herald*, p. F2.

Tousley, N. (1990, September 29). Canada hit by censorship trend. *Calgary Herald*, p. E9.

Towne Cinema Theatres v. R. (1985) 45 C.R. (3d) 1 at 12 (S.C.C.).

Walsh, B. (1991, January 19). Jury acquits rockers of obscenity charges. *Calgary Herald*, p. C8.

Zimmerman, K. (1990, October 26). Controversial disc is still available in Calgary stores. *Calgary Herald*, p. C2.

CHILDREN AND TELEVISION

Jeffrey L. Derevensky and Carolyn Klein

"Teenage Mutant Ninja Turtles," "He Man," "The Real Ghostbusters," "Pee-Wee's Playhouse," "The Simpsons" and "Sesame Street." These program titles show how dramatically children's television has changed since the early days of "Captain Kangaroo," "The Mickey Mouse Club," and "Howdy Doody." Although television, which began in the 1940s, is a relatively recent invention, few if any other innovations have had such an extreme impact. Initially invented as a novelty for the wealthy, television sets are now found in more than 98 percent of all Canadian households.

In addition to commercial and public television programming, the proliferation of cable channels has significantly altered television viewing habits since the late 1970s. These cable networks have provided a more centralized and focused approach, intended to address specific markets, such as children. Programs on the Disney Channel, Nickelodeon, and the Family Network are directly aimed at children. Statistics Canada's Report on Cable Television (1990) indicates that over 70 percent of all homes subscribe to cable television. More recently, video cassette recorders (VCRs), introduced in 1975, have become widely used by the general population. Rentals of prerecorded instructional programs and movies on cassette have similarly experienced a dramatic increase in popularity. Virtually overnight, the video rental store has created a new industry. In many communities, video stores remain open 18 to 24 hours per day. Classic adult and children's films have experienced a resurgence in popularity. Children and adults now have the ability to record specific programs while simultaneously viewing others. Large home video libraries are being developed, likely resulting in increased television viewing time.

The age at which children become video-sophisticated appears to be quite young. We are reminded of a cartoon depicting a young child and his mother seated in front of a television set. The young child proudly informs his mother that "I'm not in school yet, but I already know my numbers; zero, one, two, three, four, five, six, seven, eight, nine, pause, fast forward, rewind, play, and record" (Glasbergen, date and origin unknown). Children not old enough to tie their shoelaces often are capable of operating remote control devices for VCRs and television sets. Teachers report that many children unable to recite their multiplication tables are "walking *TV Guides*," able to accurately recite the daily sequence of programs on each and every channel.

The increased frequency with which television enters our daily lives has heightened the importance of examining its effects upon children and the family. According to a recent report (Statistics Canada, 1990), the average Canadian watches 23.5 hours of television weekly, with residents of Newfoundland and Quebec surpassing other Canadians with an average of 26.2 hours of television-viewing per week. The average North American spends more time watching television than on any other activity, save sleep and work (Huston, Wright, Rice, Kerkman, & St. Peters, 1990).

Since 1960, when television became widely accessible, television-viewing time has significantly increased. Reports indicate that the average American television set is on approximately seven hours per day (Steinberg, 1985). However, this figure may not be truly reflective of individual viewing time, since many households report that the television set is frequently on when no one is watching. Nevertheless, there is substantial evidence indicating considerable television viewing time.

Children are certainly not immune to the lure of television. Rather, parents report that their children can be found sitting mesmerized in front of a television set for hours. Children, whose parents report they have poor attention spans, often have little difficulty sustaining attention while watching their favourite television programs. It is reported that a typical six- to nine-month-old infant is seated in front of a television approximately one and a half hours per day (Hollenbeck & Slaby, 1979). By the time the child reaches three years of age, he/she will spend as many as three to four hours a day in front of the television set (Singer & Singer, 1981; Pearl, Bouthilet, & Lazar, 1982). Canadian children between the ages of two and eleven, watch an average of twenty hours of television per week (Statistics Canada, 1990).

During the preschool years, the average child will watch two and a half hours of television every day. However, viewing time has been shown to be as individual as the child, with weekly exposure ranging between 0 and 75 hours (Huston et al., 1990). From eight years of age, television viewing patterns increase steadily to approximately four hours per day during adolescence. As children's bedtime becomes later, the amount of television they watch increases. Although viewing patterns vary significantly, by the time a child reaches school age, television will likely have occupied more time than will be spent in a college classroom (Gerbner & Gross, 1976). Overall, by the time the average youth has graduated from high school, he/she will have spent approximately 15 000 hours watching television (NIMH, 1982). It is interesting to note that Saturday-morning cartoons, which are expressly aimed at children, account for a relatively small percentage of children's viewing time (13 percent for two- to five-year-olds, 15 percent for six- to eleven-year-olds) (Nielsen Report, 1988). The vast majority of viewing time is during the week, in early morning, late afternoon, and early evening hours (Comstock, Chaffee, Katzman, McCombs, & Roberts, 1978; Kunkel & Watkins, 1987). As well, evidence exists that children in elementary school exhibit viewing preferences for dramatic and adult-oriented programs, a phenomenon that likely increases their total viewing time (Comstock et al., 1978; Statistics Canada, 1990).

Research evidence has contributed to our understanding of significant variables that influence viewing patterns and behaviours. Certain characteristics have been shown to be related to television viewing habits. Ethnic minorities, women, individuals in lower socio-economic strata, and less educated individuals are reported to watch considerably more television than others (NIMH, 1982; Greenberg, 1986; Williams, 1986; Statistics Canada, 1990).

It appears that boys watch more violent action cartoons than girls (Lyle & Hoffman, 1976); however, there is some evidence that this pattern is changing as more aggressive female role models have been incorporated into cartoons (Eron, Huesmann, Brice, Fischer, & Mermelstein, 1983). Still further, children with emotional disorders watch more television overall, and more aggressive programs in particular, than typical children (Sprafkin, 1988). In their study of children's leisure activities, Medrich, Roizen, Ruben, and Buckley (1982) found that children from the least advantaged homes were roughly three times as likely to have heavy television viewing diets as compared to children from higher socio-economic groups.

Television viewing undoubtedly consumes a great deal of children's time and attention. Its role in educating and socializing children is only beginning to be understood. Successive generations of children will continue to view television. While the programs will change, its societal effects can no longer be considered a casual part of life. Rather, television has become a significant part of the acculturation process. A large-scale report of the National Institute of Mental Health (1982) concluded that:

> almost all evidence testifies to television's role as a formidable educator whose effects are both pervasive and cumulative. Television can no longer be considered as a casual part of daily life, an electronic toy. Research findings have long since destroyed the illusion that television is merely innocuous entertainment. While the learning it provides is mainly incidental rather than direct and formal, it is a significant part of the total acculturation process (NIMH, 1982, p. 87).

Television's role in society, its effects upon children and its limitations are only beginning to be understood. Its potential has yet to be fully realized.

This chapter examines how television influences children in four distinct ways: through social learning, education, entertainment, and advertising. Its potential benefits and limitations are discussed.

SOCIAL LEARNING

Television's ability to affect children's behaviour has grown stronger as social factors continue to change the structure of the family. For many years, researchers and theorists have recognized the family as the crucial socializing agent for the child. However, since the end of the Second World War, the structure of the family has been significantly altered, and other sources of socialization have taken on added importance. The demise of the extended family, and of the nuclear family (as a result of high incidence of divorce), have significantly altered the socialization process. No longer are grandparents in the home; frequently they do not even live within the same community. No longer do parents work in the home. Often children come home to empty homes in which television serves as both a friend and companion. Television viewing behaviour has become to a large extent uncontrolled, as parents are unavailable or unable to monitor its use and/or to set limits. Certainly, television has begun to play a crucial role in the child's socializing process, in his/her understanding of the world, and in his/her development of values, attitudes, and social skills.

Changes in child-rearing practices have occurred as a function of societal reorganization, due in large part to such factors as "urbanization, child labour laws, commuting, the centralization of schools, the working mother, the experts' advice to be permissive, the delegation and professionalization of child care, and the seductive power of television for keeping children occupied" (Bronfenbrenner, 1970, p. 99). Cumulatively, this societal reorganization has served to lessen opportunities for children to interact with their parents, with grandparents, and with adults in general. Rather, the segregation of society, grandparents from parents, parents from children, continues (Bronfenbrenner, 1970; Huston, Wright, et al., 1990). According to Bronfenbrenner (1970), "Children used to be brought up by their parents." This statement, made twenty years ago, is even more apropos today. As economic conditions have necessitated the two-parent working family, parents have become more reliant upon television as an educational tool, a companion, and a babysitter. Globally, today's parents are less able to set limits in general, and to specifically limit and censor the frequency and quality of their children's television viewing habits.

Television has radically changed family behaviour. Johnson (1967) reports that 60 percent of families have changed their sleeping patterns because of television programming, 55 percent have altered meal times, and 78 percent of families have incorporated television as the ultimate electronic babysitter. Leisure-time activities are often scheduled around television viewing patterns. In a study in western Canada, in which a Canadian community had only recently received television broadcasts, Williams and Handford (1986) found that although television did not determine the number of community activities available, it clearly had a negative effect upon participation in those activities. Involvement in community activities fell dramatically after television was introduced. The effect was particularly strong for sports-related activities by adolescents; however, it also affected youths' attendance at community dances, suppers, and parties, and attendance at meetings of clubs and other organizations for adults. It was further suggested that television may lead to greater age segregation and may qualitatively influence community life by reducing contact between individuals of different generations.

While most adults tend to believe that television is merely a simplistic form of entertainment, which has few negative consequences and limited social influence (Steiner, 1963), there remain serious questions as to its effects upon children's cognitive, social, affective, and personality development, and subsequently, their behaviour. Certainly recurring questions concerning the role of television in shaping children's stereotypes, attitudes, perceptions, acquisition of aggressive behaviour, and its educational utility remain to be answered.

In order to explain the influence that television has upon children, a number of theoretical positions have been proposed. One of the most cogent and widely accepted perspectives is that of Social Learning Theory, as proposed by Albert Bandura (1977). Central to this theory is the view that learning can occur through vicarious and symbolic modelling. Proponents of this theory recognize that an individual's thoughts, feelings, and actions, which are indisputably influenced by direct experience, can also be distinctly shaped through modelling and imitation.

According to social learning theory, an individual's psychological functioning is defined through continuous shared interaction between personal and environmental determinants. Figurative, vicarious, and self-regulatory mechanisms assume dominant roles. Whereas other theories, such as behaviourism, propose that learning can occur only through direct experience of behaviour and its consequences, social learning theory assumes that learning can occur vicariously by observing the consequences of others' actions (Bandura, 1977).

The ability to learn through observation permits behaviour patterns to be acquired without the lengthy trial-and-error process required for learning through performance. Learning through observation also facilitates the acquisition process, and ensures that specific behaviour will be reproduced with greater accuracy. This learning need neither be direct nor formal. Rather, incidental learning can occur without the child even being aware.

In order to fully understand television's impact upon children, knowledge of the factors that affect the modelling process is essential. If television, more specifically television characters (real life or cartoon), can influence children's behaviour, it is necessary to delineate among three sets of conditions that have been shown to influence the modelling process. These conditions include: (1) specific characteristics of the child; (2) characteristics of the observed behaviour; and (3) characteristics and attributes of the model (Bronfenbrenner, 1970).

Before children can model and assimilate observable events, they must be able to perceive to some extent the specific behaviour, they must have the physical capacity to perform such a behaviour, and lastly they must have the cognitive framework to assimilate the event.

Certainly the complexity of a behavioural act is critical for children's acquisition. Although letter sequences from "Sesame Street," as an example, are readily acquired, more complex phenomenon such as reading are not as easily acquired (e.g., "Electric Company"). More importantly, there exist certain qualities of a model that have the greatest potential for influencing children. These include the competency and status of the model, the degree of support and control the model exhibits over the environment, the similarity between the model and the child, aspirations of the child to be a member of a group to which the model belongs, and lastly, consequences of the behaviour itself will influence the likelihood of the behaviour being modelled (Bronfenbrenner, 1970).

According to social learning theory, these conditions and attributes affect the probability that a model's behaviour will be imitated. Bandura's (1965) research contends that individuals are more likely to imitate a model who has been reinforced for his/her behaviour. Similarly, observers are less likely to pattern their behaviour after models who have been punished for their actions (Bandura, Ross, & Ross, 1963; Bandura, 1973). In instances of violent depictions by television characters, it follows, therefore, that the modelled aggression should have an inhibitory effect when the protagonist is punished for his/her behaviour. Conversely, an instigative effect should arise when the protagonist is reinforced for his/her actions (Turner, Hesse, & Peterson-Lewis, 1986). Persistence of the viewed behaviour appears to be unrelated to the role model, but instead is a function of the way in which the child is reinforced for it (Bandura, 1965).

Observational learning has also been shown to vary as a function of age, with two-year-old children being able to imitate, with a fair degree of accuracy, what they view on television (Eron, Huesmann, Lefkowitz, & Walder, 1972; Collins, Berndt, & Hess, 1974), clearly a phenomenon that educational television has attempted to capitalize upon. However, since young children cannot fully understand the relationship between aggression and its underlying motives, they become most vulnerable to what they view on television.

Social learning theorists predict that viewing televised models (whether in cartoon or human form) who behave violently on television facilitates children's aggressivity. There has been considerable support from laboratory studies to show that children do indeed imitate aggressive behaviour depicted on television immediately following its presentation (e.g., Hicks, 1968). Additional research has also demonstrated that such learning occurs in more naturalistic situations as well (e.g., Parke, Berkowitz, Leyens, West, & Sebastian, 1977).

In 1972, the Surgeon General of the United States published the results of a series of examinations into the relationship between television violence and aggression. The results of these studies led the Surgeon General to conclude that a causal relationship between watching television violence and aggressive behaviour does indeed exist. Ten years later, the National Institute of Mental Health (NIMH, 1982) published results of a compendium of follow-up studies that further cemented the conclusion of the Surgeon General's report. Rubinstein (1983), in a summary of the NIMH report, states:

> Granted that the data are complex and that no single study unequivocally documents the connection between televised violence and later aggressive behaviour, the convergence of evidence from many studies is overwhelming and was so interpreted in the NIMH report (Rubinstein, 1983, p. 821).

Cartoons, representing the vast majority of programs directed toward young children, have repeatedly been shown to have the highest occurrence of violent incidents per episode (Williams, Zabrack, & Joy, 1982). Researchers and clinical investigators have placed great emphasis upon examining their violent content. Numerous studies have documented increased aggression in children following exposure to cartoon violence (e.g., Ellis & Sekyra, 1972), with no studies reporting a decrease in aggression following exposure to cartoon violence (Stein & Friedrich, 1975). This increase in acquired aggression has been noted for both boys and girls, across various socio-economic strata, and for children of different ages (e.g., Lovaas, 1961).

The prevalence of violence on commercial television remains consistently high (Signorielli, Gross, & Morgan, 1982). One cannot deny the plethora of evidence that suggests that in the short and long term, television violence influences childhood behaviour. Results gathered in the laboratory, in the field, and from studies spanning several decades, despite methodological shortcomings, have all shown that violent television elicits aggressive behaviour in children.

A critical period during which exposure to violent television has the most deleterious effects has been postulated. It appears that the greatest effects of television violence occur when viewed in the late preschool and early elementary school years (Eron et al., 1983; Huesmann et al., 1984). Still further, many of these studies report that these harmful effects are long lasting and increase proportionately with the amount of violent television viewed (e.g., Eron et al., 1983).

A variety of research studies have concluded that children's imitation of aggressive models can occur through incidental and vicarious learning. This finding is particularly important for the young child who attends intermittently to television (Anderson & Lorch, 1983), who may be unaware of and/or may fail to comprehend the links between aggressive actions and perceived punishment (Collins, 1983). Continued exposure and concomitant aggressive behaviour have repeatedly been observed by researchers across a variety of populations incorporating various methodological approaches. The physiological arousal, stimulated in large part by the fast-paced action of television programs aimed at children, and cognitive arousal, associated with children's attentiveness, may also facilitate this learning (Williams, 1986). Moreover, Williams (1986) reports that frequent observations of aggression as a successful method of conflict resolution may reduce inhibitions against aggressive behaviour. Coupled with an increased desensitization, propensity for increased tolerance for aggressive behaviour and violence may result in children's increased aggression and tolerance for verbal abuse.

Still further, a number of studies have concluded that aggressive behaviour, while being acquired, may not necessarily be immediately exhibited, but rather may occur much later. On a more positive note, research has also shown the aggressive behaviour may be inhibited and modified through viewing appropriate models (Huesmann et al., 1983; Williams, 1986).

Singer and Singer (1981) reporting on their longitudinal study of preschool children have suggested that television's effect upon children may not be so straightforward. Rather, they have attempted to examine a combination of television and family variables that place a child at risk for problematic behaviour by early elementary school age. They conclude that the high-risk child comes from a home in which (1) television viewing is uncontrolled; (2) there exists heavy viewing of television during the preschool years; (3) there has been recent heavy viewing of violent programs; (4) parents tend to emphasize physical punishment as the primary form of discipline; and (5) parents fail to stress curiosity, creativity, imagination—traits that tend to mediate the influences of television. Thus, while there appears to be overwhelming evidence that television viewing behaviour can lead to increased aggressivity and violence in children, it is not a pure unidirectional consequence; rather it may be a mediating variable. Television alone cannot negate the impact of parents.

Since the 1970s, parents and educators have been interested in how television could be used to reinforce prosocial desirable behaviours, such as sharing, helping, co-operation, and imaginative play (Lovelace & Huston, 1982). In general, studies examining television's effects on prosocial behaviour have been conducted with young children, and characteristically, only short-term effects have been reported (Eron, 1986). Over the past two decades, empirical evidence has emerged in support of the potential of prosocial learning through television (Gunter, 1984). Through observational learning, children have been shown to acquire prosocial positive behaviours and appropriate conduct from watching television characters behave in a prosocial manner (Gunter, 1984). Similar results have been shown in laboratory and field studies (e.g., Zuckerman, Ziegler, & Stevenson, 1978). Lesser (1974), in writings concerning

"Sesame Street," has noted that observational learning of prosocial behaviours need not necessarily require direct instruction. He suggests that displaying activities that convey an implicit prosocial attitude can result in effective modelling. "Altruism, kindness, courage, and tolerance can be communicated indirectly through the actions of the televised characters without explicit labelling" (Lesser, 1974, p. 86).

A study conducted by Paulson (1974) during the first season of "Sesame Street" examined the effects of special inserts modelling prosocial and antisocial behaviour as a method for teaching co-operation. During a six-month field study, children who viewed these segments demonstrated significantly more co-operative behaviour when placed in similar situations. Unfortunately, these behaviours did not transfer or generalize to other situations (Paulson, 1974).

Other researchers have demonstrated that television can encourage generosity. Bryan and Walbeck (1979) showed six- to nine-year-old children a television program depicting a child successfully playing a bowling game and winning gift certificates. In different versions, the boy either donated his winnings to charity, stating that it was the right thing to do, or kept the winnings for himself. Children who viewed the "giving" version were more likely to subsequently donate their own winnings. A replication of this study carried out in England found similar short-term effects (Rushton & Owen, 1975).

While prosocial behaviour can be acquired by watching unambiguous portrayals on television, programs of this type are rare. More common are programs that depict the "good guys" winning over the "bad guys," or good overcoming evil. Frequently, western, police, and detective programs fit into this mould. Other shows, such as "Mister Rogers' Neighborhood" and "Sesame Street," attempt to reinforce positive prosocial behaviour. A content analysis of "Mr. Rogers' Neighborhood" revealed that in a sample of twenty episodes (ten hours) 1223 (95 percent) instances of positive reinforcement and 67 (5 percent) instances of punishment (verbal criticism, ignoring) were noted (Coates & Pusser, 1975). Studies by Friedrich and Stein (1973) and Friedrich-Cofer, Huston-Stein, Kipnis, Susman, and Clewett (1979) have shown that under certain conditions, children's viewing of "Mr. Rogers' Neighborhood" promotes an increase in prosocial behaviours. Similarly, for "Sesame Street," 78 percent instances of positive reinforcement and 22 percent instances of punishment occurred. Although these programs differ in their pace, overall design, and degree of prosocial and antisocial content, they both employ conflict resolution as a means of modelling prosocial behaviour (Lovelace & Huston, 1982).

Prosocial interactions such as altruism and sympathy are portrayed in many programs (Harvey, Sprafkin, & Rubinstein, 1979). A number of films have also been used to reduce fear and anxiety in children (Lovelace & Huston, 1982), and to present appropriate social skills (O'Connor, 1969, 1972).

TELEVISION AS TEACHER OF EDUCATIONAL MATERIAL

When television first appeared in the 1940s, children's programs were an important part of the broadcast schedule. Most programs were in the form of puppet shows and other short programs. By 1953, the first educational television station began operation, and by the end of the decade, 44 stations existed (O'Bryan, 1981). Many of these stations operated with restricted budgets and had low visibility. Frequently, these stations were operated by local community groups, school systems, and universities. The preponderance of the educational programs were adult oriented, with relatively few aimed at children (Liebert & Sprafkin, 1988). Early educational television, limited by a lack of technology, colour, and sophistication, was often found to be boring, repetitive, and uninteresting.

Educational television had two distinct faces from its inception. The first to be emphasized was the master teacher model, in which teachers, appearing as "talking faces" were broadcast into the classroom via closed-circuit television. These programs were intended to combat (1) overcrowding in the classroom, and (2) the effects of poor teaching. The other type of educational television, now by far the stronger of the two, maintained that educational programming should be as interesting and as well produced as commercial television and should be considered as an aid to, and not a replacement for, the classroom teacher. By 1980, closed-circuit master-teacher television had virtually disappeared (O'Bryan, 1981), and Educational Television (ETV) had become stronger than ever.

The growth of ETV was slow due to scheduling and technical difficulties and lack of financial resources. But, in the 1960s, the industry began to appreciate its potential and a report from the Carnegie Commission (1967) proposed the establishment of a Corporation for Public Television and support from local and national sources was recommended. One year later, the Children's Television Workshop (CTW) was founded. CTW's philosophy was that children's television had to meet the standards and withstand the competition of commercial programming, and as such, a complete revamping of children's television ensued.

"In 1969 two significant events took place: Neil Armstrong set foot on the moon, and 'Sesame Street' went to air" (O'Bryan, 1981, p. 5). During the late 1960s, programs designed to educate the young child became widely noticed. Along with "Sesame Street," early child-oriented programs such as "Mister Rogers' Neighborhood" and "Mr. Dressup" began to appear. "Sesame Street" is by far the most popular and successful educational television program ever broadcast (Palmer, 1984; Rice, Huston, Truglio, & Wright, 1990). Its estimated audience of 10.4 million American households, and its target audience of three- to five-year-olds makes "Sesame Street" an ideal vehicle for teaching preschoolers a variety of basic concepts and skills. From its inception, Joan Ganz Cooney and Lloyd Morrisett, the planners and architects of the Children's Television Workshop, were concerned about the paucity of highly entertaining quality educational programs for young children. Cooney and Morrisett had a strong belief that "the wasteland of children's programming was too vast for a major effort not to attract at least some audience" (Cooney, 1974, p. xv). They were concerned about the plight of the preschoolers, about the lack of progress in educating young children, and about the predicament of underprivileged children for whom "experimental" preschool programs were then unavailable. As such, CTW became the agent by which television would begin to teach young children, regardless of socio-economic status, some basic cognitive skills, such as letter recognition and basic arithmetic, and prosocial behaviours, such as sharing and co-operation.

Today, "Sesame Street" is broadcast in nine languages to 50 countries. "Sesame Street" has been viewed by an entire generation of children, successfully broadcasting for more than twenty years, making it the longest-running television series of all time. Liebert and Sprafkin (1988) have reported that "Sesame Street" remains the world's most famous and popular television show and is viewed by almost half of all American preschoolers on a weekly basis (5.8 million children between the ages of two and five), watching an average of three episodes per week. In many cities, "Sesame Street" is broadcast several times each day. The Canadian version of "Sesame Street," "Sesame Street North," has met with considerable success. Content from "Sesame Street North" has been distributed worldwide.

As soon as "Sesame Street" was first broadcast, formative evaluation research began. Technical specialists and others, who would later become instructional designers, were contracted to improve its production. As well, senior-level producers, writers, and designers were hired from commercial television, and "Sesame Street" became "the model for the teaching face of children's television" (O'Bryan, 1981, p. 13). "Sesame Street," incorporating attention-holding attributes (e.g., fast movement, animation, short segments, humour, repetition), Jim Henson's now famous Muppets (Big Bird, Ernie, Bert, Kermit, etc.), and special guests, mesmerized children and parents alike.

Considerable research has been presented suggesting that "Sesame Street" has successfully achieved many of its initial goals, that is, teaching a number of school readiness skills (e.g., Ball & Bogatz, 1970). Instead of attempting to heighten general cognitive ability, "Sesame Street" attempts to teach specific content such as letters, numbers, and relational concepts. Summative evaluations performed after the first two seasons of "Sesame Street" revealed that children who watched the program regularly gained more new knowledge than children who did not (Ball & Bogatz, 1970, 1972). Further, benefits were found across all socio-economic groups, in that disadvantaged frequent viewers often learned as much as advantaged frequent viewers and more than advantaged infrequent viewers. Today, the Muppet characters created by Jim Henson are household names for preschoolers throughout the world. Along with the Disney characters, "Sesame Street" characters remain the most desired licenced products by parents of preschool children. However, with all the praise has come criticism, and some researchers have questioned the magnitude and longevity of the effects (Cook & Conner, 1976).

Although it has been shown that when viewed under carefully controlled situations, "Sesame Street" promotes the acquisition of certain basic school-readiness skills (Ball & Bogatz, 1972), questions remained about its effects upon other skills. A two-year longitudinal study by Rice et al. (1990) attempted to assess the relationship between naturally occurring home viewing of "Sesame Street" and vocabulary acquisition among three- to seven-year-old children. Studying the educational effects of television in a home setting, as opposed to a laboratory setting, provided a more realistic assessment of television's effects insofar as within the home, competing activities and distractions abound.

Two groups of children, within three months of their third or fifth birthdays were followed over a two-year period. Every six months, parents were asked to complete a one-week television viewing diary. Both prior to and following the two-year period children's receptive vocabulary was assessed using the Peabody Picture Vocabulary Test-Revised (PPVT), a well-accepted measure of receptive vocabulary. Parental data, such as educational and occupational level, attitudes toward television, and specific attitudes toward "Sesame Street" were also collected. Results of multiple regression analyses indicate that "Sesame Street" viewing was positively related to vocabulary scores for both the three-year-olds and five-year-olds. At the completion of the two-year period, however, "Sesame Street" viewing was seen to be a significant predictor of the child's vocabulary for the younger group only. Significantly, at all levels, the parents' level of education was found to be positively related to children's vocabulary. As well, first-born children demonstrated greater vocabulary than later-borns. "Sesame Street," by focusing children's attention, providing repeated exposure to the same material, and using visual and verbal redundancies, allows for the introduction of new word meanings to young children. Thus, the results substantiate the importance and fact that more subtle incidental learning appears to be acquired through "Sesame Street."

According to Gerald Lesser, "Sesame Street's" main lesson was to illustrate that television can directly teach children without hiding its educational intentions and yet attract a large and devoted audience while being broadcast over non-commercial, public broadcasting stations. As well, it provided new evidence of "the remarkable rate at which young children can learn from television" (Lesser, 1974, p. 234).

An evaluation of "Electric Company," another CTW production, aimed at providing remedial reading instruction to primary school students (Ball & Bogatz, 1973), revealed that although specific reading skills were learned by most viewers, these skills did not transfer to general reading ability; children in the bottom ten percentile failed to learn the intended skills; and home viewing was relatively ineffective. While helping many children, the results were viewed as disappointing. In 1985, after fourteen years of programming, "Electric Company" ceased broadcasting.

Other educational programs have evolved from the Children's Television Workshop. "3-2-1-Contact" was designed for eight- to twelve-year-old children and had three primary goals: (1) to help children experience the joy of scientific exploration, (2) to help children become familiar with various styles of scientific thinking, and (3) to help children, with a special appeal to girls and minorities, recognize science and technology as open to their participation (Children's Television Workshop, 1980). This series, broadcast in several languages and in more than 30 countries, has focused on such topics as the oceans, space, water, electricity, flight, communication, and the senses (Liebert & Sprafkin, 1988).

Although studies suggest that television can be used to promote improved vocabulary (Rice et al., 1990), positive benefits have been noted for few programs. Children's exposure to television has been found to negatively affect academic achievement in general (Gadberry, 1980), and reading skills in particular (for a review of this literature, see Hornik, 1978).

Many researchers and educators have argued that television viewing severely impedes reading development (e.g., Gunter, 1982; Morgan & Gross, 1982). There is much support for the contention that television, by occupying a significant number of hours per day (Singer & Singer, 1981; Pearl et al., 1982), limits the time children spend reading. Television often replaces reading as a leisure-time activity, which in turn has limited children's ability to use language (Gunter, 1982). These generally negative results are related to the amount of time children view television, often to the exclusion of reading, doing homework, and performing other academic-type tasks.

An eighteen-month longitudinal investigation of six- to eleven-year-old children in New York reported by Gunter (1982) revealed that a negative correlation exists between television viewing and the effort devoted to academic subjects. From her research findings, Williams (1986) concludes that comparisons among the communities in Canada prior to and two years after the arrival of television broadcasting indicated that "TV probably slows down the acquisition of fluent reading skills" amongst young pre-readers. However, she quickly noted that once reading skills were acquired, they did not deteriorate. Children who had a greater number of television viewing hours tended to be poorer readers than those who watched fewer hours, even after the effects of intellectual ability were removed. Better readers were found to use and to have a greater reliance upon print media (books, newspapers, and magazines) than less efficient and poorer readers. Gunter (1982) found that academic effort and persistence were negatively correlated to a propensity for adult-oriented and action-adventure programming. Further, for young children, a positive relation between a preference for children's educational programs and academic ability was found. Taken together, these results suggest that television may be used to promote academic achievement and provide valuable information but the types of programs watched must be carefully selected. Nevertheless, when television viewing time reaches an unreasonable level, the amount of academic tasks a child performs will likely decrease, resulting in poorer performance on achievement tests.

Zuckerman, Singer, and Singer (1980) examined the relationship between television viewing and a number of variables related to school performance (reading ability, reading habits, and attitude toward school in general) among ten- and eleven-year-old children. It was found that when compared to children who spent little time reading, children who spent more time reading scored higher on standardized tests of intelligence, had more educated fathers, and watched fewer hours of action-adventure type television programs. Children rated by their teachers as being highly imaginative also tended to be those who watched fewer of these programs. The authors conclude that it is not the violent television programs that appear to have replaced reading, but instead, it seems that programs aimed at facilitating fantasy, involving super-human characters and fast-moving action, fulfil children's fantasy needs (Zuckerman, Singer, & Singer, 1980).

It is important to note that within the educational realm, television provides a daily course on current events. Both for children and adults, large amounts of information are acquired through television viewing. Science programs, recreations of significant historical events, programs designed to teach viewers how to use computer programs, courses in cooking, psychology, fine arts, and our exploration of space are but a few examples of how the television medium can successfully be used as an educational tool.

Anecdotally, parents frequently report that their children will "rush through" their homework to be able to watch television. Certainly, there is considerable research under the heading of "time on task" (Rosenshine, 1976) that has demonstrated that the amount of time a child is working on a particular academic task is highly correlated to achievement in that domain. If television viewing time is precluding the performance of school-related tasks, albeit voluntarily, performance and achievement are likely to suffer. While television can help to fulfil the "fantasy" role in a child's development, excessive viewing behaviour can limit the school-age child's acquisition of important basic skills and concepts.

TELEVISION AS ENTERTAINMENT

Certainly, television provides a significant source of entertainment for children and adults. There is considerable evidence that children, like their parents, are committed to watching each and every episode of their favourite program. Children can sit motionless, viewing program after program. With the widespread use of VCRs, favourite shows along with popular movies can be taped, saved, and replayed at a later date.

The use of television as a primary source of entertainment and escape from reality has often been noted. Schramm et al. (1961) have suggested that the young child's process of maturation, with its concomitant difficult experiences, limitations, and frustrations, leads the child to seek escape from conflicts, to seek aid for problems, to use television as a form of pure entertainment and escapism. Through animation, the child's favourite cartoon characters come to life and perform feats that can only be realized in the child's imagination. Schramm et al. (1961) differentiate between two types of content: reality-based and fantasy. Reality-based material has the function of providing children with information. Although Huston et al. (1989) report that children's information-type programs are relatively rare on commercial television, programs such as "Pee Wee's Playhouse," "Fat Albert and the Cosby Kids," and "Pryor's Place" should be commended for their creative efforts. They have successfully provided the child with some educational and prosocial content, while entertaining them. In contrast, fantasy material is often used to vicariously solve the child's problem. According to this theoretical argument, fantasy becomes a primary function of television.

Many television programs and cartoons depict child characters in heroic and central roles. These characters have the ability to perform tasks and feats and solve problems in ways in which the child him/herself cannot. Generally, these characters are able to exert significant control over their environment, an attribute about which the child fantasizes and desires to possess. As a result, a strong attachment, albeit an unconscious one, occurs with the character. From a psychoanalytic perspective, children's identification with cartoon and real-life models would support this perspective. Several research reports have noted that children have a propensity for fantasy-type programs as opposed to reality-type programs. Still further, empirical results support the contention that for some children, television viewing is a temporary means of escapism (Riley & Riley, 1951; Maccoby, 1954; Bailyn, 1959). Although this perspective is speculative, observations of childhood television viewing patterns certainly lend some credence to it.

ADVERTISING

Children under the age of thirteen constitute more than a quarter of the North American population, a population of more than 70 million people. They spend considerable time watching television, with as much as 40 percent of their viewing time taken up by commercials directed specifically toward them.

Children have become a prime target for advertisers trying to promote toys, cereals, candy, and other childhood products (Barcus, 1977). Television remains the prime vehicle by which advertisers reach large numbers of children. Whether this advertising is aimed at a select group of children, based on characteristics of age, sex, race, etc., or children in general, the message is powerful. Children have very little purchasing power. Rather, products aimed at children are designed to have them request their parents to purchase specific products or brands. The strength of store purchases is often contingent upon the amount of money manufacturers have committed for television advertising.

Huston et al. (1989) report that a convincing body of research has been accumulated during the 1970s demonstrating that children under eight years of age have difficulty distinguishing program material from advertising. Likewise, children often do not comprehend the "selling intent" of television commercials and that misleading impressions are prevalent and created by commercials despite any accompanying disclaimers (Liebert & Sprafkin, 1988). In testimony before the Federal Trade Commission, representatives of the Action for Children's Television group alleged that intricate advertising techniques are frequently used to deceive, cajole, and exploit the youngest and least knowledgeable members of society. Naturally, marketers deny such allegations and cite evidence indicating that advertising serves mainly to reinforce existing attitudes and opinions and that parents ultimately remain the key influence in their child's cognitive development and determine which products are purchased. However, extensive research suggests that advertisers are capitalizing upon the child's ability to understand and act upon persuasive messages. Still further, they rely upon their knowledge of developmental stages to provide the most persuasive message possible.

Marketing researchers are also aware that early consumer patterns are relatively durable and are resistant to change over time (Bever, Smith, Bengen, & Johnson, 1975). Therefore, it is to the advantage of advertisers to attend to this potential market at a time when children are most susceptible to developing their consumer behaviours and brand loyalty.

Available studies indicate that children's attitudes toward television commercials and their ability to evaluate them are influenced by their cognitive development. The ability to evaluate television commercials and recognize the advertiser's intent increases with age. Moreover, as children grow older, their attitudes become more materialistic, they become more cynical and considerably more sceptical about the truth underlying television advertising. However, for the young child, seeing is believing. Children not only believe the claims presented in advertisements but they frequently perceive some underlying message. Take for example, a product called Skittlebowl, a bowling game intended for use by the "entire family." The television commercial presents a mother, father, brother, and sister playing the game. Children subconsciously believe that if their parents buy them this toy, then the entire family will play it together. Unfortunately, toys are frequently purchased in order for the child to be engaged in solitary play. Other products may be even more deceiving. What looks so very interesting in a 30-second commercial may maintain the child's interest for a similar period of time.

Still further, young children often fail to differentiate between the program and the product. Liebert & Sprafkin (1988) refer to these television shows as "program-length commercials." These television shows are focused upon programs that feature characters that represent either existing or future toys. No longer are toys developed following the success of television shows. Today, toys may precede, or be presented simultaneously, with the television program or movie. Toy manufacturers have now become the developers and producers of children's television programs. Bryant (1985) observed kindergarten children watching the television cartoons "The Transformers" and "She-Ra." Children who watched these cartoons found the Transformer and She-Ra toys to be much more appealing than children not exposed to these shows.

Regardless of conflicting results, it is clear that television advertising influences both children's social behaviour and patterns of consumption, at least in the short term. However, it has yet to be determined what effects the same advertising message has on their behaviours over longer periods of time. Advertising's potential ability to persuade children seems especially plausible when the child is unsophisticated or relies on television for her/his view of reality. This research would suggest that the group most vulnerable to television advertising is the preschooler, who is lacking in knowledge and cognitive defences.

Given the influence that powerful models have upon children (Bandura, 1977), the concept of product endorsement by an individual or cartoon character fits well within the advertisers' domain. Considerable research has found that this technique is effective in increasing consumer purchases when aimed at children (e.g., Iskoe, 1976; Ross et al., 1984).

The question of what effects television advertising has on children's attitudes and behaviours is a problem in which correlation and causal relations can get confounded. The advent of television was accompanied by dozens of other important social changes, one of them being the proliferation of television advertising. Which ones are causes of children's behaviours and which are not is still not known.

Certainly, many mediating variables are important to consider. Parental reponsivity to children's requests are critical. It is interesting to note that when parents refuse to purchase a requested product, large-scale arguments frequently ensue. In fact, Atkin (1978) reports that 65 percent of parental refusals of children's requests prompted by television advertisements were accompanied by parent-child conflicts and arguments. Still further, mothers often blame advertisers for their children's negative behaviours, since their perceptions are strong that television significantly influences their requests (Ward, 1976).

It is generally agreed that older children become jaded to commercials, pay less attention to them, and are less likely to be persuaded by their messages. Younger children, however, appear to be more persuadable. They are more passive viewers than older children and show less resistance to commercial interruptions.

Given these findings, stronger governmental legislation has been proposed. To some, television should be totally unregulated, with the onus of children's viewing behaviour and habits placed upon parents. Others would prefer to see a total banning of all aggressive programs and advertising on programs aimed at children (Linz, Penrod, & Donnerstein, 1986).

CONCLUSIONS

Technological innovations, the demise of the extended family, the incidence of divorce, and other societal reorganizations have altered childhood forever. Today's children develop and live in a world where crime is rampant, drugs are plentiful, and working mothers are the reality. Today's child is more mature and sophisticated than children in previous generations and requires more to be entertained. Parents, busier than their parents were, have come to rely upon television, video games, and other fast-paced innovations to entertain their children. Children have become more sophisticated consumers, and no longer merely entertain themselves, but instead turn to television to satisfy many of their needs.

It has been shown that television can teach children skills, such as letter and number recognition, can help develop their vocabulary, and can foster prosocial behaviour. However, considerable research has emphasized the deleterious effects of heavy exposure to television, that is, increased aggression following repeated exposure to violent television and decreased academic performance. It has been shown that the effects of television violence are cumulative and last well into adulthood.

In this chapter, we have attempted to examine several aspects of television's influence upon children. Neither governmental legislation nor more responsible programming alone will suffice. While television can help to educate and to socialize children, it cannot replace effective and responsible parenting. According to Gerald Lesser:

> Television does not hover over children with demands and expectations. They can watch without being tested, graded, reprimanded or even observed by others. They are safe from the threat of humiliation or ridicule for not living up to what is expected of them. There is little doubt that we all need retreats, some sanctuary from forces that correct and direct us. But, we have not made up our collective mind about whether they should exist. We fear that they may engulf us in escape and illusion, and that the indulgence may become addictive. Yet periodic escape from surveillance and exacting expectations need not be equivalent to escape from reality. For those children who need it, television used in moderation can provide a temporary refuge (Lesser, 1974, p. 246).

The evidence suggests that under proper parental supervision, and in moderation, television can serve to provide children with information, entertainment, and an escape from daily pressures. However, like any addictive substance, when used to excess, negative side effects are bound to ensue.

REFERENCES

Anderson, D.R., & Lorch, E.P. (1983). Looking at television: Action or reaction? In *Children's Understanding of Television: Research on Attention and Comprehension* (Eds., Bryant, J., & Anderson, D.R.). New York: Academic Press, pp. 1–33.

Atkin, C. (1978). Observation of parent-child interaction in supermarket decision making. *Journal of Marketing, 42,* 41–45.

Bailyn, L. (1959). Mass media and children: A study of exposure habits and cognitive effects. *Psychological Monographs, 73.*

Ball, S., & Bogatz, G.A. (1970). *The first year of Sesame Street: An evaluation.* Princeton, NJ: Educational Testing Service.

Ball, S., & Bogatz, G.A. (1972). Summative research of *Sesame Street:* Implications for the study of preschool children. In *Minnesota Symposia on Child Psychology* (Vol. 6). (Ed., Pick, A.D.). Minneapolis: University of Minnesota.

Ball, S., & Bogatz, G.A. (1973). *Reading with television: An evaluation of the Electric Company.* Princeton, NJ: Educational Testing Service.

Bandura, A. (1965). Influences of model's reinforcement contingencies on the acquisition of imitative responses. *Journal of Personality and Social Psychology, 1,* 589–595.

Bandura, A. (1973). *Aggression: A social learning analysis.* Englewood Cliffs, NJ: Prentice-Hall.

Bandura, A. (1977). *Social learning theory.* Englewood Cliffs, NJ: Prentice-Hall.

Bandura, A., Ross, D., & Ross, S.A. (1963). Imitation of film-depicted aggressive models. *Journal of Abnormal and Social Psychology, 66,* 3–11.

Barcus, F.E. (1977). *Children's television: An analysis of programming and advertising.* New York: Praeger.

Bever, T., Smith, M., Bengen, B., & Johnson, T. (1975). Young viewers' troubling responses to TV ads. *Harvard Business Review, 53*(6), 109–120.

Bronfenbrenner, U. (1970). *Two worlds of childhood: U.S. and U.S.S.R.* New York: Simon & Schuster.

Bryan, J.H., & Walbeck, N.H. (1979). The impact of words and deeds concerning children. *Child Development, 41,* 747–757.

Bryant, J. (1985, October 28). Testimony at hearings before the U.S. House of Representatives' Subcommittee on Telecommunications, Consumer Protection, and Finance.

Canada. Statistics Canada. (1990). *Annual television viewing in Canada: 1988 culture statistics.* Ottawa.

Carnegie Commission. (1967). *Public television: A program for action.* New York: Harper & Row.

Children's Television Workshop. (1980). *International research notes*. New York: Author.

Coates, B., & Pusser, H.E. (1975). Positive reinforcement and punishment in "Sesame Street" and "Mister Roger's Neighborhood." *Journal of Broadcasting, 19*, 143–151.

Collins, W.A. (1983). Interpretation and inference in children's television viewing. In *Children's Understanding of Television: Research on Attention and Comprehension* (Eds., Bryant, J., & Anderson, D.R.). New York: Academic Press, pp. 125–150.

Collins, W.A., Berndt, T.J., & Hess, V.L. (1974). Observational learning of motives and consequences for television aggression: A developmental study. *Child Development, 45*, 799–802.

Comstock, G., Chaffee, S., Katzman, N., McCombs, M., & Roberts, D. (1978). *Television and human behavior*. New York: Columbia University Press.

Cook, T.D., & Conner, R.F. (1976). The educational impact. *Journal of Communication, 26*, 155–164.

Cooney, J. (1974). Forward. In *Children and Television: Lessons from Sesame Street* (Ed., Lesser, G.). New York: Random House.

Ellis, G.T., & Sekyra, F. (1972). The effect of aggressive cartoons on the behavior of first grade children. *Journal of Psychology, 81*, 37–43.

Eron, L.D. (1986). Interventions to mitigate the psychological effects of media violence on aggressive behavior. *Journal of Social Issues, 42* (3), 155–169.

Eron, L.D., Huesmann, L.R., Brice, P., Fischer, P., & Mermelstein, R. (1983). Age trends in the development of aggression, sex tying, and related television habits. *Developmental Psychology, 19*, 71–77.

Eron, L.D., Huesmann, L.R., Lefkowitz, M.M., & Walder, L.O. (1972). Does television violence cause aggression? *American Psychologist, 27*, 253–263.

Friedrich, L., & Stein, A. (1973). Aggressive and prosocial television programs and the natural behavior of preschool children. *Monographs of the Society for Research in Child Development, 38* (4, Whole No. 51).

Friedrich-Cofer, L.K., Huston-Stein, A., Kipnis, D.M., Susman, E.J., & Clewett, A.S. (1979). Environmental enhancement of prosocial television content: Effects on interpersonal behavior, imaginative play, and self-regulation in a natural setting. *Developmental Psychology, 15*, 637–646.

Gadberry, S. (1980). Effects of restricting first graders' TV-viewing on leisure time use, IQ change, and cognitive style. *Journal of Applied Developmental Psychology, 1*, 45–57.

Gerbner, G., & Gross, L. (1976). Living with television: The violence profile. *Journal of Communication, 26*(2), 172–199.

Greenberg, B.S. (1986). Minorities and the mass media. In *Perspectives on Mass Media Effects* (Eds., Bryant, J., & Zillmann, D.). Hillsdale, NJ: Lawrence Erlbaum Associates.

Gunter, B. (1982). Does television interfere with reading development? *Bulletin of the British Psychological Society, 35*, 232–235.

Gunter, B. (1984). Television as a facilitator of good behaviour amongst children. *Journal of Moral Education, 13*(3), 152–159.

Harvey, S.E., Sprafkin, J.N., & Rubinstein, E. (1979). Prime time television: A profile of aggressive and prosocial behaviors. *Journal of Broadcasting, 23*(2), 179–189.

Hellman, H., & Soramäki, M. (1985). Economic concentration in the videocassette industry: A cultural comparison. *Journal of Communication, 35*(3), 122–134.

Hicks, D.J. (1968). Effects of co-observer's sanctions and adult presence on imitative aggression. *Child Development, 39*, 303–309.

Hollenbeck, A.R., & Slaby, R.G. (1979). Infant visual and vocal responses to television. *Child Development, 50*, 41–45.

Hornik, R. (1978). Television access and the slowing of cognitive growth. *American Educational Research Journal, 15*, 1–15.

Huesmann, L.R., Eron, L.D., Lefkowitz, M.M., & Walder, L.O. (1984). Stability of aggression over time and generations. *Developmental Psychology, 20*, 1120–1134.

Huston, A.C., Watkins, B.A., & Kunkel, D. (1989). Public policy and children's television. *American Psychologist, 44*, 424–433.

Huston, A.C., Wright, J.C., Rice, M.L., Kerkman, D., & St. Peters, M. (1990). Development of television viewing patterns in early childhood: A longitudinal investigation. *Developmental Psychology, 26*, 409–420.

Iskoe, A. (1976). *Advertising via famous personalities and the effects on children.* Unpublished manuscript, The Wharton School, University of Pennsylvania, Philadelphia.

Johnson, N. (1967). *How to talk back to your television set.* Boston: Little, Brown, & Co.

Kunkel, D., & Watkins, B. (1987). Evolution of children's television regulatory policy. *Journal of Broadcasting & Electronic Media, 31*, 367–389.

Lesser, G. (1974). *Children and television: Lessons from "Sesame Street."* New York: Vintage Books.

Liebert, R., & Sprafkin, J. (Eds.). (1988). *The early window: Effects of television on children.* 3rd ed. New York: Pergamon Press.

Linz, D., Penrod, S., & Donnerstein, E. (1986). Issues bearing on the legal regulation of violent and sexually violent media. *Journal of Social Issues, 42* (3), 171–193.

Lovaas, O. (1961). Effect of exposure to symbolic aggression on aggressive behavior. *Child Development, 32*, 37–44.

Lovelace, V.O., & Huston, A.C. (1982). Can television teach prosocial behavior? *Prevention in Human Services, 2* (1/2), 93–106.

Lyle, J., & Hoffman, H. (1976). Television viewing by preschool age children. In *Children and Television* (Ed., Brown, R.). Beverly Hills: Sage.

Maccoby, E. (1954, Fall). Why do children watch television? *Public Opinion Quarterly, 18.*

Medrich, E., Roizen, J., Rubin, V., & Buckley, S. (1982). *The serious business of growing up: A study of children's lives outside school*. Berkeley: University of California Press.

Morgan, M., & Gross, L. (1982). Television and educational achievement and aspiration. In *Television and Behavior: Ten Years of Scientific Progress and Implications for the Eighties,* (Vol. 2), (Eds. Pearl, D., Bouthilet, L., & Lazar, J.). Washington, DC: U.S. Government Printing Office, pp. 78–90.

National Institute of Mental Health. (1982). *Television and behavior: Ten years of scientific progress and implications for the eighties*. Rockville, MD: NIMH.

Nielsen Report. (1988). *Television: 1988 Nielsen Report*. Northbrook, IL: A.C. Nielsen.

O'Bryan, K.G. (1981). The teaching face: A historical perspective. In *Children and the Faces of Television: Teaching, Violence, Selling* (Eds., Palmer, E.L., & Dorr, A.). New York: Academic Press, pp. 5–18.

O'Connor, R.D. (1969). Modification of social withdrawal through symbolic modeling. *Journal of Applied Behavior Analysis, 2,* 15–22.

O'Connor, R.D. (1972). Relative efficacy of modeling, shaping, and the combined procedures for modification of social withdrawal. *Journal of Abnormal Psychology, 70,* 327–334.

Palmer, E.L. (1984). Providing quality television for America's children. In *The Future of Children's Television* (Eds,. Murray, J.P., & Salomon, G.). Boys Town, NE: Boys Town Center, pp. 103–24.

Parke, R., Berkowitz, L., Leyens, J., West, S., & Sebastian, R. (1977). Some effects of violent and nonviolent movies on the behavior of juvenile delinquents. *Advances in Experimental Social Psychology, 10,* 135–172.

Paulson, F.L. (1974). Teaching cooperation on television: An evaluation of "Sesame Street" social goals programs. *Audio-Visual Communication Review, 22,* 229–246.

Pearl, D., Bouthilet, L., & Lazar, J. (Eds.). (1982). *Television and Behavior: Ten Years of Scientific Progress and Implications for the Eighties* (Vol 2). Washington, DC: U.S. Government Printing Office.

Rice, M.L., Huston, A.C., Truglio, R., & Wright, J. (1990). Words from "Sesame Street": Learning vocabulary while viewing. *Developmental Psychology, 26,* 421–428.

Riley, M.W., & Riley, J.W. (1951). A sociological approach to communication research. *Public Opinion Quarterly, 15.*

Rosenshine, B. (1976). Recent research on teaching behaviors and student achievement. *Journal of Teacher Education, 27,* 61–64.

Ross, R.P., Campbell, T., Wright, J.C., Huston, A.C., Rice, M.L., & Turk, P. (1984). When celebrities talk, children listen: An experimental analysis of children's responses to TV ads with celebrity endorsement. *Journal of Applied Developmental Psychology, 5,* 185–202.

Rubinstein, E.A. (1983). Television and behavior: Research conclusions of the 1982 NIMH report and their policy implications. *American Psychologist, 38,* 820–825.

Rushton, J.P., & Owen, D. (1975). Immediate and delayed effects of TV modelling and preaching on children's generosity. *British Journal of Social Clinical Psychology, 14*, 309–310.

Schramm, W., Lyle, J., & Parker, E.B. (1961). *Television in the lives of our children.* Stanford, CA: Stanford University Press.

Signorielli, N., Gross, L., & Morgan, M. (1982). Violence in television programs: Ten years later. In *Television and Behavior: Ten Years of Scientific Progress and Implications for the Eighties* (Eds., Pearl, D., Bouthilet, L., & Lazar, J.). (Vol. 2: Technical Reports). Washington, DC: U.S. Government Printing Office, pp. 158–173.

Singer, J.L., & Singer, D.G. (1981). *Television, imagination and aggression: A study of preschoolers.* Hillsdale, NJ: Lawrence Erlbaum Associates.

Sprafkin, J. (1988). Television and the emotionally disturbed child. In *The early window: effects of television on children* (Eds. Liebert, R., & Sprafkin, J.). New York: Pergamon Press.

Stein, A.H., & Friedrich, L.K. (1975). Impact of television on children and youth. In *Review of Child Development Research* (Ed., Hetherington, E.M.). (Vol. 5). Chicago: University of Chicago Press, pp. 183–256.

Steinberg, C. (1985). *TV facts.* New York: Facts on File Publications.

Steiner, G.A. (1963). *The people look at television.* New York: Alfred A. Knopf.

Turner, C.W., Hesse, B.W., & Peterson-Lewis, S. (1986). Naturalistic studies of the long-term effects of television violence. *Journal of Social Issues, 42* (3), 51–73.

Ward, S. (1976). Effects of television advertising on children and adolescents. In *Children and Television* (Ed., Brown, R.). Berkeley: Sage.

Williams, T.M. (Ed.. (1986). *The impact of television: A natural experiment in three communities.* New York: Academic Press.

Williams, T.M., & Handford, A.G. (1986). Television and other leisure activities. In *The Impact of Television: A Natural Experiment in Three Communities* (Ed., Williams, T.M.). Orlando, FL: Academic Press, pp. 143–213.

Williams, T.M., Zabrack, M.L., & Joy, L.A. (1982). The portrayal of aggression on North American television. *Journal of Applied Social Psychology, 12*, 360–380.

Zuckerman, D.M., Singer, D.G., & Singer, J.L., (1980). Television viewing, children's reading and related classroom behavior. *Journal of Communication, 30*, 166–174.

Zuckerman, P., Ziegler, M., & Stevenson, H.W. (1978). Children's viewing of television and recognition memory of commercials. *Child Development, 49*, 96–104.

SUGGESTED READINGS

Boyd, D.A., & Straubhaar, J.D. (1985). Developmental impact of the home video cassette recorder on third world countries. *Journal of Broadcasting & Electronic Media*, 29(1), 5–21.

Bryant, J. Zillman, D., & Brown, D. (1983). Entertainment features in children's educational television: Effects on attention and information acquisitions. In *Children's Understanding of Television: Research on Attention and Comprehension* (Eds., Bryant, J., & Anderson, D.). New York: Academic Press, pp. 221–240.

Christy, P.R., Gelfand, D.M., & Hartmann, D.P. (1971). Effects of competition-induced frustration on two classes of modeled behavior. *Developmental Psychology, 5,* 104–111.

Hellman, H., & Soramäki, M. (1985). Economic concentration in the videocassette industry: A cultural comparison. *Journal of Communication, 35*(3), 122–134.

Jennings, R. (1970). *Programming and advertising practices in television directed to children.* Boston: Action for Children's Television.

Robertson, T.S. & Rossiter, J.R. (1974). Children and commercial persuasion: An attribution theory analysis. *Journal of Consumer Research, 1*(1), 13–20.

Ward, S., Reale, G., & Levinson, D. (1972). Childrens perceptions, explanations and judgements of television advertising: A further exploration. In *Television and Social Behavior. Vol. IV: Television in Day-to-Day Life: Patterns of Use* (Eds., Rubinstein, E.A., Comstock, G.A., & Murray, J.P.). Washington, DC: U.S. Government Printing Office, pp. 468–490.

WHERE ARE THE HUNKS?
"STREET LEGAL" AND THE
CANADIAN CONCEPT OF HEROISM

Helen Holmes and Helen Allison

Never in our series television has the CBC tried to build up a heroic hunk of manhood, either historical or fictional.

Mary Jane Miller, 1987

It is now trite to say that, to a large extent, media create our realities. They provide us with models of what to wear, what to buy, what is beautiful, what is despicable, and what is worthy of our attention. Media, perhaps particulary the CBC, which is mandated to do so, give us our sense of the country in which we live, and out of our mediated experience, we construct our sense of ourselves. Indeed, increasingly, much of our experience of every realm of life is mediated. What can be said then about a country whose popular culture, according to Wolfe (1985), Miller (1987), and others provides no heroes, no one who represents or reflects its ideals and values?

Mary Jane Miller, in *Turn Up the Contrast*, from which the above passage is taken, alludes to the type of leading men CBC has created in the recent past, heroes such as Wojek, who was not remotely, in the conventional beefcake sense, handsome (Miller, p. 45), the plump and easy-going Larry King of "King of Kensington," and Louis Ciccone of "Seeing Things," whose problem according to Morris Wolfe was that he "looks Canadian: he's fortyish, bald, overweight and a klutz" (p. 54). Wolfe argues, in fact, that a lack of good looks is a distinct tradition of Canadian television's leading men. Paul Rutherford, in *When Television Was Young: Prime Time Canada 1952–1967* (1990), says that while many argue that Canadian television is characterized by a taste for irony, open endings, unresolved conflicts, and a "gritty" realism that grew out of the techniques of making documentaries—a world that does not readily include heroes—he rejects the claim that Canadians have not admired Hollywood heroes and argues that much of the made-in-Canada drama "shared Hollywood's fascination with believable stereotypes, simplified conflict, wise and powerful males and the like" (p. 384). He argues that there were more handsome, dashing heroes striding across Canadian screens than there were fumbling, inept failures or mere survivors plodding through our grey and gritty documentary media world (p. 384).

Nevertheless, if you were to ask most Canadians, they would say we have few if any media heroes. Despite the fact that we bemoan their lack, their absence seems to be part of our mythology. Our ambivalence over this lack reflects our ambivalence about Canada's position in the world: on the one hand, our dearth of heroes is indicative of our status as a less-than-first-power, but on the other hand, the absence of heroes is evidence of our superiority over such profligate countries as the United States with their apparently never-ending procession of fictional and historical heroes whose virtues are sometimes dubious, heroes such as Bart Simpson and Donald Trump. We seem to take some pride in the fact that, in Morris Wolfe's words, Canadian television "tells it like it is" whereas American television tells "beautiful lies" (p. 80). We believe that if Canada were to generate heroes, we would want them to be genuinely admirable. At the same time, we criticize ourselves for taking ourselves too seriously, being unimaginative and unpatriotic, and feel that Canada would somehow be a better and stronger country if we had a roster of certifiable heroes, both English and French.

Since so much of our reality is experienced through television—we continue to watch more than twenty hours a week—and since "[p]roducers had learned by the end of the 1950s that series drama . . . was the most effective way of telling stories to the masses" (Rutherford, 1990, p. 350), it is appropriate to look at heroes, or the lack of them, in this most popular of the popular culture genres. As Rutherford points out, in order to meet public acceptance and assure advertisers, creators of series drama steeped the stories in the "mythology of the times: they embodied the icons, the clichés, the concerns, and the myths that were present in the mainstream of society" (p. 350). In other words, the narratives of popular television series, like other heroic tales of the past, help us make sense of our experience; they play a bardic role. Like the bards in oral cultures, television displays our dreams and develops a collective memory of cultural values, a cultural mythology. According to Fiske and Hartley, "Television functions as a social ritual, overriding individual distinctions, in which our culture engages in order to communicate with its collective self." Televison series offer us the mythology of ourselves (1978, p. 85).

But nationalists cannot order up a few heroes from CBC (or even less possibly from CTV or Global), even though CBC's mandate comes exceedingly close to asking it to do just that. In *The Hero with a Thousand Faces*, Joseph Campbell points out that heroes and other "symbols of mythology are not manufactured; they cannot be ordered, invented, or permanently suppressed. They are spontaneous productions of the psyche" (p. 4). Does the Canadian psyche exclude the heroic? Does the absence of home-grown heroes mean that we have no ideals or cannot agree on what qualities represent our ideals? Is there no one we can elevate to a status beyond that of the ordinary person because we have no vision of what this country is or should be? The hero, says Campbell (1968), is a boon bringer, "one whose actions bring us the answer to our prayers and requests." The hero of myth is always a powerful man (or woman or god-man or god-woman) who, through enduring trials and tests of his moral and physical strength, vanquishes evil, and in so doing, liberates his people from death or destructions and leads them out of the wilderness. He both exemplifies the dominant ideology of society and redeems and elevates that society. The evil he must vanquish takes many culturally-specific shapes; evil need not be dragons, serpents, and demons, of course. But always, says Campbell, a hero champions future possibilities; "the dragon to be slain by him is precisely the monster of the status quo" (p. 337). Does the apparent absence of heroes then mean that we are smugly satisfied with the status quo?

And parallelling the hero's moral virtues are his good looks, an external sign of his internal virtues and strength. A hero is beautiful, tall or at least physically impressive; physically as well as metaphorically, he stands head and shoulders above the rest; he doesn't "look Canadian." A hero is a hunk.

It can be argued that Canada has or has had home-grown heroes both in history and fiction. Among the earliest was the Mountie. Far from being fat, forty, balding, and klutzy, our Royal Canadian Mounted Police hero was physically and morally ramrod straight and—the issue of his uniform aside—distinctively Canadian. Unlike the American maverick hero, marked by his individuality and independence, who sought justice outside the law and often achieved success despite the law-keepers, the Canadian Mountie hero was the law; he sought peace, order, and good government and found them *through* his membership in his institution. Today, however much we lovingly and naïvely wish, it is difficult to look at the Mountie as heroic. We have become cynical; we have seen too many incidents of wire tapping and the like and too many plastic Mounties sold to tourists on Banff Ave. And television has not presented the Mountie as heroic for a long time. The popular hero must be in tune with his times, and it appears that for a long time, traditional heroes such as the Mounties have been out of step with the times.

It is perhaps worth examining Steve Wojek, the Canadian male protagonist who was the star of "Wojek," a series that aired in 1966 and 1967 and, according to Rutherford (1990), was "the best popular drama CBC-Toronto ever produced" (p. 382). The character of Wojek seems typically Canadian but was, in fact, part of a new mythology in television culture evident in both Canada and the United States, which created a variation on the archetypal mythic hero. During the revolutionary sixties when the program was made, the handsome hero was generally suspect and out of popular favour, as was the traditionally beautiful woman. (Note the immense popularity of the anorexic model Twiggy.) The less-than-handsome looks of these heroes were a physical manifestation of the feelings of a generation who felt betrayed by the traditional values of their society; because society was not pretty, neither should its heroes be. The less-than-handsome hero has affinity with people who are in the process of rejecting the structures of their society, as were many in the sixties, and to some extent the seventies. Despite Wojek's appearance, however, or perhaps, given the times, because of it, he had stature. He was compelling, impressive, and "personified justice, a justice full of moral indignation" (Rutherford, p. 394).

Canadian series television persisted in creating unhandsome television heroes long past the sixties, however. To name a few, we had Larry King, Louis Ciccone, and for a very long time, the sensitive but somehow ineffectual Nick Adonis of "The Beachcombers." An underlying motivation to create these unheroic heroes may have been, in part, a belief that handsome, wholly virtuous heroes belonged to the Americans, and in our effort to make Canadian television distinctively Canadian, we, perhaps deliberately, perhaps unconsciously, steered away from them. There are, of course, many examples of not-necessarily-handsome heroes on American television too: Lou Grant, Barney Miller, and the doctors on "M*A*S*H" to name a few. Not only are such characters not handsome, they display what we like to think of as Canadian characteristics: a sensitivity to others' needs, an appreciation of being part of a community, and a willingness to confront realistic problems and concerns of their society. So Canadians cannot lay claim to less-than-perfect heroes; nor can they claim, of course, that handsome ones are uniquely American. The tall, handsome, virtuous hero is not a Hollywood classic; he comes to us from antiquity and we, of course, have as much right to claim him for our own as anyone else.

"STREET LEGAL" AND THE NEW CANADIAN HEROES

In 1986, CBC produced "Street Legal," a series whose two male leads, over the show's long run, perhaps demonstrate through their collective qualities, a new maturity and confidence in our conception of ourselves. In their personal qualities and their actions and concerns in situations that reflect Canadians' moral and cultural dilemmas, they come close to demonstrating universal qualities of heroism, at the same time remaining distinctively Canadian. They are, as Fiske says of all heroes, socially central types who embody the dominant ideology (1987).

"Street Legal" is about a partnership of four lawyers in Toronto: Leon Robinovitch, Carrie Barr, Chuck Tchobaniam, and Olivia Novak. The storyline revolves around the trials of their business and personal lives, which often overlap. Other regular characters are Nick Del Gado, a Toronto cop and Carrie's romantic interest, and Alana Newman, another lawyer and Leon's wife. Chuck and Olivia have an on-again off-again romance. Dillon, a Crown attorney, is romantically interested in Carrie.[1]

Themes recur relating to the relationships among characters and characters' relationship to the institutions within which they work. Carrie is a criminal lawyer who often finds herself at odds with the justice system because of her concern for her clients. This often puts her at odds with Nick and Dillon, who as a cop and Crown attorney, enforce the system. Chuck and Olivia primarily value the money and prestige that come from practising law, sometimes creating conflict with the more idealistic Leon and his store-front approach to the law. Olivia's ruthlessness contributes to the on-again off-again nature of her relationship with Chuck, who vacillates between allegiance to Olivia and to his other partners, not to mention his own conscience.

The first season of "Street Legal" created two characters with heroic potential: Leon and Chuck. Leon is neither handsome nor tall, but he was under forty in the first episodes and not overweight, bald, or a klutz. And he is endowed with traditionally heroic qualities of a thirst for justice and the courage to stand up for his principles. He has a Canadian respect for the law and, as a lawyer, he uses legitimate avenues in his quest for social justice. However, the character of Leon, who was created in the Wojek mould, tended to be the least popular character in the first season, mainly, it appears, because audiences did not like his strait-laced, preachy approach (CBC, 1987). He may also have been too eccentric in his behaviour—riding his bicycle while wearing his court robes—and in his appearance—his hair standing on end and his wearing of such unorthodox attire as checked shirts and bow ties.

Chuck, the other male lead, is relatively tall and handsome—potentially a handsome hero. However, he lacks those heroic qualities of courage and a thirst for justice that Leon has. Despite this apparent flaw, he was initially more popular than Leon was, likely the result of his appearance. In focus groups conducted by CBC Research, about half of the respondents who said that they liked him referred to his physical attractiveness (CBC, 1986). His lack of idealism and propensity to succumb to the sins of commercialism made him an unsuitable Canadian hero. Over the long run, however, Chuck has been allowed to develop along more traditionally heroic lines.

During 1988–89, Leon's appearance was more conventional. His hair was combed down, and his suits, ties, and the occasional sweater were more appropriate to his position as a lawyer. His clothes, although no longer eccentric, displayed his unique style, suggesting that he was not cut from the same cloth as ordinary men. He preached less and his quest for justice was more often manifested through his court battles for constitutional rights, for protection of the environment, and against greedy landlords and employers who take advantage of new immigrants and refugees. The more radical elements of his character were skilfully placed where they would be more acceptable to contemporary audiences: back in his youth as a sixties student. Leon thus remains allied with the anti-hero of the sixties and at the same time well grounded in the conservative ethos of the eighties and nineties. We know, however, that he has not abandoned his youthful principles; he maintains his quest for justice, but now uses the peaceful and legitimate avenues of the law; rebellion is not the Canadian way. An analysis of an episode from the 1989–90 season illustrates this transformation.

In this episode, Leon defends Don Chapman, an old friend from his student days who has been charged with blowing up an industrial smokestack that he believes is a threat to the environment. Leon's radical past is alluded to in the dialogue. However, the episode stresses his development from the radical protester of the sixties to the lawyer who pursues justice through the peaceful means of the law. This can be seen in the scene where he bails his friend out of jail.

SHOT 1	DIALOGUE
Leon and Don at the police station signing his release papers. Leon, well groomed, is in suit and tie. Don wears an open, checked lumberjack shirt with a T-shirt underneath and jeans. He is unshaven and generally scruffy.	Don: I won't be sorry to see the outside of this place. Leon: You said that twenty years ago. Don: The costs of doing war, Leon. Leon: Look! There are more effective ways to change things! Don: I tried them all. Didn't stop the cruise missile, didn't close down any nuclear power plants. Leon: Yeah! Well, try harder!
SHOT 2	
Don finishes signing and walks away from the desk in disgust.	Don: What, like you? How many industrial smokestacks you shut down lately, Leon?

SHOT 3

| TS of Leon and Don. ECU of Don with an OF BECU of Leon. | Leon: Look, how many people could you have killed doing it? |

(See glossary of camera-shot abbreviations.)

In this scene, Leon is visually placed within the Canadian establishment through his conventional garb and neat grooming, which are in contrast to the non-conventional attire of his friend. Also, in Shot 3, he is out of focus. This camera technique has the effect of reducing the connection between the out-of-focus object or person and the in-focus elements in the frame. Thus Leon is visually alienated from the radical and violent Don Chapman. Linguistically, he upholds the Canadian cultural value of peace, without losing his effectiveness. In another scene, in answer to Chapman's accusation that he has deserted his earlier principles, he tells him that he "has found a better way."

Despite a sexual peccadillo in the 1991 season, Leon has remained a boon bringer, a strong, effective, idealistic hero who embodies and upholds and brings about those values of social justice Canadians hold dear, such as adequate housing, human rights, and environmental concerns. He pursues the resolution of conflicts and the spreading of human decency peacefully, through the revered institutions of the Canadian legal system. Paradoxically, the hero, says Campbell (1968), "is the man of self-achieved submission" (p. 16). Leon, in abandoning his young radicalism, has submitted to the rites and rules of his country.

On the other hand, by the 1989–90 season, Chuck had developed as all too humanly frail to fit the heroic mould: Canadians were still being deprived of their handsome hero. But they were not deprived for very long. During the previous season, the character of Nick, a Toronto cop, was introduced into the show. Tall, dark, beautifully built, and unquestionably handsome, Nick would soon emerge as CBC's first "heroic hunk of manhood."

Nick was initially introduced as a love interest for Carrie, but as he developed he became primarily an action figure, as befits his role of police officer. The connection of Nick's character with our traditional hero, the Mountie, is obvious. Nick was often seen in uniform performing his duty to serve and protect. In one episode, he bravely saves Carrie from a pathological killer and is wounded in the process. By the 1989–90 season, Nick had become a regular character.

Although Nick's role as Carrie's love interest is still quite prominent, he appears as a character in his own right, until recently as a plainclothes undercover cop. He performs heroic actions such as saving a teenage runaway from the evil clutches of a prostitution ring, capturing the head of the prostitution ring, and rescuing Leon from a violent killer. In the final episode of one season, he is shot and wounded in retribution for bringing the head of the prostitution ring to justice. However, he heroically rises from his hospital bed to save Carrie's seven-year-old adopted daughter from being harmed by members of the ring, who are threatening her in order to stop Carrie from testifying in court against Nick's assailant.

Significantly, Nick always acts within his institutional role as a member of the Toronto police force. He doesn't gather evidence illegally by using excessive violence or breaking and entering, as do many of his American counterparts. Like Leon, Nick in his official role of executor of the law, embodies and upholds the values of peace, order, and good government.

But neither Nick nor Leon hold all the attributes of the hero and "Street Legal" often presents Nick and Leon together. Each character brings to the team his own heroic qualities that make up for the other's lack. Nick's good looks and physical action complement Leon's high principles and intelligence, and Leon's dedication to the law and non-violent methods control Nick's potential violence and possible disregard for the law to which his propensity for physical action could lead.

The collective heroism in the characters of Nick and Leon was first evident in the episode aired September 12, 1989. In this episode, Leon is trying to prove that a man, whom he defended six years ago, is innocent of the murder charge of which he was convicted. His renewed interest in the case is sparked by Tom Joicey, who comes to Leon's office and insists that Grant Simon, an Olympic rower, is guilty of the murder. Joicey claims that Simon came into the rowing club the night of the murder with blood on his jacket. The murder victim was Simon's fiancée, and it seems that he murdered her in a fit of jealous rage because she was seeing another man. Joicey confesses to blackmailing Simon for the past six years, then promptly shoots himself. Leon doesn't have much of a case. He tries to have the case reopened, but neither the police inspector nor the Crown attorney will help him. So our handsome hero comes to the rescue, and Nick and Leon work together as a team to prove Simon's guilt.

Nick helps gather evidence through the official method of search warrants. However, he obtains these warrants without his superior officer's authorization. But this does not mean that Nick is in opposition to the law; both linguistic and visual signs indicate that his actions are legitimate, and Nick's alliance with Leon, who by this time is firmly established as a defender of the Good, legitimizes Nick's actions.

The first representation of their alliance takes place in the main Toronto police station. Leon has just had a fruitless discussion with Chief Inspector Morris, who refuses to investigate Simon. As he is leaving, he meets Nick, who has been relegated to office work because, although he captured the head of the aforementioned prostitution ring, he blew his cover in the process. Nick and Leon briefly discuss Joicey's suicide and the lack of evidence against Simon, and Nick offers to try to persuade Morris to change his mind.

SHOT 1	DIALOGUE
CU of Leon from Nick's perspective. Office workers in background. BECU outline of Nick. Both are dressed in shirts and ties but no suit jackets. Their ties and shirts are different colours but their ties have a similar pattern of swirls.	Leon: and it looks like I'm on my own as far as Metro's finest is concerned.

SHOT 2
CU of Nick from Leon's perspective.
BECU of Leon.

Nick: Maybe you could use a little inside help.

SHOT 3
Same as Shot 1.

Leon: Officially or unofficially?

SHOT 4
Same as Shot 2.

Nick: Strictly by the book. I'll talk to Morris. Maybe he could use a little extra manpower.

SHOT 5
Same as Shot 3.

Leon: I'd really appreciate that. Why the interest?

SHOT 6
Same as Shot 4. He indicates the paper-work in his hands.

Nick: Does this look like my kind of work? I've been pushing a pencil ever since I blew my cover.

In this scene, Nick's potential for heroism in his official capacity is stressed. Linguistically, the reference to "Metro's finest" alludes both to Canada's finest, the RCMP, and to New York's finest, the NYPD. In either case, the term "inside help" places him inside the police force. The legitimacy of the help he offers is further established in Shots 3 and 4. The camera work establishes their alliance visually. The close-ups are seen from each other's perspective, which aligns them, and the back-shots and outlines are in focus. In contrast, in the scene from the previous episode between Leon and Don Chapman, the out-of-focus back-shot of Leon alienates the characters from each other. The conventional shirts and ties they both wear, the absence of suit jackets, and the similar pattern on their ties, both allies them and iden-tifies them as adhering to the norms of conventional society but as having their own style within these conventions.

Nick does talk to Morris, but Morris refuses to grant permission for Nick to investi-gate Simon. Nick, however, ignores Morris and obtains a warrant for Simon's bank records. Morris upbraids Nick for this and threatens to charge him with insubordina-tion. But Morris's authority is undermined by linguistic and visual signs, and Nick's actions are affirmed.

SHOT 1
HL of Morris standing in backgound.
OF SECu of Nick sitting in foreground.

DIALOGUE
Morris: The search warrant he gave you was obtained without my authorization.

SHOT 2
ECU of Nick still seated. Half-turned toward Morris. He is shot from the opposite of Morris's perspective.

Nick: Sir, I believed Simon Grant's bank records would afford evidence of a crime.

SHOT 3
ECU of Morris. He holds up his hand in a halting and dismissive gesture.

Morris: Don't quote the criminal code to me.

SHOT 4
SECU of Nick. His expression and pose show intolerance. Morris is speaking off-camera.

Morris: I understand you've been talking to a cerain lawyer . . .

SHOT 5
CU of Morris.

Morris: . . . who's been bending your ear with stories of gross injustice?

SHOT 6
CU of Nick half-turned toward Morris. Again opposite to Morris's perspective.

Nick: Sir, I believe the case has some merit!

SHOT 7
Focus on Morris with OFS outline of Nick.

Morris: Oh, do you! Do you know that in he original trial your lawyer friend didn't even put his client of the stand . . .

SHOT 8
CU of Nick opposite to Morris's perspective. After Morris finishes speaking, Nick turns away to the side with a determined shake of his head.

Morris: . . . Now he's trying to re-open the case to grab headlines.

Nick: I don't think so.

SHOT 9
SCU of Nick. When Morris starts speaking off-camera, Nick half turns his head toward him. Still an oppositional camera perspective.

Morris: (off-camera) Listen to me, Del Gado!

SHOT 10
CU of Morris.

Morris: You're not involved in this investigation. If you don't stay out of it, I'll have you up on charges of insubordination. Do I make myself clear?

SHOT 11
SCU of Nick half turned to Morris.   Nick: (resentful)   Yes, sir.
Oppositional perspective.

The blocking and camera work put Morris and Nick at odds. Throughout the scene, the two are in oppositional poses, and out-of-focus side, back, and outline shots of Nick alienate him from Morris. The straight-line pattern of Morris's tie, suggesting rigidity, clashes with Nick and Leon's similar and softer pattern. By alienating Nick and Morris, the visual signs of the scene also alienate Morris from Leon, with whom Nick is allied. Linguistically, Nick's action in obtaining the warrant is legitimated through his reference to the Criminal Code, and the legitimacy of Morris's authority is undermined when he refuses to accept the higher authority of the Criminal Code. Morris's use of first-person pronouns to describe himself highlights his personal position rather than his official position. In contrast, his reference to Leon as "a certain lawyer" and "your lawyer friend" emphasizes Leon's official role. And his attempts to discredit Leon have the opposite effect of discrediting his own character because of Leon's heroic status.

Of course, Nick ignores Morris's threats and obtains another warrant, which helps Leon to find photographs taken by a private detective Simon hired to follow his fiancée. The pictures prove that Simon's fiancée was seeing another man, providing Simon with a motive. Significantly, when Leon and Nick go to the detective's office it is locked, but rather than gaining entry by illegally breaking in, Nick shows the warrant to a cleaner who lets them in with her key—all strictly in the Canadian tradition.

Once Morris finds out about the warrant, he suspends Nick. Nick then suggests to Leon that he record the conversation while they show the pictures to Simon, in hopes that he will confess. Leon goes along with the suggestion, but so as to keep within legitimate boundaries suggests that he do the recording: ". . . you're suspended, I'll wear the wire." When Simon is confronted with the pictures and Nick accuses him of the murder, he attacks Nick. Nick easily bests him and wants to use violent methods in order to make Simon confess. But Leon stops him.

Nick: I can get it out of him.
Leon: Forget it. It'll all be inadmissible. . . .

As Simon used violence first, Nick's initial physical response is justified, and as Leon was able to stop Nick from continuing to use force to extract a confession, the Canadian value of non-violence is upheld. The scene also stresses the need to gather evidence that will stand up in a court of law. Just as the Greek hero Theseus needed Poseidon to teach and guard him, and as Arthur needed Merlin, so too does Nick require the guidance of a wise and older man.

Simon is finally brought to justice when he breaks into Leon's house to steal the photographs. Leon discovers him, and Simon is about to beat him to death when Nick arrives just in time to stop him. Nick's arrest of Simon, by the way, offered Canadian viewers a rare opportunity to hear a cop read a suspect his Canadian legal rights:

SHOT 1	DIALOGUE
Nick handcuffing Simon while Leon looks on.	Nick: It is my duty to inform you that you have the right to obtain and instruct counsel without delay.

SHOT 2	
TS of Nick and Simon. Before Nick takes Simon away he stops to speak to Leon who is off-camera.	Nick: (to Leon) Nice work, partner.

Of course, Nick's remark in Shot 2 underlines his alliance with Leon and vindicates him.

As can be seen from this discussion of the September 12, 1989, episode, "Street Legal" skilfully balances the characteristics of Nick and Leon to create a recognizably Canadian heroic team. Such legal teamwork is, of course, common in both print and television series about the law, but one feels that perhaps a heroic team is particularly acceptable to Canadians who defer to the collective rather than the individual and might find the housing of all heroic virtues in one person rather suspect.

Epic heroes are not just courageous combatants of evil, however; they are also lovers. Traditionally, romantic love plays an important role in heroic narratives. In fact the meeting with the goddess, represented in every beautiful woman, is often the hero's final test, and the union of the hero and his lady symbolizes his mastery of life itself (Campbell, 1968). Contemporary television is no different in this respect. Nick and Leon are also romantic heroes.

Leon had several love interests in the early seasons, but in the fourth season, he meets and marries Alana, another lawyer and later a judge. She's a modern career woman—intelligent, caring, and beautiful. Interestingly, Alana is a Tory, whereas Leon is an NDP supporter, but true to the Canadian ideals of political freedom and peaceful co-existence, they make their relationship work without either having to give up their political affiliation. Leon respects Alana's ambitions and is sensitive to her feelings. Usually their love for each other is expressed through words and tender gestures rather than through more glandular displays, and their rather heartwarming, smooth-sailing romance makes Leon a romantic hero for the contemporary professional woman.

Nick's more tempestuous romance with Carrie is in keeping with his more physically active character. Marked by passionate arguments and equally passionate making-up, their romance is more exciting than heartwarming. And whereas Leon is cast in the contemporary romantic hero mould of sensitive, caring "new man," Nick is more in keeping with the traditional romantic hero who proves his love through action. In the same episode discussed above, Nick declares his love in a scene reflecting many elements of a medieval romance.

SHOT 1
FL TS of Carrie and Nick. She is trying
flag down a cab.

SHOT 2
CU of Carrie. She is still trying to flag
a cab.

SHOT 3
CU of Nick.

SHOT 4
CU of carrie. Outline of Nick.

SHOT 5
HL of Carrie turning and walking hastily
away.

SHOT 6
CU of Nick Looking after her, fondly
amused.

SHOT 7
Carrie walking through the crowd at a
bus stop with Nick following her.

SHOT 8
CU of Nick stopping to call after her.

SHOT 7
CU of Carrie stopping and half turning
back to him. Nick's voice off-camera

SHOT 10
CU of Nick amused.

SHOT 11
CU of Carrie. She dismisses his comment
with and exasperated shake of her head,
and continues on through the crowd.

DIALOGUE
Carrie: Look. I don't want to argue any
more, okay! That's all we ever do!
Nick: That's not all we ever do.

Carrie: Oh yeah! When was the last time
we had dinner and didn't end up biting
each other's heads off?

Nick: You're exaggerating.

Carrie: It's over, Nick! I'm a cop,
you're a lawyer. I'm too old and you're
too young!

Nick: Carrie.

Carrie: What!
Nick: I'm the cop . . .

Nick: . . . you're the lawyer.

SHOT 12
Front view of Carrie walking quickly
through the crowd. She bangs into a few
people in her distress.

Carrie: Excuse me. Sorry.
Nick: (off-camera) Carrie, wait!

SHOT 13
Nick running through the crowd to catch
up with her. In his haste, he knocks a pile
of books out of the hands of a teenage
girl in a school uniform. He stops to pick
them up for her.

SHOT 14
Carrie. She is out of the crowd and is
flagging down a cab from the sidewalk.
Nick's off-camera voice calling after her.

Nick: (off-camera) Carrie!

SHOT 15
Nick and girl picking up books. He is
facing Carrie and is on bended knee.

Nick: I don't care how old you are . . .

SHOT 16
CU of Carrie. She is still upset.

SHOT 17
Nick leaning forward to pick up the
rest of the books.

Nick: I'll wait for you to grow up.

SHOT 16
CU of Carrie. She is not amused. A cab
pulls up and she opens its door. At
Nick's request, she turns to look at him.

Nick: (off-camera) Carrie, would you
at least look at me.

SHOT 19
CU of Nick with crowd in background.

Nick: All I'm trying to tell you is you
left your car in the parking lot.

SHOT 20
CU of Carrie shaking her head in
exasperation.

SHOT 21
CU of Nick. Serious expression.

Nick: And I love you.

SHOT 22
CU of Carrie. Stunned expression. Crowd:
Applause. Music: Excerpt of signature tune.

SHOT 23
Crowd applauding and Nick still on
bended knee even though all the books
are picked up. Crowd: Applause.
Music: Excerpts of signature tune.

SHOT 24
CU of Carrie capitulating with a laugh.

SHOT 25
ECU of Nick standing up with a smile.

As in a medieval romance, Nick pursues Carrie, his lady love, and while on his
quest performs a good deed in picking up the schoolbooks—not as impressive as slay-
ing a dragon but a credible substitute. Having gained Carrie's attention, he publicly
declares his love on traditional bended knee, a gesture reminiscent of a knight swearing allegiance to his lady. The scene should be corny, but it is not. Instead, the
formulaic structure transforms the interchange of two ordinary people on a busy
Toronto street into a scene of archetypal romance.

Although such romantic pageants may be exhilarating, we tend to value the tender
peace of a mature and stable relationship more highly than the excitement and passion
of conquest and conflict. "Street Legal" reflects this trend in the romantic fortunes of
Leon and Nick: Leon and Alana's relationship is celebrated in marriage at the same
time as Nick and Carrie's romance comes to an end.

In the 1990–91 season, there were a number of changes in the tone and character of
"Street Legal" that seem to undermine the heroic stature of Nick and Leon and lessen
those elements that gave the series its distinctly Canadian flavour: Nick quit the police
force and became a private investigator, Leon betrayed his marriage in an adulterous
act, Carrie counselled one of her clients to break the law, and Chuck was implicated in
a violent murder. Our handsome hero was no longer sanctioned through his membership in an institutional peace-keeping body, our righteous hero betrayed the institution
of marriage, our heroine no longer revered the law, and the principle of non-violence
was jeopardized. Some viewers claimed with pleasure and others with regret or disgust
that "Street Legal" had become almost American.

Perhaps not, however. These changes may as readily be interpreted as reflections of
the current turmoil in this country. They need not be seen as selling out to the American
model or as evidence of a lack of integrity in the television industry. Cultural products,
including our television heroes, are spontaneous outpourings of a people's loves, fears,
and worries; these changes may well reflect our current feelings and concerns about
threats to the integrity of Canada itself. GST protests, cutbacks to Via Rail and to the
CBC, the failure of the Meech Lake Accord, the ambivalent feelings of English Canada
to threats of Quebec separation, the Oka crisis, free trade agreements with the United
States and Mexico, and Canada's involvement in the Gulf War, all shed light on
changes in the Canadian tale of "Street Legal" during this disturbing year.

Our heroes reflect this turmoil. From Ulysses to Roland, from Robin Hood to Rocky and Dirty Harry, heroes have always had to come to terms with the dark side of their personality and their own destructive powers. Our heroes, like our country, are going through tough times.

Abbreviations of Camera Terms

SHOT	One camera frame
WS	Wide-shot
TS	Two-shot. Two people in frame
FL	Full length of person/s
HL	Half length of person/s
CU	Close-up from a little above the waist to the shoulders. Establishes intimacy or hostility. The closer the shot, the more intense the emotion.
ECU	Extreme close-up
SCU	Side close-up
SECU	Side extreme close-up
BCU	Back close-up
BECU	Back extreme close-up
OF	Out of focus. Establishes alienation from the rest of shot.

NOTES

1. To the regret of her fans, Carrie was killed in an episode in January 1992, and now graces the program only in reruns.

REFERENCES

Campbell, J. (1968). *The hero with a thousand faces*. Princeton: Bollingen.

Canadian Broadcasting Corporation. (1986, November 21).Internal memo.

Canadian Broadcasting Corporation. (1987, November 13). Internal memo.

Fiske, J. (1987). *Television culture*. London: Methuen.

Fiske, J., & Hartley, J. (1978). *Reading television*. London: Methuen.

Miller, M.J. (1987). *Turn up the contrast*. Vancouver: University of British Columbia Press/ CBC Enterpises.

Rutherford, P. (1990). *When television was young: Primetime Canada 1952–1957*. Toronto: University of Toronto Press.

Wolfe, M. (1985). *Jolts*. Toronto: James Lorimer.

AMBIVALENCE AT THE 55-YARD LINE: TRANSFORMATION AND RESISTANCE IN CANADIAN FOOTBALL

Robert A. Stebbins

Lnglish Canadians are, and always have been, ambivalent toward their second national sport, Canadian football. People who are uncertain hold contradictory attitudes or emotions toward the object of ambivalence such that actions that would be taken with reference to it are often inhibited by the more or less equally strong contradictory orientations. The argument made in this essay is that, given their ambivalence toward their game at the professional level, Canadians are restrained today by their own feelings from at least one important football-related act: buying tickets to games. This ambivalence, however, has been present since the beginning, since the last quarter of the nineteenth century when football began to develop as a distinct game by separating itself from rugby and soccer. Thus, other factors besides ambivalence are needed to help explain why better than a century of ambivalence is only today making itself felt at the gate.

One might wonder how this proposition about national ambivalence is at all tenable, given the mania accompanying Grey Cup Week, an occasion held by many Canadians to be one of the major unifying national events of the year. Moreover, English Canadians do take a routine interest in their professional football, as it is served up to them through the press and as it drifts in and out of talk at work and at home. The progress of the local team is a popular topic of conversation. And discussion of its performance unfolds within the lore of great games and great names of the past. These are cultural ties that bind, and football is at the centre of them.

Yet, all this now takes place alongside the highly appealing coverage by the mass media of National Football League (NFL) games in the United States. On television such coverage has become technically impressive, constituted as it is of instant replays, zoom shots, split-screen comparisons, and the like and co-ordinated by colour commentary from American football heroes of the past. National Football League games are beamed into Canadian homes at prime time, giving Canadians an easy opportunity to compare the two versions of the game. The slick coverage and the seemingly greater precision in execution of plays in American football lead some

Canadian football fans to conclude that the game played in Canada is inferior or at least less glamorous.

As for Canadian newspaper coverage of NFL football, although hardly the technical display found on television, it does nonetheless consume a noticeable amount of space in the typical sports section. And, when combined, the television and newspaper coverage of American football are such that the CFL tries to avoid competing for television viewers who might just forsake Canadian games for more attractive ones telecast from south of the border. How much the new World League of American Football will further these tendencies remains to be seen, but with a Canadian team in the league (Montreal), there is bound to be considerable attention given to it in both the print and the electronic media.

To show how the ambivalence proposition is tenable, I shall consider five value conflicts, which have undermined wholehearted acceptance of Canadian professional football from the beginning. These are the conflicts of rules, ideals, rights, quality, and familiarity. The first two, although not entirely dead issues today, are now of only minor importance when compared with their importance in the past. They did, however, set the stage for contemporary ambivalence, an orientation that is substantially influenced by certain reporting practices in the mass media.

Early Value Conflicts

Ambivalence is not just an orientation that developed concurrently with the game of football; it is endemic to it. Past and present contradictory events and practices in football have fostered and continue to foster this ambivalence. Moreover, the Canadian game is unique among modern western sports in that it was a derivative from an influential sport, namely, American football. From the beginning, then, Canadian football has always had reason to question its identity as something distinctly Canadian. At the outset, it was a set of haphazard modifications of an upper-middle-class British sport that were being adopted and modified at the same time with more publicity and fan appeal in the United States. All this was happening against the backdrop, in the late nineteenth century as now, of efforts by English Canadians to shape a distinct national identity for themselves, particularly as separate from Britain and the United States.

The Conflict of Rules

The first of our five value conflicts emerged within this scenario. It was the conflict of rules: British rugby versus American football. It began this way: members of an English garrison stationed in Montreal during the 1860s played rugby against civilian teams composed principally of McGill University students (Cosentino, 1969, p. 1). The game caught on quickly at McGill and in English-speaking Quebec. By the early 1870s, Quebec boasted the best rugby teams in Canada, if not in North America.

It must have been Quebec's reputation for rugby that led Harvard to challenge McGill to a two-game series in May 1874. By this time, McGill students were playing with an egg-shaped ball. Their game consisted of running, kicking, passing, and tackling. There was a concept of off-sides and the use of free kicks and drop kicks. Harvard preferred the "Boston game," a variant of association football played with a round ball with which the players could run. The Boston game was unpopular with other American schools, a sentiment that forced Harvard to search elsewhere for competition. It won the first game using its rules and its ball. The second, played according to McGill's rules, wound up in a 0–0 tie.

This series is frequently cited as the most important turning point in the history of American football. The Harvard team greatly preferred McGill's rugby to their own modification of soccer. Another match was played in Montreal in September of the same year. Harvard won this first game of intercollegiate football in Canada by a score of 3 to 0. It set out at once to persuade the students at other northeastern colleges and universities in the United States that rugby was superior to soccer, the Boston game included.

A game between Harvard and Yale in 1875 was sufficient to convert the latter to rugby. During the following year, the Intercollegiate Football Association was formed in the United States. The game it organized was rugby. The game it excluded was soccer, which, by 1877, had disappeared from American campuses, not to return until shortly after the turn of the century.

Although Harvard introduced rugby to American collegiate circles, the early transition from rugby to present-day American football occurred at Yale. During the 1880s and 1890s, Walter Camp, first a player and then a coach for the Yale team, either introduced or formalized the use of the scrimmage line, the quarterback, eleven men on a team, the calling of signals, and the practice of giving up the ball unless it advanced five yards or more (later to become ten yards) by the fourth down. Except for the number of players and downs, all these changes soon drifted up to Canada.

Thus in the waning years of the nineteenth century, rugby in the United States was rapidly transformed into American football. In Canada, owing to the strong British influence, the transformation of rugby to Canadian football was slower. The English Rugby Union was established in 1871, an act that brought needed standardization to the rules of the game. The organization became a model for rugby unions in Quebec and Ontario. Now a set of official rules and regulations existed, backed by a bureaucracy to enforce them.

The history of changes in Canadian football is primarily about the outcome of the struggles between what Frank Cosentino calls the "traditionalists" and the "liberals" (Cosentino, 1969, p. 11). The former wanted it to remain as it was in Britain; the liberals wanted the game to evolve more or less as it was developing in the United States. Obviously, the liberals, who were strongest in western Canada, where ties to Britain are relatively less important than in the Canadian east, won most of these struggles, although they sometimes had to wait several years for success. But the liberals did not win them all.

The present Canadian game is distinguished in part by certain rugby features and by a legacy of resistance to complete Americanization. Hence Canadian football is not simply football as played in Canada; rather, it is a uniquely Canadian version of the game that evolved through protracted compromise. Of course that process itself is characteristically Canadian, as is the ambivalence that it evokes.

It is not always known how quickly changes in the rugby game in the United States came to Canada. The University of Michigan used the snap back with the hand or foot from a single line of seven forwards against the University of Toronto in 1879 (Howell & Howell, 1969, pp. 80–81, 195). Canadian teams were using quarterbacks in fourteen-player teams by the turn of the century. These innovations had spread from Walter Camp at Yale University to other American schools and subsequently to schools in Canada. A new scoring system put into use in Canada in the 1880s consisted in part of a four-point touchdown, two-point conversion, one-point safety touch, and one-point rouge. The rouge is awarded to the kicking team when it misses a field goal, or when the receiving team fails to run the ball out of its end zone following a punt.

The first three decades of the twentieth century saw numerous changes to the game and its equipment. By 1909, the first year of Grey Cup competition, teams were allowed substitutions for injured players during the first half of the game and, by 1915, during the entire game. By 1921, the number of men per side had dropped to twelve. Centres had dropped the practice of heeling the ball and were directly "snapping it back" between their legs. Thus the other two men of the front three forwards were no longer needed. And, despite its roughness, football in Canada was not played with built-in shoulder pads until the early 1920s. At this time headgear was still varied: some wore a helmet, some wore a cap, and some wore no protection whatsoever.

Frank Shaughnessy, the American-born-and-trained coach of the powerful McGill teams of 1912 and 1919, is usually credited with bringing the huddle to Canada. It was not used by any other team until 1925 and then only amid great controversy. Those opposed to this innovation held that it slowed the game too much. Those favouring it felt this disadvantage was outweighed by the secrecy it provided for calling signals. Before the huddle was adopted, signals were called at the line of scrimmage within earshot of the opposing team.

The Conflict of Ideals

Parallelling, and to some extent connected with the conflict of rules, was the conflict of ideals: amateur sport versus professional sport. This conflict was already apparent in the late nineteenth century. The Canadian rugby unions organized competition among the adult senior, intermediate, and junior teams sponsored by various athletic clubs in the cities of Quebec and Ontario. Disagreements between them over certain rules and regulations continued until they became affiliated in the late nineteenth century with the Canadian Rugby Union (CRU). The CRU soon became the most powerful football body in Canada and remained so for the next 65 years.

During the 1880s and 1890s games were played, sometimes sporadically, sometimes regularly, between various colleges and universities in Ontario and Quebec. A league, the Intercollegiate, which was finally formed in the late nineteenth century, also promptly became affiliated with the CRU. The Intercollegiate teams competed for the oldest annually awarded football trophy in Canada: the Yates Cup. The winner of the Yates Cup advanced to the CRU playoffs for the Dominion Championship against the senior winner of the rugby union playoffs.

The Intercollegiate teams won the majority of Dominion Championships through 1924. Even the "Big Four"—the four strongest senior teams from Montreal, Toronto, Hamilton, and Ottawa and the forerunners of today's professional teams in these cities —were unable to dominate the major university teams. The Big Four were themselves a cut above the other senior teams in the rugby unions. Hence, the other unions were weakened beyond recovery when the Big Four pulled out in 1907 to form their own rugby union.

However, the university teams sometimes refused to compete in the CRU playoffs. Between 1900 and 1904, they boycotted the Dominion Championship on the grounds that the rugby unions were using professionals. Further rule changes and hence further standardization were demanded of the CRU before the universities would return to the Dominion Championship in 1905. But professionalism continued to be a problem. A model already existed in the form of the English Rugby League, which commenced operation shortly before the turn of the century.

By the early 1930s, the growing professionalization of Canadian football was a trend to be reckoned with. Professionalism of individual players, though not of teams as a whole, had become common. Historically the common-sense notion of professionalism was what stimulated discussion, some of it acrimonious, on whether it was good or bad for football. One of the criteria used to differentiate amateurs from professionals since the late 1920s has been excellence. It was generally believed that professionals were the better players.

Another criterion was player remuneration. Occasional charges of football players being paid were made before the turn of the century. By the early 1930s, however, it was widely believed that the senior teams were paying from two to five players on a per game basis. Most of these men were Americans. Since no contracts were signed, the fiction of amateurism could persist at the executive level of the rugby unions. Still, it was clear enough to the eastern universities, when they played the senior teams, that some of the men on these teams were professionals. The university teams quit Grey Cup competition in 1934. And there were other signs about that time to suggest that professionalism was a growing force in Canadian football: Promoters tried to establish a professional league in 1932; a professional team called the Crosse and Blackwell Chiefs actually competed for several seasons against professional teams in the United States. The Winnipegs, a senior team, had nine American players on their roster in 1935.

By the late 1940s, the ideal of amateurism, to which the CRU demanded allegiance by all member teams, was being ignored. The wealthiest senior teams—the Big Four and the western senior teams—neither embraced professionalism nor renounced amateurism. Behind the scenes, they had the money to acquire more fine players than the teams in the other eastern senior leagues. The latter two leagues, which by this time were composed mostly of teams from the smaller cities in Ontario and Quebec, suffered much the same fate from the late 1930s onward that the university teams had endured ten to fifteen years earlier: A noticeable gap in excellence had developed between them and the big-city teams, accompanied by declining fan interest.

The CRU made three decisions in 1946 that unwittingly fostered the further growth of professionalism. First, it abolished the rule that an imported player had to live a minimum of one year in Canada to qualify as a player for a member team. Next, the new rule stated that he need only be a resident by the twenty-first of August of the year that he played for his team. Third, all linemen were allowed to block up to ten yards beyond the line of scrimmage. Since earlier CRU rules had prohibited downfield blocking, Canadian linemen had little experience with it. This inadvertently encouraged the further importation of American players, since they were familiar with this technique.

With contracts still a rarity, Canadian teams began to hire American players with increasing frequency in the early 1950s. The collapse of the All-American conference threw many good players out of work. The CRU's response was to raise the number of imports allowed to seven. About the same time, Canadian teams began a bidding war with the National Football League in a drive to acquire some of its more talented players. And, while NFL officials were protesting the "raids" by Canadian teams, certain NFL coaches and managers were trying to lure players from these same teams to play in the United States. The demand for players had raised their value and hence their salaries. As a result, the financial gap between the rich and poor teams in Canadian senior football grew still wider. And what Bruce Kidd refers to as the "Canadian dependence on and subordination to U.S. commercial football" was assured at this time (Kidd, 1982, p. 293).

The Canadian Football Council was established to exempt the senior teams, which were by now openly professional, from the restrictions imposed on amateurs. Yet the council was part of the CRU, an amateur organization. This lingering anomaly was eliminated in 1958 with the formation of the independent Canadian Football League (CFL).

MODERN VALUE CONFLICTS

Against this background, three present-day value conflicts continue to fuel ambivalence toward Canadian professional football. As I will point out later, sports reporting in the mass media helps foster the conflict and ambivalence of today. One is the conflict of rights: the employment of Canadians versus the employment of Americans. In a recent study of Canadian amateur and professional football players, I found that one important career contingency is the position a man has played in junior or university football, to which he hopes to get signed as a professional in Canada (Stebbins, 1987, pp. 109–10). Although there are occasional exceptions, the general rule is that Canadians hoping to play professionally are much less likely than Americans to be invited to a training camp as quarterbacks and somewhat less likely than Americans to be invited as defensive backs or wide receivers. Likewise, with certain exceptions, Americans are much less likely to be invited to a training camp in the position of kicker and the positions in the offensive line (Jones, 1984). The regulation stating that a team have no more than thirteen imported players on its active roster (plus three quarterbacks, all of whom may be imports) suggests that this contingency might be different were there no such restriction.

Another contingency bearing on employment is physical limitations. Some players, although equal to their competitors in ability and experience, are lighter or smaller. Depending on the positions they seek, these men receive few invitations to try out for the professional clubs or, if they do somehow get to a professional camp, they are quickly cut. Several interviewees pointed out that many Americans in the CFL were unable to pursue a career in the NFL, not because of a lack of ability, but because of weight or height limitations (Stebbins, 1987, p. 104). Canadians who are eliminated from the professional ranks for these reasons, of course, have no alternative professional league.

The strategy of flexibility is also of interest. By remaining flexible and useful, that is, by being willing and able to play several positions, certain categories of players influence their own employability. This strategy, which is open mostly to Canadian linemen, helps their teams achieve the optimum mix of talented Canadian and imported players. It is a strategy that benefits Canadian linemen and American backfield players.

The Conflict of Quality

One of the principal reasons for wanting to hire American players, or "import players" as they are more neutrally called in football circles, is embodied in the fourth value conflict, of quality: Canadian mediocrity of play versus American excellence of play. My study of Canadian amateurs and professionals turned up the following: The competitive nature of training fosters certain malevolent practices (Stebbins, 1987, p. 116). Many rookies are vying for the same position. When differences in ability and experience are slight to nonexistent, other criteria must be brought to bear if individual players are to distinguish themselves from their competitors.

To this end, colleges and universities are ranked according to their reputations in football. Being from a school with a poor reputation is taken as a sign that players from that school are poorly qualified to play professional football. Such players may deny the truth of this reasoning. Still, imputations of this sort do little to bolster their self-confidence in a highly competitive situation where self-confidence may be the determining factor in performing well enough to make the team. The ranking system generally accords Canadian schools a lower reputation for football than American schools. Supporting this evaluation are the facts that, on the average, Americans start playing football on organized teams earlier than Canadians, and that they have better football programs in high school and, to a lesser extent, in university.

In other words, imported players, as well as coaches and managers, generally believe that experience at a school in the United States validates their claim that they are better than Canadians, especially if the school has a strong football reputation. The following comments by a Canadian offensive linemen with five years' professional experience and four years at an American college indicate that at least some Canadians also accept this ranking system:

> If you're Canadian, you're looked down on. They'll look down on you if you're a Canadian and played Canadian college football or a Canadian who played in the States. Like I told you before, there's a ranking. They'll [the coaches] take you sight unseen if you played in the States. . . . I'm just as bad myself. I say Canadian college football sucks and all that, yet this attitude may cost us a great football player once in a while. But I'm a victim of that myself. I look down on Canadians until they prove themselves otherwise. But I've seen some great Canadian football players.

In general, imported players wind up in the so-called "skilled" positions, presumed to require the most speed, agility, and dexterity. These are quarterback, running back, cornerback, and wide receiver (Simmons, 1986).

The Conflict of Familiarity

Related to the two preceding conflicts is the issue of local familiarity. "Local" refers here to local community or national Canadian talent or both. Local talent is better known by Canadian football fans than imported talent (at least initially), since it has greater press coverage and, on the community level, greater visibility. The imported players are not normally the well-publicized stars of American college and professional football, since these men wind up in the NFL. Compared to their Canadian colleagues, players coming from the United States are less known to Canadian football fans.

In time, imported talent can become local by being present for a couple of years or more. Thus, it is possible that this value conflict could disappear once a team establishes its roster. Unfortunately for the reduction of ambivalence, established rosters are uncommon in the CFL. The tendency for many coaches and personnel managers is, when their team is having a lacklustre season, to trade and cut players in an effort to find a winning combination. Although it is doubtful that their goal is reached by these measures, there are other undesirable consequences as well (Stebbins, 1987, pp. 191–92). One is the destruction of fan allegiance. Fan allegiance may well be tested by a team in the throes of two or more losing seasons. But the problem is only exacerbated when attempts to start winning include bringing in large numbers of new players about whom the fans know little. At this point many fans begin looking for other outlets for their leisure time and money (CBC, 1986).

How is it that the mass media are implicated in all this? Modern reportage on matches and events relating to them tends to centre on, among other aspects of sport, two phenomena: great plays and great names. Play-by-play commentary as well as pre- and postgame reviews of sporting events discuss and recall outstanding athletic actions, especially those of the stars. In Canadian football, those stars are most likely to be import players, since they are rendered most visible of all team members by their passing, catching, running, and defending in the backfield. Thus fans who follow their team in the newspapers and on radio and television hear much more often about American than about Canadian players. Such an imbalance can only exacerbate the conflicts of rights, quality, and familiarity that they are presently experiencing.

CONCLUSIONS

The central proposition in this essay is that English Canadians are ambivalent toward Canadian professional football, an orientation that has been around since the beginning of the game and that is indeed endemic to it. This ambivalence is embodied in five specific value conflicts that have emerged through certain contradictory events and practices over the history of the game, three of which have been further sharpened by the reporting practices of sports journalists. And, as mentioned in the introduction, ambivalence may also be furthered by the mass media, particularly televised, coverage of NFL football and the invidious comparisons that this practice makes possible with the Canadian game. One important inhibiting result is low patronage of the games.

There are without doubt other explanations for poor ticket sales. Even if ambivalence were somehow suddenly eliminated, other factors such as attractive alternative forms of leisure, high ticket prices, and scheduling problems appear to have a bearing on fan attendance. Indeed, it might even be found, through further study, that fan allegiance is as strong as ever, but is now being expressed in ways other than going to games. Talk about team performance, watching televised games (when not blacked out), identification with one's team, and the like may still be high.

It would be interesting to know what role, if any, amateur college football in Canada plays in this situation. Except for the conflict of rules, which is comparatively weak today, college football is free of the conflicts considered here and the consequences of mass media reporting just mentioned. Are fans perhaps more attracted today to amateur collegiate football for this reason than in the past and in comparison with football? Has amateur football possibly buoyed Canadian interest in football and given the professional game a longer lease on life than it might otherwise have had?

Whatever the answers to these questions, the reduction of ambivalence does not lie in trying to change the psychology of the fans. If my argument is correct, they are responding to real conflicts and contradictions inherent in Canadian football that only changes there will resolve. In other words, the next move lies with the CFL, not with the people who buy tickets.

From a more detached perspective, however, Canadian football can be seen as a master symbol of Canadian popular culture. It is a historical compromise between British and American influences, one that is today uncertain of its loyalties to the former but stubbornly wary of becoming too much like the latter. It is ironically fitting that a "second sport" enjoys this stereotypical symbolism, and it is characteristically Canadian to be whimsically ambivalent about the whole matter. Canadian football, one suspects, will survive—whether we like it or not and despite the mass media.

REFERENCES

Canadian Broadcasting Corporation. (October 13, 1986). "Inside Track". (Radio program).

Cosentino, F. (1969). *A history of Canadian football 1909–1968.* Unpublished M.A. thesis, Faculty of Physical Education, University of Alberta.

Howell, N., & Howell, M.L. (1969). *Sports and games in Canadian life: 1700 to the present.* Toronto: Macmillan.

Jones, T. (1984). *Canadian Pro Football '84.* Markham, ON: Paperjacks.

Kidd, B. (1982). Sport, dependency and the Canadian state. In *Sport, Culture and the Modern State* (Eds. Cantelon, H., & Gruneau, R.). Toronto: University of Toronto Press.

Simmons, S. (1986, December 8). *Calgary Herald.* p. C1.

Stebbins, R.A. (1987). *Canadian football: The view from the helmet.* London, Ontario: Centre for Social and Humanistic Studies, University of Western Ontario.

MYTHS AND MARKETS:
HOCKEY AS POPULAR CULTURE
IN CANADA[1]

Martin Laba

Canada is an improbable country—a vast and daunting geography, a fractured and volatile political landscape, an unblended aggregation of regions and cultures in long-established and often visceral conflict. In historical terms, Canada has been a nation in search of symbols, in search of a vehicle by which an integrative, collective, nationalist sensibility can be structured and promoted. Government-sponsored campaigns to stir nationalist inclinations among the diverse citizenry of the country have been profoundly unsuccessful in creating a compelling and enduring nation-symbol.

Hockey is not an unlikely candidate as a symbol for a Canadian collective identity, and indeed the game has been treated in such terms since it was played with square pucks and hurly sticks. In a nation desperate for points of connection, hockey has been frequently cited as evidence that a Canadian culture exists. The game has been discussed in romantic flourishes by Canadian writers and broadcasters as a key element in the character, composition, and direction of Canadian culture. And it is this attribution of cultural significance to hockey that has both obscured and complicated the contemporary commodity status of the game—that is, hockey as a media-made commercial entertainment spectacle, defined, situated, ordered, and elaborated within the imperatives and machinations of the media marketplace.

This paper is concerned with the tensions and contradictions of hockey as popular culture in Canada, its cultural dimensions and its market realities, its mythic construction and its commercial progress. It will be argued that in the case of hockey in Canada, and indeed, in the case of any form of popular culture structured and served up in the marketplace, commercial and cultural processes are engaged in a relationship of mutual determination, even interdependence. As an article of faith for many Canadians, hockey is a ritual that embodies and articulates collective aspirations and values. It is also a ritual that often expresses the deepest and most enduring divisions, prejudices, and conflicts in Canadian cultural and political history. The contemporary framework within which the game becomes meaningful to Canadians, and through which these "rituals" are enacted, is the media-based, commercial spectacle of hockey —the business of hockey as professional sport.

AN ELUSIVE NATIONAL CHARACTER:
HOCKEY BECOMES CANADIAN?

Both the mythic abstraction of hockey and its industrialization and commodification are fundamentally tied to its nature and progress as popular culture. From the earliest versions of shinny in Kingston and the rule-ordered, indoor, varsity refinement of the game at McGill University in Montreal in the late nineteenth century, to the professional and commercial media product that is the NHL's televisual version of the game, hockey has constituted a vital and complex popular culture in Canada.

Hockey historians, writers, commentators, and broadcasters have created a repository of hockey romance and icons that suggest not only is there a Canadian collective sensibility, but that this sensibility is enacted in the origins of the game, in the connections—treated as vital, even mystical—of the game to the daunting Canadian climate and geography, and in the mythic heroics of play, as young boys move from the hockey on frozen ponds under bracing winter skies, to the hockey in professional arenas before media audiences of millions.

The identification of the distinctively "Canadian" attributes of the game has been a central theme of numerous historical treatments of hockey. In the more benign, descriptive historical accounts, the instruments of the game are understood as central to the definition of hockey as a uniquely "Canadian" game. In his discussion of the confusion of genesis theories of hockey, for example, J.W. Fitsell argues that modifications and refinements to the numerous and varied antecedents of hockey—"shinty" or "shinn(e)y," "ricket," "hurling" or "hurley," and "bandy"—were crucial to the development of hockey's Canadian character. In particular, Fitsell points to the first recorded game of hockey in Montreal, played indoors at the Victoria Skating Rink on March 3, 1875 (Fitsell, 1987, pp. 159–64). The nine-a-side teams pursued a circular wooden block, with two flat sides, an object first referred to in print in Montreal in 1876 as a "puck." As well, the flat-bladed, curved stick, uniforms, and goal nets were all introduced in Montreal. Finally and most important, the February 27, 1877, edition of *The Gazette of Montreal* published the first rules of hockey—"Playing Rules for the Game of Hockey"—by which the first game was regulated.

The first recorded game, however, involved an element that was to become more essential to the Canadian character of the sport than rules, pucks, and sticks. Although it was customary at the time to end a match after one team scored three goals, the contest played the evening of March 3, 1875, ended with a final score of 2 to 1. The reason play was not extended is given in a news account wired from Montreal to *The Daily British Whig* of Kingston: "Shins and heads were battered, benches smashed and the lady spectators fled in confusion." This incident of violence at the end of the match is elaborated in a report in *The Montreal Witness:*

> Owing to some boys skating about during play an unfortunate disagreement arose; one little boy was struck across the head, and the man who did so was afterwards called to account, a regular fight taking place in which a bench was broken and other damages caused (Fitsell, 1987, p. 36).

Hockey, as it was organized in the late nineteenth century at McGill University, was certainly not meant to be violent. In particular, the game was structured to embody and reflect the principles and virtues of Victorian sportsmanship and gentility—"Tom Brown's School Days" meets the frozen Canadian north. Hockey's initial formative period occurred within a context of new attitudes toward leisure activities in the late 1800s by which the youth of Montreal, and other Canadian urban areas, were encouraged to engage in the vigorous fair play of organized, character-building sport. As Alan Metcalfe notes, with the growth of the YMCA and Amateur Athletic Associations, fraternity, industry, honesty, and discipline were the socially useful traits promoted and acquired in a sport organized, directed, and regulated by Christian standards—a "true muscular Christianity" (Metcalfe, 1978, p. 153). From the inter-faculty and varsity teams at McGill, University of Toronto, Queen's University in Kingston, and other university and college teams in the United States, to gentry associations (the Montreal Amateur Athletic Association, for example), to private club teams (the Granite Club of Toronto, for example), Canadian hockey matches in the late nineteenth century were played by wealthy, educated, and for the most part, well-behaved young men. Sport in general, and hockey in particular, became centred on the imperatives and demands of nineteenth century Canadian Victorian morality.

While Victorian principles of virtuous and character-building recreation emphasized vigorous rather than aggressive play in the earliest forms of hockey, aggression became commonplace, even a signature of the game. The contemporary professional entertainment of hockey in which extreme aggression transmuted to violence has been institutionalized, "officially" explained, even sanctioned by the NHL, is evidence of the authority of this signature. Throughout its amateur and professional development, as hockey spread to other regions of the country, to mining, lumbering, fishing, and farming communities, to the popular classes and cultures of these communities, to the social and economic conditions of work and leisure in these communities, the game became truly Canadian. The play of hockey took on the character—the frustrations, struggles, tensions, and passions of popular class culture in communities across the country. The emotional investment in the game on the part of players and spectators was considerable and was constructed within the relationship between competitive sport and community affiliation, between its speed, its roughness, its intensity, and the realities of social life in the community. While the contemporary mass-mediated spectacle of masculinity and violence as entertainment has given another torque to hockey's aggressiveness, rough play can be referenced to broader historical issues in Canadian social and economic development.

In their analysis of the resonance of the social, political, and economic context and conditions in Atlantic Canada through the content and popular culture of song in that region, Brunton, Overton, and Sacouman argue that the force, immediacy, and relevance of popular culture is crucially tied to broader issues in history and social structure: "It is precisely in order to inform the historical-dynamic analysis of specific expressions of culture in action (of culture as a viable, creative response/strategy to lived social, political and economic conditions) that prior analysis of historical and structural conditions is appropriate" (Brunton, Overton, & Sacouman, 1981, p. 106).

As a "specific expression of culture in action," hockey similarly requires a framework of analysis of the factors of history and social structuration. The intention here is precisely to consider specific historical moments and attendant developments and changes in the definition of hockey, its styles of play, its ideologies, its connections to history, culture, and politics, its socially produced significance and meaning in a diverse Canadian cultural landscape—all considerations in the expressive force of the game as popular culture in Canada.

Hockey, as with all sport, may demonstrate and articulate local, regional, or national identities and conflicts and may serve as a vehicle for spectators, or a more general public, to express these issues for themselves. Although sporting games displace identities and conflicts from their real social basis to a realm of "play," the power of these games as popular representation is substantial. As it draws on and imparts symbolic value to social life, hockey has served to construct, articulate, and maintain identities and conflicts. As Bruce Kidd argues, in these vital connections between sport and culture, games can be refashioned according to distinctive characteristics of a community, local, regional, or national (Kidd, 1982). It is this capacity of hockey to contain, structure, and express a sense of belonging, place, and connection within a community, across a region, or a nation, that accounts for its symbolic power.

Ken Dryden and Roy MacGregor offer evidence for and detail this complex symbolic dimension of the game in terms of the commonplace, everyday means by which hockey connects to the social life of communities across Canada (Dryden & MacGregor, 1989). Through the profiles of Saskatchewan towns, and in particular, through a focus on the capacity of hockey to punctuate, direct, comment on, and at moments, give purpose to social life in those towns, Dryden and MacGregor demonstrate the social and cultural power of the game. They describe, for example, "the coldest night of the year" on the northern outskirts of Saskatoon, a night in which the extreme danger of cold and snow has caused cancellation of bingo, the Elks club, Brownies, the PTA meeting, curling, the 4-H, the dart and cribbage tournaments, and choir practice. Yet there is a jam of traffic on the Yellowhead Highway:

> . . . the road is plugged with idling, blinking cars spewing exhaust smoke as thick as toothpaste. In this unlikely place on this forbidding night, the vehicles' occupants are almost in reach of their evening's destination, Saskatchewan Place. They park in the paved field that surrounds the arena, then hurry through wind and blowing snow and air so cold their nostrils lock solid on a single breath. They are going to a hockey game (Dryden & MacGregor, 1989, p. 16).

The influence of hockey in community life in Canada, and the love of play and spectating that brings crowds out to cheer the Saskatoon Blades in the brutal inclemency of a Saskatchewan winter, are pervasive and compelling factors in the popular culture of the game. The depth of this influence is expressed poignantly in the anxieties of the people of Radisson, Saskatchewan, concerning their hockey rink, and is rendered ethnographically by Dryden and MacGregor. The old rink of Radisson, we discover, is condemned because of its structural deterioration. As residents of

Radisson engage in conversation about hockey, as they always do, in the Red Bull Café—"a highway coffee and doughnut stand that is charged, along with the elevator and arena, with the care and nurturing of the town's soul"—the crucial role of the rink in the everyday life of the community is made clear:

> "If you lose the rink," says Scotty Mundt, the retired power company employee who now as a volunteer takes care of the town arena, "people'll lose interest in the town and start looking other places. It's just as important as the elevator."

> "It's the backbone of the community," says Don Harris, who runs the elevator. "That's what draws people to town."

> Around the tables, the coffee spoons stir and the men nod. "We know of other towns that have lost their rinks," says Kyliuk. "They die overnight. It's the grand central gathering place for the young and the old. The young come to skate and the older citizens come in to watch. The arena is the gathering place for the winter months" (Dryden & MacGregor, 1989, p. 15).

In the progress and dynamic of social life in Radisson, and in other communities across the country, the rink and the game figure centrally. It is the ability of hockey to stimulate and give form and consequence to a sense of place and connection within a community, and to the social dynamic and cultural life of that community, that is a demonstration of hockey's expressive and symbolic import.

THE BUSINESS OF PLAY: "YOUR IMPERIAL OIL HOCKEY BROADCAST! BRINGING YOU ... FOSTER HEWITT!"[2]

When Lord Stanley of Preston, the sixth Governor General of Canada, donated a trophy for hockey champions in 1893, he intended it as a challenge cup among amateur teams. The challenge was open to and engaged amateur teams and leagues from across the country. As early as 1907, however, the tensions and struggles for supremacy between amateur and professional interests began to emerge. The "professional" player, paid, borrowed, or signed by new hockey club owners, changed the style and progress of hockey in Canada. As Brian McFarlane notes, after 1908, "A few teams struggled along with amateur players but the winning teams were the teams that paid their players." (McFarlane, 1989, p. 8). The Victorian spirit of the amateur intra-faculty, inter-collegiate, or inter-amateur club hockey—playing the game for its own sake —slowly eroded as the ideology of professionalism reordered the game as a commercial spectator sport. In 1910, with the formation of the National Hockey Association, the ideology of commercial professionalism was entrenched and began to dominate the way in which hockey was both defined and played. The business of hockey prevailed, and increasingly the game was dependent upon the capital and the enterprising spirit of club owners and entrepreneurs. Mining magnate Ambrose

O'Brien, for example, bought a collection of hockey stars for his newly awarded franchise in the NHA, the Renfrew Creamery Kings (later the Renfrew Millionaires), and brought a team of highly skilled professionals to his paying fans of Renfrew miners. The professional league on the west coast was similarly driven by and for profit. Lester and Frank Patrick left Renfrew and their playing days in the east and moved to British Columbia to work with the fortune of their father, lumberman Joseph Patrick. In 1911, the Patricks established the Pacific Coast Hockey Association (PCHA) with franchises in Victoria, Vancouver, and New Westminster and built two artificial ice rinks—the $110 000, 3500-seat Victoria Arena, and the $300 000 Denman Arena, home for the Vancouver Millionaires (Fitsell, 1987, pp. 131–35). By 1914, hockey was big business—a professional, profitable, spectator sport with two leagues dominating, absorbing, or forcing out of operation competing professional and amateur leagues across the country. The Stanley Cup became the prize for professionals in the annual competition held between the NHA and the PCHA.

The National Hockey League was formed in 1917 with four franchises: the Montreal Canadiens, the Montreal Wanderers, the Ottawa Senators, and the Toronto Arenas. Initially, the emergence of a single dominant professional league seemed unlikely. Bidding wars between owners, escalating players' salaries, and unstable franchises characterized this period for the new league. Owners were above all concerned with their individual profits rather than with working for the financial success of the entire league. By the mid-1920s, however, the drive for profit in professional hockey altered this situation dramatically.

Beginning in 1924, the majority of NHL owners moved their operations and franchises to the United States with the promise of substantial revenues in the larger and more lucrative U.S. markets. By 1926, the NHL was primarily a U.S. league. The NHL had set itself up as a monopoly—the only game in town. It eliminated competition—for example, the NHL bought out the PCHA and collapsed its operations and players into the league—and the NHL became the only seller of the product, professional hockey, and the only buyer of the commodity, professional players, to perform for and service its business. NHL owners began to understand the economic benefits of collusion and a scheme to maximize profits for the whole league and for the benefit of every franchise. By the late 1920s, the NHL consolidated its position as the dominant league playing the dominant version of hockey. The league moved into the large urban media markets, and the sports cartel that the NHL had become reinforced its monopolization of the game.

The role of the media in the profit drive of the NHL was central. While the NHL had sanctioned corporate sponsorship in the form of team endorsements for products such as gasoline and cigarettes, hockey owners realized that the real prosperity of their operations was dependent upon the capacity of radio to deliver audiences in massive numbers to advertisers. The Conn Smythe-Jack McLaren deal of 1929 pioneered this emerging media business of hockey (Young, 1990, pp. 38–52).

Smythe, part owner and manager of the Toronto Maple Leafs, and Jack McLaren, director of the Canadian office of the American-owned advertising agency, Campbell-Ewald Limited, agreed to an arrangement concerning radio rights, including the services of Foster Hewitt, for Leaf games. With the promise that Smythe would build a much larger arena than the 8000-seat Arena Gardens on Mutual Street in downtown Toronto where the Leafs played, McLaren had a considerable interest in working out a broadcast rights deal that involved his agency in the arrangement and ongoing business of sponsorships. Two years later, McLaren's agency secured General Motors as the first sponsor of Leaf games from the new Maple Leaf Gardens and followed in the 1938–39 season with arranging the sponsorship of Imperial Oil. Through radio, corporate sponsorship, and the revenues from advertising and broadcast rights, the business of hockey began to work the consumer landscape.

These historical notes are meant neither to deny the cultural significance, purpose, and direction of hockey in Canada, nor to suggest that economic factors alone have determined the progress and meaning of the game. Rather, these notes provide a critical perspective on the historical struggles, negotiations, and accommodations between the business and the culture of play, and on the early and enduring strategies of business and marketing by which hockey became a Saturday-night spectacle that generated substantial profit for its owners and producers.

POPULAR CULTURE AND THE GAME

Arguably twelve players engaged in gaming combat in pursuit of a rubber disc is neither intrinsically interesting nor important. What is interesting and important, however, is how and why cultural and political meanings are attached to this activity—how the game has achieved authority as a dramatization of Canadian culture, and of the social and political developments and conflicts in Canadian history.

Among the numerous and varied artistic renderings of hockey's cultural authority, Rick Salutin's 1977 play *Les Canadiens* best addresses the capacity of the game to embody, sum up, and enact crucial and complex Canadian cultural issues, concerns, and tensions.[3] Salutin analyzed this capacity in his introduction to the text of the play in terms of the sense of the visceral connection that Canadians feel to the game—a sense of possession and ownership:

> Hockey is probably our only universal cultural symbol. It is universal not because every Canadian has played the game—everyone hasn't. But even those who haven't played hockey (most women, for example), nevertheless, relate to hockey. They know what it is, connect to it in some context, and have some *feelings* about it. The point is not whether hockey is the world's best, fastest, or most barbaric game; nor whether we are the best in the world at playing it. The point about it is—as Margaret Atwood has said in a similar context about Canadian literature—it is *ours* (Salutin, 1977, pp. 1–12).

Les Canadiens begins with the epic 40-minute battle of Canada on the Plains of Abraham. As Wolfe's invading imperial army is near victory, a fallen Québécois soldier, a farmer, with his final breath of life, throws his rifle to his son to carry on the battle—and the rifle turns into a hockey stick. The battle will continue on the ice.

When Rocket Richard was suspended for striking a linesman in a game against Boston on March 16, 1955, by "that walking symbol of Anglo-Canadian authority," NHL president Clarence Campbell, a riot boiled out of the Forum and onto St. Catherine Street. Salutin treats this historical moment as, in effect, the opening volley of the Quiet Revolution. On stage, as the sounds of the riot on the streets continue, the time clock and message board record the events to follow:

19:62: "Thousands Protest in Front of CNR Headquarters."

19:64: "Bombs in the Streets of Westmount."

19:65: "Protest Against the Queen Crushed by Police."

19:67: "Huge Crowd Cheers 'Vive le Québec libre.'"

19:68: "Beatings, Arrests in Anti-Trudeau Riot."

19:69: "Riot Act Read in St. Léonard."

19:70: "War Measures Act Proclaimed."

From the Plains of Abraham, to the revolutionary movement of 1837, to the anti-conscription movements of both world wars, to the Quiet Revolution, to the unravelling of the Meech Lake Accord, the history of the cause of Quebec has been rooted in moments of resistance to real and/or felt subjugation through nationalist and independentist political movements, and through the forms and practices of popular culture. The hockey riots of 1955 connected the cause of Quebec to a singular and vital symbol of Quebec supremacy in the centuries-old battle against English-Canadian hegemony—les Canadiens. Nationalism in Quebec has always been a constituent element of Quebec popular culture and was particularly expressed and symbolized through hockey when the Montreal Canadiens were predominantly Québécois players, and when the team had the ability to sum up the character and the sensibility, the struggles and the identity of Quebec.

Hockey in Quebec is one example of the political and popular cultural dimensions and dynamics of the game in Canada. To apprehend the full meaning of hockey as Canadian popular culture demands a historical view of the moments, the locales, and the social conditions by which the game developed and achieved cultural significance, and a recognition that the game both shapes and is shaped by the experiences and the struggles of those who take pleasure from it, and who have contributed to its social definition and meaning as a form and practice of popular culture.

The popular culture of hockey also embodies the tensions and struggles in play itself—the tensions and struggles between the emotion and the art of play, and the commercial product of play, or what ex-NHL player Eric Nesterenko has referred to as "pure play" and "play as art" on the one hand, and the "corrupted" form of play as commodity on the other (Terkel, 1972). Nesterenko's reminiscence of his time playing for the Toronto Maple Leafs and the Chicago Black Hawks from the 1950s to the 1970s both articulates and analyzes this conflict from the perspective of play as professional entertainment—"play for pay":

> When you sell play, that makes it hard for pure, recreational play,
> for play as an art, to exist. It's corrupted, it's made harder, perhaps
> it's brutalized, but it's still there. . . .

> Cynicism is a tool for survival. I began to grow up quickly. I became
> disillusioned with the game not being the pure thing it was earlier in
> my life. I began to see the exploitation of players by owners. You
> realize owners don't really care for you. You're a piece of property
> (Terkel, 1972, p. 500).

Throughout the history of hockey, the tensions, conflicts, and contradictions that
have characterized the popular culture of the game have been subsumed in the enduring romance and persistent mythology surrounding the game. The exhilaration of play
and the visceral emotion in spectating have always been expressions of the fundamental appeal of hockey, and the foundations of the romance by which the game has been
explained, made meaningful, and celebrated. Its speed, its spontaneity, its complex
and "unlimited dramatic possibilities"[4]—all are aspects of the what Nesterenko refers
to as the "pure" play of hockey that sum up the game's expressive potential beyond its
commercial demands and conditions, and that inspired Nesterenko to rhapsodize on
the essential and romantic beauty of skating in hockey:

> I haven't kept many photographs of myself, but I found one where
> I'm in full flight. I'm leaning into a turn. You pick up the centrifugal
> forces and lay in it. For a few seconds, like a gyroscope, they sup-
> port you. I'm in full flight and my head is turned. I'm concentrating
> on something and I'm grinning. That's the way I like to picture
> myself. I'm on another level of existence, just being in pure motion
> (Terkel, 1972, p. 506).

A Theoretical Framework:
Commerce and "The Popular"

A view of culture as a site of struggle over meaning is well established in cultural and
communication studies. In particular, culture became understood as a social field of
interaction and negotiation between popular, "everyday" values, sensibilities, and
experiences, and the larger structures and institutions—political, economic, social, and
cultural—which frame and order popular practices. The intersection of these two component processes of culture was suggested by Gramsci's recognition that popular
sentiments and convictions proceed from the imperatives of everyday life under capitalism. Specifically, Gramsci's notion of hegemony—the continual negotiation
between dominant orders in society and the popular classes, whose consent is won for
dominance to be sustained—offered a means of understanding culture as a meeting
ground for political and economic interests and ideologies, and popular practices; that
is, as a meeting ground for social structure and human agency.

Raymond Williams elaborated this complementarity of structure and agency within
the process of hegemony (Williams, 1977, 1980). In particular, he considered the ways
in which everyday cultural practices resonate and reproduce social structure, and the
ways in which social structure provides the framework by which cultural practices are

interpreted, made relevant, and meaningful. Hegemony in Williams's formulation, was neither ideological domination or direct imposition of a dominant ideology on subordinate, popular classes. Instead, the daily experience of both work and leisure in the culture of popular classes served as a contributing factor in the creation of the social conditions and relations that shape those experiences.

Hegemony in Williams's terms was a "saturation of the whole process of living" to the extent that social structural pressures, limits, and constraints are experienced as commonplace and common sense. Cultural forms and practices then, were understood to contain the logic of political and economic interests, and the ideologies that define, situate, and sustain these interests in the social production of common sense. At the same time, cultural forms and practices were acknowledged as active and significant constituent elements in this social production of common sense. Popular culture was viewed as the "terrain," historically ordered, upon which the processes of social structuration and cultural practice interact. Tony Bennett's definition of popular culture as a historically constructed set of tensions, negotiations, and accommodations is most helpful here. He argues that popular culture is those cultural forms and practices

> . . . varying in content from one historical period to another—which constitute the terrain on which dominant, subordinate and oppositional cultural values and ideologies meet and intermingle, in different mixes and permutations, vying with one another in their attempts to secure the spaces within which they can become influential in framing and organising popular experience and consciousness (Bennett, 1986, p. 19).

The application of these views of the popular culture process, and the intersection and complementarity of social structure and cultural practice, is particularly useful in the analysis of hockey in Canadian history and culture. The popular, common sense of the game is, to employ Bennett's definitional argument, a concept that has been historically struggled over and negotiated in the range of hockey's competing values and ideologies. The apparent and experienced naturalness of hockey in Canada—in particular, both the popular and commercially manufactured senses of the game as connected essentially to Canadian culture—is the basis of its mythic character. The popular culture of hockey is the ground upon which popular and corporate conceptions of the game have interacted to create a common sense about the significance of hockey in Canada, and to stimulate and sustain through hockey a collective cultural conception.

Concluding Note: Hockey's Mythic Dimension

In a basic, anthropological sense, myth functions as creation tale, a narrative of genesis and evolution that a people tell themselves about themselves. In this way, myth has the capacity to "naturalize" history, to offer a way of understanding social conditions and cultural life as already complete—evolved, inherent, natural. Roland Barthes has argued that as myth confuses history with nature, it is "not read as a motive, but as a reason" (Barthes, 1973, p. 129). Myth, then, "glosses over" history and creates a naturalizing veneer beneath which real historical conditions cannot be apprehended. In this way, as Barthes argues, myth "deprives the object of which it speaks of all History" (p. 151). It presents the object of myth as somehow organic, "God-given," and de-historicized.

In the historical Canadian search for and anxiety over commonality, for points of connection, and for evidence of a national identity, hockey has served as a virtual creation tale. The romance of hockey is mythic—a romance that has regarded and rendered the game as a natural outgrowth of the daunting challenges of Canadian geography and climate, as organically rooted as snow, ice, forest, prairie, rock shield, and the myriad of the country's other geographic and climatic facts. "Naturally" then, and demonstrated in the historical development of the game, Canada has claimed both ownership of, and supremacy in hockey. As evidenced in past and recent international competitions, the national identity stakes are high in Canadian hockey. Indeed, these stakes prompted Alan Eagleson's admonition before the start of the 1972 Canada-Soviet series: "Anything less than an unblemished sweep of the Russians would bring shame down on the heads of players and the national pride" (Richler, 1976, p. 4).

Myth has mediated in the negotiations between the popular cultural and corporate dimensions of the sport, to the extent that hockey is presented to us, at best, in a benign gloss of hockey's "official" history as televisually constructed by the various corporate entities that "own" and design hockey's currency and hockey's memories. Myth can be manufactured, commercially produced, and marketed. As hockey has become an entertainment commodity, myth and marketing have become inextricably linked. Myths have been constructed by hockey organizations, corporate sponsors, and media interests to reinforce and maintain an abiding loyalty among fans as consumers and, of course, to build profits.

Yet it is precisely the naturalness of the game as celebrated in romantic, mythic conceptions, treatments, and experiences of hockey that has been created in and accounts for both the enduring cultural identity investments in the game, and the frenzied media advertising enterprise of corporate professional hockey. In all, the social production of hockey in Canada, and the common sense of the game's meaning and significance, have been structured in and expressed through the complex economics, politics, and history of hockey's popular culture.

NOTES

1. This study has been benefited substantially from my collaboration with Rick Gruneau in the research and script writing of a four-part documentary television series for the Knowledge Network (British Columbia) entitled, "Hockey: The Canadian Game."

2. With these words, the CBC's Charles Jennings introduced "Hockey Night in Canada," beginning in 1937.

3. *Les Canadiens* was commissioned by and first performed at Centaur Theatre in Montreal on February 10, 1977.

4. In their political, economic, and cultural analysis of hockey in Canada, Bruce Kidd and John Macfarlane discuss the dimensions of pleasure and play that make the game significant to players and spectators and that serve to explain the game in historical and popular cultural terms. See (1972), *The death of hockey*. (Toronto: New Press).

REFERENCES

Barthes, R. (1973). *Mythologies* (A. Lavers, Trans.). Frogmore, England: Paladin.

Bennett, T. (1986). The politics of "the popular" and "popular culture." In *Popular Culture and Social Relations* (Eds., Bennett, T., Mercer, T., & Wollacott, J.). Milton Keynes: Open University Press.

Brunton, R., Overton, J., & Sacouman, J. (1981). Uneven underdevelopment and song: Culture and development in the Maritimes. In *Communication Studies in Canada* (Ed., Salter, L.). Toronto: Butterworths.

Dryden, K., & MacGregor, R. (1989). *Home game: Hockey and life in Canada*. Toronto: McClelland and Stewart.

Fitsell, J.W. (1987). *Hockey's captains, colonels and kings*. Erin, ON: Boston Mills.

Kidd, B. (1982). Sport, dependency, and the Canadian state. In *Sport, Culture, and the Modern State* (Eds., Cantelon, H., & Gruneau, R.). Toronto: University of Toronto Press.

McFarlane, B. (1989). *One hundred years of hockey*. Toronto: Deneau.

Metcalfe, A. (1978). The evolution of organized physical recreation in Montreal, 1840–1895. *Social History, 21.*

Nesterenko, E. (1991, May). (Interview, Vancouver).

Richler, M. (1976, October 30) Pucksure. *Weekend Magazine.*

Salutin, R. (1977). *Les Canadiens*. Vancouver: Talon Books.

Terkel, S. (Ed.) (1972). *Working.* New York: Avon, pp. 499–506.

Williams, R. (1977). *Marxism and literature*. London: Oxford University Press.

Williams, R. (1980). *Problems in materialism and culture*. London: Verso.

Young, S. (1990). *The boys of Saturday night: Inside "Hockey Night in Canada."* Toronto: Macmillan.

APPENDIX A:
BASIC FACTS ON CANADIAN MASS MEDIA

Compiled by Janet Harkness

LIST OF FIGURES

FIGURE 1

Basic Canadian Media Statistics

Average television viewing time/week/person (Fall 1989)		23.4 hours
Average radio listening time/week/person (Fall 1989)		18.8 hours
Average attendance at regular movie theatres/person/year (1987–88)		3.2 times
		% of total
Number of households with television sets (May 1989)	9 355 000	98.7
Number of households with cable television (May 1989)	6 711 000	70.8
Number of households with cable converters (May 1989)	4 156 000	43.8
Number of households with video recorders (May 1989)	5 576 000	58.8

Source: Statistics Canada. (1990). *Cable television 1989.* (Cat. No. 56–205). Reproduced with the permission of the Minister of Supply and Services Canada, 1991.

FIGURE 2

Federal Government Expenditures on Major Communications Sectors, 1988–1989

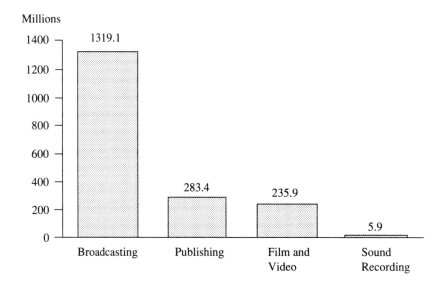

Source: Statistics Canada. (1990). *Government expenditures on culture 1988–89 culture statistics.* (Cat. No. 87–206). Reproduced with the permission of the Minister of Supply and Services Canada, 1991.

FIGURE 3

Revenue of Major Media Sectors, 1988–1989

Total Reported Revenue	$
Broadcasters, 1989	2046 million
Book publishers and exclusive agents, 1988–1989	1375 million
Cable systems, 1989	1154 million
Periodical publishers, 1988–1989	867 million
Film producers, 1988–1989	624 million
Record label companies, 1988–1989	560 million
Film distributors, 1988–1989	549 million
Motion picture theatres, 1988–1989	499 million
Videocassette wholesalers, 1988–1989	269 million
Film laboratories and post-production services companies, 1988–1989	224 million

Source: Statistics Canada. (1991). *Focus on culture*. Vol. 3 (Spring). (Cat. No. 87–0004). Reproduced with the permission of the Minister of Supply and Services Canada, 1991.

FIGURE 4

Seven Leading Media Companies in Canada, 1989

Company	Operating Revenue $
Thomson Corporation	5.11 billion
Quebecor Inc.	2.21 billion
Southam Inc.	1.68 billion
Maclean Hunter Ltd.	1.43 billion
Torstar Corp.	982 million
Hollinger Inc.	740 million
Rogers Communications Inc.	600 million

Source: Hannigan, J.A. (1991). Canadian media ownership and control in an age of global megamedia empires (which used "The top 1000 companies," *Globe and Mail Report on Business*, July 1990). In *Communications in Canadian Society* (Ed., Singer, B.D.). Scarborough, ON: Nelson Canada.

FIGURE 5

Share of Net Advertising Revenues, by Medium, 1975–1989

	1975	1980	1985	1989
	%	%	%	%
Television	13.7	16.2	16.6	16.0
Radio	10.7	10.4	9.0	8.3
Newspapers	35.0	32.5	30.3	29.5
Periodicals	13.5	14.7	14.2	16.5
Outdoor	7.1	6.4	7.5	7.9
Other print	19.9	19.7	22.4	21.8
Total	**100.0**	**100.0**	**100.0**	**100.0**

Note: Figures may not add to totals due to rounding.

Source: Department of Communications. (1991). *The economic status of Canadian television, report of the task force* (which used Statistics Canada and Maclean Hunter research). Ottawa: Minister of Supply and Services.

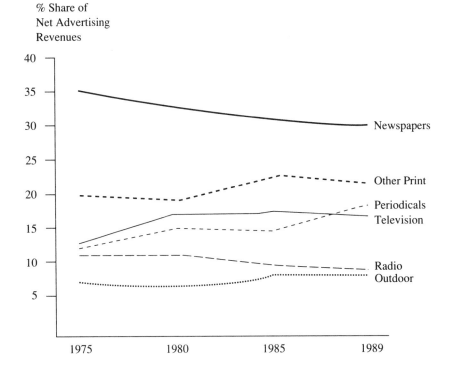

FIGURE 6

**Percentage of National Newspaper Circulation
Controlled by Nine Canadian Newspaper Groups in 1990**

Group	Percentage of national circulation
Southam	27.1
Thomson	20.5
Toronto Sun Publishing	11.0
Quebecor	8.5
Gesca	5.8
Unimedia	3.2
Irving	2.5
Armadale	2.4
St. Catharines Standard	0.9
Sterling	0.9
Total	**82.8**

Source: Kesterton, W., & Bird, R. (1991). The press in Canada: A historical overview. In *Communications in Canadian Society* (Ed., Singer, B.D.). Scarborough, Ontario: Nelson Canada.

FIGURE 7

Circulation and Controlling Group of Major Canadian Daily Newspapers

Controlling Group	City	Newspaper	Circulation (daily; weekdays)
Southam Inc.	Brantford	Expositor	33 269
	Calgary	Herald	134 417
	Edmonton	Journal	160 934
	Hamilton	Spectator	142 606
	Kamloops	Daily News	20 370
	Kingston	Whig-Standard	38 709
	Kitchener-Waterloo	Record	77 997
	Medicine Hat	News	14 150
	Montreal	Gazette	199 204
	North Bay	Nugget	24 218
	Ottawa	Citizen	184 724
	Owen Sound	Sun Times	24 301
	Prince George	Citizen	22 289

(Continued)

Controlling Group	City	Newspaper	Circulation (daily; weekdays)
Southam Inc. (continued)	Sault Ste. Marie	Sault Star	27 372
	Vancouver	Province	175 262
	Vancouver	Sun	229 692
	Windsor	Star	86 394
Thomson Ltd.	Barrie	Examiner	14 133
	Belleville	Intelligencer	18 269
	Brandon	Sun	19 300
	Cambridge	Reporter	14 306
	Charlottetown	Guardian	18 341
	Charlottetown	Patriot	5 621
	Chatham	Daily News	16 242
	Corner Brook	Western Star	11 236
	Cornwall	Standard-Freeholder	18 062
	Guelph	Daily Mercury	18 725
	Kelowna	Daily Courier	17 094
	Kirkland Lake	Northern Daily News	6 058
	Lethbridge	Herald	24 267
	Lindsay	Daily Post	5 214
	Nanaimo	Daily Free Press	11 031
	New Glasgow	Evening News	11 164
	Niagara Falls	Review	21 725
	Orillia	Daily Packet & Times	10 676
	Oshawa	Times	21 941
	Pembroke	Observer	7 491
	Penticton	Herald	8 472
	Peterborough	Examiner	27 927
	Sarnia	Observer	24 429
	Simcoe	Reformer	10 246
	St. Thomas	Times-Journal	9 928
	St. John's	Telegram	38 392
	Sudbury	Star	28 686
	Sydney	Cape Breton Post	31 791
	Thunder Bay	Chronical-Journal	30 180
	Thunder Bay	Times-News	8 669
	Timmins	Daily Press	14 001
	Toronto	Financial Times	116 178
	Toronto	Globe and Mail	318 300
	Truro	Daily News	9 187

(Continued)

Controlling Group	City	Newspaper	Circulation (daily; weekdays)
Thomson Ltd. (continued)	Vernon	News	7 727
	Victoria	Times-Colonist	77 698
	Welland	Evening Tribune	17 532
	Winnipeg	Free Press	170 443
	Woodstock	Sentinel-Review	9 938
Toronto Sun Pub. Corp.	Calgary	Sun	73 416
	Edmonton	Sun	83 503
	Fort McMurray	Today	6 126
	Grande Prairie	Daily Herald-Tribune	8 129
	Kenora	Miner & News	5 031
	Ottawa	Sun	Not Reported
	Portage La Prairie	Daily Graphic	4 622
	Toronto	Sun	286 883
	Toronto	Financial Post	208 144
Torstar	Toronto	Star	523 458
Quebecor Inc.	Montreal	Le Journal de Montréal	317 024
	Quebec	Le Journal de Québec	103 127
	Sherbrooke	Record	6 122
	Winnipeg	Sun	47 526
Unimedia	Chicoutimi	Le Quotidien du Saguenay	34 455
	Ottawa-Hull	Le Droit	37 437
	Quebec	Le Soleil	116 688
Gesca	Granby	La Voix de l'Est	16 384
	Montreal	La Presse	191 698
	Sherbrooke	La Tribune	42 200
	Trois Rivières	Le Nouvelliste	56 081
Irving	Fredericton	Daily Gleaner	27 799
	Moncton	Times-Transcript	45 346
	Saint John	Evening Times-Globe	32 198
	Saint John	Telegraph-Journal	32 465
Armadale	Regina	Leader-Post	70 082
	Saskatoon	Star-Phoenix	59 785

(Continued)

Controlling Group	City	Newspaper	Circulation (daily; weekdays)
St. Catharines Standard Group	Cobourg	Daily Star	5 525
	Port Hope	Evening Guide	3 590
	St. Catherines	Standard	43 944
Sterling Publications	Cranbrook	Daily Townsman	4 164
	Dawson Creek	Peace River Block News	3 135
	Fort St. John	Alaska Highway News	3 185
	Kimberley	Daily Bulletin	Not Reported
	Nelson	Daily News	5 500
	Port Alberni	Valley Times	6 878
	Prince Rupert	Daily News	Not Reported
	Trail	Times	5 892
Independently Owned	Amherst	Daily News	4 500
	Brockville	Recorder & Times	16 290
	Flin Flon	Reminder	7 600
	Halifax	Chronicle Herald	80 274
	Halifax	Daily News	23 895
	Halifax	Mail-Star	57 870
	London	Free Press	126 971
	Montreal	Le Devoir	29 528
	Red Deer	Advocate	23 171
	Stratford	Beacon-Herald	13 205
	Whitehorse	Star	4 620

Source: Circulation figures: *The Canadian encyclopedia*. (1988). Edmonton: Hurtig Publishers and *Gale directory of publications and broadcast media*. (1992). 124rd ed. New York: Gale Research Inc.

Ownership data: Kesterton, W., & Bird, R. (1991). The press in Canada: A historical overview. In *Communications in Canadian Society* (Ed., Singer, B.D.). Scarborough, Ontario: Nelson Canada.

FIGURE 8

CBC and CTV's Top 25 English Network Television Programs, Ranked by Persons Age 2+
(Week of February 4–February 10, 1991)

Program	Audience (000's)	Audience Rankings	Network
America's Funniest Home Videos	3 131	1	CTV
America's Funniest People	2 689	2	CTV
Unsolved Mysteries	2 370	3	CTV
CTV Tuesday Movie Special	2 268	4	CTV
Full House	2 216	5	CTV
CTV Sunday Movie	2 158	6	CTV
Magical World of Disney	1 877	7	CBC
Cosby Show	1 775	8	CTV
Matlock	1 632	9	CTV
Knots Landing	1 614	10	CTV
Rescue 911	1 593	11	CTV
Barbara Walters Special	1 574	12	CTV
Dallas	1 531	13	CBC
* CBC National News	1 497	14	CBC
Designing Women	1 322	15	CBC
* W5	1 318	16	CTV
Fresh Prince/Bel Air	1 303	17	CBC
CTV Monday Movie	1 295	18	CTV
Night Court	1 285	19	CTV
* Road to Avonlea	1 285	20	CBC
Different World	1 268	21	CTV
* Hockey Night in Canada	1 252	22	CBC
* CTV News	1 210	23	CTV
* CBC News – Sunday Report	1 179	24	CBC
Golden Girls	1 172	25	CBC

* Canadian Program

Source: CBC Research (A.C. Nielsen), 1991.

FIGURE 9

**Percentage Share of Viewing by Station Groupings for
English- and French-Language Television, for Persons Age 2+ (1985–1989)**

English-Language	1985 %	1987 %	1989 %	Change from 1985 to 1989 %
U.S. stations	30	29	30	0
CTV	29	27	23	- 6
Independents	11	13	15	4
CBC	21	22	19	- 2
Global	6	6	7	1
Pay & Specialty	2	2	5	3
TVO	1	1	1	0
Total	**100**	**100**	**100**	

French-Language	%	%	%	%
TVA	52	43	42	- 10
SRC	30	24	22	- 8
TQS	–	15	19	19
SRC affiliates	12	9	7	- 5
R-Q	5	6	5	0
Pay & Specialty	1	2	5	4
Other	–	1	–	0
Total	**100**	**100**	**100**	

Note: TQS: on air September 1986

Source: Department of Communications. (1991). *The economic status of Canadian television,
Report of the task force*, (which used Marketing Research, Marketing Analysis
Division, CRTC). Ottawa: Minister of Supply and Services.

FIGURE 10

**Percentage Distribution of Television Viewing Time, by
Program Origin and Genre, for Persons Age 2+ (Fall, 1989)**

Program Genre	Canadian Programs	Foreign Programs	Total
Drama	4.0	23.8	27.9
News/Public Affairs	16.6	4.0	20.6
Comedy	0.9	14.4	15.3
Variety/Games	5.6	5.5	11.1
Sports	5.6	2.0	7.6
Instruction	2.1	0.9	3.0
Documentary	0.7	0.5	1.2
Music/Dance	1.1	0.1	1.1
Religion	0.3	0.1	0.4
Other	–	11.9	11.9
Total	**36.8**	**63.2**	**100.0**

Note: Figures may not add to totals due to rounding.

Source: Statistics Canada. (1991). *Television viewing in Canada 1989 culture statistics.* (Cat. No. 87–208). Reproduced with the permission of the Minister of Supply and Services Canada, 1991.

FIGURE 11

**Viewing of Canadian and Foreign Programming on
English and French TV, 1984–1989 (6:00 a.m.–2:00 a.m.)**

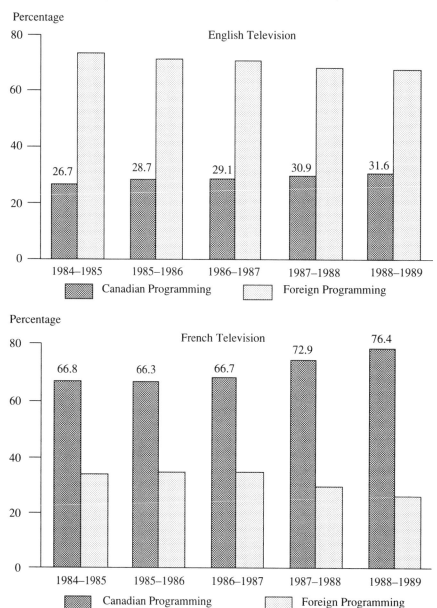

Source: Department of Communications. (1991). *The economic status of Canadian television,
report of the task force* (which used CBC Research [A.C. Nielsen, September–March]).
Ottawa: Minister of Supply and Services.

FIGURE 12

Number of Film and Video Productions 75+ Minutes in Length Distributed in Canada, by Country of Origin of Copyright, Ownership of the Production, and Market, 1988–1989

Origin of Copyright	Theatrical	Pay/ Specialized	Conventional TV	Home Video	Non- Theatrical	Total
Canada	130	122	285	52	861	1450
France	172	97	157	35	68	529
U.K.	35	217	318	9	2180	2759
U.S.	458	433	4295	407	1501	7094
Other	256	81	66	42	76	521
Total	**1051**	**950**	**5121**	**545**	**4686**	**12 353**

Note: Government-sponsored agencies and all TV stations and networks are excluded.
Table includes new and previously released feature films.

Source: Statistics Canada. (1991). *Film and video 1988–89 culture statistics*. (Cat. No. 87–204). Reproduced with the permission of the Minister of Supply and Services Canada, 1991.

FIGURE 13

Number of Motion Picture and Drive–in Theatres in Canada, 1977–1986

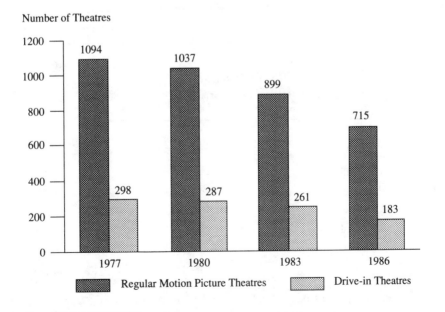

Number of Theatres

Source: *Film Canada yearbook 1989* Toronto: Cine-Communications.

FIGURE 14

Percentage Distribution of Radio Listening Time, for Persons Age 7+, by Station Format (Fall, 1989)

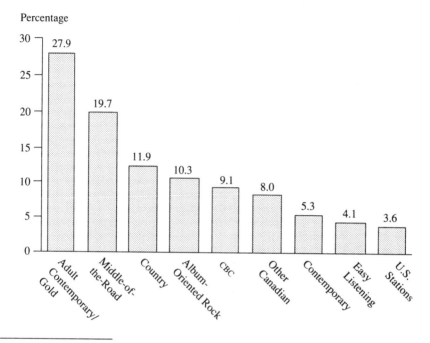

Source: Statistics Canada. (1990). *Focus on culture.* Vol. 2 (Winter). (Cat. No. 87–004). Reproduced with the permission of the Minister of Supply and Services Canada, 1991.

FIGURE 15

Number of Book Publishing Firms and Titles in Print, by Language and Ownership of Firm, 1988–1989

	No. of houses	No. of titles
English Language		
Canadian-Controlled	176	22 979
Foreign-Controlled	29	12 703
French Language		
Canadian-Controlled	97	17 258
Foreign-Controlled	5	1 546
Total	**307**	**54 486**

Source: Statistics Canada. (1990). *Book publishing 1988–89 culture statistics.* (Cat. No. 87–210). Reproduced with the permission of the Minister of Supply and Services Canada, 1991.

FIGURE 16

**Number of Canadian-Authored Titles in Print,
by Language and Ownership of Publishing Firm, 1988–1989**

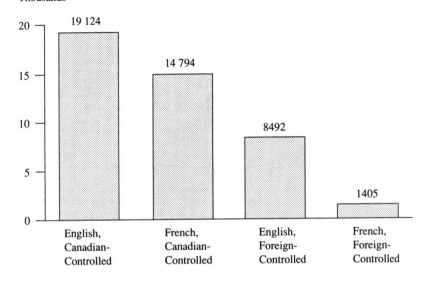

Source: Statistics Canada. (1990). *Book publishing 1988–89 culture statistics*. (Cat. No. 87–210). Reproduced with the permission of the Minister of Supply and Services Canada, 1991.

FIGURE 17

Circulation, Revenue, and Number of Periodicals Published in Canada, by Category, 1988–1989

	No. Periodicals	Total Annual Circulation	Ad Revenue ($000s)	Total Revenue ($000s)
General interest	439	341 270 659	241 523	468 141
Special interest	914	214 868 167	295 155	371 502
Scholarly	181	1 616 672	2 208	11 697
Total	**1534**	**557 755 498**	**538 886**	**851 340**

Source: Statistics Canada. (1991). *Periodical publishing 1988–89 culture statistics*. Reproduced with the permission of the Minister of Supply and Services Canada, 1991.

APPENDIX B

The Broadcasting Act of 1991

38-39 Elizabeth II

An Act respecting broadcasting and to amend certain Acts in relation thereto and in relation to radiocommunication.

[Assented to 1st February, 1991]

Her Majesty, by and with the advice and consent of the Senate and House of Commons of Canada, enacts as follows:

SHORT TITLE

1. This Act may be cited as the *Broadcasting Act.*

PART I

GENERAL

Interpretation

2. (1) In this Act,
" broadcasting" means any transmission of programs, whether or not encrypted, by radio waves or other means of telecommunication for reception by the public by means of broadcasting receiving apparatus, but does not include any such transmission of programs that is made solely for performance or display in a public place;

"broadcasting receiving apparatus" means a device, or combination of devices, intended for or capable of being used for the reception of broadcasting;

"broadcasting undertaking" includes a distribution undertaking, a programming undertaking and a network;

"Commission" means the Canadian Radio-television and Telecommunications Commission established by the *Canadian Radio-television and Telecommunications Commission Act*;

"Corporation" means the Canadian Broadcasting Corporation continued by section 36;

"distribution undertaking" means an undertaking for the reception of broadcasting and the retransmission thereof by radio waves or other means of telecommunication to more than one permanent or temporary residence or dwelling unit or to another such undertaking;

"encrypted" means treated electronically or otherwise for the purpose of preventing intelligible reception;

"licence" means a licence to carry on a broadcasting undertaking issued by the Commission under this Act;

"Minister" means the Minister of Communications;

"network" includes any operation where control over all or any part of the programs or program schedules of one or more broadcasting undertakings is delegated to another undertaking or person;

"program" means sounds or visual images, or a combination of sounds and visual images, that are intended to inform, enlighten or entertain, but does not include visual images, whether or not combined with sounds, that consist predominantly of alphanumeric text;

"programming undertaking" means an undertaking for the transmission of programs, either directly by radio waves or other means of telecommunication or indirectly through a distribution undertaking, for reception by the public by means of broadcasting receiving apparatus;

"radio waves" means electromagnetic waves of frequencies lower than 3000 GHz that are propagated in space without artificial guide;

"temporary network operation" means a network operation with respect to a particular program or a series of programs that extends over a period not exceeding sixty days.

(2) For the purposes of this Act, "other means of telecommunication" includes wire, visual or other electromagnetic system or any optical or technical system.

(3) This Act shall be construed and applied in a manner that is consistent with the freedom of expression and journalistic, creative and programming independence enjoyed by broadcasting undertakings.

Broadcasting Policy for Canada

3. (1) It is hereby declared as the broadcasting policy for Canada that

(a) the Canadian broadcasting system shall be effectively owned and controlled by Canadians;

(b) the Canadian broadcasting system, operating primarily in the English and French languages and comprising public, private and community elements, makes use of radio frequencies that are public property and provides, through its programming, a public service essential to the maintenance and enhancement of national identity and cultural sovereignty;

(c) English and French language broadcasting, while sharing common aspects, operate under different conditions and may have different requirements;

(d) the Canadian broadcasting system should

(i) serve to safeguard, enrich and strengthen the cultural, political, social and economic fabric of Canada,

(ii) encourage the development of Canadian expression by providing a wide range of programming that reflects Canadian attitudes, opinions, ideas, values and artistic creativity, by displaying Canadian talent in entertainment programming and by offering information and analysis concerning Canada and other countries from a Canadian point of view,

(iii) through its programming and the employment opportunities arising out of its operations, serve the needs and interests, and reflect the circumstances and aspirations, of

Canadian men, women and children, including equal rights, the linguistic duality and multicultural and multiracial nature of Canadian society and the special place of aboriginal peoples within that society, and

(iv) be readily adaptable to scientific and technological change;

(e) each element of the Canadian broadcasting system shall contribute in an appropriate manner to the creation and presentation of Canadian programming;

(f) each broadcasting undertaking shall make maximum use, and in no case less than predominant use, of Canadian creative and other resources in the creation and presentation of programming, unless the nature of the service provided by the undertaking, such as specialized content or format or the use of languages other than French and English, renders that use impracticable, in which case the undertaking shall make the greatest practicable use of those resources;

(g) the programming originated by broadcasting undertakings should be of high standard;

(h) all persons who are licensed to carry on broadcasting undertakings have a responsibility for the programs they broadcast;

(i) the programming provided by the Canadian broadcasting system should

(i) be varied and comprehensive, providing a balance of information, enlightenment and entertainment for men, women and children of all ages, interests and tastes,

(ii) be drawn from local, regional, national and international sources,

(iii) include educational and community programs,

(iv) provide a reasonable opportunity for the public to be exposed to the expression of differing views on matters of public concern, and

(v) include a significant contribution from the Canadian independent production sector;

(j) educational programming, particularly where provided through the facilities of an independent educational authority, is an integral part of the Canadian broadcasting system;

(k) a range of broadcasting services in English and French shall be extended to all Canadians as resources become available;

(l) the Canadian Broadcasting Corporation, as the national public broadcaster, should provide radio and television services incorporating a wide range of programming that informs, enlightens and entertains;

(m) the programming provided by the Corporation should

(i) be predominantly and distinctively Canadian,

(ii) reflect Canada and its regions to national and regional audiences, while serving the special needs of those regions,

(iii) actively contribute to the flow and exchange of cultural expression,

(iv) be in English and in French, reflecting the different needs and circumstances of each official language community, including the particular needs and circumstances of English and French linguistic minorities,

(v) strive to be of equivalent quality in English and in French,

(vi) contribute to shared national consciousness and identity,

(vii) be made available throughout Canada by the most appropriate and efficient means and as resources become available for the purpose, and

(viii) reflect the multicultural and multiracial nature of Canada;

(n) where any conflict arises between the objectives of the Corporation set out in paragraphs *(l)* and *(m)* and the interests of any other broadcasting undertaking of the Canadian broadcasting system, it shall be resolved in the public interest, and where the public interest would be equally served by resolving the conflict in favour of either, it shall be resolved in favour of the objectives set out in paragraphs *(l)* and *(m)*;

(o) programming that reflects the aboriginal cultures of Canada should be provided within the Canadian broadcasting system as resources become available for the purpose;

(p) programming accessible by disabled persons should be provided within the Canadian broadcasting system as resources become available for the purpose;

(q) without limiting any obligation of a broadcasting undertaking to provide the programming contemplated by paragraph *(i)*, alternative television programming services in English and in French should be provided where necessary to ensure that the full range of programming contemplated by that paragraph is made available through the Canadian broadcasting system;

(r) the programming provided by alternative television programming services should

(i) be innovative and be complementary to the programming provided for mass audiences,

(ii) cater to tastes and interests not adequately provided for by the programming provided for mass audiences, and include programming devoted to culture and the arts,

(iii) reflect Canada's regions and multicultural nature,

(iv) as far as possible, be acquired rather than produced by those services, and

(v) be made available throughout Canada by the most cost-efficient means;

(s) private networks and programming undertakings should, to an extent consistent with the financial and other resources available to them,

(i) contribute significantly to the creation and presentation of Canadian programming, and

(ii) be responsive to the evolving demands of the public; and

(t) distribution undertakings

(i) should give priority to the carriage of Canadian programming services and, in particular, to the carriage of local Canadian stations,

(ii) should provide efficient delivery of programming at affordable rates, using the most effective technologies available at reasonable cost,

(iii) should, where programming services are supplied to them by broadcasting undertakings pursuant to contractual arrangements, provide reasonable terms for the carriage, packaging and retailing of those programming services, and

(iv) may, where the Commission considers it appropriate, originate programming, including local programming, on such terms as are conducive to the achievement of the objectives of the broadcasting policy set out in this subsection, and in particular provide access for underserved linguistic and cultural minority communities.

(2) It is further declared that the Canadian broadcasting system constitutes a single system and that the objectives of the broadcasting policy set out in subsection (1) can best be achieved by providing for the regulation and supervision of the Canadian broadcasting system by a single independent public authority.

Application

4. (1) This Act is binding on Her Majesty in right of Canada or a province.

(2) This Act applies in respect of broadcasting undertakings carried on in whole or in part within Canada or on board

(a) any ship, vessel or aircraft that is

(i) registered or licensed under an Act of Parliament, or

(ii) owned by, or under the direction or control of, Her Majesty in right of Canada or a province;

(b) any spacecraft that is under the direction or control of,

(i) Her Majesty in right of Canada or a province,

(ii) a citizen or resident of Canada, or

(iii) a corporation incorporated or resident in Canada; or

(c) any platform, rig, structure or formation that is affixed or attached to land situated in those submarine areas adjacent to the coast of Canada and extending throughout the natural prolongation of the land territory of Canada to the outer edge of the continental margin or to a distance of two hundred nautical miles from the baselines from which the breadth of the territorial sea of Canada is measured, whichever is greater.

(3) For greater certainty, this Act applies in respect of broadcasting undertakings whether or not they are carried on for profit or as part of, or in connection with, any other undertaking or activity.

(4) For greater certainty, this Act does not apply to any telecommunications common carrier when acting solely in that capacity.

PART II

OBJECTS AND POWERS OF THE COMMISSION IN RELATION TO BROADCASTING

Objects

5. (1) Subject to this Act and the *Radiocommunication Act* and to any directions to the Commission issued by the Governor in Council under this Act, the Commission shall regulate and supervise all aspects of the Canadian broadcasting system with a view to implementing the broadcasting policy set out in subsection 3(1) and, in so doing, shall have regard to the regulatory policy set out in subsection (2).

(2) The Canadian broadcasting system should be regulated and supervised in a flexible manner that

(a) is readily adaptable to the different characteristics of English and French language broadcasting and to the different conditions under which broadcasting undertakings that provide English or French language programming operate;

(b) takes into account regional needs and concerns;

(c) is readily adaptable to scientific and technological change;

(d) facilitates the provision of broadcasting to Canadians;

(e) facilitates the provision of Canadian programs to Canadians;

(f) does not inhibit the development of information technologies and their application or the delivery of resultant services to Canadians; and

(g) is sensitive to the administrative burden that, as a consequence of such regulation and supervision, may be imposed on persons carrying on broadcasting undertakings.

(3) The Commission shall give primary consideration to the objectives of the broadcasting policy set out in subsection 3(1) if, in any particular matter before the Commission, a conflict arises between those objectives and the objectives of the regulatory policy set out in subsection (2).

6. The Commission may from time to time issue guidelines and statements with respect to any matter within its jurisdiction under this Act, but no such guidelines or statements issued by the Commission are binding on the Commission.

7. (1) Subject to subsection (2) and section 8, the Governor in Council may, by order, issue to the Commission directions of general application on broad policy matters with respect to

(a) any of the objectives of the broadcasting policy set out in subsection 3(1); or

(b) any of the objectives of the regulatory policy set out in subsection 5(2).

(2) No order may be made under subsection (1) in respect of the issuance of a licence to a particular person or in respect of the amendment, renewal, suspension or revocation of a particular licence.

(3) An order made under subsection (1) is binding on the Commission beginning on the day on which the order comes into force and, subject to subsection (4), shall, if it so provides, apply with respect to any matter pending before the Commission on that day.

(4) No order made under subsection (1) may apply with respect to a licensing matter pending before the Commission where the period for the filing of interventions in the matter has expired unless that period expired more than one year before the coming into force of the order.

(5) A copy of each order made under subsection (1) shall be laid before each House of Parliament on any of the first fifteen days on which that House is sitting after the making of the order.

(6) The Minister shall consult with the Commission before the Governor in Council makes an order under subsection (1).

8. (1) Where the Governor in Council proposes to make an order under section 7, the Minister shall cause the proposed order to be

(a) published by notice in the *Canada Gazette*, which notice shall invite interested persons to make representations to the Minister with respect to the proposed order; and

(b) laid before each House of Parliament.

(2) Where a proposed order is laid before a House of Parliament pursuant to subsection (1), it shall stand referred to such committee thereof as the House considers appropriate to deal with the subject-matter of the order.

(3) The Governor in Council may, after the expiration of forty sitting days of Parliament after a proposed order is laid before both Houses of Parliament in accordance with subsection (1), implement the proposal by making an order under section 7, either in the form proposed or revised in such manner as the Governor in Council deems advisable.

(4) The Minister shall consult with the Commission before a proposed order is published or is laid before a House of Parliament under subsection (1).

(5) In this section, "sitting day of Parliament" means a day on which either House of Parliament sits.

General Powers

9. (1) Subject to this Part, the Commission may, in furtherance of its objects,

(a) establish classes of licences;

(b) issue licences for such terms not exceeding seven years and subject to such conditions related to the circumstances of the licensee

(i) as the Commission deems appropriate for the implementation of the broadcasting policy set out in subsection 3(1), and

(ii) in the case of licences issued to the Corporation, as the Commission deems consistent with the provision, through the Corporation, of the programming contemplated by paragraphs 3(1)*(l)* and *(m)*;

(c) amend any condition of a licence on application of the licensee or, where five years have expired since the issuance or renewal of the licence, on the Commission's own motion;

(d) issue renewals of licences for such terms not exceeding seven years and subject to such conditions as comply with paragraph *(b)*;

(e) suspend or revoke any licence;

(f) require any licensee to obtain the approval of the Commission before entering into any contract with a telecommunications common carrier for the distribution of programming directly to the public, using the facilities of that common carrier;

(g) require any licensee who is authorized to carry on a distribution undertaking to give priority to the carriage of broadcasting; and

(h) require any licensee who is authorized to carry on a distribution undertaking to carry, on such terms and conditions as the Commission deems appropriate, programming services specified by the Commission.

(2) Notwithstanding subsections (1) and 28(3), no licence of a distribution undertaking may be made subject to a condition that requires the licensee to substitute replacement material for commercial messages carried in a broadcasting signal received by that licensee.

(3) Subsection (2) does not apply in respect of a condition of a licence renewed after October 4, 1987 where before that date the licensee was complying with such a condition.

(4) The Commission shall, by order, on such terms and conditions as it deems appropriate, exempt persons who carry on broadcasting undertakings of any class specified in the order from any or all of the requirements of this Part or of a regulation made under this Part where the Commission is satisfied that compliance with those requirements will not contribute in a material manner to the implementation of the broadcasting policy set out in subsection 3(1).

10. (1) The Commission may, in furtherance of its objects, make regulations

(a) respecting the proportion of time that shall be devoted to the broadcasting of Canadian programs;

(b) prescribing what constitutes a Canadian program for the purposes of this Act;

(c) respecting standards of programs and the allocation of broadcasting time for the purpose of giving effect to the broadcasting policy set out in subsection 3(1);

(d) respecting the character of advertising and the amount of broadcasting time that may be devoted to advertising;

(e) respecting the proportion of time that may be devoted to the broadcasting of programs, including advertisements or announcements, of a partisan political character and the assignment of that time on an equitable basis to political parties and candidates;

(f) prescribing the conditions for the operation of programming undertakings as part of a network and for the broadcasting of network programs, and respecting the broadcasting times to be reserved for network programs by any such undertakings;

(g) respecting the carriage of any foreign or other programming services by distribution undertakings;

(h) for resolving, by way of mediation or otherwise, any disputes arising between programming undertakings and distribution undertakings concerning the carriage of programming originated by the programming undertakings;

(i) requiring licensees to submit to the Commission such information regarding their programs and financial affairs or otherwise relating to the conduct and management of their affairs as the regulations may specify;

(j) respecting the audit or examination of the records and books of account of licensees by the Commission or persons acting on behalf of the Commission; and

(k) respecting such other matters as it deems necessary for the furtherance of its objects.

(2) A regulation made under this section may be made applicable to all persons holding licences or to all persons holding licences of one or more classes.

(3) A copy of each regulation that the Commission proposes to make under this section shall be published in the *Canada Gazette* and a reasonable opportunity shall be given to licensees and other interested persons to make representations to the Commission with respect thereto.

11. (1) The Commission may make regulations

(*a*) with the approval of the Treasury Board, establishing schedules of fees to be paid by licensees of any class;

(*b*) providing for the establishment of classes of licensees for the purposes of paragraph (*a*);

(*c*) providing for the payment of any fees payable by a licensee, including the time and manner of payment;

(*d*) respecting the interest payable by a licensee in respect of any overdue fee; and

(*e*) respecting such other matters as it deems necessary for the purposes of this section.

(2) Regulations made under paragraph (1)(*a*) may provide for fees to be calculated by reference to any criteria that the Commission deems appropriate, including by reference to

(*a*) the revenues of the licensees;

(*b*) the performance of the licensees in relation to objectives established by the Commission, including objectives for the broadcasting of Canadian programs; and

(*c*) the market served by the licensees.

(3) No regulations made under subsection (1) shall apply to the Corporation or to licensees carrying on

programming undertaking on behalf of Her Majesty in right of a province.

(4) Fees payable by a licensee under this section and any interest thereon constitute a debt due to Her Majesty in right of Canada and may be recovered as such in any court of competent jurisdiction.

(5) A copy of each regulation that the Commission proposes to make under this section shall be published in the *Canada Gazette* and a reasonable opportunity shall be given to licensees and other interested persons to make representations to the Commisssion with respect thereto.

12. (1) Where it appears to the Commission that

(*a*) any person has failed to do any act or thing that the person is required to do pursuant to this Part or to any regulation, licence, decision or order made or issued by the Commission under this Part, or has done or is doing any act or thing in contravention of this Part or of any such regulation, licence, decision or order, or

(*b*) the circumstances may require the Commission to make any decision or order or to give any approval that it is authorized to make or give under this Part or under any regulation or order made under this Part,

the Commission may inquire into, hear and determine the matter.

(2) The Commission may, by order, require any person to do, forthwith or within or at any time and in any manner specified by the Commission, any act or thing that the person is or may be required to do pursuant to this Part or to

any regulation, licence, decision or order made or issued by the Commission under this Part and may, by order, forbid the doing or continuing of any act or thing that is contrary to this Part or to any such regulation, licence, decision or order.

(3) Where an inquiry under subsection (1) is heard by a panel established under subsection 20(1) and the panel issues an order pursuant to subsection (2) of this section, any person who is affected by the order may, within thirty days after the making thereof, apply to the Commission to reconsider any decision or finding made by the panel, and the Commission may rescind or vary any order or decision made by the panel or may rehear any matter before deciding it.

13. (1) Any order made under subsection 12(2) may be made an order of the Federal Court or of any superior court of a province and is enforceable in the same manner as an order of the court.

(2) To make an order under subsection 12(2) an order of a court, the usual practice and procedure of the court in such matters may be followed or, in lieu thereof, the Commission may file with the registrar of the court a certified copy of the order, and thereupon the order becomes an order of the court.

(3) Where an order that has been made an order of a court is rescinded or varied by a subsequent order of the Commission, the order of the court shall be deemed to have been cancelled and the subsequent order may, in the same manner, be made an order of the court.

14. (1) The Commission may undertake, sponsor, promote or assist in research relating to any matter within its jurisdiction under this Act and in so doing it shall, wherever appropriate, utilize technical, economic and statistical information and advice from the Corporation or departments or agencies of the Government of Canada.

(2) The Commission shall review and consider any technical matter relating to broadcasting referred to the Commission by the Minister and shall make recommendations to the Minister with respect thereto.

15. (1) The Commission shall, on request of the Governor in Coundil, hold hearings or make reports on any matter within the jurisdiction of the Commission under this Act.

(2) The Minister shall consult with the Commission with regard to any request proposed to be made by the Governor in Council under subsection (1).

16. The Commission has, in respect of any hearing under this Part, with regard to the attendance, swearing and examination of witnesses at the hearing, the production and inspection of documents, the enforcement of its orders, the entry and inspection of property and other matters necessary or proper in relation to the hearing, all such powers, rights and privileges as are vested in a superior court of record.

17. The Commission has authority to determine questions of fact or law in relation to any matter within its jurisdiction under this Act.

CONTRIBUTORS

Helen Allison is a graduate student in the graduate program in Communication Studies at the University of Calgary. She is currently studying cultural messages in Canadian television.

Patricia Baranek is Manager of the Health Human Resources Policy Unit, Ontario Ministry of Health. She is the co-author with Richard Ericson and Janet Chan of three groundbreaking studies of the Canadian media: *Visualizing Deviance*, *Negotiating Control*, and *Representing Order*.

William Boot is the pen name of Christopher Hanson, the Washington correspondent for the Seattle *Post-Intelligencer*. Hanson is also a contributing editor of the Columbia *Journalism Review*.

Janet Chan is a lawyer and lecturer in sociology and social policy at the University of New South Wales. She is the co-author with Richard Ericson and Patricia Baranek of *Visualizing Deviance*, *Negotiating Control*, and *Representing Order*, all major studies of the news-gathering process in Canada.

Jeffrey Derevensky is Associate Professor and Director of Graduate Programs in Educational Psychology in the Department of Educational Psychology and Counselling; Associate Professor, Department of Psychiatry; and Associate Professor, Department of Community Dentistry at McGill University. Dr. Derevensky is also Director of McGill University's Ready Set Go Parent Education Child Enrichment Project.

Peter Desbarats is Dean of the Graduate School of Journalism at the University of Western Ontario. A former TV news anchor for Global TV, Desbarats has also worked for the *Toronto Star*, the CBC, and the *Montreal Star*. He is the author of *Guide to Canadian News Media* and a biography of René Lévesque.

Nancy Duxbury is a graduate student at the Canadian Centre for Studies in Publishing, Simon Fraser University. Her bachelor's degree is in business. Her present work focuses on examining government support for book publishers in Canada.

Ross A. Eaman teaches the history of communication and Canadian broadcasting in the Mass Communication program in the School of Journalism at Carleton University. He is the author of *The Media Society: Basic Issues and Controversies* and a forthcoming work on the history of CBC audience research.

Richard Ericson is Professor of Criminology and Sociology at the University of Toronto. He is the author of *Reproducing Order: A Study of Police Patrol Work* and co-author with Patricia Baranek and Janet Chan of *Visualizing Deviance*, *Negotiating Control*, and *Representing Order*.

Seth Feldman is editor of two anthologies on Canadian cinema: *Canadian Film Reader* and *Take Two*. His commentary on film and television has appeared in professional journals, the popular press, and on CBC radio and television. Professor Feldman is currently Associate Dean of Fine Arts at York University.

Robert Hackett teaches communication at Simon Fraser University. His research interests include social movements and the media, the politics of social democracy, and ideological roles of news and journalism. He is the author of *News and Dissent*, a book on news reporting of the peace movement and a number of significant articles on media and politics in Canada.

Helen Holmes is Director of the Communications Studies program at the University of Calgary. She teaches communication history and Canadian media courses.

Tom Kent, a former editor of the *Winnipeg Free Press*, advisor to Prime Minister Lester Pearson and Deputy Minister of Employment and Immigration, headed the Royal Commission on Newspapers. He is the author of *A Public Purpose* and *Getting Ready For 1999: Ideas for Canada's Politics and Government*.

Carolyn Klein is a doctoral candidate and Faculty Lecturer in the Department of Educational Psychology and Counselling at McGill University. Ms. Klein is a licensed applied development psychologist.

Stephen Kline is a Professor of Communication and Director of the Media Analysis Laboratory at Simon Fraser University. He is a co-author of *Out of the Garden: Childhood in the Age of Marketing* (1991). His recent research includes studies of political advertising, social marketing, and children's marketing, and he is currently studying the communication of emotion in advertising.

Martin Laba is the Chair and Associate Professor in the Department of Communication at Simon Fraser University. He is the author of numerous articles, book chapters, and reports on issues in communication, popular culture, media, and Canadian culture. He is the co-editor of *Media Sense* and is the author of a new book on youth, popular media, and the marketplace entitled *Manufacturing Youth*. He has written, produced, and directed a number of media productions, including "Video, Vinyl and Culture" (half-hour television program on music video, 1985) "Youth and Popular Music" (twenty-minute radio documentary, 1988); "Looking Ahead" (six video productions for the Canadian International Development Agency, 1989); and "Hockey: The Canadian Game" (a television documentary series, 1990).

William Leiss is Professor of Communication, Director of the Centre for Policy Research on Science and Technology, and Vice President, Research, at Simon Fraser University. He is the author of *Domination of Nature* (1972), *Limits to Satisfaction* (1976), *C.B. MacPherson* (1988), and *Under Technology's Thumb* (1990), and co-author of *Social Communication in Advertising*. He is presently working an a new book, *Towards Consensus in Environmental Controversies*.

Rowland Lorimer is a Professor of Communication and Director of the Canadian Centre for Studies in Publishing at Simon Fraser University. He is co-author of *Mass Communication in Canada* and *Creating Ideas and Information* and author of *The Nation in the Schools*. The focus of his recent work has been on the Canadian publishing industry and mass communications in Canada and abroad.

Janice Dickin McGinnis, a lawyer and historian, teaches in the Faculty of General Studies at the University of Calgary. She was awarded an SSHRC Canada Research Fellowship in 1988. Professor Dickin McGinnis is the co-editor with Wendy Mitchinson of *Essays in the Social History of Canadian Medicine* and is currently researching a biography of Aimee Semple McPherson.

Joshua Meyrowitz is Professor of Communication at the University of New Hampshire. He is the author of *No Sense of Place: The Impact of Electronic Media on Social Behaviour*, a book that won the Best Book on Electronic Media Award of the National Association of Broadcasters and Broadcast Education Association in the United States.

Richard Pinet teaches in the Department of Communication at Simon Fraser University.

Marc Raboy is an Associate Professor in the Departement d'information et communication, Université Laval. A former journalist with the *Montreal Star* and CBC radio and television, his major publications include *Movements and Messages: Media and Radical Politics in Quebec* and *Missed Opportunities: The Story of Canada's Broadcasting Policy*.

Gertrude J. Robinson is Professor and past Director of the Graduate Program in Communications at McGill University. She is also editor of the *Canadian Journal of Communication*. Her recent research is on international news-flow patterns and the democratization of the media in eastern Europe. Professor Robinson is writing an intellectual history of the field of communications in North America.

Myles Ruggles is a Ph.D. candidate and teaches in the Department of Communication at Simon Fraser University.

Robert A. Stebbins is Professor of Sociology at the University of Calgary. He is a past president of the Canadian Sociology and Anthropology Association and of the Social Science Federation of Canada. Professor Stebbins is the author of thirteen books and of numerous articles and book chapters. His most recent book, *Amateurs, Professionals and Serious Leisure* will be published by McGill-Queen's University Press.

David Taras, a political scientist, is Director of the Canadian Studies Program at the University of Calgary. He is the author of *The Newsmakers: The Media's Influence on Canadian Politics* and co-editor of *A Passion For Identity: Introduction to Canadian Studies, Prime Ministers and Premiers,* and *Meech Lake and Canada: Perspectives from the West* among other books.

John Herd Thompson is an historian of post-Confederation Canada whose best known book is *Canada 1922-1939: Decades of Discord*. He teaches the history of Canada in the Canadian Studies Program at Duke University. He discusses the U.S.–Canadian cultural relationship more fully in *Canada and the United States: Ambivalent Allies* (co-author Stephen J. Randall), forthcoming in the series *America and the Americas* from the University of Georgia Press.

Linda Trimble is in the political science department at the University of Alberta. She has published articles on the CRTC policy on sex-role stereotyping and on women and politics in Alberta and is currently writing a book on gender politics and public policy in Canada.

Gail Guthrie Valaskakis teaches in the Department of Communication Studies at Concordia University. Professor Valaskakis has done a number of significant studies on communications and Native peoples in the Canadian North.

To the Owner of this Book:

We are interested in your reaction to *Seeing Ourselves: Media Power and Policy in Canada* edited by Helen Holmes and David Taras. With your comments, we can improve this book in future editions. Please help us by completing this questionnaire.

1. What was your reason for using this book?
   _____ university course _____ college course
   _____ continuing education course _____ personal interest
   _____ other (specify)

2. If you used this text for a program, what was the name of that program? _____

3. Which school do you attend? _____

4. Approximately how much of the book did you use?
   _____ 1/4 _____ 1/2 _____ 3/4 _____ all

5. Which chapters or sections were omitted from your course? _____

6. What is the best aspect of this book? _____

7. Is there anything that should be added? _____

8. Please give your reaction to the readings, listed here in the order of their appearance in the book:

Author	Pertinent	Unrelated to your study objectives
Hackett	_____	_____
Kent	_____	_____
Task Force	_____	_____
Eaman	_____	_____
Desbarats	_____	_____
Feldman	_____	_____
Lorimer	_____	_____
Kline	_____	_____
Trimble	_____	_____
Raboy	_____	_____
Taras	_____	_____
Thompson	_____	_____
Valaskakis	_____	_____
Meyrowitz	_____	_____
Ericson	_____	_____
Boot	_____	_____
Robinson	_____	_____
McGinnis	_____	_____
Derevensky	_____	_____
Holmes	_____	_____
Stebbins	_____	_____
Laba	_____	_____

9. Please add any comments or suggestions _____

Fold here

- -

Business
Reply Mail
No Postage Stamp
Necessary if Mailed
in Canada

POSTAGE WILL BE PAID BY

Heather McWhinney
Editorial Director
College Division
Harcourt Brace Jovanovich Canada Inc.
55 Horner Avenue
Toronto, Ontario
M8Z 9Z9

Tape shut